Daniel Ross

Psychopolitical Anaphylaxis
Steps Towards a Metacosmics

with an Afterword by Bernard Stiegler

CCC2 Irreversibility

Series Editors: Tom Cohen and Claire Colebrook

The second phase of 'the Anthropocene,' takes hold as tipping points speculated over in 'Anthropocene 1.0' click into place to retire the speculative bubble of "Anthropocene Talk". Temporalities are dispersed, the memes of 'globalization' revoked. A broad drift into a de facto era of managed extinction events dawns. With this acceleration from the speculative into the material orders, a factor without a means of expression emerges: climate panic.

Daniel Ross

Psychopolitical Anaphylaxis
Steps Towards a Metacosmics

with an Afterword by Bernard Stiegler

OPEN HUMANITIES PRESS

London 2021

First edition published by Open Humanities Press 2021
Copyright © 2021 Daniel Ross
English Translation Copyright © 2021 Daniel Ross

Freely available at:
http://openhumanitiespress.org/books/titles/psychopolitical-anaphylaxis/

This is an open access book, licensed under Creative Commons By Attribution Share Alike license. Under this license, authors allow anyone to download, reuse, reprint, modify, distribute, and/or copy their work so long as the authors and source are cited and resulting derivative works are licensed under the same or similar license. No permission is required from the authors or the publisher. Statutory fair use and other rights are in no way affected by the above. Read more about the license at creativecommons.org/licenses/by-sa/4.0

Cover Art, figures, and other media included with this book may be under different copyright restrictions.

Print ISBN 978-1-78542-090-0
PDF ISBN 978-1-78542-089-4

OPEN HUMANITIES PRESS

Open Humanities Press is an international, scholar-led open access publishing collective whose mission is to make leading works of contemporary critical thought freely available worldwide. More at http://openhumanitiespress.org

Contents

Introduction: Just This, Written Just Here and Just Now,
By Just This Individual in Just This Mood — 9

1. Bereft and Adrift in an Entropic Universe
   After Bernard Stiegler — 27

2. Protentional Finitude and Infinitude
   in the Anthropocene — 50

3. Shanghai, 2018:
   An Introduction to Technics and Time, 1 and 2 — 64

4. The Question of Elon Musk
   and the Aporia of Sustainability — 144

5. Carbon and Silicon: Contribution to an Elemental
   Critique of Political Economy — 179

6. Psychic and Collective Anaphylaxis:
   For an Organological Critique of Sovereignty — 203

7. For a Neganthropology of Markets — 239
   With a Communication From Bernard Stiegler

8. Towards an Exergue on the Future of Différance — 292

9. The End of the Metaphysics of Being
   and the Beginning of the Metacosmics of Entropy — 315

Afterword: On Positive Pharmacology — 357
   by Bernard Stiegler

Notes — 369

References — 419

Permissions — 436

For Bernard, with infinite gratitude and unending friendship.

Introduction: Just This, Written Just Here and Just Now, By Just This Individual in Just This Mood

> Every species of living being, and every specimen of each species, is affecting and modifying the biosphere by its efforts to keep itself alive during its brief lifetime. However, no pre-hominid species has ever had the power to dominate the biosphere or to wreck it. On the other hand, when a hominid chipped a stone with the intention of making it into a more serviceable tool, this historic act, performed perhaps two million years ago, made it certain that, one day, some species of some genus of the hominid family of primate mammals would not merely affect and modify the biosphere, but would hold the biosphere at its mercy.
>
> *Arnold Toynbee, Mankind and Mother Earth*

The turn towards curtailment

Let me begin by expressing my sincere gratitude for your decision to crack open at least the first page of this volume. Given that mass literacy is an idea that has only been around a few centuries, given that thus far some 130 million titles have been published and more than two million new ones are added each year, given that a human being who dedicated his or her life to reading books would still only be able to get through a few thousand tomes cover-to-cover over the course of a lifetime, and given that the desire and the habit of regularly reading whole books is on the decline, an author in the twenty-first century should be thankful that anyone should happen to choose *their* work from among all the other possible options vying for their careful attention. Given the vastly greater number of possible choices compared with the number any individual can read, the set of books read by any particular man or woman amounts, we could say, to one way in which the uniqueness or the singularity of the psychic individuation process that characterizes his or her existence is expressed: the corpus of books read over a lifetime is an expression of that particular individual's way of participating in the process of the transindividuation of literary significance, their way of drawing nourishment for their noetic soul from what the philosopher Bernard Stiegler called the noetic necromass, that artificial treasure of wealth corresponding psychically and culturally to the wealth of nutrition that the necromass, composed of dead life, makes available to the biomass.

In the ecological sense (rather than the renewable energy sense), the biomass is the sum total of all the living biological organisms occupying an ecosystem, and the ecosystem that encompasses all the smaller ecosystems has been known since the work of Vladimir Vernadsky as the biosphere. Vernadsky reflected on the way in which biochemistry interacted with and also transformed geochemical processes, hypothesizing that it was indeed possible, across geological timescales, for the combined biochemical processes of the biomass to reshape the whole 'terrestrial envelope'.[1] The book in which he made this case, *The Biosphere*, was published in 1926, the same year in which Martin Heidegger was still settling upon his conception of temporality while writing the final draft of *Being and Time*. The last of these books, *Being and Time*, was read by Stiegler early in his philosophical life, and his first book argues that, even though Heidegger does consider the place of artefacts in the constitution of Dasein's historical temporality, he ultimately rejects the possibility that 'determining the undetermined' could grant access to the true character of time. For Stiegler himself, on the other hand, the possibility of such access can arise only from the world opened up by artefacts of all kinds, from the most basic tools to books to computer technology – the question of 'technics and time' lying in this possibility of a *world opened up* beyond the 'milieu' described by Jakob von Uexküll for the animal (or the sensible soul, in Aristotle's terms).[2]

The first of these books, *The Biosphere*, was not read by Stiegler until many years later, I believe, when he had begun to ask not just about technics but about what he called 'exosomatization', a notion derived from reading the work of Alfred Lotka, a mathematical biologist, on 'exosomatic evolution'.[3] Exosomatic evolution refers to the unfolding of a form of life that is no longer just the *endosomatic* evolution of the biological life of the biosphere, but rather technical life, that produces organs extending outside the body of the organism, without which it cannot survive. Exosomatic evolution thus names the process that in *Technics and Time, 1* Stiegler mostly referred to as hominization (a process that *precedes* the human).

What was crucial for Stiegler about the work of Lotka, however, was not just the *distinction* between exosomatic and endosomatic evolution, but the fact that these were considered to be distinct forms of the struggle against *entropy*: 'as was pointed out years ago by Boltzmann, the life struggle is primarily a competition for available energy'.[4] In other words, if, asking in Dublin in February 1943 about the fundamental character of life, Erwin Schrödinger referred to 'negative entropy', then Lotka shows in 1945 that we must ask this question in a specific way when life operates not just through natural selection, but artificial selection. Vernadsky himself would cite earlier work of Lotka, but whereas Vernadsky still believed that technology is a 'universal, peaceful and civilizing force',[5] Lotka, writing in the immediate aftermath of the Second World War, was far more conscious of the fact that, for exosomatic life, technical power (the 'receptors and effectors') requires processes of 'adjustment' through knowledge, wisdom and care, if the perpetual threat of disaster is to be avoided:

> It is precisely this that has gone awry in the schemes of men: The receptors and effectors have been perfected to a nicety; but the development of the adjustors has lagged so far behind, that the resultant of our efforts has actually been reversed. From the preservation of life we have turned to the destruction of life; and from expansion of the human race we have, in some of the most advanced communities, turned to its curtailment.[6]

Stiegler, too, would characterize human existence in terms of this struggle between advance and delay, as a being constantly capable of leaps ahead but also of lagging behind, this corresponding as well to the 'intermittency' of the noetic soul according to Aristotle, that is, of the fact that this soul may be perpetually noetic in potential, but is noetic in actuality only at certain moments, and always at risk of falling back, both individually and collectively, a risk that is bound to occur, time and time again.

Arnold Toynbee and the enigmatic question

Another of the books that Stiegler chose to read seemingly towards the last few years of his life, since he referred to it only latterly in his work, is *Mankind and Mother Earth*, by the British historian Arnold Toynbee, written in 1973 but published posthumously in 1976. The life of Arnold Toynbee, from 14 April 1889 to 22 October 1975, occupies an almost identical stretch of time as that of Martin Heidegger, from 26 September 1889 to 26 May 1976. This span stretches from: (1) a youth that coincided with the industrialization of production and faith in 'progress' characteristic of the world prior to the unprecedented destruction of the First World War; to (2) a major period of work, a period that also saw the industrialization of consumption and the withering of faith in progress that accompanied the catastrophic convulsions of the twentieth century; and eventually to (3) late reflections, occurring at a moment when the 'glorious' post-War years were at an end, and the world was entering a new age of computational technology which by the 1970s had only begun to unfold into the vast process of transformation still underway in 2020.

In the third of these periods, Toynbee, like Lotka after the Second World War, had become highly conscious of the fact that humankind was now confronted with the reality of this curtailment, and the fact that the preservation of life had turned to destruction:

> Man is the first species of living being in our biosphere that has acquired the power to wreck the biosphere and, in wrecking it, to liquidate himself.[7]

Toynbee does not discuss the second law of thermodynamics, and nor therefore does he discuss life in terms of the struggle against it, let alone exosomatic evolution. Nevertheless, the conception of the character of the 'mankind' of the title resonates with Stiegler's Promethean and *Epimethean* description of neotenic man in *Technics and Time, 1*. Toynbee writes about the process of hominization as follows:

> By the time that Man had become human, he had been stripped of all built-in physical weapons and armour, but he had acquired a conscious intellect which could think and plan, and two physical organs, his brain and his hands, which were the material instruments for his thinking, his planning, and his attempt to achieve his purposes by physical action.[8]

Furthermore, just as Friedrich Engels had said as early as 1883 that the hand 'implies the tool',[9] just as Stiegler will argue in 1994 that the evolution of this brain and this hand are co-constitutive with the evolution of the tool, so too Toynbee argues in 1973 that 'tools are coeval with human consciousness'.[10] Hence the situation with which we are confronted today, the power if not the likelihood that we will wreck the biosphere, is one whose roots lie so far back in time as to precede the appearance of *Homo sapiens* itself, in that coeval unfolding of hominization and technicization, of brain and hand, that gave rise to an exosomatic being who slowly but surely began to encroach further upon the biosphere, in the competition for available energy. Yet even if these roots lie far back, it is a transformation in the *conditions* of this competition that has produced a decisive turn from preservation to destruction:

> Since the beginning of the Upper Palaeolithic Age, perhaps 70,000/40,000 years ago, Man has been taking the offensive

> against the rest of the biosphere; but it is only since the beginning of the Industrial Revolution, no more than two hundred years ago, that Man has become decisively dominant. Within the last two centuries, Man has increased his material power to a degree at which he has become a menace to the biosphere's survival...

Like Lotka, Toynbee sees this in terms of a lag in the adjustors, that is, a failure of knowledge, wisdom and care to keep up with this acceleration:

> ...he has become a menace to the biosphere's survival; but he has not increased his spiritual potentiality; the gap between this and his material power has consequently been widening; and this growing discrepancy is disconcerting; for an increase in Man's spiritual potentiality is now the only conceivable change in the constitution of the biosphere that can insure the biosphere – and, in the biosphere, Man himself – against being destroyed by a greed that is now armed with the ability to defeat its own intentions.[11]

Only an increase in spiritual potentiality can save us. If we do not wish to take this as a mystical invocation, then we must hear it as a diagnosis of current pathologies and a call to address them by changing the conditions of our psychic and collective formation. The exosomatic being may be in possession of a noetic soul, but there is no guarantee it will not be lost, in gaining the world (and it is for this reason that Stiegler will refer, in invoking and updating Weber's account, to the lost spirit of capitalism).

What then is the pathology? It is a recklessness, a carelessness that Toynbee identifies as a kind of civilizational suicidal tendency:

> Mankind's material power has now increased to a degree at which it could make the biosphere uninhabitable and will, in fact, produce this suicidal result within a foreseeable period of time if the human population of the globe does not now take prompt and vigorous concerted action.[12]

Forty-five years later, this prompt and vigorous concerted action has utterly failed to materialize, and we cannot discount that the moment may already have passed, that we have already slipped the hangman's noose we have fashioned for ourselves around our neck, climbed atop the chair and are now teetering on the edge of the precipice and staring down into an abyss that can no longer be avoided. This is the point to which we have been brought by those two centuries that are now called the Anthropocene; it seems to be the point to which the Covid-19 pandemic is bringing us; it is the threshold that some noetic souls have already found themselves unable not to cross. As Toynbee says in the last lines of his book, in the case that we have just referred to as the Anthropocene, such a suicide cannot be divorced from a murder – on the scale of the biosphere:

> Will mankind murder Mother Earth or will he redeem her? He could murder her by misusing his increasing technological potency. Alternatively he could redeem her by overcoming the suicidal, aggressive greed that, in all living creatures, including Man himself, has been the price of the Great Mother's gift of life. This is the enigmatic question which now confronts Man.[13]

Overshooting the mark, life itself

How should we characterize such a tendency towards civilizational suicide and biospheric murder? Is it not precisely the embodiment of the meaning of entropy, applied not just to thermodynamics or to biology (but incorporating them all, and at the macrocosmic scale of the biosphere), but rather the entropy that is peculiarly characteristic of the kinds of beings that we ourselves are? In this tendency towards lagging behind, towards falling back from the noetic heights, towards destruction rather than preservation, towards disorganization rather than organization, towards the closing of what with so much difficulty had been opened, towards laziness and cowardice, hubris and denial, towards failing to do what one knows without a doubt must be done, towards suicide and towards murder, do we not see all of the elements that define the real meaning of this strange word designating *that turn within*, as it applies not just universally, but cosmically, and for us?

Such a question may sound like an affront to physics, as if philosophy has overshot the mark of its questions and landed in foreign territory over which it claims no rights. Nevertheless, in this book, all of these tendencies, taking the form of overreactions, underreactions, denials, suicides, murders and so on, will be considered as a kind of entropy, one peculiar to the exosomatic beings that we are and that Stiegler calls exorganisms. We will follow Stiegler in arguing that such tendencies are irreducible and ineliminable, that the struggle against them is a temporary and local effort, even if the biological struggle of endosomatic evolution has lasted a few billion years within that largest locality that is the biosphere, that this struggle to decrease entropy here and now can never occur without also producing an increase of entropy 'elsewhere', and that for the kinds of beings that we ourselves are, this struggle is not just against the second law of thermodynamics that is named by the concept of entropy, but against the peculiar regressive tendency it possesses that Stiegler calls anthropy. For Stiegler, the struggle for the preservation of exosomatic life is conducted under the sign of neganthropy, and the potential for unexpected turns and bifurcations it contains, and must always contain as the différance we must *make*, relies on our anti-anthropic capacity.

At the same time, this book will see such tendencies, such reactions, such suicides and such murders – individual, collective, civilizational and biospheric – from a slightly different perspective: if the struggle against entropy is always a question of 'organization' (leading to Stiegler's distinction between the endosomatic organic and the exosomatic organological), and if this organization is always a question of strongly-interrelated local and temporary dynamic systems (such as a cell, an organism, an ecosystem, or an exorganism, a family, a tribe, a society, a civilization), then this organized locality always involves a relationship between interior and exterior that we can consider in terms of what in biology are known as immune systems. More than that, we will follow Georges Canguilhem in considering that the difference between a 'normal' immune response and a supersensitive immune response – such as the kind that produces a shock reaction that can even prove fatal to the organism itself, so that a protective mechanism in fact functions as a destructive agent – can be understood in terms of the difference between tendencies that are propulsive for the locality (leading it towards a future metastability) and those that are repulsive (destabilizing the organism or exorganism).[14] Canguilhem himself reflects on the distinction that characterizes exosomatization when he refers to the 'technical form of life', but it is precisely *this* form of life that, he says, bears within it the '*temptation* to fall sick',[15] and hence we argue for the possibility of seeing the shocks and reactions of contemporary existence as tendencies towards a form of anaphylaxis that is not biological but *psychosocial*.

This affront thus risks being one not just against physics, but against biology and medicine too. Nevertheless, we have already seen Lotka citing Ludwig Boltzmann that the life struggle is a question of available energy, and we are inclined to extend the question of energy past the thermodynamic and to the libidinal, if not beyond. In terms of physics, what led to the discovery of the second law of thermodynamics was the inefficiency of the steam engine, and the effort to decrease that inefficiency through theoretical and practical means. From the consideration of the engine as a closed system, it was recognized that inefficiency itself is irreducible, and that *some* energy must always be lost by the system: it was the generalization of this realization to the universe considered as itself a closed system that led to the formulation of the concept of entropy.

At the time of Rudolf Clausius, however, atomic theory was not yet accepted, and so it was not possible to consider the entropic tendency of a gas, for example, in terms of the statistical consequences of vast numbers of atomic or molecular collisions. Only seven years later, in 1872, the situation with regard to atomic theory had not changed, but it would nonetheless fall to Ludwig Boltzmann to formulate this law in statistical terms, which is to say, as the tendency for the probable to eliminate the improbable, which, over the vast numbers of such collisions involved in any macroscopic phenomenon, becomes an overwhelming and highly predictable progression. It is this characteristic of statistical dependability and this alone that makes this tendency susceptible to being described as a *law*.

How then did Boltzmann himself, who was a frequent lecturer willing to consider the relationship between scientific discovery and 'philosophical' questions, conceive biological life in relationship to this tendency? In an address on the second law given in 1886, a year before the birth of Schrödinger and three years before the births of Toynbee and Heidegger, Boltzmann recognized that all of terrestrial life depends on a constant source of energy from outside the biosphere, the Sun, allowing it to behave not as a closed system but as an open one. As a result, endosomatic life is, in sum, an effort to decrease and postpone the entropic tendency by taking advantage of this seemingly eternal source of 'free' energy:

> The general struggle for existence of animate beings is therefore not a struggle for raw materials – these, for organisms, are air, water and soil, all abundantly available – nor for energy which exists in plenty in any body in the form of heat [...], but a struggle for entropy, which becomes available through the transition of energy from the hot sun to the cold earth. In order to exploit this transition as much as possible, plants spread their immense surface of leaves and force the sun's energy, before it falls to the earth's temperature, to perform in ways as yet unexplored certain chemical syntheses of which no one in our laboratories has so far the least idea. The products of this chemical kitchen constitute the object of struggle of the animal world.[16]

The struggle for existence is a 'struggle for entropy', or, as Schrödinger will say, in a slightly less confusing way more than half a century later, the organism 'feeds on negative entropy' to 'compensate the entropy it produces by living'.[17]

In 1905, almost twenty years after this statement about life and entropy, the chemistry of photosynthesis was still not understood, but Boltzmann would turn to the question of *value*, which is to say, the criteria for behavioural selection for exosomatic beings. While endosomatic beings are bound by instinct, or may partially modify it as a means of adapting to lessons learned in the life of an animal, and where the criteria for these bound selections are themselves the result of endosomatic evolution, this is no longer the case for exosomatic life. In the latter case, behavioural selection becomes a *problem* of existence, unbounded by the dictates of instinct even if still tied to the material reality of biology, and imposing the necessity of asking the question: what to do?

We are in the habit, Boltzmann says, of 'assessing everything as to its value', and of doing so 'according to whether it helps or hinders the conditions of life'. 'Life', whatever is named by this grand term, is the source of the judgment about values, and what has value is what promotes life. From here, however, Boltzmann takes a perhaps surprising turn, if not to say a twist:

> This becomes so habitual that we imagine we must ask ourselves whether life itself has a value.[18]

What inner turn in the psychic individuation process of Ludwig Boltzmann produced this question?

Boltzmann intends to put before us evidence of a kind of perversion or distortion of thought. 'Metaphysics', having acquired the habit of pursuing questions and seeking out further territory to be conquered by those questions, applies that habit in ways that forget that the source of the possibility of such a habit is life itself qua archi-criterion of value. This problem does not arise for endosomatic life, which does not open up the gap into which the world enters and questions impose their necessity. Only for exosomatic beings, possessing a noetic soul that must *select* its behaviour, does it become possible to *ask* about 'value', to make life into a *question*, a question of value.

Yet only for these beings, too, does the possibility of an inner turn arise, an *en-trope*, so to speak, allowing the question to rebound upon the source of its own unboundedness. It is the circuit through this outside that is the opening onto questions that introduces the possibility of this perversion or this distortion, which is inherent to questioning itself, and insofar as to question is *always* a question of responding to the problem of the exigencies of exosomatic life or the shocks it encounters or brings upon itself. It is a matter of the pharmacology of the question (in the sense of the Greek *pharmakon* that is a remedy that can always become a poison). And this is what Boltzmann himself understands, and why he raises this example:

> This becomes so habitual that we imagine we must ask ourselves whether life itself has a value. That is one of those questions utterly devoid of sense. Life itself we must accept as that which has value, and whether something else does can only be judged relatively to life, namely whether it is apt to promote life or not [and] this means whether life is apt to promote life, a question that has no sense.[19]

It is the characteristic of human beings to ask questions in general and questions of value in particular, to rise up above phenomena in order to see what chances it affords, and it is for this reason that Whitehead will say that the 'function of Reason is to promote the art of life'.[20] In asking the question of the value of life itself, however, in trying to measure that which provides the criteria for the measuring stick, it becomes a 'mental habit that overshoots the mark'.[21]

In fact, this trope of 'overshooting the mark' occurs repeatedly in Boltzmann's writing, like a habit of thought that occupies him constantly: the tendency for behaviours that begin as beneficial adaptations to be extended to an excessive point at which they become harmful. For example, in 1904:

> Many inappropriate features in the habits and behaviour of living beings are provoked by the fact that a mode of action that is appropriate in most cases becomes so habitual and second nature that it can no longer be relinquished if somewhere it ceases to be appropriate. I express this by saying that adaptation overshoots the mark. This happens especially often with mental habits and becomes a source of apparent contradictions between the laws of thought and the world, and between those laws themselves.[22]

What should regulate the relationship between thought and world is law, but the susceptibility of law to become a kind of automatism, repeated beyond all measure, leads to a kind of maladaptation, and this is precisely the case when, through a kind of repetition compulsion, we are drawn from asking about value within life to instead asking about the value *of* life, whether of the individual or of humankind:

> Similarly something is called useful or valuable if it furthers the living conditions of the individual or of mankind, but we overshoot the mark if we ask for the value of life itself, when for example it seems to us pointless because it has no purpose outside itself. [...] I regard it as a central task of philosophy to give a clear account of the inappropriateness of this overshooting the mark on the part of our thinking habits.[23]

Yet it is 'metaphysics' itself that tends to fall into this trap, to overshoot the mark in a kind of excess that is also a kind of automatism – an excessive automatism. The task of philosophy must be precisely to aim at 'appropriateness' and eliminate 'inappropriateness' so as to approach a lawful expression without tangles and contradictions. Despite this seemingly straightforward, not to say naïve commitment to philosophical perfection and the removal of all dogma, Boltzmann seems at the same time to recognize that a problem arises in this adoption of life as value of values, of life as the seemingly 'natural' archi-criterion of values, and that it is a problem, *precisely*, of the various scales of locality of this thing called life:

> In this we try of course to talk the individual into believing that what has value for him is not what promotes his own life but that of his family, tribe or even mankind as a whole.[24]

What is the root of this need for persuasion? The implication, here, is that the values that promote the art of life and decrease the rate of entropy at least appear in different guises depending on the vantage point from which they are examined or sought, and more specifically depending on the scale of the locality with which one is preoccupied. Boltzmann seems to recognize that this unimpeachable value of values that is life 'itself' qua archi-criterion in fact involves a composition of standpoints that is hard to reconcile with any kind of 'pure' Reason, that this merging of perspectives always requires a kind of stereoscopic trick or illusion. Is it not to effect this illusion, to pull of this trick, that the force of rhetoric is required?

Only such a trick or illusion of a depth that crosses scales can *guarantee* the unsocial sociability necessary to overcome an anti-social tendency towards preferring 'one's own' point of view, the wish to stay within the filter of one's own bubble. Yet without this guarantee, which always involves instruments to generate this depth and achieve this illusion, the social organism itself consumes itself entropically and anaphylactically. This is what Boltzmann seems to acknowledge here with his admission of the need for persuasion, but it is difficult to reconcile this apparent recognition of the need to conduct such a composition, to generate an always partly illusory or fictitious depth of field capable of crossing the scales of locality, with Boltzmann's immediate conclusions concerning the task of philosophy in the aftermath of the second law of thermodynamics, which seem premised, instead, on the possibility of eliminating this aspectival or perspectival implication:

> The task of philosophy for the future is, in my view, to formulate the fundamental concepts in such a way that in all cases we obtain as precise instructions as possible for appropriate interventions in the world of phenomena. This requires first that if we follow different paths we never reach different rules for further thought and action, that is we never meet internal inconsistencies [...]. That sort of event is always a sign that the laws of thought still lack the last finish.[25]

Surely what we know from the second law of thermodynamics is that no system ever receives that last finish, that there is only entropic becoming or unfinished individuation.

Boltzmann gave many such lectures and lecture series in the latter part of his life. Himself a 'democratic radical and a resigned republican',[26] Boltzmann lived within the contradictions of Robert Musil's Kakanic Vienna,[27] and faced with hostility towards atomic theory, especially from those around Ernst Mach, Boltzmann's initial taste of success turned to pain, anxiety and restlessness, and a powerful urge to convey to anyone who would listen the importance of his theories, ideas and discoveries – which were, after all, destined to be proven correct. Cuts in finances, health problems, overwork, swings between mania and depression, thirty lectures in English at Berkeley in 1905 that his listeners struggled to understand – in the latter part of that year, Boltzmann visited a mental hospital but decided against staying. Mach (who was the subject of Musil's PhD) informs us that there had been earlier attempts at suicide, and it was understood he required constant supervision. Boltzmann was forced to postpone his lectures of summer 1906 due to 'his nervous condition', but then travelled to Duino with his wife and daughter: apparently it was her idea, but he seemed to improve.

As I am writing these lines, I realise with a sudden sense of shock that today is 5 September 2020, precisely one month after the death of Bernard Stiegler on 5 August 2020 at 68 years old, and precisely 114 years to the day after 5 September 1906, when Ludwig Boltzmann, aged 62, due to return to Vienna the next day to commence his lectures, and apparently having 'showed himself particularly excited' earlier on that day, made and carried out the decision to hang himself.

A final birth? The last escape?

Among those who would be affected by this event was Erwin Schrödinger, then nineteen years old:

> The old Vienna Institute, from which shortly before Ludwig Boltzmann had been torn away in a tragic fashion [...], engendered in me a direct empathy for the ideas of that powerful spirit. For me his range of ideas played the role of a scientific young love, and no other has ever again held me so spellbound.

The budding physicist, registering the shock of the tragic, not to say violent loss of the voice that had spoken to him like no other, the one who, *binding* him with the spells that were his ideas, incantations that had opened the enchanted realm that would become Schrödinger's discipline, would, by adopting this accident and striving to make it his necessity, participate in the transindividuation of the significance of the life and work of one who, for him, amounted, we could say, to a kind of saint – however improbably. Almost forty years later, in lectures given in Dublin, Schrödinger would, as we know, postulate the thesis that life must be considered a form of 'negative entropy'.

At some point in the last few years of his life, Boltzmann had begun a poem with the following lines:

> *With torment that I'd rather not recall*
> *My soul at last escaped my mortal body.*
> *Ascent through space! What happy floating*
> *For one who suffered such distress and pain.*

It is difficult not to hear in these lines the sense of mortality as a release from suffering yearned for by the distressed and unstable thinker of entropy as the statistically guaranteed triumph of the probable. Yet later in the poem, we read the following:

> *The saint who suffers pain and grief*
> *Redemption's rays illuminate his way.*
> *No man achieves a hero's worldly fame*
> *Who has not forced himself with all his power;*
> *And as it caused his aching heart to tremble*
> *His valiant deed will live in song immortal.*

Only a few years later, in his *Duino Elegies*, Rainer Maria Rilke would refer in similar terms to the *klēos* of the hero:

> *Begin again. Try out your impotent praise again;*
> *think about the hero who lives on: even his fall*
> *was only an excuse for another life, a final birth.*

A 'final birth', *seine letzte Geburt*, that lives on 'in song immortal'. Gilbert Simondon, in his own reflection upon the fate of the noetic soul of the mortal, will say a 'second birth', *une seconde naissance*.[28] What does it mean to say that there is a second birth that survives the first death? In fact, this involves the same question that animated Schrödinger's consideration of the animate as negentropic, the same question that Lotka asks concerning the doubling of the struggle against entropy that occurs with exosomatic evolution, and which is to say, as well, the question just barely but already opened up by Boltzmann concerning the shifts of scale involved in the consideration of 'life' as the source of neganthropic value.

For Simondon, the second birth becomes possible when 'life' is no longer just a matter of vital individuation but of psychic and collective individuation. The psychic individual belongs not just to a vital milieu, an ecosystem with which it negotiates its metastability until the moment of its eventual demise, but rather exists in relation to other psychic individuals, and, more than that, exists *only* in relation to other individuals. Already while still living, after the first birth, the individual is both drawing from the collective and *secreting* himself or herself *into* the collective, through which alone the individual has the chance of becoming the one who they are or will be. The individual remains unfinished in life, and *continues* to be unfinished even after death, so long as there are psychic individuals who remain, and collective individuals that remain, affected by the life of the lost individual, by the work of the individual, if not as well by the shock of losing them, and who, so affected, carry something on – a survival. As the individual is withdrawn from life, that absence becomes the gap that opens the call to the work of 'reactualizing this active absence' as a 'seed of consciousness and action'.[29]

Yet for all that to be possible, the remains are definitive, less the corpse than the corpus, the traces, through which what has been secreted may become the transindividuation of meaning, of significance – significations that become, precisely, transindividual. As a result, what has closed remains open, 'not contained, locked, in an individual enclosure that will degrade'.[30] Instead, 'converted into meaning, perpetuated in information', or in other words, entered into a song immortal (and here we must not forget that a song, whether mortal or immortal, is always something technical, as is the act of singing), the instability of the fragile individuation of a noetic soul can be overcome and can join the 'only and definitive metastability', that of the collective, 'perpetuated without aging through successive generations'.[31]

Nevertheless, we would like to introduce two wrinkles into the tapestry we are here weaving between Toynbee, Boltzmann, Rilke, Schrödinger and Simondon (not to mention Lotka and Stiegler), two discordant notes into this cosmic melody concerning the posterity of the mortal individual sung by the chorus of the collective, amounting in the final assessment to an unending 'ode to man', and to his *deinon*.

The first is to suggest that, sometimes, the existence of a psychic individual is not only cut short, but cut short having left traces and memories of unfulfilled promise, of work yet to be carried out, of leaps yet to be taken, but indicated, prepared-for, initiated, promised. Secretions remain, unextruded, and no longer extrudable. Sometimes those promises, unfulfilled, are of a singular kind utterly dependent on the unique characteristics of the particular soul who conceived possibilities and bifurcations that were not yet brought to fruition – in the case of genius, for example. No doubt continuation, a second birth, is still possible, and even more so, yet in another direction, a turn off and probably a turn in, and where the collective, insofar as it is a genuine collective, cannot but be aware of how the *direction* in which that living on continues involves a deviation from the initial path, and, perhaps, in a weaker direction, as a shadow.

The second concerns Simondon's thought that it is the collective alone, constituted through the immortal song of transindividual signification, that ever and always bears any lasting metastability. Maybe so, but if this song is technical, and this technics is a necessary medium and support through which alone the transindividual is possible, then we are confronted with what Stiegler calls a *pharmakon*, and with the fact that the collective individuation process opened up through this song need not just progress, but is always and irreducibly exposed to the risk of regress, just like the psychic individuation processes of which it is necessarily composed. The collective soul, too, is only ever intermittently capable of its noetic potential, and its greater stability is by no means divinely guaranteed.

In short, while Simondon speaks as though, by being translated into transindividual meaning, the psychic individual is being absorbed or reabsorbed into something larger, something of a broader amplitude, not a universe but a cosmos, nevertheless it may be that scales become skewed and reversed, that what is larger suddenly becomes smaller, and that the smaller scale of the psychic soul suddenly proves to be too vast for any such reabsorption. The whole world may shrink, and shrink before the task given to it by a loss that, precisely, exposes its shrunken character. In such a case, when the collective has suffered a proletarianization and denoetization (to use Stiegler's terms) that leaves it bereft and adrift, then the adoption of the shock of the event may not just be the improbable necessity of quasi-causally turning the accidental into the necessary: it may have become a strict and irreversible impossibility. Whether overshooting the mark in overreactions, or underreactively failing to fire a shot for want of ammunition or will, it may turn out that there is no longer anyone left to measure up to the task of thinking and caring in the Anthropocene. In the struggle between the upward trend and the downward, as Whitehead calls it, and so long as entropy remains an irreducible tendency of the universe, inevitably it eventuates that we one day reach the cosmic inflection point.

What is the Anthropocene? What is it, futurally, but the arrival of a moment when nihilism is fulfilled, when there is no longer any way to 'talk the individual into believing that what has value for him is not what promotes his own life but that of his family, tribe or even mankind as a whole' – or the biosphere as a whole? And when this is so because there is no longer any voice, speaking or singing, capable of resonating with a sense of the scale of the problem that exosomatic life in the biosphere has become, no signification immortal or mortal capable of weighing the gravity of the task.

It is possible, after all, for the last such voice to be silenced, in this Anthropocene whose probabilistic and entropic character Boltzmann was the first to open up mathematically, and who, perhaps, was also the first to perceive this epoch's permanent and impending closing, foreshadowed by his own dramatic spiralling in upon himself. Other voices, too, have opened up our awareness of the general character of entropy, for instance philosophically, or organologically, calling us to the task of healing this sur-real cosmos, yet they too can close, perhaps are closed, perhaps once and for all. Can we still dream that they might live on, a second birth? What else than a dream could they ever have been? It is this conjunction of closures, psychic, collective and biospheric, that, more than anything, confronts us with the appalling and dreadful likelihood of the Anthropocenic and anaphylactic fate that beckons us – the last escape.

How to read this book

This book is suffused with the work of Bernard Stiegler, in a way that is apparent on almost every page, but it is not the great synthesis of

Stiegler's philosophy that the world still lacks. Would that it were so, but for that it is still necessary to wait, if it is not indeed still too soon, however urgent. More modestly than that, it is a compilation of texts written over the past five years or so, and then rewritten to various degrees, each chapter responding to certain aspects of Stiegler's work, at times starting to open a dialogue that is now destined to remain closed. More specifically, several of the chapters take up themes from the Internation Collective project that occupied the last few years of Stiegler's work, and resulted in the book entitled in English, *Bifurcate: 'There is No Alternative'*. Nevertheless, this book does not respond to that one, and readers of some of the chapters in this book would benefit from reading some of the chapters of that collectively-composed volume.

Because a number of the chapters were written as a kind of engagement with an existing project, they tend to assume some familiarity with Stiegler's work. One way around this potential problem for less familiar readers is to read the introduction, written by this author, to Stiegler's collection entitled *The Neganthropocene*. At the same time, the first chapter of the present work was written subsequently to the others, and is intended to serve as a kind of introduction to the theme of Stiegler and the Anthropocene. Chapter 3 is also intended as another kind of introduction again, one written for students at Tongji University in Shanghai, and focused only on the first two volumes of *Technics and Time*. Additionally, Chapter 4 was in part written as yet another kind of introduction. Yet another choice, and probably the best one, would be to go straight to the Afterword, 'On Positive Pharmacology', written by Stiegler.

There are thus a number of different introductions available in this book and outside of it, and a number of chapters that engage in forms of discussion in need of an introduction. But then, it has always seemed that Stiegler's work was in need of being introduced again and again, a mark, perhaps, of his departure from some of the conventional expectations of philosophical writing over recent decades. It is also a sign, however, of the fact that his work has yet to achieve the reception it deserves, at least in the clear view of the present author.

In preparing this book, the decision was made to present the chapters in the order they were written (with the exception of Chapter 1), because it seemed to the author that they formed a kind of progression, and that each chapter served to some extent as a way of leading in to the next. Nevertheless, the sequence of arguments in each individual chapter does not really add up to a coherent line of thought extending from beginning to end, and it is entirely reasonable and possible to read the chapters in any order whatsoever. In short, it is a case of spirals within spirals…

Daniel Ross
Melbourne, Australia
September 2020.

1 Bereft and Adrift in an Entropic Universe: After Bernard Stiegler

Eons, eras, periods, epochs and ages – to the Anthropocene

The planet on whose surface dwells all the current or extinct living matter that has ever been discovered anywhere in the Universe was formed some 4.5 billion years ago, and the accidental terraforming of this surface began some 3.5 billion years ago, resulting in what, after Vladimir Vernadsky, has become known as the biosphere. Since that time, this planet and its biosphere have undergone many transformations and seen many stages, which geologists divide into four eons, themselves neatly and progressively subdivided into various eras, periods, epochs and ages. The most recent of these four eons is the Phanerozoic (meaning 'visible life'), commencing some 541 million years ago with the Cambrian explosion and distinguished by the widespread proliferation of multicellular life – plants and animals.

The most recent of the three *eras* of the Phanerozoic Eon is the Cenozoic ('new life'), corresponding to the rise of mammals and beginning around 66 million years ago. The most recent of the three *periods* of the Cenozoic era is the Quaternary that began approximately 2.5 million years ago and was characterized by a series of climatic changes in which ice sheets and glaciers repeatedly formed and receded. The Quaternary itself is divided into two geological *epochs*, the second of which, the Holocene ('wholly new'), begins some 11,650 years ago, after the last glacial event.

The commencement of the Holocene epoch thus occurs at approximately the same time as, or just before, what is known in the divisions of the stages of human evolution as the Neolithic age, when *Homo sapiens* became farmers, cultivating plants and domesticating livestock. This development also implied replacing the nomadic lifestyle hitherto necessary for subsistence with an increasing tendency to build permanent settlements. In other words, it is at this very recent point that the 3.5 billion-year-old biosphere first begins to be *anthropized* – significantly marked by the effects of one particular species' efforts to survive, efforts that consist in *organizing* (via artificial selection) the reproduction of various forms of biological life, and in covering the terrestrial surface with more or less long-lasting forms of *organized* inorganic matter (by making technical artefacts, a process that of course began much earlier). The Holocene epoch, or the Neolithic age, thus occupies approximately 1/375,000 of the entire span of time in which the Earth has existed.

How should we marry this very long history of organic life with the much shorter history of what Bernard Stiegler will call organological life, that is, a form of life composed of the inextricably entwined evolution of somato-psychic organs, social organizations and technological organs? How do these organic and organological strands of terrestrial history culminate in what has come to be called the Anthropocene? The notion that we have entered the Anthropocene corresponds to the idea that at a certain point the Holocene ended, and to the idea that some large-scale change befell that series of social and technological evolutions that can be traced back over ten or twelve millennia to the beginning of the Neolithic, in a way that transforms and threatens to seal the fate of this biosphere. Does a chance remain that we can influence the fate of this Anthropocene epoch, which seems almost to be over and done with when it has but barely begun, less fading into its twilight than succumbing to a violent and irresistible suicidal impulse – however long may linger its agonizing death throes?

When *did* it begin? For geologists, the scientific question of whether, within this infinitesimal fragment of Earth's history, a new epoch has begun *after* the Holocene requires asking whether changes are visible in stratigraphic rock layers, such changes needing to be observable all across the planet. In other fields, however, what matters are not so much the official standards by which stratigraphers institutionalize the division of geological time, but rather the very noticeable *acceleration* in the processes of anthropizing the biosphere, which is to say, the accelerating encroachment of what has been called the *technosphere upon* the biosphere. This acceleration gets going a little more than two centuries ago, which is to say between 1/50 and 1/60 of the span of time covered by the Holocene epoch or the Neolithic age, when human beings begin to employ new means in this process of anthropization: new forms of energy production and consumption with the development of heat engines and new forms of automation with the development of machinery and factories.

If we date the commencement of the Anthropocene from these developments, then it corresponds to the beginning of what, in terms of technological history, is usually called the industrial revolution, and what, in terms of economic history, corresponds to the rise of industrial capitalism or what Karl Polanyi called the great transformation. In the twentieth century, this acceleration intensifies with the development of vast electricity grids, mass production and consumerist capitalism. It is transformed once again in the twenty-first century, with the development of global digital networks and what has been called platform capitalism – *but*, thus far, the sources of energy production have *not* greatly changed (though of course, the post-war sources of electricity were extended to include nuclear power, which has already given us Chernobyl and Fukushima), or, at least, not greatly enough.

From the tragedy of oi thanatoi to Gestell

Some hundred centuries after the dawn of the Holocene and the Neolithic, in the context of a crisis of that settled area known as the Greek *polis* of Athens, Socrates questioned whether the sophists really knew the things they thought they knew, whether they knew how to distinguish between what they knew and what they didn't know, and whether they knew how to pursue a question to its origin, so that the unknown might become known. In so doing, and with the trial and punishment of Socrates by that *polis*, and then Plato's retrospective written record of the spoken words of Socrates, there began a long chain of inquiry and recording concerned with knowledge and its crises that would be known as *philosophy*, which has continued until this day – or, at least, almost until this day.

At the time of philosophy's commencement, and throughout most of the twenty-five centuries since then, none of the facts concerning the eons, eras, periods, epochs and ages of the history of Earth or its biosphere were known to philosophers or to anyone else, and nor were the ages of the history of hominization. Nor could the founders of philosophy or most of their heirs ever have imagined how anthropization, which was already well underway in their lifetimes, would proceed to cover the biospheric surface of the Earth and transform the very conditions of both biological (or endosomatic) life and technological (or exosomatic) life – to the point of threatening to destroy the conditions necessary for the very continuation of the human adventure. They could thus have imagined neither the Neolithic or Palaeolithic past of hominims nor the apocalyptic nightmare that currently threatens to engulf them, not just because they had yet to uncover the scientific facts of terrestrial history, but more importantly because the *pace* of the exosomatic process of anthropization (the pace of *exosomatization*) was still too slow to be noticeable to those living through it.

For that reason, the cosmic conception that underlay philosophy and the concepts it produced was founded on the distinction between those things that change and those things that remain unchanged – a cosmos divided between the sublunary world and the astral universe. All of the concepts and categories of philosophy were characterized by this opposition between being and becoming, the timeless and the temporal, the eternal and the transitory, and the interrelationships between living things dwelling within what we have come to think of as 'nature' were inevitably conceived in terms of notions of balance and harmony, rather than as a dynamic process and perpetual war unfolding through the struggle and proliferation of countless generations of organisms and species unfolding across an unimaginably long timescale.

In Greek mythology and thought, an element of disorder or disharmony appears only with the disruption that we ourselves introduce into the world of *physis*. In the famous 'ode to man' chorus of Sophocles' *Antigone*, human beings are described in terms of *deinon* and *deinotaton*, 'man' being the uncanniest and most frightening of beings, constantly caught in one or another trap, but more adept than any other at finding their way beyond them – this is his *mētis*, his cunning intelligence.[32]

We see this character again in the myth of human origins told via Prometheus and Epimetheus, where, because of Epimethean oversight, humans are alone among the creatures in having no pre-given qualities defining their place among living things. Instead of being granted such skills, talents or abilities by Zeus or by 'nature', human beings have the *foresight* to fashion their own qualities by taking advantage of the gift of fire, stolen from Zeus and Hephaestus, allowing them to *acquire* the ability to escape from all those traps into which they fall due to their own disordered being. It is as a consequence of this theft and the unnatural power it brings, however, that human beings have the possibility of falling *into* disorder, in the form of war and strife. And it is only *after* this theft, as a late and compensatory *afterthought*, that the primordial feelings of *dikē* and *aidōs* are distributed to human beings, forming the basis of the potential for *philia*, that is, the possibility of acquiring the art of learning to live together – opening onto the always risky and fragile capacity for making wise collective decisions that would come to be called politics.

Human beings, *Anthropos*, or better to say mortals, *oi thanatoi*, between the beasts and the immortals, are for the Greeks tragic beings caught in the dramaturgy of rise and fall, bearers of a noetic soul (as distinct from the sensible soul and the vegetative soul described by Aristotle for animals and plants) and so granted the perpetual possibility of ascending to all the possibilities afforded by reason, yet only intermittently so, more often finding themselves falling back, regressing to the level of the sensitive soul of the beasts. Despite this drama of the disorders of the noetic soul, however, this will not become a *historical* drama until the time of Hegel. And only with the work of Karl Marx and Friedrich Engels in *The German Ideology* would it be suggested that Darwin's theory of the evolution of sensible and vegetative souls should be doubled by an account of the evolutionary dynamic within which the existence of noetic souls would itself unfold: a theory of the evolution of what these two thinkers would call the 'means of production', or in other words, technics:

> Men [...] begin to distinguish themselves from animals as soon as they begin to *produce* their means of subsistence, a step which is conditioned by their physical organisation. [...] This mode of production must not be considered simply as being the production of the physical existence of the individuals. Rather it is a definite form of activity of these individuals, a definite form of expressing their life, a definite *mode of life* on their part.[33]

To this thought of a technical mode of production defining the very conditions of life for those dwelling within it, Engels would later add an account of the complex interrelationship of the evolution of the hand, the tool and the brain, emphasizing not just that the hand sets human beings apart from animals by its ability to grasp tools, but that the hand 'implies the *tool*'.[34] What is implied by this implication is that hand and tool (and by extension, brain) evolve in a dynamic historical relationship of co-constitution.

In the twentieth century, Martin Heidegger would add to this the thought that the fate of this noetic soul in modern technology now consists in the prevailing of calculation over all earlier forms by which the world reveals itself, so that the future would henceforth be planned via a thoroughgoing use of calculation, rather than existentially projected. This cybernetic tendency is progressing, he argues as early as the late 1940s, to the point that the co-evolutionary dynamic between the hand and the tool, between the human being and technology, would not just be revealed by the unfolding of human history, but would increasingly *displace* the role of human beings themselves *in* this dynamic, where the latter increasingly find themselves to be just one more *object* of that provocation or challenging-forth that is its basis. It was for this reason that Heidegger would eventually posit that our uncanny destiny consists in the necessity of 'thinking being without beings', that is, without that guiding being who in *Being and Time* was named Dasein, that is, that being who may not be 'man' but is nothing other than man – or in other words, the kind of being that we ourselves are.[35]

From phylogenesis, through epigenesis, to epiphylogenesis

Bernard Stiegler further complicates the account of this dynamic in the first volume of *Technics and Time*, through a close reading of the work of the palaeo-anthropologist André Leroi-Gourhan. The commencement of this new dynamic involving the co-implication of hand, tool and brain occurs long, long before the Neolithic evolution, long before the appearance of *Homo sapiens*, and even before the appearance of the genus *Homo*. Already with Lucy, that is, with *Australopithecus afarensis*, more than three million years ago, hammerstone tools were being produced; with Zinjanthropus, maybe two million years ago (more or less), Oldowan tools were in use. Only with *Homo erectus* would finer Acheulean flint tools be developed, and only with *Homo sapiens sapiens* would fires be systematically built and maintained for warmth and cooking. At the same time as the slow advancement of techniques in tool production, brain size would also progressively increase, from 365–417cc for Lucy, 450–550cc for *Paranthropus boisei*, 546–1251cc for *Homo erectus* and 1400cc for the beings that we ourselves are (and where this increase is not just uniform, but involves the development of the frontal lobes and so on, that is, those parts of the brain that extend beyond the limbic system).

In such a gradual, *simultaneous* evolution of hands, tools and brains, it is strictly impossible to assign *one* of these elements as the driver of the process. All three are inextricably entwined in a single co-evolutionary process, and it is therefore as true to say 'that the *what* invents the *who* [...] as much as it is invented by it'.[36] If by the *who* we imply a being (a Dasein, in Heidegger's terms) in possession of an 'interiority' (or what Husserlian phenomenology will call 'intentional consciousness'), a consciousness that apprehends the world *as* world, then it is as true to say that *exteriorization*, the process of putting oneself outside oneself in the prostheses of inorganic and exosomatic technics, invents the interiority of this *who* as much as it is invented by it. And all this, long before anything that we can call 'the human' even appears on the evolutionary stage, or in other words, long before the appearance of those creatures in whom we can conceivably recognize ourselves, long before 'men like ourselves',[37] as Georges Bataille will say about those who painted the Lascaux caves, and who are already very much closer to the Neolithic age.[38]

In putting forward this way of conceiving the dynamic of hominization, Stiegler is to an extent following Jacques Derrida's attempt to undo (or deconstruct) the oppositions between the natural and unnatural, animal and human, that have, the latter says, perpetually structured the metaphysics of presence characteristic of the history of Western thought. In *Of Grammatology*, Derrida, too, will refer to Leroi-Gourhan (albeit on a single page), and to his concept of exteriorization, in order to undertake this deconstruction. Derrida will refer to an exteriorization always already begun, in order to maintain that the history of life, whether biological or technological, *is* the history of différance, that is, the history of traces opening up new possibilities of life as the unfolding of a process of deferral and differentiation.[39] As Stiegler later summarizes:

> In his most famous work, *Of Grammatology*, and after *Speech and Phenomena*, Derrida advanced his central thesis through a critique of Saussure – and by shifting from the question of structure (which was, for example, still the 'common understanding' of the journal *Tel Quel*) to more general questions of the *grammē* and *différance* – that is, to the question of a process that, by deferring its own accomplishment, differentiates itself, this differentiation producing traces, which is also to say, *grammēs*, forms of writing and of what *Of Grammatology* called 'supplements'.[40]

Yet despite their similarities on this score, Derrida, unlike Stiegler, never quite conceives différance *as* a process, let alone one through which there occurs the *differentiation* of *Anthropos*:

> On the basis of reading Leroi-Gourhan, something became clear to me: it is necessary to think what Jacques Derrida calls différance – which constitutes *the process of the production of traces*, which he also calls supplements – precisely *as* a process, while the possibility of considering this process, starting from what Georges Canguilhem calls the technical form of life, should be understood as a process of *exteriorization*, in the sense proposed by Leroi-Gourhan, with the formidable philosophical problem being that [...] exteriorization is a paradoxical concept, since it is not preceded by an interiority, and therefore is not exactly an exteriorization.[41]

Far more than Derrida, Stiegler will emphasize this processual character of différance, not just through reading Leroi-Gourhan, but by marrying this account with Gilbert Simondon's account of individuation, and the latter's description of the shift from the vital individuation of biological or endosomatic evolution to the *psychic and collective* individuation of technological or exosomatic evolution. What Stiegler will add is that the opening of this bifurcation, from out of which psychic and collective individuation unfurls a new process of différance, cannot be conceived without recognizing that this new regime of individuation is composed of *three* intertwined strands: the psychic, the collective and the *technical* (thus coinciding with the three kinds of organs that define organology). In the passage from vital individuation to psychic and collective individuation, *technical* individuation introduces cleavage that opens this gap between the psychic and the collective, because it opens a new form of temporality (or temporality as such, in the Heideggerian sense), in the sense that every technical artefact functions, accidentally or deliberately, as a new support of *memory*.

Stiegler thus shows that the history of life qua différance should be grasped as a very long history of several great epochs of *memory*, where the latter is understood very broadly as the improbable possibility of the past persisting into the present. This possibility of conserving order in matter is in turn understood as constituting the fundamental means of all life in its struggle against the tendency towards the probable, that is, towards the disordering of its matter. The first of these great epochs is genetic memory, encoded and transmitted via the genome but incapable of learning lessons – *phylogenetic* memory, beginning with the commencement of terrestrial life.

The second great epoch is that of nervous memory, engraved not in the molecular structure of the DNA molecule but in 'grey matter' – *epigenetic* memory that arises with animal life and makes it possible for individual organisms to learn lessons, that is, to vary their behavioural selections according to the past experience *of* the organism, but where all of those experiences are lost with the perishing of the organism and its nervous system. Both of these forms of memory have existed for billions (in the case of phylogenetic) or hundreds of millions (epigenetic) of years, and they constitute the means by which endosomatization – vital individuation – postpones the march of the probable through a diversification of organs and species that runs counter to the overwhelming tendency of the so-called 'arrow of time'.

With the advent of exteriorization, however, it is not just grey organic matter that is engraved but inorganic matter such as stone or clay, so that the lessons conserved in that engraving (for example, the gestures recorded in the form of a flint tool) are *not* lost with the loss of the individual who made them, but are instead preserved and transmissible – what Stiegler names *epiphylogenetic* memory. Again, this is something that begins long before the appearance of *Homo sapiens*, and thus the *distinction* that is marked by the advent of this third kind of memory simply cannot be ascribed to any kind of 'anthropocentrism', and nor can it ground any *opposition* between the human and the animal. What the recognition of this new and distinct process *can* do, however, is open a pathway to understanding what *difference* this event in the history of différance makes, when the processes of natural selection operating through phylogenetic and epigenetic memory are *supplemented,* if not in fact *suspended,* by epiphylogenetic memory.

It is only after this history of epiphylogenetic exteriorization has progressed quite far that forms of exteriorization arise whose *function* it is to exteriorize memory. Every flint tool *in fact* functions as such a memory, because, for example, a careful examination can still divulge the lessons it contains about how that tool was crafted, but this is only an accidental feature of a hand axe. With phenomena such as cave painting, however, that is, forms of aesthetic decoration in which, Bataille says, we can at last recognize 'ourselves', there begins the deliberate recording of past experience, making it possible not only for lessons to be transmitted, but to be *accumulated,* and in a systematic way through those processes of intergenerational training we refer to as education. From cave painting to forms of writing in stone or clay, or on papyrus or paper, and then of printing and eventually within the circuitry of silicon chips, this exteriorized memory becomes *hypomnesic,* as Stiegler calls it, ultimately giving rise to formalized knowledge whose canon is geometry.

Hypomnesis, grammatization, proletarianization

What is the significance of this term, 'hypomnesic', and do we really need 'philosophy' to make sense of any of these multiple histories whose stories we have been telling? Aren't these questions and stories scientific more than they are philosophical? Have we really located any grounds for considering that the Stieglerian perspective on the 'Anthropocene' distinguishes itself in any crucial way from any archaeological, anthropological, economic, sociological or political account of the implications to be drawn from delineating such an epoch? To approach such questions, it is necessary to shift from the first stage of Stiegler's work, on technics, to the second, when he begins to refer to 'general organology' and insists that it must also be a 'pharmacology'.[42]

In *Phaedrus,* Socrates draws attention to the ambivalent character of writing, on which the sophists rely so heavily. On the one hand, writing functions as an aid to memorization, but it can also have the opposite effect, when it becomes a crutch on which one leans instead of internalizing what one knows. Because writing has this duplicitous characteristic of being both a remedy for faulty memory and poisonous for that same memory, Socrates refers to it as a *pharmakon* (a drug may cure us, but if not used well, it can poison us; a bandage may help us heal, but if not used well, it can encourage infection). Stiegler argues that all forms of exteriorized memory, not just writing, and in fact all forms of technical exteriorization in general, possess this same duplicity, the consequence of which is that writing, epiphylogenetic memory and technics in general can never be described as good or bad in themselves: they *always* require *care* to be taken in the practice of these *pharmaka, just as* the gift of fire (that is, technics) stolen by Prometheus required the *late* gift of the possibility of *philia*, failing which the *polis* is bound to fall into strife.

In Socratic terms, the epistemological significance of this argument can be seen by drawing it into a relation with the conclusion reached in *Meno*. This early Platonic dialogue ponders how to know the meaning of virtue: on the one hand, a list of examples of virtue drawn from experience cannot tell us what virtue is *as such*; on the other hand, where can we find the unity of these examples, if we cannot find it in our experience? What this aporia raises for Socrates is the question of the origin of knowledge, and of our access to it, and his answer is that all knowledge comes to us as a recollection, an *anamnesis*, of what we once knew, in a past life of our soul, but have since forgotten. The question of the location of knowledge can no longer lead *us* to the notion of past lives of an immortal soul. Yet the significance of the aporia of *Meno* remains, and the question it raises is still *our* question: from whence arises the possibility of ascribing unity to the concepts with which we think, and without which *anamnesis* is not possible, that is, thinking for oneself through that revealing that Heidegger too ascribed to *an-amnesis*?

Despite some vacillation in *Being and Time* about the place of monuments and other hypomnesic *pharmaka* in exposing the world-historical character of Dasein, the possibility of such unconcealment ultimately depends for Heidegger on the opposition between the determined, which forms the basis of calculation, and the indeterminate, which opens the possibility of genuine thinking. This opposition between calculation and authentic thinking will be borne out and intensified in his later thought. For Stiegler, on the other hand, determination amounts to a necessary condition of any access to the indeterminate, and this means, firstly, that every prosthetic artefact can function as a *hypomnesis*, and that this alone gives rise to the possibility of any such *anamnesis*.

In Heidegger, determinate 'clock time' simply closes off the possibility of 'authentic time', which cannot be determined by the calculability of mechanical timekeeping. Stiegler does not disagree that mechanical timekeeping, calculably determining duration, may close off the possibility of a remembrance of our existential thrownness between past and future, as Heidegger thinks. Yet, he argues, it is equally true that if Dasein is the being who is *capable* of knowing such authentic time, it must be because Dasein is the being that is *capable of seeing* that it is thrown into time, because it is capable of gazing upon the artefacts of its own past, which open up, as the already-there, the fact of Dasein's having to *run ahead* to its past, opening up its authentic and singular future, and opening Dasein to the existential fact of its mortality. What's more, if this is so, it is because *every* artefact, as a *record* of the past of Dasein and of every exosomatic being, *is* a kind of clock – not just because for Anaximander a stick was sufficient to create a gnomon, but because every artefact is a mirror in which one sees reflected one's own past or the past of others, and which alone, and through that maieutic, opens up the possibility of a relationship to the indeterminate future.

It is because this artefactual mirror reflects not just the past one has lived oneself, but a past that one has not lived but that can thereby *become* one's own past, that it answers to *both* Heidegger's inability to constitute the grounds of the distinction of Dasein as the noetic being thrown into the possibility of authentic time, *and* the aporia of *Meno*: through the reflective waves made possible by the hypomnesic artefact, the beings that we ourselves are can access, internalize and recapitulate the lessons of lives other than our own. In this way, the lessons of past lives become a primordial and collective fund on which we can draw, from the mythological storytelling that occurs in ancient rituals to the geometry textbook that grants the student the possibility of acquiring a capacity for geometrical reasoning that required millennia before a Euclid would arise capable of setting down its fundamental axioms and theorems. Rather than the past lives of the immortal soul, it is the continuous recommencement of knowledge through the circuit we form with the past via the hypomnesic memories of exteriorized artefacts that supplies the funds through which we can *believe in* the unity of the concepts with which we hope to reason and decide about our future. But these hypomneses can, as well, and as Socrates knew, always also become the very thing that stands in the way of the possibility of knowledge and reason – not just for oneself, but in general.

What follows from this analysis is that the stages, epochs and rhythms of the history of epiphylogenesis (the evolution of exosomatic memory) are just as crucial to the unfolding of the history of life qua différance as the stages, epochs and rhythms of the evolution of phylogenetic and epigenetic memory. Unlike the geological timescale of neatly divided subdivisions, however, these epochs of exosomatization involve a strange pattern of advance and delay, of technical developments that run ahead of the ability to take care of them, provoking shocks and consequently requiring the invention of new practices and forms of care; or, alternatively, of moments when changes yet to come seem to be anticipated in advance of their arrival, which may take quite some time, such as the two hundred years that Nietzsche forecast would be necessary for the fulfilment of nihilism. In this way, these successions of advances and delay are the collective extension of the irreducible intermittency of the noetic soul that may leap forward or, more often, regress – of that noetic soul that belongs to the organological being that we ourselves are.

In order to elucidate the epochs of the organological life of the noetic soul, Stiegler draws on the work of the linguist Sylvain Auroux and his concept of 'grammatization'. Grammatization is Auroux's name for the process necessary for the temporal flow of speech to be turned into the spatial and material forms of alphabetical writing, necessarily involving the discrimination and analysis, not necessarily conscious, of the discrete phonetic elements that would become the letters.[43] The processual reinterpretation of grammatology implies the necessity of such a process of grammatization, we could say.

Stiegler's genius was to recognize that a process of spatialization, materialization, discretization and analysis lies at the root, not just of the alphabetical writing that made possible the Greek *polis* and its tragedy, philosophy and democracy, but also of the industrial revolution. In the latter case, however, this was a process of grammatization applied not to the temporal flow of speech but to the temporal flow of *gesture*, and more specifically, of the gestures of the tool-equipped hands (those hands that are the exosomatic *consequence* of the pre-hominim *foot* that becomes *implied* with the tool) of workers possessing the knowledge of how to craft material objects, from the weaver to the potter to the blacksmith and beyond. It was this gestural knowledge of the worker that had to become subject to a process of grammatization in order for the mechanization and automation of industrial manufacturing to be established in the nineteenth century.

This process is exactly what Marx describes in the *Grundrisse*, albeit without the concept of grammatization at his disposal. The 'Fragment on Machines' is a precise account of how the knowledge possessed by the worker is inscribed into fixed capital, that is, into Arkwright's spinning frame, Jacquard's loom and a thousand other inventions based on the mechanization of processes that previously required manual skill. The formation of the great division of classes diagnosed by Marx as the division between capital and labour is made possible by this dispossession of workers of the means of production, but where these means must be identified above all as the knowledge of how to use tools, which in the act of dispossession is transformed into a discrete and analytical form programmable into machines. In this act of dispossession, then, knowledge, which is incalculable, is turned into information, which is inherently and necessarily defined by its calculability.

What makes possible this dispossession of gestural knowledge is not its *technologization* (such knowledge was always already tool-equipped, that is, technical, and this is precisely what opens it up *as* knowledge), but its *industrialization* (which is to say, its mechanization, or in other words, its automation).[44] The industrial machine, like writing, may open up the possibility of new knowledge, but, in the industrial revolution, which is to say at the dawn of the Anthropocene, its use mainly consisted in destroying the knowledge possessed by workers, who in this way literally disappear, becoming labourers deprived of the potential to pursue or transform their knowledge of how to work.

It is for this reason that Stiegler occasionally refers to Socrates as the first thinker of *proletarianization*, this term being understood firstly and in this way as the destruction of knowledge. In both ancient Athens and nineteenth-century Manchester, it is the process of grammatization that makes this destruction possible, by inscribing it into the fixed capital of writing and then into the machines of industrial production. Conceived in this way, Marx and Socrates share the distinction of being the thinkers who conceived the pharmacological basis of the technical transformations that gave rise to their troubled epochs, but it is only in Marx's time that such proletarianization becomes systematic and systemic.

Organology of tertiary retention in the twentieth and twenty-first centuries

There is an at least twofold problem, however, with the fate of Marx in becoming Marxism: first, this analysis does not appear in *Capital*, while the *Grundrisse* was not published until 1939; second, the process of grammatization did not end in the nineteenth century, and new epochs of grammatization would in the twentieth century completely transform industrial society. These two problems, combined with a dialectical approach that would fallaciously ascribe negative power to this process of proletarianization, and with Engels' rejection in the *Dialectics of Nature* of the concept of entropy, prevented Marxism from developing an adequate account of the fate of industrial society as it comes increasingly to be founded not on the industrialization of production but on the industrialization of consumption. Furthermore,

Stiegler effectively demonstrates that for any such account to be adequate, it will also require a consideration and critique of the Husserlian description of the time-consciousness.

The forms of grammatization that will develop in the twentieth century are first and foremost those of the temporal flows of sight and sound – the grammatization of the auditory and visual sensible realms that was necessary for the invention of the gramophone, radio, cinema and television. These forms of grammatization again gave rise to new forms of proletarianization, but the knowledge destroyed by the systematic use of these instruments would not just be concerned with the work made possible by the use of tools, but rather with all the forms of knowledge associated with ways of life, from politeness to education to courtship and ritual, and to all the other details of everyday life. Although the so-called leisure or consumer society of the twentieth century was referred to by Alain Touraine and Daniel Bell as 'post-industrial', for Stiegler it is in fact *hyper*-industrial, marked by the rise of the culture industries and functionally premised on the capacity of these new grammatization technologies to influence and control desire (and from an increasingly young age), and through that, behaviour, making possible mass production, which required the ability to *count on*, that is, invest in, mass consumption.

Why is Husserl's phenomenology of the temporality of intentional consciousness (that is, the noetic soul's experience of the passage of time) necessary for this account? Because it is through the description of the consciousness of temporal flow offered by Husserl at the beginning of the twentieth century that we can understand how these new grammatizing technologies are able to systematically interfere with the very process of forming a relationship to the future. Husserl's distinction between primary retention and secondary retention will, when supplemented with Stiegler's concept of tertiary retention (*as* supplement), make apparent the way in which the deliberate and systematic introduction of audiovisual imagery offers a way of conditioning the basis of perception – and does so pharmacologically, for better and for worse.

Husserl's problem was to understand how it is possible to perceive the passage of time itself, and his assumption was that time cannot be composed of a series of 'now points' strung together, since this would not constitute the *flow* of time. His thesis was that the way to conduct a phenomenological investigation of this question is to reflect on the perception of an object whose existence cannot be divorced from the flow of time because its existence consists only *in* this flow: he called this a temporal object, the paradigmatic case of which is the melody. By examining the way we intend towards such a temporal object, it would be possible to distinguish the perception of the object's existing in time from the perception of the temporal flow within which the object itself flowed, and it would thereby become possible to pay attention to the experience of time-consciousness itself.

To perceive a melody, or even a single note, Husserl argued, it is necessary for the moment just past to be retained in the present, so that the 'now-apprehension is, as it were, the head attached to the comet's tail of retentions relating to the earlier now-points',[45] just as it must also be conjoined to the expectation of the immediate next moment, which he called *protention*. This keeping of the just-past as *constitutive* of the present is what Husserl called *primary retention*, that retention involved in the very passing of the present, distinct from the *secondary retention* that would be illustrated, for example, when I run through a melody again in my mind that I heard yesterday – former primary retentions that have been added to my epigenetic memory and that, in becoming secondary, are able to be recalled. This distinction between primary retention and secondary retention is what Derrida will deconstruct in *Speech and Phenomena*, showing that Husserl falls into contradiction in the play of presence and absence at work in the opposition between past and present, and that *both* primary and secondary retention must be considered as 'two modifications of non-perception [...], two ways of relating to the irreducible nonpresence of another now'.[46] Stiegler will accept this critique without question, while nonetheless insisting that the *distinction* if not the opposition between primary retention and secondary remains crucial, but that to it must be added the concept of 'tertiary retention', exteriorized memory, as that which opens the very ground of the play of the primary and the secondary.

What difference does all this make? Stiegler points out that Husserl conducts his phenomenological investigation of the temporal object that is the melody at around the same moment as the invention of the gramophone. Furthermore, this invention makes it possible, for the first time in history, for a listener to *repeat* an identical auditory reception: the recorded sound that is emitted remains unchanged from the first time I listen to an album until the second. What this new possibility of identical auditory repetition exposes is that, for the *listener*, the experience is *not* identical.

The question is why, and the only possible conclusion is that if there has been change, it must be in the listener – they must have individuated themselves in the interval between the first listening and the second. What this implies is not that they have aged or undergone some other physiological alteration, but that the store of primary retentions that have become secondary has been added to and rearranged in the interval between the two occasions, and firstly by the fact that, second time round, the 'content' has become less unfamiliar. If this second experience really is different from the first, however, then this further implies that the very act of perception, of primary retention, is not just a passive reception of the 'given' that is provided by the 'data' on the gramophone record: the reception involved in primary retention must always already be a *selection* from among possible primary retentions, and the *criteria* for this selection must be provided by the arrangement of secondary retentions, that is, from the stock of past experience.

The upshot of this consideration is that *tertiary* retention, the artificial memory producing the process of epiphylogenesis, makes it possible to manipulate the arrangement of secondary retentions, which in turn makes it possible to influence the selection criteria involved in primary retention, or in other words, to condition the character of experience itself. And, along with it, to condition protection, that is, the whole gamut of the relationship to the future that is covered by the concepts of expectation, anticipation, hope, fear and desire, along with will, belief, faith, confidence and trust.

On the one hand, it is this possibility of control that is positively exploited in every process of education (conducted via what Stiegler calls the 'programming institutions',[47] starting with parental care and including every level of schooling), where systematic access to the tertiary retentions containing the accumulated knowledge of past generations makes it possible to *re-interiorize* what has been exteriorized in books or other hypomnesic artefacts, so that it becomes possible, for example, to memorize a poem, and through that re-interiorization to produce a differentiation of experiences of that poem, which is to say, to open up the possibility of a new *interpretation* of that poem. In this sense, the automatisms of education are the condition on which it becomes possible to reach that state of autonomy that Kant called maturity and that amounts to the possibility of critique and thinking for oneself. At the same time, any such educational process is perpetually threatened with becoming impotent with respect to changes occurring in the technical system that leave existing ways of life in want of new knowledge and practices of care, an impotence and sterility reflected in knowledge becoming dogma, that is, negatively pharmacological.

On the other hand, it is this very same possibility of control that is exploited by marketing as the basis of twentieth-century consumer capitalism (conducted via what Stiegler calls the 'programming industries', that is, the culture industries), which, in the twentieth century, takes advantage of the mass broadcast capabilities afforded by audiovisual grammatization technology to target, not the desires that form the basis of all long-term cultivation required by every kind of education, but rather the drives, in order to condition behaviour towards the pursuit of the most short-term satisfactions imaginable. In this way, consumer capitalism is founded on systematically short-circuiting the libidinal economy, undermining every form of long-term cultivation, and taking advantage of this proletarianization of everyday life by offering readymade substitutes.

At the *end* of the twentieth century, a new form of grammatization begins to dominate: digital grammatization (grammatizing literally *everything* in binary code), combined with the global networks of the internet based on the HTML protocol and so on. In the twenty-first century, this is combined with the invention of the ubiquitous handheld computer known as the smartphone and the simultaneous rise of the gargantuan so-called 'social' networks, making possible a vast two-way traffic of data (which was *not* possible with the mass-broadcast terrestrial networks of twentieth-century radio and television) that could be combined with algorithmic processing to target individual brains in a highly segmented and particularized way.

This leads to a third stage of generalized proletarianization, targeting not just the knowledge of how to use tools in order to perform work, not just the knowledge of how to conduct everyday life, but every form of formalized, conceptual and theoretical knowledge as well. Beyond proletarianization, this amounts to what Stiegler calls *denoetization*, reflected not just in the Cambridge Analytica scandal that contributed to the rise of a president himself (dis)connected to/from the world via Fox News, but also Lancetgate, which showed the reliance of researchers publishing in the oldest and most prestigious medical journals on datasets about which they themselves remained completely blind. In the Covid-19 pandemic of 2020, the owners of the platforms involved in this algorithmic form of governmentality are doing their utmost to take advantage of this 'shock' to introduce a new doctrine, raising the prospect of what Naomi Klein refers to as a 'screen new deal'.[48]

From organology to neganthropology – there is no alternative

Bernard Stiegler himself did not begin to refer to the Anthropocene *as such* until the third phase of his work, in which he begins to elaborate, in a much more serious way, a question that can be found in his earlier work, but without the same emphasis: the question of entropy and its corresponding counter-tendency most often referred to as negentropy. Already in 2001, for example, Stiegler describes the 'diversity of possible interpretations' involved in reading a text – and specifically for Kant himself in *re*-reading the *Critique of Pure Reason* and through that re-*writing* it – in terms of being the production of negentropy 'as the chance of thought itself', whereas the 'industrialized production of tertiary retentions for masses of consciousnesses' amounts to a mass standardization producing a 'homogeneous entropic soup' that risks 'an entropic synchronization of consciousnesses that would add up to nothing less than the end of time'.[49] 'End of time': because temporality is nothing but the maintenance and multiplication of the improbable against the arrow of probable becoming, consisting firstly in the struggle of endosomatic life, and secondly in that unfolding negentropic diversity of singular interpretations produced by singular noetic souls weaving a fabric of primary, secondary and tertiary retentions and opening the possibility of a future rather than sinking and regressing into becoming. In later texts, this 'end of time', which is not an 'end of history' in the sense of Francis Fukuyama but rather an inability to obtain the conditions of a relationship to past and future necessary for the constitution of an epoch, will be referred to by Stiegler as our current state of subsisting within an 'absence of epoch'.

It is only with a series of lectures and papers, probably beginning with 'The Anthropocene and Neganthropology', given in November 2014 at the University of Kent, and then the publication of *La société automatique* in March 2015, that the relationship will be established between the second law of thermodynamics and the planetary crisis conceived as an Entropocene.[50] A new set of terms will then proliferate in Stiegler's work, on the basis not just of Erwin Schrödinger's 1944 account of life as a kind of negentropic and asymmetrical process of crystallization,[51] but also the 1945 work of the mathematician Alfred J. Lotka,[52] who emphasizes the fact that *exosomatic* evolution is a kind of *second* negentropy, in the sense that it may, indeed, belong to and emerge from endosomatic evolution, but it also *suspends* that evolution and, more importantly, the criteria by which it operates. Rather than involving the finite aims of genetic instinct, or some latitudes of freedom in the expression of those aims granted by epigenetic memory, the behaviour of the noetic souls of exosomatic beings becomes detached from what Freud called the exigencies of life, and can instead be reattached to desires and expectations that are no longer finite, but singular and infinite, aiming at what does not exist but consists,[53] including all the forms of knowledge.

This doubling of the counter-entropic tendency by the advent of exosomatization leads Stiegler to refer not just to negentropy but to *neganthropy* and *anti-anthropy*, which struggle against not just thermodynamic entropy (for example, the warming of the atmosphere due to greenhouse gases), nor just biological entropy (for example, the loss of biodiversity resulting from habitat destruction), but *anthropy* (the psychic and collective devastation wrought by the reduction of knowledge to information, the incalculable to the calculable). The question of the origin of the human was, as we said at the beginning, of little interest to Stiegler: what mattered was not *Anthropos* but the appearance of epiphylogenesis, a third kind of memory associated with what, after Lotka, he will call exosomatization.

In the third phase of his work, noetic souls will be what are possessed by what Stiegler begins to call 'simple exorganisms' (a contraction of exosomatic organisms), which always belong to both 'lower complex exorganisms' (a factory, a hospital, a school, a club) and 'higher complex exorganisms' (such as a nation), where it is the latter alone who can appeal to what does not exist but consists (justice, democracy, etc.), even if only at infinity, through that providing the overarching criteria for behavioural selection. Stiegler is not concerned with the human, but with our undeniable potential to become *in*human. What matters is not *Anthropos* as such, but *anthropy*: anthropy as the risk of the noetic soul's regression, as 'anthropogenic forcing', as all those tendencies towards stupidity and madness that are both the irreducible possibility of the noetic soul and the systemic consequence of a technical and economic system that is based on an ideology of market absolutism and drives us ever-increasingly towards proletarianization and denoetization.

The infinity of knowledge, as that towards which simple and complex exorganisms must aim, consists first of all in the fact that whenever we come to *know* something, and not just to acquire information, we add something to the world that it previously did not contain. In this way, knowledge does not just maintain the improbable against the tendency towards the probable: more than that, it always involves something of the *incalculably* improbable. Furthermore, like every kind of negentropy, knowledge and exosomatic life are always only ever *local*, the result of singularly local histories, even while they may be perpetually de-localizing (both positively and negatively), and only ever *temporary* (there is never any final victory against entropy): the production of negentropy within a locality (a cell, an organism, a tribe, a nation, a biosphere) always *also* produces entropy, and thus always involves risk.

This functional yet local, temporary and open characteristic of knowledge applies equally to whatever knowledge we may acquire of anthropy and neganthropy themselves, and for this reason it calls for a new relationship to the knowledge pursued in the physical, social and human sciences, including philosophy: whereas in the final pages of *Tristes Tropiques* Claude Lévi-Strauss proposes re-spelling anthropology as 'entropology' to reflect the overwhelmingly destructive agent that *Anthropos* has proven to be,[54] Stiegler calls instead for a 'neganthropology' of exorganic life. The neganthropic character of knowledge is a question of the incalculably improbable because it is a question of the new, of an addition that in this way opens up the possibility of a change – a bifurcation – making possible and necessary the pursuit of still further knowledge. It is to name the global scale of such a necessity, and against the anthropic tendencies that are leading to an increase of entropy of all kinds as the technosphere overwhelms the biosphere, that Stiegler refers to the need for a planetary bifurcation taking us to what he calls the Neganthropocene – however improbable a dream that may be.

Such a bifurcation entails a reinvention of work as a knowledgeable and knowledge-producing activity, less to prevent the new wave of automation that may well be coming than to take advantage of the chances it affords. Similarly, it cannot possibly be a question of rejecting or resisting 'algorithms', but of reinventing the operational characteristics and architecture of computation at a fundamental level so that it can serve the function of reason and the overarching value of neganthropy. And it requires the elaboration of new therapeutic approaches to the psychosocial disorders of contemporary life, which have their roots in the anthropic characteristics of the present-day use of hypomnesic tertiary retentional technologies. These were goals that Stiegler pursued collaboratively at his institute affiliated with the Centre Pompidou, experimentally as part of the Plaine Commune project that aimed to create a Contributory Learning Territory in the northern suburbs of Paris, and theoretically in his last book, the collective work published in French under the title *Bifurquer: 'Il n'y a pas alternative'*.

The evil reign of anthropy and the probably closed fate of the Entropocene

Nevertheless, we should not let these hopeful aims and positive projects cloud our awareness of the depths of the abyss before which we find ourselves, nor of the depths of the abyss to which Bernard Stiegler himself was led. In the preface of his first book (repeated on the back cover), he already wrote:

> That a radical change in outlook and attitude is demanded induces all the more reactivity because it is unavoidable. *Ressentiment* and denegation are factors of ruin as well as

irreducible tendencies, which Nietzsche and Freud placed at the heart of their reflections a century ago.[55]

In *Acting Out*, writing about the twenty-five years that had passed since his release from prison, he says that, indeed, the world marked by 'the organization of the *loss of individuation*' has 'revealed itself to be appallingly inhospitable'.[56] In *The Age of Disruption*, a work on all the forms of madness produced by the 'disruption' pursued via computational capitalism, he describes how, in August 2014, he found himself 'increasingly obsessed by death, that is, by what I *projected* as being my death, and by the latter as my deliverance, waking up every night haunted by this suicidal urge'.[57] Later in the same chapter, in a section entitled 'Suffering', he relates this intimate and private haunting to a much more general spectre haunting our world or lack of it:

> Today, however, melancholy and more generally all forms of ὕβρις are shaped by the retentional and protentional specificities of the *pharmaka* of the absence of epoch, and this absence of epoch produces disruption inasmuch as these automated retentions and protentions are treated by algorithms operating more quickly than any form of care. Because of all this, madness, which becomes ordinary and general, is today a question that is inextricably medical, economic, juridical, political and industrial, that is, technological.[58]

More recently still, in *The Immense Regression*, he returns to the statement he had made in the preface of *Technics and Time, 1*, observing that, twenty-five years later, the 'explosion of resentment [...] has exceeded all my fears'.[59] Stiegler is thereby led to write a book that reflects on the fact that today, our problem is less a politics of repression than a vast tendency towards the regression of the noetic soul, in the course of which he undertakes to re-read Nietzsche through the prism of the relationship between entropy and nihilism, showing that the machine, the railway and the telegraph, which Nietzsche thinks in terms of a 'combination', lead Nietzsche to a profound dread steeped in his awareness of the second law but without the means to conceive its negentropic and neganthropic counterpart. The Entropocene, Stiegler concludes, is what accomplishes nihilism in the form of so-called disruption, no matter that its totalitarian character may so often remain unperceived. Agreeing with Nietzsche that today our philosophy must begin not with wonder but with dread, he sees before us a becoming without future that brings to reality all the threats swept along by the current of nihilism, which is also a drowning of singularities in and by averages via technologies of scalability, which saturate the technosphere thanks to intensive computing – *informational democracy*, which has liquidated the *democracy of opinion*, moves like the sorcerer's apprentice swept away by his broom.[60]

And it is in this world that, in his final book, he sees the arrival of Greta Thunberg as a sign, an Antigone, but a *more-than-tragic* figure. Greta Thunberg confronts us not just with the loss of the remembrance of divine law, but with the loss of everything: in the age of tragedy, death proves to be inevitable and every artifice to be ambiguous and pharmacological, yet the cosmos remains inalterable; today, it is the cosmos itself that succumbs to the anthropic tendency as every improbable locality and singular place tends to be reduced to an undifferentiated entropic space.[61]

In one of his final texts, not yet published, Bernard Stiegler refers once again to the historian Arnold Toynbee, and to his 1976 book, *Mankind and Mother Earth*, where, in Stiegler's words, Toynbee diagnoses the imminent possibility of a catastrophe that 'would result both from a suicidal tendency of civilizations and from excessive exploitation of the biosphere':[62]

> Collective suicidal tendencies appear in a civilization when the credit it grants to itself, and which founds the power of its organic solidarity, is for any reason compromised – invasion, natural catastrophe, corruption, famine, disease. Aristotle called *philia* the solidarity that creates the sustainability of societies – which he himself observed from the perspective of the city, the *polis*, and this standpoint constituted what since Plato has been called politics.[63]

What he had in the earlier quotation called 'informational democracy', which seems to algorithmically and performatively close off every possible neganthropic future, amounts to this elimination of the possibility of granting the credit necessary for *philia*.

The credit necessary for any possible establishing of a sustainable future involves the entire field of belief, faith, trust, confidence and hope, but it is also a question of the existential dimension of philosophy itself: without the '*existential* dimension of *all* philosophy', the latter 'would lose all *credit* and sink into scholastic chatter'.[64] This existential dimension must be felt, as must its loss, which Stiegler, perhaps, felt more keenly than anyone, a loss that is also a loss of credit, leaving us in 'absolute *mécréance*':

The latter is characteristic of the nihilism that will thus have been *accomplished* fifty years earlier than Nietzsche had foreseen, which presents itself in the form of an accursed age, corrupting the twenty-first century as if in advance, and which will become the general reality of the Anthropocene era as the latter turns out to be *an accumulation of reasons for doubt* in all domains, if not of counter-truths – modern certitude thereby literally *collapsing*.[65]

What now remains of Stiegler's project, recalling that for him, meaningful political action, if these remain terms with which to face what is coming, could never consist in designating scapegoats, nor in resenting what was, nor in resisting power, nor in opposing an enemy (who is only ever a bearer of a tendency)? Was it nothing more than a dream, like so many others?

A dream, what else?

His loss leaves us, leaves me, caught in a vast entropic current, seemingly without any realisable dreams in which any longer to believe: bereft and adrift. Are we, am I, perpetually trapped in a more-than-tragic situation of overwhelming anthropy, bound as a result to become or remain evil? A strange question, perhaps. On this, we will allow the final word to go to Bernard, neither quite a saint nor a hero nor a father nor a king, but a generous and warm and truthful friend, and undeniably a philosopher, a great one, and possibly – perhaps even probably – the last:

> As for *evil*, it is above all, as the *replacement of thought with the denunciation of evil*, OUR renunciation, *we* who worry about the future of the *we*, *our* renunciation of *critique* and *invention*, that is, of *combat*.[66]

2 Protentional Finitude and Infinitude in the Anthropocene

Introduction

Casting a glance at the world today inevitably means peering into the ubiquitous screens now occupying the attention of consumers for the great bulk of their waking life.[67] Doing so equally inevitably brings into focus a picture of a world that seems to be running off the rails and out of control, in which disorder and strife are intensifying in unforeseen ways, and where a torrent of populist events seems to have consigned truths hitherto assumed to a kind of twilight zone, if not a rapidly darkening twilight of truth itself. The future has never seemed so unpredictable, our disadjustment and misalignment never so unreadjustable and out-of-joint, and our protentional capacities never so correspondingly limited.

But when did this torrent begin its onrush? Everyone knows that today's sense of chaos, privation and powerlessness was not born yesterday, as surely as they doubt that faith, or trust, or certainty will be reawakened tomorrow or the day after. Is this rising madness an industrially-manufactured populism peculiar to the twenty-first century, or do the worrying images propagating across our screens reveal the return of those secularized, disenchanted, technocratic, yet wildly irrational movements of the twentieth, such as the fascism and Nazism hurriedly evoked by so many of those trading in diagnoses of the present day? Ought we seek yet older roots in the industrial revolution itself, in the harnessing of fire's motor force and in the philosophical 'importation' of thermodynamic ideas?[68] Or has this irrationality been harboured and ushered forth via the very notions of progress and enlightenment themselves, bound, despite themselves, to lead to a new kind of barbarism?[69]

Is there a madman who, by dint of an uncommon willingness to peer more deeply into the shadowy parts of our collective souls, can illuminate these tenebrous sources, and so aid in re-orienting our disorientation? In July 2004, Peter Thiel, whose entrepreneurial persona certainly consists in an unusual composition of contradictory personal, political and religious elements, proffered his own stab at a kind of barometer of the times, in a lecture entitled 'The Straussian Moment'. Thiel begins with the rather arch assertion that the twenty-first century began 'with a bang', and it is notable that, at this apogee of 'neocon' influence, when, in the wake of 9/11, Paul Wolfowitz and his ilk had indeed seized hold with great force and even greater hubris of the American military apparatus,[70] Thiel suspects these putative geopolitical world-shapers and will-revivers may have 'missed something fundamental altogether'.[71] And what Straussians miss is precisely the hubris of their own visions: they tend to downplay the violence, indeed the murder, lying at the foundation of all social formations, the scapegoating that is the perpetual temptation in the face of that violence, and the way all forms of secularization repeat, mimetically, the sacrificial inscription of that founding crime (sacrifice being itself an attempt to prevent repetition that paradoxically ensures it). In short, for Thiel, René Girard trumps Leo Strauss, and the neoconservative faith in the ability to conjure some new political will fails to reckon with the duplicity of the ritual tomb that simultaneously elevates the victim and conceals the crime that lies always at the origin.

Hence for Thiel the great pseudo-schism of American politics between 'liberals' and 'conservatives' requires temporal interpretation: liberals wish to know nothing of this foundational violence, while conservatives wish to know nothing of the transformational character of the future.[72] If it is clear that Thiel, the conservative libertarian, the pious disruptor, wants to stretch himself out along the contours of this schism between past and future, the practical implications are less clear: to counter the tendency towards 'the limitless violence of runaway mimesis' he offers only the elusive advice that 'the Christian statesman or stateswoman would be wise, in every close case, to side with peace'.[73]

Nevertheless, *one month* after delineating the Girardian character of the Straussian moment, Thiel took the practical step of becoming the first outside investor in the largest mimetic experiment in human history, Facebook, and did so because Girard's work gave him to understand that social media are doubly the embodiment of mimetic desire, both in the way they spread, and in what they are 'about'.[74] Facebook: which is now relentlessly approaching two billion members, and which algorithmically regulates the content to which each of those members is screenically exposed, with the effect of auto-propagating microcosmological 'bubbles', a mimetic crisis that would, twelve years after Thiel's investment, contribute to the election of a scapegoating candidate supported and assisted by Thiel himself.

Somewhat paradoxically, Thiel, who in 2004 was already a founding member of the PayPal mafia, has not one word to say in 'The Straussian Moment' about network technology or its disruptions. There is only the hint of a suggestion that these transformations that conservatives fail to envision may not just be social and political, but technological, perhaps even primarily so, yet how this goes in Thiel's mind remains unstated. If this amounts to a suppression of the technological, however, it is a characteristic common also to Girard: in his own contribution to the 2004 Stanford University conference that would be published as *Politics and Apocalypse*, for instance, Girard argues that the duplicitous tomb (the 'rotting corpse inside and the beautiful structure around it') is homologous with culture itself, because, with 'the exception of tools, the most ancient traces of human culture are tombs, and tombs may well be the original monuments of humanity'.[75] But what justifies this 'exception'? Even if ritualized burial sites date back 300,000 years,[76] and thus vastly predate the Neolithic myths and rituals that Claude Lévi-Strauss understood to be those concerned with the origin of agriculture and the dispersal of groups, they would not predate the Palaeolithic myths concerned with the domestication not of plants and animals but of fire, the 'seed' of which must, in the hearth, itself be cared for and tended, and so cultivated, and so worshipped.[77] On what basis is such a repression of the tool, that is, of technics, to be grounded, and what are its effects? Are not the duplicity of the tomb, and of the sacrificial structure that both forbids and ensures violent repetition, not in this light something more like instances of a more general duplicity, so that the Platonic *pharmakon* would not then function, as Girard contends, '*like* the human pharmakos',[78] but would instead, in its broadest generality, as technics in general, be rather more its source?

From Peter Thiel to Theodore Kaczynski, the struggle to the death between self-propagating supersystems and nuclear war as the lesser evil

One madman who cannot be accused of sweeping the technological under the carpet, who all too clearly sees its ubiquitous figure adorning every terrestrial surface, who feels the night closing in, hears the noise of the gravediggers and smells the stench of decomposition that these sometimes beautiful structures cannot conceal, currently resides in a federal prison in Colorado. While Theodore Kaczynski's technological apocalypticism unambiguously opposes the rampant digital utopianism of Silicon Valley billionaires, not unrelated anxieties are clearly detectable among the latter, too, most openly thematized by Thiel but evidenced as well by their predilection for diverting wealth to potential escape routes, whether these be seasteading, the elixir of youthful blood, colonizing Mars (or, even more improbably, New Zealand), but also by rising fears of the consequences of fully unleashed artificial intelligence. A brief examination of the Unabomber's logic, as expressed most recently in *Anti-Tech Revolution: Why and How* (2016), may expose, despite the locked prison of its delirium, how high are the theoretical walls and practical stakes raised by what is now termed the Anthropocene.

For Kaczysnki, as for innumerable others, it is self-evident that 'modern society is heading toward disaster' and that what links together the dangers besetting it is modern technology.[79] What sets him apart is his other founding premise, which we venture to describe as *protentional finitude*: the highly limited capacity of collective social formations to anticipate future events or predict the long-term consequences of collective action. His entire first chapter catalogues historical examples of failed attempts at 'rational human control'. Of course, to assume from the outset the impossibility of control is to stack the deck: the technophilic hopes of the geoengineers and disruptors and the sociophilic dreams of progressive planners like Naomi Klein are equally deluded, according to such a perspective, equally symptomatic of a denial that wants, regardless of the calculable probability of impending disaster, to do anything but acknowledge that only the total elimination of the destructive factors could significantly deflect the inexorable trajectory of what has become a global system.

Not content with drawing inductive conclusions from historical examples, Kaczynski presents a sequence of deductive propositions intended to elaborate a metaphysics of 'self-propagating systems', dynamic formations that tend to promote their own 'survival and propagation'.[80] He thus aims to develop a quasi-Darwinian understanding of both vital and psychosocial individuation processes, where these localized metastable systems are nested within one another in such a way that microcosmological *subsystems* tend to accommodate to and become dependent upon macrocosmological *supersystems*. Such self-propagating systems are in perpetual competition, but their a-teleological character has the perverse consequence that those with advantageous short-term strategies tend to eliminate those with better long-term strategies: fitness for long-term survival does not translate into an increased *likelihood* of surviving, *even if* the long-term consequence of the advantageous short-term strategy may be the destruction of all (say by the incomplete voidance of the destructive products of their own processes).

Throughout most of the history of life, and of the history of *Homo sapiens*, self-propagating systems have been limited by geographical conditions and their own restricted capacities for expansion, and when such systems have collapsed, the repercussions have only been local. But today, the globalization of human systems encounters other limits, encouraging the formation of a few massive supersystems and tending to eliminate smaller, less successful systems, producing intense competition between the remaining rivals – let's say a mimetic crisis. In such circumstances, the slightest deviation from the most immediate short-termism (by unilaterally attempting serious climate mitigation strategies, for example) can result only in negative feedback for that system and corresponding gains for its rivals: a vast competitive potlatch in which, purely through the impact of selections effected through 'trial and error', the immediate destruction of resources will always triumph over the benefits of the whole, in this case the whole world. The strict irreversibility of this logic is so stark that Kaczynski advocates the immediate destruction of the entire global technological framework. Even the possibility that efforts to undo this destructive, supersystemic competition themselves risk provoking geopolitical chaos, potentially triggering nuclear conflict, is no deterrent: the biosphere would likely survive the latter holocaust, he argues, and so, 'if we had to choose between a major nuclear war and the continued existence of the system, we would have to take nuclear war as the lesser evil'.[81]

Light and heat, inertia and entropy

Kaczysnki expresses what everyone fears but tends to repress: that no process of collective decision-making may any longer be capable of curtailing destructive intensifications of systemic disruption. He ostensibly evinces a kind of social Darwinism, but one whose outcome, when the imprisoned eco-terrorist obsessively runs simulations of this model through his mind, is, instead of the survival of the fittest, always just 'game over'. This 'terroristic conception of human history'[82] is absolutely antithetical to that of Immanuel Kant, for example, who, though 'without the mind of a seer', foresaw progressive improvement no longer subject to 'total reversals'.[83] Friedrich Nietzsche already saw this as a symptom of Kant's becoming an idiot, action compelled by the 'instinct of life' having nothing to do with Kant's 'automaton of "duty"'.[84] Yet if, with this sense of the life instinct as the only real arbiter in the struggle of existence, Nietzsche, too, embraced some more complex mutation of Darwinism, he himself arguably failed to reckon with what ultimately lies behind this theme and all its variations: the second law of thermodynamics.

For Georges Canguilhem, the discovery of this law corresponds to a shift in the locus of the question of progress, from light to heat.

> Now, in the nineteenth century, the physical phenomenon that symbolizes progress is no longer light, but heat. Unlike

light, whose continuous emission is regarded as being guaranteed by the stability of the solar system, heat requires non-renewable deposits of earthly combustibles if it is to be used as an industrial tool.[85]

Canguilhem does not fail to observe that the steam engine was a machine both invented and improved *'before and without* the elaboration of the theory that made its workings intelligible'.[86] Industrial mechanization arose, then, not from progressive improvements in the understanding of becoming, but *in advance* of that understanding, bringing with it a transformation of the social and working environment whose duplicitous face was immediately obvious in the darkened skies of industrial cities and pitiful conditions of proletarian labour. Only *subsequently* would the *concept* of entropy arise, precisely as the generalization of that theoretical elaboration enabling innovative gains in engine efficiency. It is these transformations of the productive economy, together with the philosophical importation of the concept of entropy, that, according to Canguilhem, will then lead to the 'decline of the idea of progress', a decline that reaches a kind of limit in Kaczynski's terroristic conception of the fatal destructiveness of globally-extended self-propagating supersystems.

And yet, a glance at the dominant theoretical apparatuses elaborated in the second half of the twentieth century doesn't *exactly* confirm this hypothesis about entropy's philosophico-political impact. In Jean-Paul Sartre's attempted reconciliation of existentialism and Marxism, of freedom and its natural and historical limits (1960), scarcity figures extremely prominently, yet the struggle it provokes is associated not with entropy but 'controlled inertia':

> labour, as we have seen, is *primarily the organism* which reduces itself to a controlled inertia so as to act upon inertia and satisfy itself as need. Clearly this does not in itself mean either that labour exists in the field of scarcity, *or* that it must be defined as a struggle against scarcity. But given a social field which is defined by scarcity, that is, given the historical human field, labour for man has to be defined as *praxis* aimed at satisfying need *in the context of scarcity* by a particular negation of it.[87]

The word entropy does not appear.

In *Tristes Tropiques* (1955), Claude Lévi-Strauss does indeed advocate the re-spelling of anthropology as entropology, on the grounds that the former studies nothing more than the 'highest manifestations of this process of disintegration' that is civilization. Yet the entropologist reveals his own confusion, when he describes this civilization as an extraordinarily complex mechanism whose function is 'to produce what physicists call entropy, *that is inertia*'.[88] It is by this seemingly minor substitution alone that the entropologist allows himself to believe that the 'inertia' of human (all too human) institutions can be *opposed* to the anti-entropic proliferations of biological evolution, as if the latter were not as bound as the former to produce an overall increase of entropy within their local ecosystems, and, at the largest scale, within the biosphere.

Prior to both these instances, Martin Heidegger begins to think the problem of what he, too, will call modern technology (1949). Like Canguilhem, he argues against the idea that science precedes technology, which 'then only later would have emerged as the application of this'. Yet he does maintain that modern technology 'begins its reign with the commencement of modern natural science some three and a half centuries ago', as the fate of modern physics that is destined to converge with the history of being, which then becomes the latter's (cybernetic, informational) fate. And so, it does indeed make a difference *how* science apprehends nature:

> But how does science take the material of nature? It conceives it as matter. What is the fundamental characteristic of matter for physics? It is inertia. What does the physicist understand by inertia? Physically conceived, inertia is continuance in a state of motion. Rest is also such a state, which counts in a physically calculable manner as the limit case of motion. [...] For physics, nature is the standing reserve of energy and matter.[89]

At the inceptions of existentialist Marxism, structural anthropology, and *Bestand* and *Gestell*, therefore, we don't *quite* see Canguilhem's replacement of light by heat, but, overlaying it, a confusion between inertia and entropy, or, in other words, between the (Newtonian and mechanical) first law of motion and the (probabilistic and irreversible) second law of thermodynamics. Beyond this confounding of mechanical and statistical notions, however, what this tends to show is that this 'importation' has brought little corresponding reflection on the persistence of order and ongoing complexification characteristic of the *negative* entropy that Erwin Schrödinger would describe in 1943.[90] If the nineteenth century did indeed grasp something of this replacement of illumination with entropic heat – whose irreversibility and 'calculus of probabilities' would be, for Oswald Spengler's terroristic philosophical anthropology, the most 'conspicuous symbol' of decline and a new kind of mythology of *Gotterdammerung*[91] – the twentieth century, in its great philosophical currents, failed to take heed of Schrödinger's thought that a vital counter-tendency exists, consisting in the struggle to organize the entropic.

From différance to neganthropology

These counter-tendencies, detours in the form of eddies provisionally and locally organized within the stream of entropic disorder, are another name for Kaczynski's self-propagating systems. What the *extremity* of the latter's eco-terroristic conception exposes is therefore that a sense of the negentropic does not, in and of itself, insure against an apocalyptic judgment unblinking even at the prospect of nuclear fire. What ultimately authorizes his rejection of 'rational control', however, is the failure to make distinctions (which are not oppositions) *within* the negentropic field: the negentropy of 'nature' and the negentropy of 'culture' remain undifferentiated, and the axiom that short-termism will always win out is, beyond historical example, founded on this assumed unity: beyond improbable, it is simply impossible for the Unabomber that any more-than-biological will could constructively intervene in the conservation or transformation of these counter-entropic eddies, which are bound as a consequence to destructively drag the entire biosphere down into the torrent of becoming. Hence Kaczynski's metaphysics is, in this, congruent with Sigmund Freud's account of the infusorian that, 'left to itself, dies a natural death owing to its incomplete voidance of the products of its own metabolism',[92] which Freud then extends to the mortal character of all higher animals, or, indeed, with Jacques Derrida's différantial continuum extending 'from the elementary programs of so-called "instinctive" behavior up to the constitution of electronic card-indexes and reading machines'.[93]

Between *Beyond the Pleasure Principle* and *What is Life?*, however, Alfred North Whitehead did, in 1929, pronounce what amounts to a counter-entropic conception, according to which the tendency to 'the slow decay of physical nature' and the 'degradation of energy' are matched by another, 'upward' tendency.[94] If this is the negentropic tendency of life itself, then, for the 'higher forms of life', it includes not just living but 'living well', that is, forms of life actively engaged in anti-entropically 'modifying their environment'. And for we ourselves, insofar as we remain noetic beings, beings *amenable* to reason, this 'attack on the environment' lives not just well but *better*, and does so precisely because 'Reason', whose primary function this is, is the 'art of life' attaining ends 'realized in imagination but not in fact'.[95]

It is to this latter conception of contending tendencies (tendencies within, emerging out of and falling back into other tendencies) that Bernard Stiegler turns when approaching the question of the Anthropocene, precisely in order to avoid the terroristic conceptions of contemporary apocalypticism and crepuscular madness, whether mimetic, technophilic, transhumanist, entropological or ecological. As the *differentiation from* and *deferral of* the entropic tendency, the counter-entropic detour that is the vital process of individuation ('life', in Schrödinger's terms) is, as Derrida thought, no more nor less than the process of différance. But for Stiegler, noetic beings are those whose milieu is not just 'natural' but always already 'technical', a pre-individuality enabling the intermittent and improbable capacity to strive for ends in imagination, for what does not exist yet consists – a potential for living better that amounts to a différance of différance. The conditions of noetic existence are therefore technological, or better, *organological*: the self-propagating systems that are the psychic and collective processes of individuation identified by Gilbert Simondon are possible *only* via their mutual dependence on processes of technical individuation, which in turn depend on psychosocial adjustments and transformations, failing which technical processes are indeed bound to sink into entropy, along with the psychic and collective individuations they support.

More than a question of nature and culture, this différance of différance involves the tendency for natural selection to be suspended when it makes way for processes of artificial selection.[96] This is a new regime of individuation, not just because tools represent a new means of attack on the environment, but, *more importantly*, because the inscriptive character of every artefact also renders it an exteriorized form of memory, in addition to those forms of behavioural conservation and programming constituted by genetic and nervous memory. The transmissibility of exteriorized memory, combined with its ability to be lastingly conserved beyond the death of the individual who inscribes it into one or another form of matter, opens up new individuation processes, enabling and requiring the intergenerational transmission of accumulated knowledge so as to cultivate the capacities opened up by technical means, just as one must tend the seed of fire. With the advent of hypomnesis – technical compensations for retentional finitude *specifically dedicated* to the exteriorization of knowledge, turning it into exteriorized information but also opening up new processes of *re-interiorization* – it becomes possible not just to conserve knowledge but to accumulate it, build upon it, interpret it and criticize it. And to forget and destroy it.

Hence the attack on the environment in which technical life consists is, for Stiegler, unlike for Whitehead, explicitly *pharmacological*, simultaneously the remedy and the poison, containing the possibility of promoting the art of life or of undermining it, contributing to processes of interiorization or short-circuiting them, pursuing processes of individuation or attenuating them. Because these pharmacological possibilities are dependent on the hypomnesic conditions of exteriorized memory, the commencement of the Anthropocene is, for Stiegler, as conditional upon Gütenberg, Jacquard and Vaucanson as it is on Watt or Newcomen. And this is also why, when it comes to anticipating the *fate* of the Anthropocene, Stiegler understands the shift to twenty-*first* century capitalism in terms of a kind of reversal of Canguilhem's move from light to heat: for Stiegler, we are at the beginning of a long shift from the 'carbon-time' of industrial mechanization, internal combustion engines and road networks to the new pharmacology of 'light-time', that of ubiquitous screens, digital networks and 'big data'.[97]

As a question of hypomnesis, that is, of the *conditions* of reason, this is a matter not just of the new weapons of the productive economy, but of the fruitful or destructive weapons that transform or capture the *libidinal* economy as the engine of systems of anticipation and control in general, and consumerist systems in particular. The différance involved in contemporary exosomatization thus involves the question not just of an attack on the environment, but of the *politics* of that attack. Ultimately, the pharmacological character of exosomatization stems from the way it participates in processes leading both to probabilistic, cosmological, entropic indifferentiation or to the conservation and transformation of local differences that is the highly improbable and (finally) unwinnable, noetic struggle against entropy. Hence the theory and practice of this politics is what Stiegler calls 'neganthropology':

> If the hyperbolic negentropy in which the organological becoming of the organic consists installs a neganthropology that accelerates (entropic and anthropic) becoming, it nevertheless also transforms this acceleration into a future that differs and defers this becoming, according to the two senses of the verb *différer* mobilized by Derrida in his term différance. Hence a (negentropic and neganthropic) future *could* be established from this infinitizing form of protention that is the object of desire as an agent of (psychic, social and technical) individuation and integration – failing which, différance will remain merely formal.[98]

The dramaturgy of modern technics and the question of desire beyond anthropocentrism

Long before he adopted this new terminology – neganthropy, neganthropology, Entropocene, Neganthropocene – Stiegler had already noted that the 'dramaturgy of modern technics begins in the eighteenth century with a phase of optimism', but that this enters into crisis with the doubly entropic, tool-equipped, thermodynamic machine, which both pollutes the milieu and destroys the worker's knowledge.[99] But where Simondon, whose 'mechanology' Stiegler is discussing in this passage, conceives the advent of cybernetics in the twentieth century as the rise of a new, negentropic machine, requiring only the accompaniment of a new mechanological discourse to conduct the orchestra of machines, Stiegler worries that the increasing automation of the functions and faculties of reason could lead 'to an ever-greater dilution of the interior milieu into the exterior one', as knowledge degrades into information.[100] Stiegler's notion of 'reason' has thus always been suspicious of any residue of the metaphysics of mastery,[101] and has always been concerned with the *conditions* of reason's actualization.

Reason, for Stiegler, has always referred to a broad spectrum of projective illumination (always casting shadows) extending through expectation, motive, desire and conceptual thought, everything that amounts to a différance of desire from drive and drive from instinct (à la Whitehead's tripartite schema: living, living well, living better) effected through an originary technicity undecidably emerging from and inaugurating a primordial and necessary default. Hence it has always also required the re-interiorization of exteriorized contents: data, the given, must circuit back into the brain qua organ for making decisions, aiming at, desiring, reasoning towards what does not exist but consists. But this 'brain' is not itself some pure interiority, but is better understood as the product of the very long maieutic between the organic and the inorganic that began at the dawn of human evolution and intensified with the birth of hypomnesic exteriorization in the Upper Palaeolithic: it is, then, an extended psychic apparatus that, as organological, cannot itself exist without being embedded in the social and technical networks of knowledge that form the system of intergenerational education in the broadest sense.

For Erich Hörl, writing prior to this terminological innovation, this foundation of Stieglerian thought in '(de)fault and lack' (a highly problematic conjunction of what must in fact be distinguished) amounts to an 'anthropocentric bias', 'a de-anthropologizing as well as a re-anthropologizing operation', exposing the 'inherent limit' of Stiegler's libidinal ecology and resulting in a 'neo-humanistic position'.[102] Hörl repeatedly suspects that the 'negativity' of 'lack and default'[103] has been superseded by cyberneticization that so redefines the difference of human and non-human actors as to require a new 'general ecology' exposed to 'the new sense that springs forth under the technological condition'.[104] If the question of the fate of interiorization therefore seems to hang over this 'new sense', Hörl nevertheless situates such an ecology within the orbit of a 'pharmacology of participation' capable of distinguishing between alienating and counter-alienating tendencies,[105] distributed between 'hyperindustrially controlled' and 'openly relational' possibilities.[106] How this critique of a purported re-anthropologizing, neo-humanizing anthropocentric bias is to be composed with such a pharmacology therefore awaits a fuller account of this proposed general ecology.[107]

Mark Hansen takes this line further, arguing that Stiegler sees technics *'exclusively as a support of human becoming* and [...] as a support for an account of human becoming *that does not put the human itself into question* (or, at least, does not do so in radical enough terms)'.[108] This alleged deficiency is shown by Stiegler's 'investment in desire and libidinal economy', which is merely a 'throwback to a moment in cultural history that has been superseded'[109] by more recent technology, leading Stiegler to a pharmacological prosthetics 'restricting technics *to a human-centered operationality'*.[110] The more radical trajectory would consist in moving beyond 'any imaginable organologic whatsoever': it is necessary to 'overcome the logic of human know-how',[111] to 'repudiate the operation of interiorization [...] so central to Stiegler's account of libidinal economy',[112] and to elaborate a *'resolutely nonprosthetic* account of technics [...] as a component in a larger system of individuation'[113] where psychic and collective individuations can be understood only from within 'larger, thoroughly technical, environmental processes'.[114]

In a quasi-Girardian manoeuvre, Hansen mobilizes first Catherine Malabou then Gabriel Tarde to argue for a 'cerebrality' that 'remains radically open' to the 'radically exterior', because it is constituted on a purely *imitative* basis, 'without requiring any form of interiorization'.[115] Hansen wonders if such an account of imitative repetition might not 'furnish the very motor mechanism for the entire individuation complex and might in this way make a crucial contribution toward situating individuation beyond organology'.[116] This technologization of the Girardian account of mimesis and abandonment of organological pharmacology, however, seems 'radically' *in*capable of mounting a *critique* of the neo-technophilic Thielian acceptance of a resolutely post-democratic world of algorithmically-engineered crowds and audiences.

Leaving aside the radically *false* assertion that Stiegler does not put the human into question, such criticisms fall for a philosophical red herring consisting in imagining that virtue today means adopting the most radically post-humanist or trans-humanist or anti-humanist pose. In short, the *distinction* between vital différance and noetic différance in no way implies an *opposition* between the animal and the human. For Stiegler it is clear that noetic 'cerebrality' has *always* been 'radically open' to the exterior. What matters is not 'the human' but technical existence, insofar as, on the basis of biological and techno-cultural automatisms, it is capable of autonomizing its existence only by aiming at what does *not* exist except in imagination.

Only through the operations of interiorization does technical life bear this capacity for protentional infinitude, for quasi-causally anticipating and realising the highly improbable.[117] Kaczynski's desperate metaphysical prison of self-propagating structures may be naïve in its failure to question what *difference* exteriorization makes to the individuation processes it purports to describe, just as, conversely, Thiel's entrepreneurial acceptance of algorithmic mimesis seems highly cynical. Yet in blithely accepting if not celebrating the breakdown of the operations of interiorization and the circuits of libidinal economy, is not Hansen at risk of locking himself *outside*, of discovering that his discourse is equally impotent, if not cynical, when confronted with today's sinking of negentropic and neganthropic processes into entropic twilight?

Between our protentional finitude and infinitude, the future consists. Our Anthropocenic challenge consists in struggling to live psychosocially and biospherically better by striving for ends existing in imagination but not in fact, or, in other words, that exist only at infinity – that do not exist at all yet consist. Such as, for example, justice, but also love, for Stiegler also writes, 'Today, in a time of lovelessness…'.[118] Two conclusions. Firstly, the *living* better and the art of *life* that promote it are a question neither of 'nature' nor the 'human', but of inventing new forms of *neganthropy* via new processes of interiorization on the basis of new potentialities of exosomatization. Secondly, the question of the libidinal economy is the question of the possibility of reviving love in a loveless age, of opening up a new love of and care for the world bearing the chance of fostering the will to invent that new, as yet unapproachable cosmology currently barely existing in our imagination, if at all. 'Duty' cannot be discarded as nothing more than an automaton antithetical to 'life', but nor can it do without automatisms not just negentropic but neganthropic: without processes of interiorization capable of fostering this new will, the apocalyptic fantasies fuelling the terroristic conceptions of telecratic populism have every likelihood of ending in the 'limitless violence of runaway mimesis', and not just in imagination. 'Siding with peace', today, consists not in raising new anthropic tombs but in inventing the conditions for the emergence of the highly improbable without denying the undoubtedly probable. If this neganthropological politics requires new ways of living, new forms of normativity in Canguilhem's sense, what remains to be elucidated is how any new, imaginable or unimaginable metastability is to be effected: not just in the face of algorithmic mimesis that captures attention and attenuates interiorization; nor just in the face of media theorists all too willing to conclude that the wish to revive such interiorization is merely the conservatism and nostalgia produced by misplaced anxiety about the transformations taking us into the age of full cybernetic automation; but confronted, as well, with a psychosocial milieu where potential allies in this struggle remain caught within a cultural politics that defines 'normativity', whether in terms of love, sexuality, gender, kinship or society in general, as that which, in every case, is to be 'opposed' and 'resisted'.

3 Shanghai, 2018:
An Introduction to Technics and Time, 1 and 2

1 What is Philosophy?

> That a radical change of perspective and attitude is needed induces all the more reactivity in that it is unavoidable. Resentment and denial are putrefying agents as well as irreducible tendencies, which Nietzsche and Freud placed at the heart of their reflections a century ago.
>
> Bernard Stiegler, *Technics and Time, 1*.

Opening remarks

I would like to begin by thanking Tongji University, and Professor Lu Xinghua in particular, for the invitation that made it possible for me to come here to speak with you in these lectures. I am extremely happy for the opportunity to do so, not just because it gives me pleasure to talk with you about a subject that I am 'interested' in, but because the philosophy of Bernard Stiegler is something I *care* about, and because I would like to show you why *you too* should care about it, and why you should care about it *just as much as I do* – which is to say, *a lot*.

In opening with such a statement, I am highly conscious that I am speaking in a way that does not necessarily have the ring of an 'academic lecturer': I sound, perhaps, more like a faithful *disciple*, and a disciple is someone whom the academy ordinarily *does not want* to hear from, because the *discipline* this seems to invoke would seem to involve a submission to authority that runs counter to the 'academic freedom' that has long been the academy's founding principle. So I have to very quickly *deny* that I am a disciple, and assert instead that I am a *translator* of Stiegler's work, where every translation is always also an interpretation, which is to say a reinterpretation, and where, nevertheless, this reinterpretation, despite its freedom, *still* involves discipline and fidelity. In wanting to interpret the work of Stiegler for you, I am hoping that you, in turn, will reinterpret my interpretation (and in fact, there is no other possibility, other than to *not listen* to my lectures, which is a perpetual possibility), as well as retranslate and reinscribe that interpretation into the *singular* context that is Chinese civilization and the world of contemporary China.

This process of translation and retranslation, interpretation and reinterpretation, is extremely difficult and highly complex: this is why it still involves discipline. We may think this is becoming *less* so, because, for example, we have apps and programs that will *automatically* translate from one language to another, one idiom to another. When we are exchanging 'information', such as instructions about how to do this or that, where this is or that is, this automation of translation can be extremely *helpful*, and perhaps one day not so far away this is how we will *always* translate between languages and idioms. And maybe we will do so by voice, and discover that we no longer have much use for reading, and even less for reading languages into which we have not been 'raised'.

With developments of this kind, we may well think that the *gulf* between idioms, languages, philosophies or civilizations can indeed effectively be *bridged* by this and other similar processes, giving rise to the possibility of many and richer forms of cultural exchange and cross-pollination. And this is undoubtedly the case. But we should also not forget that these automatic translation programs do not *know* the languages they are translating, and that even the computer programmers who design them do not need to know the languages: they work by statistical and algorithmic procedures that treat vast amounts of calculable data derived from previous translations. This is a process that reduces singular differences to calculable particularities, eliminating what is unique or infinite and therefore incalculable, and it does not just apply to languages or computer programs: it can be applied to the way movies are made, music is produced, art is created or the way we attempt to teach philosophy. Do such processes *enable* translation and thus lead to a genuine proliferation of diversity and pollination, or do they produce an *illusion* of diversity that in fact conceals a much vaster process of standardized deterritorialization?

Without answering that question straightaway, but keeping it in mind, it is thus worth pausing for a moment to reflect on the strangeness of the fact that I am here in China speaking with you today. On 2 November 2018, I find myself here in Shanghai, a city of some twenty-five million inhabitants, 70% of whom I am told were not born here, being therefore *new* to the city, in a country and a civilization dating back some forty centuries, here to talk with you about a philosopher from France, French philosophy being part of Western philosophy that amounts to a continuous chain of teachings and philosophies given and devised by individual philosophers (the community of philosophy being in this way, and unlike science, *essentially* individualized, that is, *limited*) dating back some twenty-five centuries, and where I myself originate from Australia, also with twenty-five million inhabitants, which has existed as a 'nation' for barely one single century, but on whose land so-called indigenous inhabitants have lived for more than four *hundred* centuries, making it possibly the oldest continuous culture on Earth, or at the very least the oldest outside of Africa. So who is old and who is young?

What made it possible for this strange possibility to be realised? Most immediately, it depended on two things: firstly, the jet-powered airliner that flew me here, taking eleven hours to travel from Melbourne to Shanghai, and more generally the immensely complex and wildly successful global civil aviation industry that has arisen in the one hundred and fifteen years since the first flight at Kitty Hawk; secondly, the global networks of digital communication that mean that many many emails, messages and other forms of electronic exchange could occur between myself and Bernard Stiegler, myself and Lu Xinghua, Xinghua and Bernard, publishers, visa offices, landlords of AirBnB apartments, and so on.

In truth, such concrete realities of contemporary life are highly *uncanny*. If a question arises in the course of these lectures about Stiegler's work that I am unable to answer, for example, I could, potentially, simply remove my smartphone from my pocket and immediately tap out an email to Stiegler, and in only the time it takes for him to reply on *his* smartphone, or tablet, or laptop or desktop computer, I could read to you his response (while he is writing to me from France, or from anywhere in the world, you would have time to check your WeChat messages). This is a possibility that no lecturer in philosophy ever before had the opportunity to do. But this is not something I will do during these lectures, because I don't want to take the risk that he could be busy – for example, he might be in an important meeting, or he might be going to the toilet, and this could mean that I will be forced to wait five minutes before receiving in Shanghai a reply from this person in Paris. Five minutes is so long – too long!

What makes this strange situation uncanny, then, is, at least in part, the incredible fact of *speed*, the speed with which I was able to physically travel across oceans and continents, the speed with which I am able to send information across oceans and continents. The fact that I could think that five minutes is too long to wait, that I cannot afford to waste this time, shows how easily we can absorb new situations, situations that are completely unprecedented in the four-billion-year history of life on Earth and unimaginable even only a few decades ago, and how *difficult* it can become to *perceive* what it is that we have so easily absorbed. After a very short interval, all this apparatus simply *becomes* our milieu and we simply *expect* it to function.

For Heidegger, it is when our equipment *fails* to function, when it breaks down, that we first notice that particular piece of equipment, that tool, that smartphone, that internet, for what it is, in its being present-at-hand, it's *whatness*. And in fact, there is another good reason why I will not interrupt this lecture to send Bernard Stiegler an email: my account is with *gmail*, and I have yet to set up a VPN. For me to be in China is thus uncanny for another reason, because of how it makes me *so conscious* of what I ordinarily find so difficult to perceive: the degree of my *automatic* entanglement with all these devices and networks, and of their entanglement with each other, in the vast global automated systems that pervade the contemporary world. How can it possibly be that Google is not here *with* me? As we shall see, it is through a sudden, unexpected revelation of this perceptual difficulty that Bernard Stiegler begins to think philosophically, and from which his philosophy has drawn nourishment ever since.

Beyond the end of history and the clash of civilizations

Dating back four thousand years, as we have said, traversing numerous dynasties and provinces, persisting through several revolutions, and containing one fifth of the current world human population, it is obvious that China is not just a nation or a culture but a civilization (even if a civilization is always a kind of fiction that lasts only so long as there are those who believe in it). It belongs, in other words, to the highest order of magnitude of what, as we shall see, Bernard Stiegler has begun to call higher complex exorganisms – psycho-socio-techno-organisms. The *hyper*-complex exorganisms that are civilizations, lasting centuries or millennia, are what secrete the most elemental criteria for selecting from among exosomatic possibilities, that is, for making decisions: in *Western* civilization, for example, this secretion has included the notions of truth, beauty and justice, along with theological criteria that seem no longer to be 'in force' – if any of them are.

With the collapse of the Soviet Union towards the end of what the Gregorian calendar calls the twentieth century, there were some Americans who immediately saw this as the final 'victory' of Western civilization understood as 'liberal democracy', an event to be celebrated despite the inevitable ambivalence associated with the seeming rise to prominence of Nietzsche's 'last man'.[119] The 'last philosopher' may have prophesied that the European nihilism of the last man would give rise to 'immense wars of the spirit',[120] but Fukuyama, unlike Nietzsche, was confident that 'the liberal project of filling one's life with material possessions [...] appears to have worked', and hence that it is 'hard to detect great, unfulfilled longings or irrational passions lurking just beneath the surface'.[121]

Other Americans very soon raised their voices to contest Francis Fukuyama's ebullience in seeing this event as the beginning of the 'end of history' and the pacification of these 'immense wars of the spirit'. Samuel Huntington, for example, dismissed this 'one world' paradigm as merely an 'illusion of harmony'.[122] Contrary to such harmonious fantasies, Huntington's disillusioned *realpolitik* foresaw a coming 'clash of civilizations' in which 'culture and cultural identities' would shape 'the patterns of cohesion, disintegration, and conflict in the post-Cold War world'.[123] His was a kind of rudimentary attempt to outline the present and future of these hyper-complex localities in what he called a 'multi-civilizational world', but the terms in which he framed this clash essentially belong to a nineteenth-century social physics. These hyper-complex localities were treated by Huntington as great ships traversing a vast, cold and dark ocean, each more or less navigating their own, independent path, and, when these paths did cross, the geopolitical decisions to be made about the competitive relationships between civilizations were framed in terms of a balance of 'international relations', expressions of geopolitical power whose possibilities would range from soft diplomacy to thermonuclear devastation.[124]

In the twenty-first century, this way of conceiving the relationship between civilizations as a geopolitical battle between very large but more or less spatially discrete and socially cohesive entities (as *cartographic* entities) continues to propagate, especially at the level of the mediatized politics of spectacle and rhetoric, but it can do so only through a kind of denial that refuses to see that localities, even at the geopolitical scale, are today fundamentally embedded, technologically, economically and ecologically (but also *screenically* and *informationally*), within a planetary locality that is at once a biosphere, technosphere, exosphere, infosphere and cinesphere. And what we now know, and in truth already strongly suspected then (in the 1990s), is that the biospherical system on which all these other systems and entities depends has been severely compromised due to the effects generated by the rapid expansion of these anthropic spheres. In addition, all of these civilizational ships seem today to be at risk not just of colliding, but of running aground upon the shores of a seemingly boundless desert, or else of succumbing to a putrefying disease stemming from deep within their bowels that threatens to send them into the abyss. Today, irrational passions do not seem to be lurking beneath the surface but can be found right out in the open, and immense civilizational wars of the spirit appear more likely than ever (but this requires us to ask: do we know what is meant by this word, *spirit*, or what it could mean or should mean?).

The most important meaning of globalization is that no one locality can save *its* world at the expense of other localities: it is the *inextricability* of our common (but still differentiated) technical, economic and psychosocial fates that is the real 'one world' paradigm today, a fate that we now understand could be mortal. This undeniable but often denied 'extinction risk' raises completely new and urgent questions that are 'existential' in every sense, and that necessitate a return to the very origins of the problems from which they have arisen over the last two centuries, and especially the last few decades. These questions are those of *limits*: limits reached, limits needed. But which limits? The necessity of these new questions arises at the beginning of the twenty-first century, whose conditions and tone might reasonably be said to have been fundamentally set by four events:

- the opening of the World Wide Web to global public access in 1993;
- the signing of the Kyoto Protocols in 1997, bound from the outset to fail.[125]
- the worldwide television broadcast of the Twin Towers attacks on 11 September 2001, a vast passive synthesis of collective consciousness and a kind of cinematic or televisual (but of course not *only* televisual) performative confirmation, or illusion of confirmation, of the ideology of civilizational clash, itself the outcome of a series of disastrous decisions, key among which were those leading to America's first war with Iraq in 1990;
- three months to the day after 9/11, China's accession to the WTO, which paved the way for a transformation of manufacturing and a new phase of unrestrained global consumerist economic 'growth' (recollecting that deserts, too, are said to 'grow').

If we are inclined to observe that the questions raised by these four events are 'philosophical' in the sense given to this word in Western civilization, then such an observation must be immediately circumscribed by an acknowledgment that this would:

- necessarily entail a deterritorialization of 'Western' philosophy that inevitably raises ethical questions, that is, questions of the *ethos* proper to any such globalized philosophical locality;

- involve dilemmas of civilizational translation that vastly exceed those of any 'archaeology of European translation'[126] between related languages, recollecting again that translation is *always* an interpretation (within the limits we have already stated);
- raise the *possibility* that 'philosophy' itself, despite its 2500-year history and its pretensions to 'universality', may itself be an idiomatic remnant that is too parochial or regional or metaphysical or ontological or obsolete to be suitable as a way of describing the field to be traversed by these questions and problems;
- necessitate consideration of the possibility that it is *questioning itself* that ultimately gives rise to that calculability of everything and the ever-accelerating *speed* of calculation that ultimately *initiates and becomes* the most threatening problem of all – that the horizon of all questioning may become enclosed within an algorithmic and performative exosphere operating according to rhythms and speeds that vastly escape and exceed those of human cognition, and hence that the rise of questioning could ultimately lead to its very elimination;
- force us to acknowledge that this is the true meaning of what Heidegger called *Gestell*, but *also* to acknowledge that this computational, algorithmic and performative governmentality has, in the West, brought with it an intensification from Reagan's 'government as the problem' (1981) to Trump's 'government as the disaster'[127] (2017), and that it is in this context of accomplished nihilism that Chinese governmentality seems to have become an absolutely critical *question*, insofar as it remains capable of being asked, and as we await in *Gestell* what can *no longer* be just *another* questioning, but something *wholly other*: what Heidegger called *Ereignis*, but an alternative that we are suggesting here should be understood in terms of what Stiegler calls the Neganthropocene.[128]

But however difficult this set of problem-questions obviously is, and however opaque these opening elucidations may have been, it is as an initial step towards responding to this necessity of rational inter-civilizational engagement that these lectures are aimed (and where this must result in a *trans*-civilizational process that *exceeds* any possible outcome of Huntington's multi-civilizational competitive negotiation, which is, before anything else, a highly destructive *economic* war). With that in mind, however, what follows pursues that first step by way of an introduction to the thought of a particular Western philosopher, which is undoubtedly to double up and double down[129] on all the questions and problems that have been raised in these opening paragraphs.

Philosopher and/or philosophy

When giving a series of lectures in a university philosophy department devoted to a particular philosopher, it is customary to begin by situating his or her work within the context of the philosophy that was being done by preceding philosophers, in order to begin to pinpoint the gap or flaw or obstacle that would, so it would be claimed, provide the opportunity and the necessity for the particular step or transformation of thinking that would have been accomplished by the thinker in question: philosophy as a history of mistakes, of mistakes corrected, and of corrections that inevitably introduce new mistakes requiring new corrections. In giving a series of lectures on the work of Bernard Stiegler, such a way of beginning immediately avails itself to any such lecturer, given that on the first page of his first book, Stiegler explains in what way his work fits into just such a mould:

> The object of this work is technics, apprehended as the horizon of all possibility to come and of all possibility of a future. [...] This calls for a work whose urgency is still hardly grasped despite the high stakes of the issue and the disquiet it arouses [...]. Here I would like to warn the reader of this difficulty and of its necessity: at its very origin and up until now, philosophy has repressed technics as an object of thought. Technics is the unthought.[130]

With this warning, the step that requires a transformation of thinking could thus not be more clearly stated: just as Martin Heidegger claims, on the first page of *his* first book, that the question of being has been forgotten since Plato and Aristotle, for whom this question sustained the philosophical work with which they inaugurated Western philosophy, just as Jacques Derrida claimed on the first page of the first chapter of *Of Grammatology* that everything gathered under the name of language has by a 'hardly perceptible' movement been slowly transferred to 'the name of writing',[131] so too Stiegler postulates that from the outset and 'up until now' (in 1994), philosophy has borne within it a fundamental question that it has never allowed truly to rise to the surface of visibility, even if, in more recent times, this question has become *blindingly* obvious. From its very beginnings, he argues, Western philosophy got underway by separating *epistēmē* from *tekhnē*, the knowledge of *beings that have their principle of movement, their origin, within themselves,* from the knowledge of *beings that are produced by 'art', and whose origin, whose principle of movement, would thus lie outside themselves*. On the basis of this separation, he asserts, technical beings and technics *itself*, were consigned by this philosophy to a subordinate status *beneath* the level of philosophical thinking.

But such a way of beginning a series of lectures already tends to presume that what truly counts in the attempt to understand the work of the particular philosopher in question is earlier work by other philosophers that falls *within* the bounds of that academic field known as philosophy, just as it presumes what would count as the 'level of philosophical thinking'. Such lectures are perhaps often leavened, admittedly, with some social or personal context from the world and life in which the work was written, just as Stiegler himself begins by stating that the initial subordination of *tekhnē* that more or less *inaugurated* philosophy occurred in a 'political context' in which the philosopher accused the Sophist of 'instrumentalizing the *logos*',[132] a context and a conflict that would then become our philosophical inheritance. Were we to adhere to this latter dictum, we would be obliged then to mention, for instance, that the philosopher in question in these lectures was born in Paris, the French son of a technician and electrical engineer with German heritage, that his youth unfolded during the 'thirty glorious years' of economic prosperity and his transition to adulthood during the disruptions and rebellions of the 1960s, that he did not complete his secondary schooling but became himself actively involved in these rebellions, joining the PCF *after* 1968 and through that receiving a kind of Marxist philosophico-political education, that his becoming a philosopher occurred later and in the highly unusual circumstances of five years of incarceration for a non-political crime, that in this unusual if not desperate existential situation his work towards becoming a philosopher was made possible by a great deal of solitude, by a single friend who was himself a philosopher and by the books of which this inmate was able to avail himself *in* this solitude and *from* this friend, and that the possibility these circumstances furnished of *doing* this work in turn gave rise to a keen sense of indebtedness, but which combined in the thirty-five years following his release with an increasingly ominous feeling of unease if not alarm about the social, political and technological paths being followed by France and by the world, and that these feelings of obligation and anxiety then became the governing moods orienting the philosophical work that he has undertaken across the more than thirty books that he has published since being released from prison, years that very few in the West would be inclined to characterize with adjectives akin to 'glorious'.

But to so begin a series of lectures on the work of a philosopher, by leaping directly into such summaries of circumstances, lives and events, comes at the risk of avoiding the question of what this 'thing', 'philosophy', actually is, if it is anything at all. This question is avoided for several reasons, but first among them is the fact that such a question *always* exposes an 'academic' holding a position within a department of philosophy to the risk of discovering that he or she may not be a philosopher, or may not even know what one is, or why this thing, philosophy, whatever it is, is worth the effort of actually doing. And the risk entailed by this question in turn produces a doubt that eats away at the courage required to ask this question – what is philosophy? – whose initial answer was provided by the very separation of philosophy from the allegedly 'instrumentalized' and technical discourse of the Sophist, a separation first effected through Socrates's courage to pursue and to teach the mysteries of what he termed the true, the good and the beautiful.

What I would like to propose, here, and from the outset, is that it would be better not to avoid asking this question, and that what we ought actually try to do is not just ask it but answer it, that is, to discover the answer, which is always in some sense to *invent* the answer, which implies that this answer may well contain an irreducible element of *fiction*. And what should motivate us to pursue this answer is the *further* risk of discovering that we do not know *why* we are trying to do philosophy, or whether we *should* be doing it, or whether we should *instead* be doing something *else*: *is* philosophy *in fact* what we should be doing *today*?

Again, these elementary, almost childish-seeming questions, far from the heights of philosophical maturity or sophistication, are not ordinarily the terms in which philosophical lectures are framed. We might well be tempted to think that the very significance of contemporary French philosophy lies in the abandonment of such a search for origins, in much the same manner as Jean-François Lyotard defined postmodernity as suspicion about grand narratives: contrary to this temptation, we would argue that the very *lesson* that post-structuralism learns from structuralism is that the *absence* of a simple origin *in no way* legitimates the abandonment of the search. We argue instead that there is a sense in which the genuine pursuit of questions *always* involves a return to origins, even if such a return may prove to be impossible, where this absence of origin, this ab-originality, *combined with its repression*, might prove to be the very movement of complication that gets going what, in its idiomatic singularity, will come to be known as the 'history of Western philosophy'.

What is philosophy?

So, animated by this problem, this motive and this risk, we ask: what is philosophy? Of course, the first reaction upon hearing such an unseemly question uttered out loud may well be muffled uproar at what it seems so obviously to contain: less courage than hubris. What possible answer could one give to such a question that could ever hope to circumscribe the vast diversity of philosophical approaches, interests and standpoints? And would any such answer not inevitably amount to an attempt to violently stamp the authority of one's own perspective, or the perspective of the thinker one has chosen to explicate, over this vast diversity, in a way bound to prove ultimately indefensible? And is it not possible that all the critiques, suspensions, *Destruktions* and deconstructions of 'Western metaphysics' undertaken in the last century have closed off any possible future horizon for a discourse that would seek to keep itself lodged 'within' the boundaries marked out by the word 'philosophy', or in other words is it not possible that, as Derrida mused in 1964, philosophy may have 'died yesterday'?[133] Such possibilities are in fact inevitabilities, and as such these are *already* 'problems put to philosophy as problems philosophy cannot resolve'.[134]

But might it be that hubris itself forms a *part* of that answer, not just in the sense that to presume to offer an answer to such a question would constitute an example of it, but in the sense that there can be no final separation of courage and hubris, which is to say crime, that they are therapeutic and pathological versions of one and the same motive, one and the same affect – to push past to the *limit*, or *beyond* the limit – and hence that these, and not just wonder, may turn out to be a necessary aspect of what it is that has always gotten philosophy going? It was the aforementioned Socrates who, after all, through the text of Plato, and in the earliest dialogues such as *Meno*, taught us that, although a 'what is...?' question may have many exemplars to which one may point, this possibility does not discharge us of the responsibility of asking how it is that all such examples *cohere* as signs pointing towards answers, a coherence that ought to *precede* the diversity of examples. Hence in teaching us not to avoid this responsibility, he teaches us also that this search for what unites the examples, what gives them their coherence, is always a search back to the *origin* of the question, and that *at* this origin, which is a question of the origin of *knowledge*, there lies only an aporia: this search can only be for what we *already* know, *even if* what we know doesn't exist, could never have existed and will never exist, because either we do not know what we are seeking, in which case we will not recognize it if and when we happen across it, or else we already knew it, and must have been only pretending not to know. Socrates's answer, as any student of philosophy knows, is: we did know it, but we have forgotten it, and hence all knowledge is really the recollection of something forgotten – *anamnesis*.

For Stiegler, it was this question that formed the starting point, the opening question, of what became his philosophy, and what led him to the question of technics:

> I did not first question technics but memory and, through Plato, *anamnesis* as the possibility of knowing and as the origin of knowledge itself [...]. Besides, I continue to believe that there is no other possible way to *arrive at* philosophy than by questioning the origin of knowledge, which also constitutes the very possibility of knowledge.
>
> It was on this path of memory that I found 'technics'.[135]

It will be crucial for us to understand this path that goes *from* memory *to* technics, which will also be, strangely enough, a path that goes from technics to memory. But in any case, the hubris or the courage of philosophy is in part a matter of the *insistence* on this necessity of 'going back to the origins' (of knowledge), despite the fact that this 'origin' is always *complicated*, if not *missing*: in want of an origin, in default of an origin. In the case of the original separation of beings of *phusis* from beings of *tekhnē*, the fact that the latter do not have their principle of movement, their *origin*, within themselves becomes the very historico-philosophical basis for the argument that to understand technical beings does not require a form of thinking that seeks those origins: they will have been deemed *unoriginal* beings. To think technics would, according to such a way of thinking, then not require philosophy, which would instead pursue something *more* original, something that would, unlike the products of artifice, be *worthier* of philosophical thinking: *epistēmē* and *tekhnē* are fundamentally distinct, opposed to one another. Against such a separation, such an *oppositional* manner of thinking, it would then be necessary to look back *before* this opposition, to seek a coherence of 'technics' older than its opposition from 'physics': even if such an originary technics does not exist, might it be that it *consists*?

To go back beyond this understanding of the distinction of philosophical discourse can only mean, then, understanding why this separation of technical knowledge from epistemic knowledge, on the basis of which the *repression* of technics *by* philosophy first got going, why this separation may be necessary (in the sense of unavoidable, or in the sense of an accident that then *becomes our* necessity[136]) but not sufficient for truly delineating what it is that distinguishes philosophy. Or does it simply mean that a discourse that would *no longer* live by this opposition of two kinds of beings would therefore no longer count as philosophical? For Socrates, this subordination of the technical is allied to the *doggedness* of his pursuit of the question, 'what is…?', beyond what for the Sophists would be all reasonable limits, beyond all instrumentalizable purpose: in the eyes of the Sophists, what Socrates teaches has no *function*. But here, this notion of an instrumentalizable purpose is *itself* a function of the Sophist's place within the 'political context' that determines the boundaries within which sophistic thinking is free to move. In insisting on his *own* questioning, on pursuing the questions that arise from out of his own singular individuality, because this is what philosophy *always* does, he implicitly accuses the Sophists of allowing their own individuality to be diluted, and hence he in turn finds *himself* accused of a *surfeit* of individuality, that is, of excess, of hubris. As Stiegler says:

> In fact, this inscription of the philosophical at the heart of the very intimacy of the individual is what is testified to by the life and by the death of that proto-philosopher Socrates – with that sacrificial dimension which is undoubtedly part of an existence completely devoted to thought. The singularity of Socrates's existence, his individuality, was precisely Anytus's accusation, before the trial that would condemn him.[137]

But when Socrates *exceeds* those boundaries that determine what it is legitimate to think or say, when he cannot remain content within those boundaries, when he pursues a question *all the way* to the aporia of its origin, he does so because he is himself *moved* to do so by a political context that amounts to a *problem* that gives rise to his question: Socrates is not *only* his individuality; his individuality is fundamentally an individual *co-existence* with others, which means that he *cares* about these others and the collective they form *together with him*.

To answer a question such as 'what is philosophy?' requires, before anything else, seeking to understand the provenance of that question, which in turn means, firstly, going back to the origin of the question, and, secondly, to understanding how that origin consists of a *problem*. Philosophy, then, would be the teaching of this necessity: to understand the genesis of the question from out of a problem. It will be *this* relationship of (philosophical) questioning to its provenance in a problem that makes of philosophy, not an *instruction* or even a *prescription* (for life), but always a matter of participation in and contribution to a *critique*.

So now we have another question: what is a problem, or, better, *why* is there a problem? What gives rise to a problem? What *makes* a problem? In promising answers, questions are piling up, and how could we fail to be exposed to the accusation of making false promises, promises that cannot hope to be kept?

But is this not ultimately the accusation of 'corruption' that Socrates himself faced, and for which he was condemned to drink the hemlock: the accusation that, by insisting on leading the youth of Athens so far along his own path of questioning, he could not deliver on the promises of a knowledge that could ever be beneficial for the city? And if so, what *difference* does it make that Socrates accepted this judgment, this punishment meted out by the city, that he *preferred* it to exile, and preferred it on the grounds that, despite the political context, it is *better* for his children to be orphans of Socrates than to become orphans of the city? And what difference does it make to *us*, who are also orphans of Socrates, and to our understanding of the question of philosophy inasmuch as this question arises from out of this problem of Socrates (hearing here the double genitive)?

This, of course, is the question that Socrates addresses in *Crito*, where he rejects Crito's plan for him to make an escape from Athens. Such an escape, Socrates argues through the voice of the laws, would only give rise to the suspicion that he was, after all, a 'destroyer of laws' (53c), and so would, with such an escape, only confirm the judgment that his questioning, his engagement of maieutic dialogue, far from constituting a genuine teaching, really amounts to a wholly negative destruction, a dismantling of the instrumentalization of justice embodied in the technical apparatus of the law.

But it would also be to break the injunction that 'one ought not to return a wrong or an injury to any person, whatever the provocation is' (49c–d), which in this case means that, if the city injures us, we ought not want to exact revenge by injuring those who have injured us, city-dwellers, citizens. In short, Socrates does not *resent* the sentence that has been imposed: that he suffers, that he is caused to suffer, does not mean that he wants to assuage his suffering by causing others to suffer in turn – neither those who are his direct accusers nor the city of whom they are the representatives. And nor does he want any such resentment to be transmitted to those who are his heirs, that is, to his children, that is, to *us*. In other words, even at that moment when his own being-towards-death becomes inescapable and undeniable, Socrates maintains an *affirmative* relationship to the city and to the future, to a being-towards-life together in the *polis*, an affinity with life itself and life-to-come in its onward struggle, in all its productive ab-originality and all the mistakes that follow, until it reaches us.

Nietzsche against Socrates

To describe this mood of Socrates as 'affirmative' is unavoidably to draw attention to the way in which such an interpretation of the character of the philosopher Socrates, as portrayed in the fiction that is the dialogue of *Crito* as composed by Plato, is utterly at odds with the interpretation of the 'problem of Socrates' that Nietzsche describes in *Twilight of the Idols*. For Nietzsche, such a *characterization* of Socrates could only be completely false. 'The Problem of Socrates' opens by declaring that Socrates and those of his kind, the 'wise', far from affirming life, have always *resisted* it:

> The wisest men in every age have reached the same conclusion about life: *it's no good*... Always and everywhere, you hear the same sound from their mouths, – a sound full of doubt, full of melancholy, full of exhaustion with life, full of resistance *to* life.[138]

For Nietzsche, such judgments, attitudes and moods can only ever be symptoms of a pathological relationship to life, and as such stupidities, for *'the value of life cannot be estimated'*.[139] Socrates is for Nietzsche nothing but a decadent who *wanted* to die, who took it upon *himself* to drink down the poison, whose *in-sistence* on the dialectical method was nothing more than *re-sistance*, a last resort of the defeated, his 'irony' no more than an expression of *ressentiment* and as such a booby trap of revenge.[140]

Nietzsche does acknowledge that with this dialectics Socrates touched on the 'agonistic drive of the Greeks', and that he was, in this, also 'a great *erotic*'.[141] Furthermore, he argues that this was possible because it was Socrates who perceived that, among the Athenians generally, the drives were in disarray, excessive, leading to the clash of Greek civilization with itself. In other words, Nietzsche acknowledges that Socrates perceived the political context as a *problem*, and as a problem of desire disordered. If dialectics is seen as a last resort, it is because for Nietzsche the tyranny of reason arises as a possible expedient only in the midst of a crisis, a state of emergency [*eine*

Notlage], producing a 'rational' 'moralism' that is thus 'pathologically conditioned'.[142] And in this pathology, the error consists in the misbegotten hope that to wage war on decadence by such means could ever succeed in overcoming it:

> Socrates was a misunderstanding; *the whole morality of improvement, including that of Christianity, was a misunderstanding*... The most glaring daylight, rationality at any cost, a cold, bright, cautious, conscious life without instinct, opposed to instinct, was itself just a sickness, another sickness – and in no way a return to 'virtue', to 'health', to happiness... To *have* to fight the instincts – that is the formula for decadence: as long as life is *ascending*, happiness is equal to instinct.[143]

Again, our pursuit of a coherent answer to the question, 'what is philosophy?', appears to have stumbled, in this case on this *opposition* between Socrates (conjoined by Nietzsche to Christianity) and Nietzsche with respect to life and the city, or life in the city, or in other words on this vast antipathy that Nietzsche seems to have for 'the cleverest of all self-deceivers'.[144] Is it conceivable that we could muster a *sympathetic* co-understanding of Socrates and Nietzsche capable of *overcoming* this antipathy, and if so, on what basis?

At present, Western civilization is undoubtedly suffering from a crisis of resentment, that is, the proliferation of a widespread feeling that the fact of my suffering deserves compensation in the form of the expiatory suffering of others. Contrary to any end of history, this has led to the unprecedented election of an American president on the basis of a campaign that appealed to and exploited this widespread feeling by *giving it what it wants*, that is, by supplying a set of scapegoats onto which these feelings can be fixed and discharged, sometimes violently, sometimes explosively. This is just the most visible symptom of what, in his most recent work, Stiegler refers to as an 'immense regression'. China has not succumbed to this process, not yet, but it must surely have an interest in prophylactically tracing its causes back to their origins, because at the very least it risks catching this disease, and a strain that has had time to mutate to a high level of virulence, and against which the immune system of Chinese civilization may find itself unprepared and sorely tested, in particular if that system is itself on the way to becoming computationally algorithmic.[145]

This *potential* for *ressentiment* that inevitably leads to the 'spirit of revenge' that Nietzsche describes in *Thus Spoke Zarathustra* is that of which he was the master pathologist, and for which, as a thinker of reactive forces and tendencies, he today remains more indispensable than ever. Just as Socrates in the eyes of Nietzsche was the one capable of seeing what 'was quietly gaining ground everywhere'[146] (the problem), but was unable to fight this diagnosis other than with weapons that themselves *stemmed from* the disease – that is, a dialectics according to which 'any concession to the instincts, to the unconscious [and hence a dialectics opposed, so Nietzsche argues, to the affirmation of life], leads *downwards*'[147] – so too Nietzsche sees with dread that what is quietly gathering itself in the nineteenth-century industrializing West (*its* problem) is that 'average man' afflicted with nihilism and resentment, and dwelling within a growing desert prophesied to last two centuries. The average man: that is, the *Anthropos* who is the product of averages, of the law of large numbers, of population statistics, later to become marketing statistics and user profiling – *calculable* man.

But with this notion that 'to *have* to fight the instincts' is the 'formula for decadence', and hence with his conclusion that, on the contrary, 'happiness is *equal* to instinct', or, we might say, to the *drives unbound* (by 'rational' 'morality'), we are forced to ask ourselves whether Nietzsche's diagnosis of Socrates (of philosophers and moralists generally), that 'what they choose as a remedy, as an escape, is itself only another expression of decadence', applies also to his own prescriptions.[148] If so, could Socrates amount to Nietzsche's scapegoat, his *pharmakos*, thanks to which he, too, could be accused of being one of those 'philosophers and moralists [who] are lying to themselves when they think that they are going to extricate themselves from decadence'?[149] Yet obviously we must not be too hasty: we must *also* remember that Nietzsche is the thinker from whom Georges Canguilhem learned that we are the animal with the ability to make ourselves sick, that we are perpetually *tempted* to do so, and that there is no cure and no health other than *through and with* that which makes us sick? With this thought, we have already arrived at the problem not just of the *pharmakos* but of the *pharmakon* – and of the relationship between them.

On what basis could we attempt such a sympathetic co-reading of Socrates with Nietzsche? In common between them is this question of collective life, of collective life beyond familial life, larger than familial life, as a *problem* (of disarray, of decadence) whose causes must be traced back to their origins, in the absence of which it is a problem that is bound to be exacerbated, and so to *descend* into incivility, if not into civil war, and as a problem and a question whose teaching always opens onto the problem and the question of the *future* of collective life.[150] What distinguishes Socrates and Nietzsche, at least in the eyes of the latter, is some relationship between a series of terms: life, instinct, reason.

More specifically, we find an opposition between the Socratic notion that only the *rationality* of life in the city counts as 'ascending' and the Nietzschean notion that sees the rationality of Socrates as indelibly 'opposed to instinct', Nietzsche affirming on the contrary that only *instinctual* life is ascending, life *as such*. For Nietzsche, the 'most profound instinct of life' is 'directed towards the future of life' and contrary to '*ressentiment against* life', but is it not this very *exclusion* – of anything 'descending' *from* the peak that would be life lived according to the 'instincts' – that legitimates the all too common, all too human interpretation of the 'eternal joy of becoming' as simply a matter of going with the flow of existence, with '*tragic* feeling', perhaps, but without the tragic necessity of *decision*?[151] Beyond deconstruction and its undecidability, such a sympathetic reading would thus need also to be a critique of what Nietzsche *lacked* that enabled *his* instincts to fall back, to the extent that he does (or in other words, perhaps, what makes possible *misinterpretations* of Nietzsche that go in this direction), into this last metaphysical (and biological, if not 'Darwinian') opposition between instinct and reason (even if reversing the metaphysical sign in order to privilege the former over the latter), and what can lead us beyond that opposition. This philosophical question, which necessarily entails asking how this 'future of life' is distinct from merely its becoming, forms the horizon of, and will be indirectly pursued in, the lectures that follow.

Philosophy today

Let us recap. From the assertion that we should not avoid asking and answering the question of what it is that philosophy actually is, we passed to a consideration of the figure of Socrates, and to his preference that his children (and we are all his children) be orphans of Socrates rather than orphans of the city, which we interpreted as a desire not to transmit resentment to these heirs on the grounds it is a perpetual threat to the modicum of sociability without which collective existence is impossible. From there, we were forced to acknowledge that this affirmative interpretation of Socrates is completely at odds with the 'problem of Socrates' as delineated by Nietzsche in 1888, where Socrates is portrayed as the prototypical resentful philosopher for whom life is ultimately worthless (as opposed to being that which is priceless), which, fifteen years earlier, had been the way that Nietzsche characterized the contemporary philosopher, for whom the 'drive toward truth' leads only to the question, 'And what is life worth, after all?'[152]

We are, then, led to the thought of philosophy as always involved with the *actual* problem of collective existence, with the *action* required in the here and now of a city in this or that epoch, or mired in this or that crisis, and where this involves tracing the genealogy of this or that problem, so to speak, to its origins. But if the intention here is to overcome the Nietzschean antipathy towards Socrates through the location of some kind of common ground between the 'gadfly' and 'first philosopher' and the 'last disciple of Dionysos' and 'last philosopher' with respect to the questions of life and the city, how, once again, could we hope to extend this to a definition of philosophy that could ever hope to include the notoriously divided kaleidoscope of approaches from the strictest 'logician' to the vaguest 'postmodernist'? The only possible answer, which is something other than the location of common ground, is if by 'life', here, we understand the problem of existence for those beings for whom this problem, becoming a question, is amenable to resolution through 'reason', understood in the broadest possible sense, where such reason is therefore understood as itself a *function of life*, and ultimately as that 'special embodiment in us of the disciplined counter-agency which saves the world'.[153] In other words, where it is understood in the Whiteheadian sense according to which the art of life has a tripartite division between 'living', 'living well' and 'living better',[154] in life's perpetual tension between what Whitehead calls history's

> two main tendencies. One tendency is exemplified in the slow decay of physical nature. With stealthy inevitableness, there is degradation of energy. The sources of activity sink downward and downward. Their very matter wastes. The other tendency is exemplified by the yearly renewal of nature in the spring, and by the upward course of biological evolution. In these pages I consider Reason in its relation to these contrasted aspects of history. Reason is the self-discipline of the originative element in history. Apart from the operations of Reason, this element is anarchic.[155]

How do we relate this *twofold* tension between a descending tendency and an ascending counter-tendency to the *tripartite* division between being alive, being satisfactorily alive and transforming life and its satisfactions, where the function of reason, as the promotion of this 'art of life', according to Whitehead, consists primarily in directing 'the attack on the environment', and where he concludes that this function amounts to a factor that 'directs and criticizes the urge towards the attainment of an end realized in imagination but not in fact'?[156]

With this strange question, *between two and three*, we are equipped to find a way of entering into the thought of the philosopher whose work forms the subject of these lectures, and for whom the question is not just of what life is worth, but, very specifically, of what *makes* life worth (the effort and the toil of) living – and where we must interpret this, not just as a question for the individual, or even for the collective, but as a question of *technical* life, or as the problem and the question of the *work* involved in a (collective and technical) *education* in technical *existence*. Or in other words, if we take this as an *existential* question involving our fundamentally technical *ethos*, then it is a question of how to live in a way that is *worthy* of the technical power we have so manifestly acquired. And this is, furthermore, a *civilizational* question, and it is now, that is, in the Anthropocene, a question that is not just *multi*-civilizational but *trans*-civilizational. If this question of how to collectively and worthily live the technical life inevitably entails 'affirming our trans-civilizational future', then for *philosophy* this can only be, today, and insofar as this remains the name of a discourse capable of approaching this problem, a matter of coming to know *on what basis* to conduct a revaluation of all values, where these revaluated values must form the criteria for deciding in what possible, improbable future *to invest* (which is also a question of knowing what investment *means* or *could* mean).

If we must ask this question 'today', that can only mean in a world, and on a planet, that is today deeply threatened by ecological disaster (for instance, irreversible climate change), economic disaster (for instance, the collapse of the consumerist 'perpetual growth' model) and political disaster (for instance, the dangerous rise of what is often referred to as populism), at a moment when the ability to *think and care* about all these possible futures is itself deeply threatened by the automated, algorithmic production of industrial temporal objects operating at extremely high speed. There is thus a vast gulf between Fukuyama's idea of an 'end of history', in which a 'final' geopolitical equilibrium would supposedly bring an end to 'events', and the punk notion of 'no future', where plenty can still happen even as we enter a fatal downward spiral.

Philosophy, according to this delineation, this delimitation, is a functional application of understanding and reason directed towards learning and teaching what it could mean to *take care* of collective existence, which can only mean to take care not just of its present but its *future*, and where today this 'collectivity' is that of the entire biosphere – fundamentally at risk, and in all the biological and noetic diversity that it contains, and on which it depends. This cannot be a matter of awaiting the god who could save us from economic or ecological catastrophe – from 'extinction risk'. Nor can it be a matter of blindly accelerating the disruption – the ideology of 'crash or crash through' – as if gathering enough speed will make it possible to burst through and beyond the systemic limits with which we are currently threatened. It can only be a matter of struggling against denial and resentment, and through that of investing ourselves (politically, economically, libidinally, existentially) in the urgent, careful invention of a new existence worthy of the accident that has befallen us as a result of the awesome and manifold technical powers we have ourselves terrifyingly unleashed.

For the question with which we are left is: why are *we* the beings for whom this question of taking care arises? Why are we the beings who find ourselves confronted with instabilities that *bring* questions to the fore? Why are we the beings who find ourselves in situations in which thresholds have been crossed, limits of tolerability that produce crises, requiring critique and reinvention? Why are we the beings who find ourselves thrown into questions, and through that into question? Why, thrown into questions and into question, are we the beings who must seek new ways of living, and living worthily? Without *opposing* ourselves to other beings, must we not ask ourselves, what *distinguishes us*?

With all of these questions in mind, what follows is by no means a *summary* of Stiegler's work across his thirty or so books, let alone a *summation*. Instead, these lectures will navigate an at times wayward path into and through his corpus, focusing on certain eddies in the general flow of his philosophy, the tensions and counter-flows giving rise to these eddies, and the unusual currents by which they are conjoined, sometimes across great conceptual distances. In so doing, it will constantly be a matter of giving thought to the *philosophical* import of Stiegler's work, but where this adjective must be heard together with all of these preceding questions, and in a context where the putrefying agents that are resentment and denial, along with numerous agents of ecological degradation, are visibly contributing to the potential closure of all future horizons.

2 Exteriorization and Différance

The unfurling of French theory

As we have already seen, the movement of Stiegler's philosophy takes as its point of departure the thought that what remains unthought throughout the history of philosophy is technics. That technics is repressed does not mean that it never appears in the history of philosophy, but that when it appears, it does so symptomatically, derivatively, and not as a cause or as the ultimate destination to which any legitimately philosophical question is thought to trace back. If the two great regions of beings as they have been conceived in the metaphysics of modern philosophy and modern science are (1) inorganic beings whose dynamic is merely physical and in that historically 'anarchic', and (2) organic beings whose dynamic is biological and evolutionary, then, within this schema, technical beings are metaphysically conceived merely as 'hybrids', unoriginal mechanical beings whose origin and movement lie in the beings that we are ourselves, whether we are conceived as merely beings of *phusis* or as beings who exceed the 'natural realm'.

It is Karl Marx who begins to conceive the possibility of thinking a technical dynamic that would be something other than merely derivative of physical processes and biological dynamics. In *The German Ideology*, Marx and Engels argue that men may be distinguished from animals by many criteria, but they *begin* to distinguish themselves 'as soon as they begin to *produce* their means of subsistence', through which 'men are indirectly producing their actual material life'.[157] Contrary to idealist metaphysics, 'production' and 'mode of production' become the originative element in history that conditions the forms of the attack on the environment, which, more than 'the production of the physical existence of the individuals', amounts to 'a definite *mode of life*', where this mode is then affected by '[e]ach new productive force, insofar as it is not merely a quantitative extension of productive forces already known'.[158] Heidegger will then see the possibility that such a dynamic could evolve to the point of absorbing *phusis* 'itself', ultimately outstripping and overtaking the very possibility of control and even of the very possibility of thinking.

What remains doubtful, however, is whether either Marx, thinker of the industrial revolution, machines and the 'general intellect', or Heidegger, thinker of 'modern technology', *Gestell* and cybernetics, ever pursued the technical question all the way back to the beginning, or saw in that complicated commencement the inauguration not just of a solution but of a problem, a problem that later becomes the possibility of the question *as such*, and hence, subsequently, the possibility of what Heidegger will call the question of the meaning of being, and where the meaning of *Gestell* would then be that this overtaking of thinking by the *problem* of *Gestell* amounts to the possibility that this questioning could come to an end, dissolved into a technical problematics that would then become *our* problem, the problem of whether we are any longer up to the task of thinking, and specifically of the problem of needing to think what (and that) we have not yet even begun to think.

One thinker and scholar who *may* aid this pursuit of the technical question back to the beginning is André Leroi-Gourhan. Who is André Leroi-Gourhan? He was a French prehistorian, archaeologist and palaeontologist who, among many other activities, studied under Marcel Mauss, was a member of the French Resistance, and became a professor at the Sorbonne before being appointed to a chair in prehistory at the Collège de France. It is necessary to ask this question, 'Who is Leroi-Gourhan?', because there was a long period of time in which he seemed almost to have been erased from the history of French thought, and especially from its Anglophone reception, and in the first place by another scientist profoundly influenced by Mauss, Claude Lévi-Strauss, whose Saussurean structural anthropology will set the scene for the great structuralist movement as well as for the post-structuralism that will follow it soon thereafter.

Now, Jacques Derrida's work gets going with the question of *genesis*, not in Lévi-Strauss but in Husserl, and the first published lecture he ever gave continues this theme by deconstructing (before 'deconstruction' had been coined, and long before it became something like a brand name) the distinction between genesis and structure in Husserlian phenomenology, which he pursues by noting that there is, in Husserl, an 'initial distinction between different irreducible types of genesis and structure', but that these inevitably lead back to a question of 'genesis *in general*' and 'structure *in general*'. It is on this basis that 'Husserl *operates*', but without himself asking about 'the meaning of his operative instruments *in general*' because, as that which forms the very possibility of posing the question of the transcendental reduction, to do so would imply asking 'the question of the possibility of the question' that strictly exceeds the Husserlian project.[159] And when in 1966 Derrida presents what we can consider the foundational text of this so-called post-structuralism, 'Structure, Sign and Play in the Discourse of the Human Sciences', he plainly states that Lévi-Strauss's 'respect for structurality' comes at the cost of a 'neutralization of time and history' that works by 'omitting to posit the problem of the transition from one structure to another',[160] Derrida giving the example of language that according to Lévi-Strauss 'could only have been born in one fell swoop'.[161]

Yet even though Derrida begins his work by indicating the deficiency of structuralism with respect to genesis, history, diachrony, genealogy, the destructuring process of shifting from one structure to another and so on, nevertheless post-structuralism remains marked by its own genesis in a form of thought that is perhaps not *entirely* free of this neutralization of time and history. And hence even though it is Derrida himself who draws attention to this deficiency, who rejects this refusal of history, and who therefore calls for a positive displacement towards a new concept of history, nevertheless Derrida does not himself produce this new concept, as Anne Alombert has recently pointed out.[162] And when he comes to consider Althusser's 'scientism', Derrida again understands the Althusserian gesture that consists in a critique of the 'Hegelian' metaphysics of history, but nevertheless calls for 'a new logic of *repetition* and the *trace*' aimed not at 'one single history' but 'rather histories *different* in their type, rhythm, mode of inscription',[163] but without himself producing this new logic.

How might the history of French thought have unfurled otherwise, and how might it have produced a different concept of history, had Leroi-Gourhan not been kept behind the scenes of these questions, so to speak, had not become someone about whom it is still necessary to ask and answer the question, 'Who is André Leroi-Gourhan?'? Of course, such counterfactual questions are impossible to answer, and can lead only to pointless speculation. Nevertheless, posing them can at least serve as a worthwhile reminder of the contingency and potential deficiency of the intellectual inheritance that continues to set the conditions of intellectual production in the academy.

Such counterfactual speculation would surely be tempted to conclude that, had Leroi-Gourhan occupied a place somewhere closer to centre stage in the theatre of French thinking, we might have found ourselves *much further along the way* to this new approach to history in its types, rhythms and modes of inscription. Already in 1943, Leroi-Gourhan was proposing a distinction between 'technical tendencies' and 'technical facts', where the former are not determined or localized within what he called 'ethnic groupings', that is, within particular *localities*, even though it is *only* in ethnic groupings that these tendencies are concretized – in the *form* of such technical facts, such actually realised *instances* of technical artefacts, facts that are always contingent or accidental. Already in this case, it is clear that the *idiomatic* technical expression of these *localized* tendencies indicates a kind of behavioural programming operating at a level (the 'ethnic' level) *other* than the *species* level.

Furthermore, when in 1945 he comes back to the question of the relationship between the ethnic grouping, he formulates a distinction between the *exterior milieu*, meaning the geography, climate and ecosystemic locality within which the ethnic grouping is located, and the *interior milieu*, meaning the shared past and shared ways of living of those within the ethnic grouping. The means by which the interior milieu and the exterior milieu are articulated is the 'curtain of objects', the 'interposed membrane', the 'artificial envelope' formed by the ethnic grouping as the basis for its attack on the environment (as Whitehead would say). And so, with this distinction, we can understand his concept of technical *tendency* as, in the words of Leroi-Gourhan, 'a movement, within the interior milieu, that gains progressive foothold in the exterior milieu',[164] a foothold that, nevertheless, is only ever *expressed* in the localized differentiation of technical facts. What forms of articulation are at play in this articulation of the interior and the exterior, what complexities of advance and delay, negotiation and renegotiation, between artefacts and the practice (or behavioural regulation) of those artefacts? With such questions, it becomes possible to think another approach to the temporality of the technical beings that we are (which extends before and beyond the question of the history of humanity), one that can begin to think in terms of tendencies, rhythms, epochs and modes of inscription.

For Leroi-Gourhan, the technical tendency on the one hand possesses its *own* dynamic: it involves a dynamic relationship between exterior and interior that exceeds localization and individual will. But on the other hand, it cannot do so without the *intentionality* involved in the negotiation of that dynamic: how could innovation or invention ever occur *without* intentional foresight? (This is similar, in other words, to the way in which the evolution of a particular language occurs without any conscious decision to do so by any of the speakers of that language, exceeding the level of the individual, yet is the product of nothing other than the totality of decisions of individual speakers about what to say.) In that way, Leroi-Gourhan was perhaps ripe for deconstruction, so to speak: a key question that Stiegler formulates in *Technics and Time, 1,* via Gilbert Simondon (and Bertrand Gille, who thinks the relationship between 'technical systems' and *other* systems, these 'others' being all those social systems that regulate or cope with or take care of the functioning of the technical system and its consequences), is whether this progression of technical tendencies can really any longer be said to arise *from* the interior milieu, or whether it is not rather the case that this interiority is progressively dissolved into a planetary exterior that itself finds itself progressively anthropized (that is, technicized) as technics becomes thoroughly industrial.[165] This, once again, ultimately leads to the question raised by Heidegger with the concept of *Gestell* – but in other terms.

Leroi-Gourhan, Derrida, Stiegler

It is not just a question of finishing a project whose necessity Derrida makes clear without himself carrying it to completion. More than that, it is a question of understanding the impediments, whether 'internal' or 'external', that prevented him from doing so. Because absent such a critique, those undiagnosed impediments will likely remain in force for any future attempts to so 'displace' the notion of history.

When Derrida refers to 'modes of inscription' or to the trace, these inscriptions and traces cannot simply be ascribed to 'materiality', because this would be to assign precedence to one side of a metaphysical opposition whose very possibility would for Derrida be opened up by this trace, as for example the opposition of matter and form, or the material and the ideal, the material and the spiritual, or, ultimately, presence and non-presence. But given that metaphysics is according to Derrida that from which it is strictly speaking impossible to escape, the *refusal* of *any* such materiality, the attempt to conceive traces and inscriptions as *purely* immaterial, would be exposed to the very same risk.

For Derrida, of course, this question of the trace therefore implies the notion of *archi-writing*, the originarily inscriptive character of even vocal language prior to the existence of the 'narrow and historically determined concept of writing', which is how Derrida complicates that 'one fell swoop' by which Lévi-Strauss conceives the advent of language. Before there can be inscription that opens technics, there must be the inscriptive possibility, and hence Derrida states his belief about the *priority* of writing:

> I believe [...] that a certain sort of question about the meaning and origin of writing precedes, or at least merges with, a certain type of question about the meaning and origin of technics.[166]

It may be that everything hangs on the significance of the little phrase, 'or at least merges with', or, perhaps, that the whole issue is left hanging on that phrase. We can at least wonder whether Derrida ever truly *analyses* this possible merger, and, in the absence of such an analysis, we are forced to wonder *what is at stake* in placing it under the very specific sign of 'writing', no matter how qualified this word may be. Are we not at least entitled to question this *preference* for this particular word, given that the history of inscription in matter begins some *three million years* prior to the narrow and historically determined concept of writing? What *exactly* is the relation between this 'concept' and the *choice* of this word to describe the condition of possibility of something lying not only *outside* this concept but prior to its historical determination *by such a vast distance*? If everything is already there with the first inscriptive gestures, then is not the choice of this one word, writing, historically and philosophically loaded?

If archi-writing is the condition of possibility of something like carved stone, then can the fundamental possibility of something so old (flint tools dating from at least 3.3 million years ago, that is, pre-dating not only *Homo sapiens* but the entire *Homo* genus) be unproblematically approached by way of something much, much newer (perhaps around 8000 years old)? And even if we refer not to inscription in stone, but to the first engraved markings whose *function* is to conserve or communicate meaning, as for instance with prehistoric cave painting, do not these, too, predate 'writing' by a significant margin? Is there not a risk that the use of the term 'writing' to name what predates all these epochs of inscription implies some kind of reasoning by *analogy*? Finally, if archi-writing refers to the opening, beyond the metaphysics of presence, of the inscriptive possibility from out of which the event of meaning can occur, does this non-concept contain sufficient resources for conveying not just the retentional character of such 'inscriptivity' but also its protentional character, which is to say, its *projective* character as the engine of *dreams and images*, some of which will then become *realised* dreams, that is, materialized ones, materialized specifically in artefacts?

It is with Leroi-Gourhan's two-volume major work, *Gesture and Speech*, published over 1964 and 1965, that we can begin to approach these questions, and specifically with his concept of 'exteriorization', a technical concept that, unfortunately, did not manage itself to gain a progressive foothold for at least thirty years, up until the publication of *Technics and Time, 1* in 1994. The leap effected by the concept of exteriorization consists in retying the question of the technical to the question of inscription, because Leroi-Gourhan's insight was that *every* technical artefact, whether by design or accidentally, *functions as a kind of memory*, and does so precisely because it is *inscriptive*, an inscription of living gestures into dead matter, that is, an inscription of time into space. With the concept of exteriorization, Leroi-Gourhan understands the specificity of the process of *hominization* as lying in the advent of what amounts to a *third kind of memory*.

Why do we say, a 'third' kind of memory? What is memory? Could we say that memory refers to the means by which localized systems keep the past in the present, so as to preserve a record of the past and the lessons it contains, and thereby to increase the chances of success in the attack on the environment in which living consists? Or, to put it another way, memory can be described as the capacity of localized systems to retain improbabilities against the overwhelming tendency towards the probable characteristic of the universe and described by the second law of thermodynamics. This *counter*-tendency to retain past improbabilities is, as far as we know, only a characteristic of those localized systems that are associated with life in the terrestrial biosphere. Describing the relationship between memory and behavioural anticipation, Leroi-Gourhan says that memory is to be understood 'in a very broad sense' as 'the medium for action sequences'.[167] With this in mind, we may indeed feel justified in referring to three great epochs of memory that have developed on this planet.[168]

Let us briefly outline this vast genealogy. The first kind of memory is that of molecular genetics, beginning some four billion years ago with the first articulation of organic evolutionary processes *from out of* inorganic matter: a first complicated moment, no doubt, but, in any case, involving a 'before' and an 'after'.[169] Of course, the DNA molecule does not 'remember' the past in the strict sense in which we ordinarily use this word: the molecule itself is precisely *incapable* of learning lessons. Nevertheless, this macromolecule reproduces itself *almost but not quite perfectly* (so that we should really say that DNA is not 'one' molecule but a perpetually unfolding chain of variations upon a molecular theme), thereby allowing for a *stability* of reproduction necessary for the survival of species, while also enabling the proliferation of *differentiation* across the expanse of evolutionary time (while about 1.5 million species have been formally described, estimates of the number of currently-existing species range into the billions[170]). In so doing, this dynamic of synchronic and diachronic reproduction *effectively and efficiently,* but *accidentally,* preserves the lessons of experience at the genetic level, as a kind of 'species-related memory'[171] honed by the very long-term effects of selection pressure, even if the individual has no *awareness* of those lessons as it follows genetically-based behavioural patterns within the conditions set by the exterior milieu in which the individual finds itself.

The second kind of memory is that which begins with the development of nervous tissue, some 550 million years ago. With the evolution of life forms possessing such tissue, it became possible for the individual to respond in a primitive way to changes in environmental conditions.[172] With the subsequent evolution of the *central* nervous system, it became possible for the individual to co-ordinate sensory reception with behaviour, involving the kind of sensorimotor loops that von Uexküll studied in relation to the tick. And with the further development of the executive functions of that central nervous system, parts of the brain evolved to become dedicated to preserving a record of the *outcomes* of these sensorimotor loops, that is, a 'potential memory' through which it becomes possible to learn and remember the lessons of individual experience, and so to evolutionarily benefit from the introduction of greater latitudes of behavioural variability with respect to the genetic program, *even if* the *content* of those lessons cannot be transmitted from the nervous system of one individual to the nervous system of an individual from the succeeding generation: again, the *species* benefit operates simply through the law of large numbers applied to selection pressures.

So we have one kind of 'memory', genetic memory, which is preserved and gradually transformed from generation to generation, but which cannot itself learn directly from the experience of the individual other than through the effects of the pressures of selection. And we have another kind of memory that allows the individual to modify behaviour on the basis of experience, but where those lessons are lost with the death of the individual and the destruction of its central nervous system. Furthermore, the capacity and accuracy of nervous memory is itself limited – finite – for the individual organism endowed with such a nervous system.

With the advent of what Leroi-Gourhan calls *exteriorization*, however, it becomes possible for those lessons learned by the individual to be *put outside* the central nervous system of the organism, because they can be inscribed into dead matter. This begins to make possible:

1. the sharing of a lesson learned by an individual (for example, the sequence of gestures required to make a tool), opening up the possibility of a *community* of knowledge and *cooperative* systems between groups of individuals;

2. the *lasting* of that lesson beyond the life of the individual (for example, we can still learn from prehistoric tools how they were made, and learn to make them ourselves, which is a branch of archaeology and one practised by Leroi-Gourhan[173]);

3. the eventual formation of methods of exteriorization that are designed *specifically* in order to record these lessons, such as cave painting, writing and so on (forms of exteriorization that Stiegler refers to as *hypomnesic or mnemotechnical retention*, where this *hypomnesis* would then become the condition of possibility of Platonic *anamnesis*, the *recollection* that, in *Meno*, is for Socrates always the movement that opens the path to knowledge);

4. the development of a *cumulative* set of lessons that build from generation to generation, so that any individual may

enter a process of *compressed* learning of lessons that *they have not themselves lived through,* lessons that may have taken many generations to be collectively discovered and understood;

5 the proliferation and metastabilization of these conserved lessons as all the forms of knowledge, but also their transformation, so that this building of a cumulative set of lessons becomes the *Bildung* embedded in a localized culture or civilization and transmitted via systems of education, including the transmission of the knowledge of how to use such hypomnesic retentional systems (how to read and write, for example), and where these educational and retentional systems are themselves periodically transformed, and where all of this introduces a retentional dynamic that absolutely cannot be reduced to biological evolution (and to a great extent *suspends* biological selection).

When it comes to the question of the advent of this third kind of memory that is exteriorization, however, Leroi-Gourhan cannot avoid the problem that Derrida points out with respect to Lévi-Strauss: how to explain the genesis of a structure, or a system? Did the process of encephalization (the evolutionary increase in brain size) just happen to 'naturally' reach a point where the possibility of conceiving tools and then producing them simply became 'spontaneously' possible and therefore inevitable? Or was a gesture somehow 'accidentally' inscribed in rock, *prompting* reflection on this accidental action? But could such an accident *happen* without in *some* way being both *anticipated* and *recognized*, in which case how could it be considered *just* an accident? Does the process of exteriorization derive from the interior, from the being who 'thought' to exteriorize, who *imagined* doing so, or is it the process of exteriorization that reflectively makes possible the constitution of something like an interior in the first place, and, even more so, something like imagining, or dreaming, or eventually, thinking?

This is the question of invention, and, as Stiegler says, of the *who* and the *what* of invention, where it is not at all clear which is the inventor and which the invented. It is not difficult to show that answering such a question one way or the other is strictly *impossible*:

> To enter these questions, we shall focus on the passage into the human leading from the Zinjanthropian to the Neanthropian. This ground breaking [*frayage*], which is that of corticalization [or encephalization as it becomes focused

on the expansion of the neocortex], is also effected in stone, in the course of the slow evolution of techniques of stonecutting. An evolution so slow – it still occurs at the rhythm of 'genetic drift' – that one can hardly imagine the human as its operator, that is, as its inventor; rather, one much more readily imagines the human as what is invented.[174]

In other words, speed matters: if the rhythm of the evolution of tool production occurs at a pace measurable in hundreds of thousands of years, and if the expansion of the neocortex occurs at a similar rate and over the *same* period of time, then it becomes strictly impossible to ascribe causality to one or other of these, the prosthetic tool or the hominid brain. For instance, the Oldowan stone tool is associated with the *Australopithecus garhi* hominim species living some 2.5 million years ago and with a brain volume of 450cc, whereas the development of the Acheulean hand-axe is associated with the significantly larger-brained *Homo erectus* and dated from around 1.76 million years ago (and where neither of these species are what we would call 'human').

What happens in the vast space of time over the course of which this evolution of the complexity of tools and the size of brains occurs? There is no scientific way of deciding that one or other of them is the originator or the driver of the process by which both are invented and transformed. We can only refer to a dynamic *co*-origination between the tool-equipped hand (the hand that is defunctionalized and refunctionalized by the advent of bipedalism) and the corticalizing brain. The process of exteriorization is also and simultaneously a process of interiorization, that is, the process of the elaboration of a psychic interiority (which will also become the social interiority that is the ethnic grouping, and where bipedalism, freeing the hands from walking, also frees the mouth from needing to grip, opening the possibility of that *subsequent* exteriorization that is speech).

Yet despite the revolutionary perspicacity of the notion of exteriorization as a third kind of memory, Leroi-Gourhan is himself not free of a tendency to conceive the inception of this process as needing to happen suddenly, just as Lévi-Strauss saw the inception of language as bound to have occurred 'all at once'. If Lévi-Strauss in this way cannot avoid seeing the exterior as being constituted from the interior, in Leroi-Gourhan the movement tends to go the other way: the exterior invents the interior. This is, at least, the basis of Stiegler's claim that the concept of exteriorization needs to be radicalized still further: the movement of exteriorization is a paradoxical opening of *both* exteriority *and* interiority:

> Hominization is for Leroi-Gourhan a rupture in the movement of freeing (or mobilization) characteristic of life. This rupture happens suddenly, in the form of a process of exteriorization which [...] means that the appearance of the human is the appearance of the technical. [...] The movement inherent in this process of exteriorization is paradoxical: Leroi-Gourhan in fact says that it is the tool, that is, *tekhnē*, that invents the human, not the human who invents the technical. [...] But here the human is the interior: there is no exteriorization that does not point to a movement from interior to exterior. [...] Interior and exterior are consequently constituted in a movement that invents both one and the other: a moment in which they invent each other respectively, as if there were a technological maieutic of what is called humanity. The interior and the exterior are the same thing, the inside is the outside, since man (the interior) is essentially defined by the tool (the exterior).[175]

This complication at the origin, and this co-implication of interior and exterior qua *processes* opening the possibility of the human, are what lead Stiegler to refer to a 'default of origin', an origin that, as an accident in becoming, becomes the *necessity* of adopting this accidentality without essence that is an originary de-fault. But to pursue this further, we need to inquire as to what this Stieglerian analysis means for the Derrida of 1967 (*Speech and Phenomena* and *Of Grammatology*), and then for the Heidegger of 1927 (*Being and Time*).

Deconstruction and différance

Derridian thought has a plurality of sources but the most crucial undoubtedly lie in the thought of Husserl and Heidegger. 'Deconstruction' begins firstly as a way of approaching the legacy of the 'metaphysics of presence' (the opposition of presence and non-presence and the privileging of the former, as the presence of the present, over the latter) that residually remains within these phenomenologies and ontologies deriving from the first half of the twentieth century, as well as within the whole history of what Heidegger called the history of metaphysics. 'Deconstruction', however, also maintains an inextricable relationship, via the reference contained in the word, to that *structuralism* which is also undoubtedly a key source of Derrida's approach. That deconstruction is so defined by its relation to structuralism is much more than a choice: it is a necessity.

Yet that necessary choice nevertheless has consequences for Derridian thought. Derrida will never cease drawing attention to the remnants of the metaphysics of presence in the human sciences in general, and structuralism in particular, but despite its own operation, deconstruction itself tends to lead to the reproduction of the very same privileging of the structural and the synchronic, the very same neutralization of time and history, to which Derrida himself points *in* structuralism. When it comes to thinking 'invention' or the future, for example, Derridian thought tends to be able to do so *only* in terms of an absolute break or rupture, rather than, as Simondon will conceive it, as a systemic characteristic of a dynamic process itself. In other words, where Simondon will see invention starting from the process, as the emergence of a possibility involving the reorganization of the dynamic field arranging organism and milieu, Derrida will tend to see invention as the origin of the dynamism of the process, which we might well take as evidence of deconstruction's *difficulty*, despite itself, with respect to the attempt to think the *temporality* of processes.[176]

We say 'despite itself' because, as a deconstruction of so-called 'binary oppositions', it can in fact *only* be a compositional style of thinking, which seeks the originary complication that unfolds as the process by which distinctions rigidify into the *oppositions* of so-called 'metaphysics'. A compositional style of thinking is one that seeks the emergence of such distinctions-cum-oppositions from out of an origin and across a dynamic, that is, as a struggle of tendencies and counter-tendencies. In this sense, deconstruction would, despite how the term sounds to the ear, be an *essentially* processual form of thinking, and for Stiegler it will be crucial to interpret Derridian thought in a way that takes this processual character as fundamental. Deconstruction's goal is to cause the foundations of an opposition to tremble, so as to expose what metaphysics forgets – the composition that is 'older' than the opposition – making possible a transformational reading, defunctionalizing an opposition so that it might be refunctionalized as a productive distinction, often through the introduction of an invented term that *cannot be placed* within the oppositional logic of metaphysics.

(But one question that this will leave is whether Derrida can think, not just processes of composition but processes of *de*-composition, *factual, objective or material* deconstructions that entail the need to think not just what is *older* than a distinction, but its future in the necessity and the virtue of *re*-composition, which is something other than a quasi-transcendental 'to-come': it is *here most of all* that we can understand that it may not be *completely* false to say that Derrida neutralizes history and time. Compositional thinking *should* be a form of thinking that sees the complexity at the origin as an accidentality, and that this means that the *end* is not *determined* by the origin: composition is an accidental process, and, in this way, to think in terms of composition would be a *tragic* style of thinking. One crucial question for the future of deconstruction is the degree to which Derrida himself let go of this tragic *insight* when he dropped the questions of the monstrosity of the present and the pharmacology of the trace in favour of the aporias of quasi-transcendentality, and, in so doing, *lost* sight of the de-compositional *possibility and danger*.)

One key instance of an invented term introduced by Derrida in order to exceed the limits of oppositional logic is 'différance', and it is perhaps the most important, at least for Stiegler's transformational reading (or refunctionalization) of Derrida's thought as processual, compositional and tragic. And what makes the introduction of this term in *Of Grammatology* immediately relevant is the fact that he does so at the one moment in the entire course of 'post-structuralism' when Leroi-Gourhan's argument concerning the very long epochal history of exteriorization is put on stage, even if this appearance of Leroi-Gourhan in *Of Grammatology* is rather accidental,[177] and even if this reference by Derrida to Leroi-Gourhan seems scrupulously avoided by almost the entire subsequent history of deconstruction, whether in Derrida's own work or that of his epigones – with the very notable exception of Christopher Johnson.[178]

And yet, for Derrida himself, epochality is the very *reason* for putting this term, 'neither a word nor a concept', on the scene of philosophy:

> I would say, first off, that *différance*, which is neither a word nor a concept, strategically seemed to me the most proper in order to think, if not to master [...] what is most irreducible about our 'epoch'. Therefore I am starting, strategically, from the place and the time in which 'we' are, even though in the last analysis my opening is not justifiable, since it is only on the basis of *différance* and its 'history' that we can claim to know who and where 'we' are, and what the limits of an 'epoch' might be.[179]

With this statement, Derrida indicates as clearly as could be that différance and its history *ought* to be the basis upon which it becomes possible to think who we are, our epochality, the irreducibility of *today's* epochality, and the *limits* of our epochality, the question of its *reaching its limits*. But at the same time, he immediately suspends this 'most proper' starting point, on the grounds that it is différance that opens up the very possibility of such a start – of a thinking of epochality and its limits. Derrida thus operates a kind of 'give and take' with respect to the relationship between différance and epochality, where each becomes something like the originator of the other's possibility, in a way that may ultimately prove *too* 'suspensive' in order to allow *any further step to be taken* in relation to this 'most proper' beginning.

That said, as for these limits, they must undoubtedly be circumscribed in relation to Derrida's statement at the end of the 'Exergue' of *Of Grammatology*:

> The future can be anticipated only in the form of an absolute danger. It is that which breaks absolutely with constituted normality and can only announce itself, *present itself*, as a kind of monstrosity. For that world to come and for that within it which will make tremble the values of sign, speech and writing, for that which guides our future anterior, there is still no exergue.[180]

If Derrida will, despite the introduction of this neologism, leave this exergue unwritten, despite the proliferation of Derridian works, then it becomes imperative to ask whether Derrida's *way* of conceiving différance has in some manner historically functioned as an impediment to this futural necessity for which he seems implicitly to call.

Auto-affection and inscription

Over the past half-century (for it has been that long), students of 'French theory' have perhaps become too familiar with the idea of thinking of différance as the origin of the play of difference, maybe even taking for granted somewhat that this non-concept can be placed safely under their conceptual toolbelt. For there is undeniable pleasure in the feeling of having mastered the notions of a master thinker, in feeling confident that one knows what is meant by the sign's or the trace's perpetual openness to retrospective reinterpretation as differences proliferate, a proliferation made possible by the fact that there is no sign whose meaning does not refer to others signs, no signified that is not itself a kind of signifier, différance thus amounting to the inscriptive detour that is necessary for anything like language or speech to arise.[181] To this can be added the certainty that Derrida's critique of the structuralist tendency to neutralize time and history is *also* a critique of the structuralist gesture that consists in wanting to 'totalize' structure, that is, to *close* the system that is to be elucidated, to repress the element of excess or default that gets that system or structure going, and that leaves it perpetually exposed, that is, *open*. 'Différance' would be the deconstructive term with which Derrida tries to undo this repression, and to find a path by which to think systems and structures without totalizing them and to think them precisely *as* processes. But perhaps there remains significantly more to say about this 'term' whose difference from difference cannot (in French) be heard but only read.

Before getting to *Of Grammatology*, we must consider how 'différance' is deployed in *Speech and Phenomena*, where it is introduced in the course of Derrida's deconstruction of the remnants of the metaphysics of presence to be found in Husserl's notion of the 'pure auto-affection' of 'hearing oneself speak'. The argument for the purity of this form of auto-affection lies in the 'immediacy' involved in speaking and then, without delay, seemingly without exteriority, *hearing* what one has oneself said. Derrida notes the oddness of this argument premised on the 'absolute proximity of the signifier and the signified',[182] given that Husserl also attributed the possibility of the ideal objects of scientific truth to *writing*, that is, to inscription. But if for Husserl this necessity of inscription lies in reactivation and repetition – being able to 'repeat the original sense, that is, the act of *pure thought* which created the ideality of sense', inscription also brings with it (as Socrates already argued in *Phaedrus* with respect to the *pharmakon* of writing, which Derrida will not mention until later texts) 'the ever growing risk of "forgetting" and loss of sense' as it becomes

> more and more difficult to reconstitute the presence of the act buried under historical sedimentations. The moment of crisis is always the moment of signs.[183]

It is in the context of what we could call (getting ahead of ourselves) this 'pharmacological' argument concerning the duplicity of writing that Derrida introduces the notion of 'différance'. Despite all of his efforts to absolutely distinguish presence and non-presence – that the 'body' that is spatialized writing means something only if it is 'animated' by an intentional act of meaning enacted by the temporalizing voice of a speaker – Husserl, through this phonocentric repression of difference 'by assigning it to the exteriority of signifiers', 'could not fail to recognize its work at the origin of sense and presence', because this supposedly pure auto-affection that is hearing oneself speak still 'supposed that a pure difference comes to divide self-presence'.[184] Derrida concludes:

> In this pure difference is rooted the possibility of everything we think we can exclude from auto-affection: space, the outside, the world, the body, etc. As soon as it is admitted that auto-affection is the condition for self-presence, no pure transcendental reduction is possible. But it was necessary to

> pass through the transcendental reduction in order to grasp this difference in what is closest to it [...]. We come closest to it in the movement of differance.
>
> This movement of differance is not something that happens to a transcendental subject; it produces a subject.[185]

The introduction of the notion of differentiating-and-deferring différance in *Speech and Phenomena* thus functions as the repressed complication lying at the origin of difference, beyond the metaphysics of presence and non-presence, and opening the very possibility of space, exteriority (and interiority), world and 'self', or 'subject'. And, in relation to these last, 'self', 'subject', Derrida's 1968 lecture on différance will reiterate in other terms that it is by this temporalizing deferral opening a divided self-presence that this 'self' can be constituted as a localized economy: 'to temporize, to take recourse, consciously or unconsciously, in the temporal or temporizing mediation of a detour that suspends the accomplishment or fulfillment of "desire" or "will"'.[186] With this thought that différance lies at the root of an economy not just of an auto-affective 'subject' but of a *desiring* subject, that is, at the root of a libidinal economy, we can see the opening of a thought that Derrida does not in fact pursue very far, but that Stiegler *will* pursue, even if for the latter it is crucial to understand this not as a suspension or deferral *of* desire, but rather of what is not yet desire but no longer an instinct: the drives, where such a différantial detour proves to be the very *condition of possibility* of desire.

But the question we will have to ask via *Of Grammatology* is: is it *just*, is it *right*, to understand the *inscriptivity* of différance as *necessarily* and primordially a question of *writing*? For Derrida, the phonocentric opposition is always a matter of opposing the human and the animal, and, with the argument that speech was always already a kind of writing, he means to contest the opposition of nature and culture. But that still leaves the *question* of the *passage* from one mode of inscription to another. As Derrida himself asks, and does not hesitate to ask, despite différance being 'neither a word nor a concept': 'What differs? Who differs? What is *différance?*'[187] And what is its *history*?

The history of life and its epochs

The 'grammatology' for which Derrida calls can be neither 'one of the *sciences of man*' nor 'just one *regional science* among others', because this grammatology would ask 'the question of the *name of man*',[188] or in other words because the object of grammatology is anterior to the question of what 'defines' humanity. With such anteriority, grammatology can be neither a scientific anthropology nor a philosophical anthropology. In *Of Grammatology*, Derrida introduces the notion of 'différance' to describe that process of differentiation and deferral through which actual, material traces of all kinds are produced. Such traces are for Derrida *firstly* those of writing, but they are not *only* so, and, importantly, in introducing this term he evokes the work of Leroi-Gourhan (even if, as mentioned, he does so somewhat accidentally). So as to clarify this anteriority of grammatology, Derrida aims to inscribe 'man' into a much larger adventure, whose terms fall on both sides of the metaphysical opposition of 'animal' and 'human'. Hence Derrida *answers* the question that he will ask in the 'Différance' lecture, and answers it *loud and clear,* in a manner matched only by the degree to which this page of *Of Grammatology* has remained *unheard* by most Derridian readers of Derrida, who have for the most part remained deaf to this reference to Leroi-Gourhan:

> Leroi-Gourhan no longer describes the unity of man and the human adventure thus by the simple possibility of the *graphie* in general; rather as a stage or an articulation in the history of life – of what I have called differance – as the history of the *grammè*.[189]

The vast chasm between what Derrida says explicitly and what Derrida has been understood to have said or not said about différance means that it is worthwhile reiterating:

> the history of life – of what I have called différance.

And we must go slowly enough to understand what it means to *identify* this conjoint and originary difference and deferral that Derrida names différance *with* the history of life, and what it means to do so from within the heart of the grammatological project.

This already clearly implies another necessary question, and to the one that was raised twenty-three years earlier, but which, raised in this way, was, too, and despite everything, ignored by Derrida as by French philosophy of the 1960s in general: what is life? Consideration of Schrödinger's *bio-thermodynamic* question means that we cannot avoid asking: is the *notion* of life that Derrida raises here one that is *opposed* to non-life, or rather something with which it composes? But then we will also have to ask: what is *non-*life? And finally, what is the relation between this 'history of life' and the history of what we call the 'human adventure', where the latter might indeed turn out to amount to a new composition of life and non-life, *whatever it is that these words name before being the name of man?* All these necessities arise because scholars and students of Derrida have, at least in the

Anglophone world, spent the past five decades skipping straight over this reference to Leroi-Gourhan at the heart of the grammatological project: that is, the thirty years prior to the English-language publication of *Technics and Time, 1*, and the twenty years since.

If this is a question of the 'history of life', then what is being deferred, in what kind of economy, in order to produce the play and proliferation of what kinds of differences? And this question will raise another question: in relation to this economy of deferral and difference that characterizes the history of life, does the history of deferral and difference that will characterize the history of *our* (noetic) life constitute a *rupture* or a *continuum* – what exactly is meant by 'a stage or an articulation' in this history of life, and why does Derrida feel the need to introduce this 'or' in the first place? What is at stake *between* a stage and an articulation and what possible uncertainty is reflected in the suggestive hesitation between them?

Whatever may be the case in that regard, for Derrida it is a question of a shift to a new basis into which all such concepts must be reinscribed:

> Instead of having recourse to the concepts that habitually serve to distinguish man from other living beings (instinct and intelligence, absence or presence of speech, of society, of economy, etc. etc.), the notion of *program* is invoked.[190]

For Derrida, the import of this 'notion of program' lies in its causing the opposition of animal and human to tremble: as Stiegler puts it, for Derrida, here, the human is nothing more than 'the appearance of a new type of *grammē* and/or program'.[191]

But what is this notion of program? Naturally one thinks of cybernetics and computation, which are clearly in Derrida's mind, but the reference to 'instinct and intelligence' shows that he may well be thinking of the subchapter of *Gesture and Speech* that bears this title, and which is indeed a point at which Leroi-Gourhan complicates the question of the human distinction. There, Leroi-Gourhan argues that what we refer to as either instinct or intelligence, imagining that these are the names of what *causes* particular animal or human behaviour, are not in fact causes but *effects*: action programs whose sources lie in the three kinds of memory we have already outlined. Such action programs may be short or long, simple or complex, depending on whether the species under consideration is an earthworm, an ant, a reptile, a bird or a mammal (the latter, according to Leroi-Gourhan in 1964, for the first time possessing the ability to choose *between* action sequences and of 'checking' the adequacy of the outcome of a particular sequence, meaning that ultimately the 'individual's memory

[...] takes precedence over the species memory').[192] The 'program' invoked by Leroi-Gourhan thus refers to action sequences determining the attack on the environment, a 'double movement' from past to future whose anticipatory potentials are drawn from the 'information' contained in the 'medium' that is memory, understood in a very broad sense that encompasses genetics, brain and exteriorization.

If we say 'information', here, it is to draw a link to what Derrida will state in his next sentence when he does indeed refer explicitly to cybernetics, but in a way that, as it were, immediately demands that we place this under erasure: 'information' is invoked here only with great precaution, as we are far from having determined whether it can really be deployed in relation to what is 'stored' or 'communicated' genetically by the earthworm, nervously and pheromonally by the ant, or in paintings or textbooks by 'we' ourselves.[193] But Derrida himself understands perfectly well the difficulty and the necessity of avoiding 'mechanist, technicist, and teleological language', as well as the scope of the questions all this raises, as he immediately indicates:

> It [the notion of program] must of course be understood in the cybernetic sense, but cybernetics is itself intelligible only in terms of a history of the possibilities of the trace as the unity of a double movement of protention and retention. This movement goes far beyond the possibilities of the 'intentional consciousness'.[194]

The question, then, is how Derrida's *extension* of retention and protention far beyond 'intentional consciousness' and to the whole history of life relates and does not relate to the creation of this new science of communication and control that is cybernetics.

The inscriptive character of the trace whose possibility is opened up by différance here extends from the pre-intentional, pre-conscious memory/programs of genetics, through the retentionality and protentionality of Husserlian intentional consciousness (where this extends, as we have seen, to questions of will and desire that are those not just of consciousness but of the *unconscious*, as well as that movement of retention and protention that is the mortality of Dasein stretched out between unremembered birth and the indeterminate determinacy of death), and far beyond, that is, through the artificial memory that is 'writing' and towards cybernetics 'as such', the cybernetics of electronic card indexes and computational programs. It is here that Derrida stakes his claim for différance as an inscriptive emergence amounting to the entire 'history of life':

> Since 'genetic inscription' and the 'short programmatic chains' regulating the behavior of the amoeba or the annelid up to the passage beyond alphabetic writing to the orders of the logos and of a certain *homo sapiens*, the possibility of the *grammè* structures the movements of its history according to rigorously original levels, types, and rhythms.[195]

This history is thus an epochal history, where the epochs are those of the varying modes of inscription and anticipation unfolding over the course of this history of life. But for Derrida, this lesson concerning the necessity of treating epochs in their specificity and their rhythms, a lesson learned from Leroi-Gourhan, ultimately and irreducibly depends on 'the most general concept of the *grammè*'.[196] And this is so because for Derrida it is *always*, and always *already*, a question of exteriorization:

> If the expression ventured by Leroi-Gourhan is accepted, one could speak of a 'liberation of memory', of an *exteriorization always already begun* but always larger than the trace which, beginning from the elementary programs of so-called 'instinctive' behavior up to the constitution of electronic card-indexes and reading machines, enlarges differance and the possibility of putting in reserve.[197]

With this *'exorbitant'*[198] thought, beyond the oppositions of the system, Derrida outlines his grammatological answer to the question of what différance *is*. As Francesco Vitale puts it:

> Derrida does not simply say that, thanks to Leroi-Gourhan, it is possible to retrace the emergence of writing, in its restricted sense, back to a much greater history, which would find its roots in the emergence of *Homo sapiens* in prehistory. [...] Above all [...], the *grammè* would allow us to point out that *différance* is a genetico-structural condition of the life of the living and of its evolution.[199]

That is, différance would, according to Derrida, be the genetico-structural condition of the history of life qua history and economy of deferral and differentiation opened up by the originary possibility of the movement of inscription, from the genetic, through the alphabetical, and to the analog and the digital.

Indecision

What are we to make of this phrase, 'an exteriorization always already begun'? Why does the 'liberation of memory' that unfolds across the whole evolutionary process necessarily amount to an exteriorization *always already begun*, given that for Leroi-Gourhan, exteriorization is the name of that bifurcation *within* the liberation of memory (and mobility) that consists in the advent of an organism or species that puts (itself) outside itself (so to speak) by inscribing its gestures in dead matter – or, as Derrida puts it, by 'articulating the living upon the nonliving in general'?²⁰⁰ Is a process that continually *enlarges* différance always and necessarily a process of *exteriorization*, which is also to say a process of the *production* of a distinction between exterior and *interior*? Perhaps we must indeed respond affirmatively here, but *only* if we then understand 'exteriorization' *as* this production of a progressively larger *delimitation of locality* between interior and exterior, and where such delimitations are those membranes, exoskeletons, epidermises, skins, frontiers and borders of localized systems at different orders of magnitude (of the unicellular organism, of the single cell *within* a multicellular organism, of the multicellular organism itself, of the ecosystem, of the tool-equipped multicellular organism that is *exteriorized as such*, of the infra-specific groups that such organisms form at various scales, from the tribe to the civilization, and of the biosphere as a whole).

But in that case, is it not that we are no longer talking about *Leroi-Gourhan's* exteriorization, but about some more general relationship between the interior milieu and the exterior milieu characteristic of the whole movement of life? Is Derrida justified in so enlarging Leroi-Gourhan's concept? Is he right to keep the same name, and to do so in the name of a grammatological project that in this way seems to erase the distinction and difference that Leroi-Gourhan intends to make with this concept? In other words, is what unfolds from the advent of what Leroi-Gourhan calls exteriorization still a question of *this* 'history of life', or are we forced to ask what difference it makes when this history becomes the 'pursuit of life by means *other* than life', when it becomes not just a matter of the articulation of the living upon the disorganized inorganic (of inanimate matter), but of its articulation upon the *organized* inorganic (the tool, technics)? This is the question with which, in *Technics and Time, 1*, Stiegler introduces a critique of Derrida whose implications for Derridian thought and beyond are, we claim, far-reaching:

> To articulate the living onto the nonliving, is that not already a gesture from after the rupture when you are already no longer in pure *phusis*?²⁰¹

And this is the question raised by Derrida when he describes this articulation of the living onto the non-living as the 'origin of all repetition, origin of ideality', the originary trace of which is 'not more ideal than real, not more intelligible than sensible, [...] and *no concept of metaphysics can describe it*'.[202] The question is: on what *condition* can this still be ascribed to the 'history of life' and its economy? It is a question by which Stiegler is able to make Derridian différance tremble:

> There is something of an indecision around différance: it is the history of life in general, but this history is (only) given (as) (dating from) after the rupture [...]. The whole problem is that of the economy of life once the rupture has taken place: life is, after the rupture, the economy of death. The question of différance is death.[203]

In other words, once the articulation of the living onto the non-living has commenced, it is no longer a question *only* of a history and an economy of *life*: it is then a question of *another* economy, or of an economy *properly speaking* (because it starts not from the organism or the ecosystem but from the house), a pursuit of life by means of an economy that is no longer just biological but inclusive of the non-living, that is, of what is dead. And also of death: Stiegler relates this default of origin of mortality in technics to the reflective character of the tool, functioning as a mirror in which we can first see our own gestures, retained, but also, in being retained, can see for the first time that there was an existence before mine and will be an existence after it – 'technical life – that is, dying'.[204] So it becomes a question of reconciling or deconstructing the relationship of this 'history of life – of what I have called différance' with what Derrida will say the following year:

> culture as nature different and deferred, differing-deferring; all the others of *physis* – *tekhnē, nomos, thesis*, society, freedom, history, mind, etc. – as *physis* different and deferred, or as *physis* differing and deferring. *Physis* in *différance*.[205]

Hence, with 'all these others of *physis*', it becomes a question not only of what differs or who differs in différance. We must also ask: *when* is différance, for Derrida? Stiegler notes:

> Now phusis as life was already différance. There is an indecision, a passage remaining to be thought.[206]

The Stieglerian rethinking and reinvention of différance *operates* on this indecision in the surgical pursuit of this passage. Stiegler stakes his claim with respect to his Derridian inheritance on the possibility of this operation and this pursuit.

From Heidegger to Stiegler

Stiegler will not invoke 'neganthropology' or 'exosomatization' until twenty years after the publication of *Technics and Time, 1*, when the question of entropy will be brought to centre stage via the works of Claude Lévi-Strauss, Nicholas Georgescu-Roegen and Alfred Lotka, and in confrontation with rising problems associated in particular with ecological destruction, self-defeating consumerism and the potential consequences of a new wave of automation. But with this association – non-living, the dead, death – the question he raises with respect to Derrida is already inscribed in a field that will be delimited by an 'economy of death' that connects our *mortality* to our inextricable relationship to *inorganic (but organized) matter*. And it is through this that the argument with respect to différance – which, as an economy of life and death that both conserves and transforms, is *already* a matter of the perpetual and exosomatic struggle against entropy – becomes the foundation of the argument with respect to the existential analytic of Dasein:

> To think the articulation [of the living onto the non-living] is also to think the birth of the relation we name with the verb 'to exist'; this is to think anticipation.[207]

What is at stake here is *existence* in the Heideggerian sense: there is no tool production without anticipation and delay, and as soon as there is the opening of anticipation and delay, have we not already opened the way to the ecstatic horizon of the mortality of existence? So Stiegler will argue.

In *Being and Time*, Heidegger sets out in pursuit of the meaning of being, repressed in the history of thought just as Derrida will argue concerning writing and Stiegler concerning technics, but the problem Heidegger identifies at the beginning of this pursuit is that being is not just forgotten but elusive: we perpetually find ourselves only amidst beings, stuck at the ontic rather than the ontological level. *How* to retrieve the question of being is a *problem*. Hence he argues that we must *first* go in pursuit of the exemplary being *for whom* being is a question, which can function as a guide and through which it will become possible to undertake the destruction of metaphysics necessary to think the meaning of being as such. The being for whom being is a question is, of course, the one he names Dasein: not humanity as such, yet nothing other than we ourselves, the *who* in its distinctness from all those beings that are inevitably *whats*. Dasein would thus be that being who possesses the possibility of seeing past or through or into the *what* – to the meaning of being itself.

Characterizing Heidegger's opening moves in this way already begins to indicate how he makes an *opposition* between the economy of death (existential mortality) and the economy of the non-living (the *what*). For Heidegger, Dasein is the being who *knows* it is mortal, and knows this not *because* of its relationship to the *what*, but, *mostly*, in spite of it. Unlike other beings, Dasein's existence is fundamentally circumscribed by the knowledge of its mortality, that is, a knowledge that *exceeds* the determinacy of beings and of itself as a determinate being. Nevertheless, its way of being mortal consists in *knowing something in the mode of not knowing it*. Its way of comporting itself to beings exceeds those ways that take beings as ready to hand (exorganically available for use, let's say) or as present to hand ('objects' in their whatness as such, initially revealed when objects such as tools *fail* to be at hand): knowing that it is mortal, and that this mortality is irreducibly *its own* mortality, that its world is irreducibly *its own* world, Dasein's relationship to beings involves the way they *matter* to it in an 'existential' way, as objects of an always future-oriented (that is, anticipatory) *care, Sorge*.

As circumscribed by care, however, Dasein both knows and forgets that it is mortal, which is to say, not yet finished, perpetually unfinished: Dasein knows it is mortal in the sense of being primordially certain of it and of being unable to escape it, but it does not know it in the sense that what it knows about its mortality is indeterminate (in its circumstances, for example), and in the sense that it can *flee* from what it can nevertheless not escape – it can 'forget' what it knows, as it does in its average, everyday way of living and its way of living as 'one' does, in the mode of the 'they'. That Dasein *knows* it is mortal means that all of its projects exist in a relationship to this certain but indeterminate future – it is a futural being – but the fact that it can also *not* know means that it inevitably finds itself tempted to live *as if* this knowledge does *not* matter to it, getting caught up in or sliding back down towards all the *whats* of everydayness and busyness, *Besorgen*. Dasein exists as perpetually caught between knowledge and non-knowledge.

Dasein is thus that being who is capable of existing in an 'authentic' way towards the futural knowledge it possesses, projecting itself towards and anticipating its end, but also the being who can fall back into ways of existing that tend to eliminate this *tension* between knowing and not-knowing by forgetting what it knows, denying the singularity of its existence, assimilating the mineness of its existence to that of the de-singularized group, and *determining the indeterminate*. With respect to the latter, to determine temporality is to see it in terms of what is measured by the clock, to make time into something 'objective', into a *calculable* object. Dasein's authentic existential possibility consists in the capacity for *recollecting* its indeterminate mortality and on that basis making a decision, in the 'resoluteness' with which it has the possibility of tearing itself away from all the *whats* of concern, away from 'clock time', even if this tearing away only ever seems to amount to a 'modified grasp' through which Dasein *adopts* its ownmost possibility, that is, the *singularity* of its existence. But it is through this possibility of tearing itself away (which is in this regard still conditional upon a *relationship* to whatness, which is why we said that the relationship to mortality is for Heidegger 'mostly' in spite of its relationship to the what) that Dasein can expose the originary character of the meaning of being *as* temporality as such.

Resoluteness is thus a kind of différance with respect to ordinary everydayness, the possibility of an anticipatory decision that extends past everyday concern with all the *whats* that preoccupy *das Man*, a differing and deferral of those concerns through an economy of care. But then, like Derrida, we have to ask: What differs? Who differs? From whence arises the possibility of Dasein, and the possibility of resolutely adopting its existence, and what *is it* that is thereby adopted?

What actually is this *who* that is Dasein? Heidegger says that Dasein '*is* its past'.[208] The italicization is his. Dasein 'finds its meaning in temporality', and this temporality is 'the condition of the possibility of historicity', where 'historicity is prior to what is called history'[209] (just as for Derrida archi-writing will be prior to what is called writing). What Heidegger *wants* to say, by stating that temporality is the condition of historicity and historicity is prior to history, is that originary temporality belongs to this being who is Dasein, and that this is anterior to the busyness of history that unfolds and is recorded and thematized in the minutiae of its everydayness. Yet as he has already just said, this search for the temporality of Dasein, like all research, consists in 'an ontic possibility of Dasein',[210] that is, it moves within the realm of beings, within the 'factical' realm of *whats* that *always* constitutes Dasein's field of existence. What exactly does it mean to say that Dasein *is* its past, that it 'always is how and "what" it already was'?[211] Heidegger continues:

> It is its own past not only in such a way that its past, as it were, pushes itself along 'behind' it, and that it possesses what is past as a property that is still objectively present and at times has an effect on it. Dasein 'is' its past in the manner of *its* being which, roughly expressed, on each occasion 'occurs' out of its future. In its manner of existing at any given time, and thus also with the understanding

of being that belongs to it, Dasein grows into a customary interpretation of itself and grows up on that interpretation. It understands itself initially in terms of this interpretation and, within a certain range, constantly does so. This understanding discloses the possibilities of its being and regulates them. Its own past – and that always means that of its 'generation' – does not *follow after* Dasein but rather always already goes ahead of it.[212]

By the past of Dasein, then, Heidegger means that 'already there' (before it) that it must adopt 'out of its future'. Dasein's concern with its past derives from the fact that it is always (getting) ahead of itself, not that it *is* but that it *has to be*, that it has to *care* from out of its futurity. Because this past is already there, it is that into which Dasein must grow, in the sense of finding for itself the singular interpretation of its singular past that will both *disclose* its (futural) possibilities and regulate them (through which it can *economize* its possibilities, so to speak). It is not just the facts of its demise that Dasein knows in the mode of not knowing: it is also Dasein's own past that has *not yet* been discovered by Dasein, not yet discovered its *significance*, but that awaits Dasein's resolute taking upon itself *of* that past.

Hence it is because Dasein must *discover* this past that precedes it that, *for* that Dasein, the past is what 'always already goes ahead of it', awaiting Dasein's discovery, interpretation, transformation and adoption. That about which Dasein cares in resolutely projecting itself is an interpretation of its past that is singular, in contrast to the 'dominant interpretation' to which Dasein adapts in the mode of everydayness and *das Man*. This is so because Dasein's past is *its* past, because that which counts as its past is different from the past of any other Dasein, and therefore, that future from out of which this past can become *its* past is also singular. Yet this past, even if it is *its own* past, is never *just its* past, the past of a solitary Dasein, but also and indissolubly 'that of its "generation"', which is to say, that of a collective of singular Daseins who together, and *with the world that surrounds them and that they make together*, form a generation, that is, an *epoch*.

Now, as we said, Heidegger *wants* to say that originary temporality is the *condition* of historicity and *precedes* history. That is, Heidegger's existential analytic arguably *remains* metaphysical inasmuch as he argues that, ultimately, the *who precedes* the *what*, insofar as originary temporality is always the temporality of a Dasein *itself*. And he remains metaphysical in that he wants to say that this *growing* of Dasein into its past by *interpreting* its past, and by interpreting it in terms of a future that it also *projects*, is, in the end, something fundamentally *disconnected* from all those *whats* with which Dasein is concerned in that busyness that flees such possibilities. Among the questions that Stiegler puts to this account are therefore the following:

1 *on what basis* is this 'already there' *accessed* by Dasein?
2 on what basis is Dasein's growing into (and transforming) its past, its heritage, a *deferral* that works by producing and *adopting* a *different* interpretation into which it grows?

With respect to these two questions:

1 Dasein's past differs from the past of other beings because it is a past that is inscribed, not just in DNA, or in the nerve cells recording the memories of the experiences it has lived through, but in the records that remain of experiences it has *not* lived through:

> What Heidegger calls the already there, constitutive of the temporality of Dasein, is this past that I never lived but that is nevertheless my past, without which I never would have had any past of my own. Such a structure of inheritance and transmission [...] presupposes that the phenomenon of life *qua* Dasein becomes singular in the history of the living to the extent that, for Dasein, the epigenetic layer of life, far from being lost with the living when it dies, conserves and sediments itself, passes itself down.[213]

It is the différance of différance that is technical exteriorization qua artificial memory, and it is *only* this, that makes it possible for Dasein to have a past that always already goes ahead of it and that it must grow into and out beyond. Stiegler does not at all disagree with Heidegger that existence exceeds what can be measured by the clock, and, furthermore, there is a sense in which *every* artefact is a kind of clock, determining time, which is to say, making it into something spatial and material, and therefore calculable. But he argues that only *through* the *whats* into which this past has been inscribed, which are determinate and inanimate, an articulation of the living onto the non-living, only through this spatialization and materialization of time, only through this 'epiphylogenetic' process, is it possible for Dasein to access this past that awaits it and that it must *make* its own by exceeding its determination and sedimentation, and through which it exists as such.

> This is not a 'program' in the *quasi*-determinist biological sense, but a cipher in which the whole of Dasein's existence is caught;

this epigenetic sedimentation, a memorization of what has come to pass, is what is called the past, what we shall name the *epiphylogenesis* of man [...]. We come now to Heidegger after having opened up the questions of the temporality of différance *qua* the movement of life in general because there is in Heidegger an opposition between the time of technical measurement and concern, which is the loss of time, and authentic time, which is proper to Dasein – wrenched from the technical horizon of concern. Now if it is true that only epigenetic sedimentation can be the already-there, this is only possible when the transmission allowing for the sediments is of an absolutely technical, nonliving essence: made possible by the organized albeit inorganic matter that the trace always is – be it a matter of tool or writing – let us say of the *organon* in general.[214]

2 Lacking the notion of différance as inscription in general, that is, the spatialization of the temporal, Heidegger wants to keep a privilege for one side of the distinction between the *who* and the *what*: the *who* that is Dasein precedes the *what*, and the *whats* involved in the technical determination of time are *only* what reduce temporality to technics and *not* that on the basis of which Dasein opens itself to a temporality beyond clock time. Sedimentation in artefacts is *only* that deathly loss of existence and forgetting of its ownmost possibility to which Dasein can fall prey; not the fertile soil (the humus and, as Stiegler will say much later, the 'noetic necromass'[215]) from out of which it projects its possibilities.

This is the price Heidegger pays for not being able to dwell within the ambiguity and tension of the genitive involved in the 'invention of the human'. Yet for Heidegger, the tradition that is Dasein's past, and that of its 'generation', is nothing but the consequence of that rupture in the history of life that brings a new kind of organization, that of the tribe, the ethnicity, the 'people' (*das Volk*, he will say), and so on, which is the result of a new kind of *shared memory*, on the basis of which it becomes possible to imagine and to realise (to project) a new kind of shared *future*. Dasein can anticipate, can project itself futurally, run ahead of itself, only on the basis of the already there of its inherited past, which can *be* inherited only on the basis of its artefactual sedimentation.

But if Dasein can do more than remain caught in the dominant interpretation of *das Man*, if it bears within it the possibility of projecting *another* interpretation, one founded on the singularity of *its* past, this is ultimately because it can *return* to this past in *repetition*. Repetition is the foundation of the possibility of interpretation, because by repeatedly coming back to the same, to what remains *unceasingly the same*, it is possible to create, from out of this recursivity, a dynamic and an economy of différance that finds the resources for the new precisely in the old. And this possibility depends on the *recording* of the past, and on the *exactitude* of that recording: to read the text of Plato today is to read precisely the same marks and signs that were read by the Greeks, and it is for this reason that it remains possible today to discover *new* interpretations of that old text. The openness of that text comes *because* of its spatialization in the form of a durable *what*, not despite it. But to interpret or reinterpret a text (whether it is a philosophical text, a literary text or a legislative text), to come back to a text, is to *re*-temporalize what has been spatialized, to re-interiorize what has been exteriorized, because it must pass through the temporal processes of a noetic Dasein. Ultimately, this is what makes every text uncanny, but this uncanniness consists precisely in the fact that what is dead, non-living, and which opens an originary economy of death *within* the text, nevertheless *remains*, and always bears within it the potential for revival, that is, for reinterpretation, re-temporalization.

Heidegger justifies his disengagement of the *who* from the *what* by the critique of horological instrumentality, of the measurability and calculability of clock time. But this instrumentality is thought exclusively in terms of its end – precision, that is, exactitude. For Heidegger, this is what means that clock time amounts to a technical attempt to determine the indeterminate. But if Stiegler is right that *every* artefact is a kind of clock, through which we 'see' time materialized, then, while it may be true that Dasein is a temporal being *before* it possesses sundials, clocks and watches, it is *not* true that it is a temporal being prior to being an instrumental being: it is all of these instruments, from the outset, and irrespective of their intended function, that *in fact* open up the temporality of the being who will become Dasein. Dasein is *temporal* because it is born and invented from out of the articulation of the *who* and the *what*, an articulation that must then also be *socialized* as 'our' articulation of the *who* and the *what*. Exactitude – for example, the exactitude of *written public laws*, requiring knowledge, interpretation and decision, that is, judgment – becomes the very basis of the *openness* of that socialization process, and of its open *idiomaticity*, that is, the openness of what unfolds as the processuality of open local systems emerging from a default of origin, that is, from a complication.

Far from it being the case that technical beings are subordinate to 'human' beings, because the former are merely 'hybrids', lacking their own dynamic, lacking the existential infinitude of the latter, they are what open the very possibility of such a dynamic beyond biological evolution. Heidegger was indeed among the first to perceive that '*modern* technology' bore the potential to form a dynamic of such magnitude as to potentially eclipse the very horizon of the world of Dasein: this is what he would later call *Gestell*. But in failing to see the limits of his disengagement of the *who* and the *what*, in failing to see the way in which the *what* was the very basis by which Dasein could access its past and project itself towards indeterminacies and infinities beyond calculability, in failing to give the *what* any genuinely constitutive role, he failed to grasp the full depth of the mystery of *tekhnē* as that which lies both before and beyond the anthropological horizon of Dasein. Hence Stiegler's concluding questions in *Technics and Time, 1*:

> Is not the consideration of *tekhnē*, as the originary horizon of any access of the being that we ourselves are to itself, the very possibility of disanthropologizing the temporal, existential analytic? When 'Time and Being' gives itself the task of thinking being without beings (without Dasein), is it not a question, ultimately, of radically shifting the above understanding of time in terms of *this* finitude?[216]

It is to these questions that Stiegler will return twenty years later.

3 Tertiary Retention

Husserl, Heidegger, Stein, Celan

Thus far we have focused on Derrida's notion of différance, and on broadening and critiquing what already for him was something beneath and beyond the level of a concept. For Derrida, this being more and less than a concept means that it was already something that exceeded the distinction between philosophy and science, and this is also the case for Stiegler: it is neither a matter of *reducing* différance to a 'materialist' scientific account, nor of *raising* science to the 'spiritual' level of philosophical ideas, but rather of *exposing* each of them to the processual, compositional conditions of their emergence from out of that originary complication that Stiegler calls the default of origin. We were thereby led to reflect upon two kinds of temporality relating the *who* and the *what*: (1) at the palaeo-archaeological level, the co-invention of the anthropic and the technical through the emergence of a third kind of memory, exteriorized or exosomatic memory; and (2) at the level of the existential analytic, the emergence of projective, mortal Dasein, stretched between birth and death, from the conditions of access provided by exteriorization, making possible the formation, adoption and transformation of 'tradition' and 'heritage', that is, of a past that Dasein has not itself lived.

We have seen that for Derrida, the significance of Leroi-Gourhan's account of exteriorization lies in the possibility of *extending* the Husserlian concepts of retention and protention beyond their Husserlian provenance in 'intentional consciousness'. As Stiegler puts it:

> In Husserl, retentions and protentions are phenomena existing in the temporal flow of a consciousness itself proper to a noetic soul – in Aristotle's sense – which is also the soul of a 'transcendental subject'. In Derrida, the trace as retention and protention concerns every living organism – if only because DNA, as it was understood at the time he developed this grammatology, as genetic pro-gram, is a kind of retentional as well as protentional system.[217]

And we should add that for Derrida, it was the relationship between this genetic program and the cybernetic program that meant he could conceive that this extension, operating 'far beyond' intentional consciousness, did so on *both sides* of 'the human'. In this way, Derrida would seem to be led towards the questions concerning both technology and humanism that would occupy the later Heidegger. The latter, as we have seen, did not succeed in formulating the question of how it was possible that an epoch could commence in which there arose a being concerned not with survival but existence, that is, with a form of temporality not just calculable but existential: what Heidegger could not quite manage to think was how such a possibility depends on conditions of access to knowledge of the flow of time, and where these conditions are inevitably *technical*.

Even if Stiegler will agree with the thrust of this challenge to 'humanism', that is, this deconstruction of the *opposition* of the animal and the human, he will nevertheless insist that, in the history of life, a new regime of individuation *is* introduced when, to genetic (DNA) and epigenetic (cerebral) memory, there is added a third kind of memory, which is epiphylogenetic (that is, artificial): it is necessary, not to oppose the animal and the human, but to *distinguish* the epoch that begins with the advent of technical life. Nevertheless, it would be a mistake to conceive Stiegler as a philosopher of technology: if he is a philosopher 'of' anything, he is a philosopher of memory, or more specifically, of *retention*. Technics, or what he will later follow Lotka in calling exosomatization, always has retentional properties, and, for the exosomatic beings that we are, technics *conditions* all the forms of retention of which we are capable. If indeed Stiegler *becomes* a philosopher of technics, it is *through* the question of memory, and where technics *becomes* not a 'region' of philosophical knowledge but the question of philosophy as such, or the question that *exceeds* philosophy, if it is true that philosophy has always unfolded as the repression of this question. It is for this reason that Stiegler has said that his project amounts to a 'hyperphilosophy'.[218]

Tertiary retention is a uniquely Stieglerian term, but it is built upon, extends and transforms Husserl's account of the phenomenology of time-consciousness, for the elucidation of which Husserl created the concepts of primary retention and secondary retention (and primary and secondary protention). But Heidegger *already* long ago argued that by making 'lived experience' the sole reference point for phenomenological analysis, Husserl inevitably found himself stuck within a metaphysical form of phenomenology unable to think the constitutive role of tradition and heritage, of the historicity and singularity of language and ideas, in the very possibility of philosophical thinking (though he himself did not finally confront the question of the *conditions of access* to that tradition and heritage, as we have seen[219]). Why, then, would it be necessary to go back now *from* Heidegger *to* Husserl, and to formulate this post-Husserlian concept of tertiary retention?

Before elaborating upon Stiegler's reading and critique of Husserl, then, it is worth complicating what it means to 'go back', because it is perhaps not so clear as all that what comes before what, and what comes back after what, what is remembered and what is forgotten, what is retained and what is portended. That there is indubitably a before and an after is no guarantee of the validity of any strictly linear narrative. This will certainly prove to be the case for anyone who considers the 'place' of the 1905 lectures on internal time consciousness, and what it means for the relative positions of Husserl and Heidegger in a set of widening spirals that do not come to a halt at the boundaries of phenomenology or of philosophy.

It is through Rudolf Boehm, editor of *Husserliana X*, translated into English as *On the Phenomenology of the Consciousness of Internal Time*, that we know many of the immediately relevant chronological details of the documentation and publication of these lectures, as the English translator John Barnett Brough recounts.[220] They were first published in 1928, with Heidegger credited as their editor, but what this conceals is that it was Husserl's assistant Edith Stein who in 1917 received from Husserl all the written notes on which these lectures were originally based, but to which Husserl had periodically added and deleted pages at will over the dozen years transpiring since. Despite working 'zealously' by herself and with Husserl to arrange and re-edit the texts, however, Stein did not in 1917 succeed in having them published.

So how did Husserl's later assistant, Martin Heidegger, come to be credited as their editor when they were eventually published in 1928?

> According to Heidegger's recollection, as reported to Boehm, while Husserl and Heidegger were spending their spring holidays in the Black Forest in 1926, Heidegger showed Husserl the manuscript of *Sein und Zeit*, which was almost complete at the time. It was this that prompted Husserl to propose to Heidegger that the latter undertake the publication of Husserl's investigations of time-consciousness, which meant the draft Edith Stein had prepared in 1917 [...]. Heidegger agreed, stipulating, however, that he could not get underway with the task until *Sein und Zeit* had appeared, and even then could do no more than give Stein's manuscript a careful reading.[221]

For the Heidegger who was completing *Being and Time*, then, these edited pages of Husserl's 1905 lectures on time may have been his past, but they were, in an explicit way, a past that 'does not *follow after* Dasein but rather always already goes ahead of it', awaiting him. We cannot simply say that these lectures preceded *Being and Time*, because, for the Dasein that was the author of that work, and who *knew of* these lectures while still finishing his own manuscript, they still lay in his future. We can ask whether he ever really himself *came to* these lectures that lay in wait for him. And for we who read these lectures now, we must ask ourselves whether it makes a difference *for us* that it was Stein who had edited them together, twelve years after they were delivered and eleven years before they were published by a Heidegger who had already just published *Being and Time*, that is, his work dedicated (with the infamous exception of certain editions) to Husserl and to a complete reformulation of phenomenology focused on the question of temporality and the impossibility of divorcing lived experience from the non-lived past.

How Stein edited Husserl's pages is clearly significant: in the 1905 notes, for example, there is in fact *no mention of 'retention' whatsoever*. This fact would not have been apparent to a reader in 1928 because Stein's attempt to render a coherent whole caused her to introduce later texts into the earlier lectures, or simply to substitute 'retention' for other terms such as 'primary memory' or 'fresh memory'.[222] Such a substitution may be an act both of philosophical *justice* and *historiographical* distortion.

What else would it be worth our while to know about this Edith Stein, assistant to Edmund Husserl? Like Husserl, she was born into a Jewish family, and like Husserl, she would convert from Judaism to a form of Christianity (Husserl to Lutheranism in 1886, Stein to Catholicism in 1921/22). In other words, she underwent a transformational experience, a leap of individuation, consisting in the adoption of a past that was not hers and that she had not lived: the Christian past.

Stein, Heidegger and Husserl were all together in one room on 8 April 1929, for the occasion of the celebration in Freiburg of Husserl's seventieth birthday, when Heidegger, Husserl's 'closest friend',[223] gave a speech in honour of his mentor, presenting Husserl with a bust of himself by Arnold Rickert, along with a volume dedicated to his work. In this speech, Heidegger stated that Husserl's

> breakthrough consists in nothing less than the radicalization of how we do philosophy, bending it back onto the hidden path of its authentic historical happening as this is manifested in the inner communion of the great thinkers. [...] But those who want to transform must bear within themselves the power of a fidelity that knows how to preserve. The only way to feel that power grow within oneself is to be caught up in wonder. And the only way to be caught up in wonder is to travel to the outermost limits of the possible.
>
> Yet the only way to become the friend of the possible is to remain open to dialog with the powers at work in the whole of human existence. And in fact that is the philosopher's way of being: heeding what has already been sung forth and can still be perceived in each essential occurrence of the world.[224]

These are the words to which Stein and Husserl listened in 1929, framed in terms of inheritance and transformation. How did they hear these words? Did Stein hear them differently than did Husserl? Did either of them hear them in any way similarly to the way they would have resonated auto-affectively for Heidegger himself? One might well imagine that this audience asked itself, as it listened, whether Heidegger was genuinely attempting to describe the way he conceived Husserl's 'breakthrough', or whether he was actually offering a sly – if not passive aggressive – account focused on what he considers to be *his own* breakthrough, that is, his transformation *or rejection* of the Husserlian inheritance, itself following his own conversion *to* philosophy, where this conversion amounted to a 'transformation of [his] fundamental standpoint' that 'made the *system* of Catholicism problematic and unacceptable'?[225]

Only four years later, Husserl's view of Heidegger had undergone a complete reversal, having taken note of the latter's anti-Semitism, 'which [Heidegger] came to express with increasing vigor […] around the department', as well as the fact that Heidegger had 'discounted [Husserlian phenomenology] as something entirely surpassed and superfluous, not worth studying any more'.[226] At the same time, the rise of Hitler had forced Stein to resign her recently gained teaching position, and so, instead of continuing her academic career, she entered a Carmelite monastery in Cologne, where she wrote on Heidegger's work. Being cloistered as a Catholic nun did not mean that she was no longer threatened by the effects of Nazism, however, and in 1938 she was forced to move once again, this time to a monastery in the Netherlands.

For the Nazis, Stein's adoption of a past that was not hers made no difference to the Jewish 'racial' heritage that for them was the fundamental, 'biological' criterion of discrimination: she was arrested by the SS on 2 August 1942 and sent to a camp at Westerbork. While there, we are told, and *just like Socrates*, Stein was offered a chance to escape before facing the unimaginable horror of being sent to Auschwitz, but now it was neither her birth nor her adopted past that decided her response, but simply her relation to all those to whom she was conjoined through a common fate:

> If somebody intervened at this point and took away her chance to share in the fate of her brothers and sisters, *that* would be utter annihilation. But not what was going to happen now.[227]

For Stein, both a nun and a phenomenologist of empathy, my death is not so exclusively mine as it is in the orthodox interpretation of the existential analytic. She interprets the Heideggerian account of being-towards-death in terms of the possibility of being transformed through experiencing the death of those close to us, but also in terms of 'the question of the *destiny of the soul*'.[228] For Stein, this latter question is obviously interpreted in relationship to her adopted faith, which Heidegger would no doubt have concluded ultimately falls back into the metaphysical opposition between the temporal and the timeless that structures the Catholic system, as when she writes of 'the way in which the temporal touches something which is not itself temporal, but which reaches into its temporality'.[229] But even if this may well be judged as a regression from Heideggerian philosophy back to metaphysics-as-ontotheology, it still raises the question of whether 'a bond between Dasein and a being which is not its own' can in fact lead to a 'breaking open of temporality', not in the sense of being a passageway to 'eternal life', but in the sense of participating in a futurity of life beyond Dasein's 'own' mortality. Does being-towards-death, or being-for-death, contain a counter-tendency that could be described as being-for-life, for life *after* 'mine' has ended?

Stein died at Auschwitz on 9 August 1942, less than a week after refusing the offer of escape. Fifty-six years later, she was canonized by Pope John Paul II as Saint Teresa Benedicta of the Cross, and was thus herself fully adopted at the highest level of veneration as a member of the Catholic community. Her bust can also be found in Walhalla in Regensburg, and thus she numbers among those venerated and distinguished individuals of German history represented in that 'classical' temple, too, eventually adopted by the Germans as truly, and after all, one of their own.[230] The official posthumous transformation of the Jewish philosopher into Catholic saint and German heroine was thereby completed.

Is this, then, the last chapter of a narrative that is already anything but linear? We would perhaps need to add at least the following: in 1959, Paul Celan purchased a biography of Edith Stein, marking a quotation from her that reads, 'I spoke to the Savior and said to him, I knew it was his cross that was now laid on the Jewish people.'[231] Can this decision to mark this quotation then be used to *retrospectively* interpret a poem such as 'Tenebrae', written in 1957, as John Felstiner suggests? 'Tenebrae' is a poem whose darkness precisely seems to stage a confrontation between Christianity and those who met their fate at Auschwitz: is that confrontation a reconciliation or an accusation (no doubt these terms are far too simple for any convincing reading of Celan)?

While 'Tenebrae' draws a phrase, *ineinander verkrallt* ('clawed into each other'), from an early account of the unimaginable suffering that must have been felt in the gas chamber, it has been interpreted by some German readers as nevertheless invoking a kind of Christian existentialism, combining the Holocaust theme with that 'inner communion' with the other that lies at the heart of Christian ritual, 'as if / each of our bodies were / your body, Lord'.[232] Hans-Georg Gadamer gives a kind of semi-Heideggerian, semi-Steinian account of the figuration of mortality in the poem, arguing that, in dying, 'each of us is as alone and forsaken as the dying Jesus on the cross', before concluding that with the poem's repetition of the word 'Lord', 'the person speaking for us recognizes finally that the Jesus who died on the cross remains our Lord'.[233]

But if the 'Near are we' with which the poem opens (which might also be thought to hearken towards Hölderlin's 'Patmos', the poem through which Heidegger thinks the *Ereignis* in terms of the saving power that grows only where the danger also lies) is mirrored by the 'We are near' with which it closes, should this be taken as a *communion* of solitude that confirms Gadamer's interpretation, or does this 'nearness' imply, with the darkest irony, the entrance into death and extermination (with implications of Catholic complicity, and without failing to recollect that, in addition to the famous (non)meeting between them that would take place in Todtnauberg in 1967, Celan and Heidegger had long read each other's work, and that Celan would himself commit suicide in 1970)? These words – 'death', 'extermination', 'Auschwitz' – cannot be found in the poem, of course, awaiting an irreversible witness to irreversibility, perhaps, and for reasons that are both congruent with and extend far beyond the Heideggerian observation that death is both what we know most fundamentally and what can never be known. Or, as Günter Grass expressed it, what he, Grass, owes to Celan is 'the knowledge that Auschwitz has no end'.[234]

How, then, should we interpret Celan's marking of this *pre*-Auschwitz quotation from Stein? How do we read Celan differently before and after knowing about his marking of a quotation? How do we read Stein differently, which is to say, how do we hear it differently? Should Celan be interpreted through Stein or Stein through Celan, Stein's 'breaking open of temporality' with Celan's 'deep in time's crevasse', for instance, and what would this mean for the interpretation of temporality in Husserl and Heidegger? These questions, which build upon each other as dense layers of textual and historical sedimentation and transformation (crystallizations and turns of breath), and which rebound upon each other through loops and spirals of reading and hearing, imply those that will need to be addressed to Husserl concerning the *thickness* of the temporality of, for instance, reading poetry – or of reading philosophy, viewing paintings, listening to melodies or indeed gazing at busts – both before and after Auschwitz.

And all this is also just ('also just': that is, 'not just, but also') to serve as a reminder that the questions opened by Husserlian phenomenology 'remain open to dialog with the powers at work in the whole of human existence' – as long as there remain readers capable of (re)interpreting them.

The things themselves and the non-lived past

Husserl's 'breakthrough' starts with the phenomenological motto, 'to the things themselves', which essentially states the dictum that there should be no basis for philosophy other than lived experience, and that the phenomena apprehended in that experience arise from intentional acts, from the fact that perception or consciousness is always perception or consciousness *of* such 'things'. If this is a breakthrough, it is because it is an attempt to leave the opposition of subject and object behind: what is apprehended in intentionality is not an 'objective' content passively received by the senses, nor is it a merely 'subjective' illusion produced by consciousness. Husserlian phenomenology argues that to understand what *happens* in intentional acts in terms of subject and object would be to commit a philosophical error of a kind that arises from the unreflective familiarity with which we ordinarily grasp the relationship we have to our own existence. For this reason, the *method* of phenomenology consists in a *suspension* of that relationship, an *epokhē* or a 'reduction' of the so-called 'natural attitude'.

These 'things themselves', these intentional objects, are *eidetic*, Husserl says, but such *eidē* are neither *outside* (lying there in advance of consciousness, 'in the world') nor *inside* ('in our minds'): despite the fact that 'things' are not 'there' in advance, awareness of the *eidē* still requires an intentional act that moves *towards* them. Stiegler summarizes the aim, notion and problem of Husserl's philosophy in the following terms:

> Husserl's *Logical Investigations* asserts that all consciousness is consciousness-of-something, constituted out of its object of consciousness. The phenomenological, which for Husserl cannot be constituted in advance, must neutralize all hypotheses of existence and its objects: the phenomenon is constituted in lived experience whose intentional goal is always that of an *eidos*. [...] The object could not be already given in advance, but through the object an *eidos* – in advance – is being sought. The *eidos* is not in the world: it is, rather, an ideal object. But it is also not in consciousness: if it could be discovered there already, it could not be the

> objective of a process of completion that could always fail
> [...]. The issue, then, is: where are the *eidē* [...]?[235]

The question, then, is: where are the idealities, where are ideal objects, if they are not just in consciousness or just in the world? What 'third place' could there be, or is this just a matter of 'the space in between', in which case, on what basis is such a space constituted – where is the between?

In fact, this is largely a contemporary repetition of the famous question that Socrates raised when he asked how it is that all the *examples* of (for instance) virtue can hope to be unified as a coherent *idea* of virtue. Again, Meno's paradox argued that either we *already* know what we are looking for, in which case we cannot 'find' it, or we *never* knew and so will never find it. Socrates's conclusion was that someone who is seeking knowledge can *only* find what he has already known but somehow forgotten, and in Husserl this becomes the intentionality of the object: it is only in the process of enunciating knowledge that it can be constituted; it is never received; there is *only* (intentional) conceptualization. The question is: from out of what dynamic does this possibility of constituting ideal objectivities arise, that is, objects occurring in the perpetual flow of consciousness whose 'coherence' seems *stable*? And secondly, *who* is the one seeking: can it be reduced to the *I*, or will it be that the cumulative character of (for example, geometrical) knowledge means that the dynamic of knowledge necessarily exceeds (or transcends) the *I*?

For Husserl, even though we tend to think of such idealities as timeless, or as in some way lying 'outside time', it is nevertheless the case that they can be explored only through lived experienced. Given that consciousness and what is apprehended by consciousness both occur only as a *flow*, however, means that Husserl comes to realise that the way to seek these objectivities inevitably passes through the question of the experience of temporal flow. Stiegler again:

> It is necessary to replace the subject/object relationship with
> that of flow / (real content → ideal content).[236]

In other words, it is not a relationship between a subject and an object that is at stake here, but rather between two kinds of flow: on the one 'side', the flow of consciousness, and on the other side, the movement of intentional apprehension that seeks the *eidos* in the movement from 'real' to 'ideal'. Rather than a movement from 'subjective' to 'objective', or vice versa, it is a question of a shift from inadequate to adequate perception, and it is to this that Stiegler was referring when he said that this process of 'completion' can always fail:

> All adequate perception is internal perception, but not all internal perception is adequate perception. Between internal inadequate perception and internal adequate perception, there is a tendency towards completion – which can always fail. [...] *What must be studied* [according to the phenomenologist] *is not the inadequation of subject to object, but rather the inadequation of the always-internal perception that is lived experience, which constitutes the external object and therefore external perception, to the ideality aimed at within lived experience.* The inadequation of the subject as sphere of internal perceptions to the object as source of external perceptions thus becomes the inadequation of the *real content* of lived experience that is essentially internal perception to the *ideal content* of lived experience – which is neither internal nor external: *where is it?*[237]

What this makes clear is that, despite appearances, Husserl is in fact in many ways a compositional thinker of processes – phenomenology is *always* a question of temporality. Instead of the metaphysical opposition of subject and object, it is a matter of the complicated unfolding of the flow of consciousness and the movement from a raw apprehension of contents, of the data of the 'given', to a unified apprehension in an ideal object. This movement may not always succeed, but it is that towards which consciousness or perception aims, towards which it *intends*. But, once again, the question is: if the idealities are neither internal nor external, where are they? Or in other words: how should we conceive the internality of what has hitherto been called the subject and the externality of what has hitherto been called the object, where the oppositional way of understanding this relationship would now be seen as the outcome of a 'natural attitude' towards phenomena that in fact arises from a prior compositional movement?

It is at this point that Stiegler introduces an article of reasoning that he will also deploy on future occasions, but the context in which he will do so is not usually a reading of Husserl. Rather, he will in subsequent texts mostly do so in order to describe the compositional, 'transductive' relationship between what Simondon calls psychic individuation and what he calls collective individuation, and to describe how this process opens up a space *between* the psychic and the collective, a space in which different processes of individuation are bound *never* to share an absolute coincidence of meaning, but where they nevertheless aim *towards* such, and a space whose conditions of possibility (where this is what is *missing* in Simondon) are *technical* (including the techniques of language). What we can see here, therefore, is that this explanatory trope with respect to Simondon has its roots, not in Simondon, but in Stiegler's understanding of the specificity of the Husserlian 'breakthrough' with respect to the approach to consciousness in terms of 'flow', and of the questions that ultimately lie behind and *haunt* that breakthrough (as that which seems bound to *return* in Husserl's thinking). Stiegler writes:

> What *you* read of what *I* write is not what I *write*; it is what you *read* of what I write: the reality of your 'external perceptions', of what you perceive of my writing, these are not my writings, they are the productions of your flow of consciousness, the purely internal sense of your flow of consciousness that you generate on the basis of my writings. If our internal perceptions could coincide, thus eliminating my exteriority (which makes up the ideal scientific community that Husserl would later call a *transcendental We*), it is because my written expressions aim at an ideal sense that you *too* intend/read [*visez-lisez*] and that we attempt to complete together in 'reading/visualizing/intending' [*livisibilisant*] it.[238]

In the breakthrough that consists in the shift from an opposition of internal and external to a compositional movement from inadequate to adequate, Stiegler concludes, Husserl thus 'inscribes, at the heart of consciousness, *an inadequation that is nothing other than temporality*',[239] and which Stiegler then relates to the Heideggerian question of being-towards-death:

> What is the *nature of this tension between real and ideal* and of its *possibility of completion*? Heidegger will say: death is the achievement of this completion, the end of intentional consciousness in the living qua difference-completion, completion in différance, and as different: as other. But this gesture will depend on *abandoning the privileging of lived experience* and the introduction of a historial non-lived-experience.[240]

With this thought, we may well conclude that the *Heideggerian* breakthrough, the 'radicalization of how we do philosophy, bending it back onto the hidden path of its authentic historical happening as this is manifested in the inner communion of the great thinkers', does in fact spring from the Husserlian breakthrough that first sees that the question is that of a flow, and a movement that depends on an originary inadequation. What Heidegger adds would then be that this inadequation is the mark of Dasein's mortality, not just in terms of the indeterminacy of its end but in terms of the complexity of its origin in the relationship between lived experience and the non-lived past. And what Stiegler will then add (in *Technics and Time, 1*) is that the question of this non-lived past cannot be divorced from the question of the conditions by which it can be accessed, where these conditions are technical, and where the history of these conditions is itself a movement, that is, a technical dynamic composed of epochs.

In fact, this critique of Husserl is already foreshadowed in *Technics and Time, 1*, precisely in order to elucidate the critique of Heidegger that he develops in that first volume:

> It is easy to see in what Heidegger's critique of Husserl *ought* to consist: the historical conception of temporality such as it constitutes the *who* would demand that the already-there that is *not lived* but inherited, constituted outside any perception, is nevertheless constitutive of presence as such – and this is why temporality cannot be conceived in terms of the 'now'. The response would be an argument in favor of a radical revision of the oppositions between the primary, the secondary, and the tertiary.[241]

It is this radical revision that Stiegler will undertake in *Technics and Time, 2*, as we shall now see.

The temporal object

If phenomenology exceeds the metaphysics of subject and object by reinscribing these within the flow of consciousness and the movement between inadequacy and adequacy, what does this mean for the *I*, the ego *for whom* these flows flow? On what basis can this *I* form an identity that persists in its unity *across* the time of this flowing? Is it not that the *I* can then be *nothing but* the time of lived experience itself, *as* this flowing? And if so, *how is it* that we are able to have a lived experience of the flowing of time *at all*?

The first phenomenological step towards responding to these questions consists in recognizing that if we are able to have a lived experience *of* temporality, then this means that we are capable of taking temporality as an intentional object itself: we can be conscious of the passage of time, we can make ourselves aware of it, pay attention to it, and hence it seems that the *passing* of time can in some way itself become an intentional object. If we then wish to conduct a phenomenological investigation of temporality, perhaps the way to do so is therefore through an object that itself exists in time and as the flow of time, that is, through what Husserl calls a 'temporal object'. It is this thought that Husserl pursues in the 1905 lectures, taking as his exemplary case of a temporal object the melody, or even just a single extended tone (but the question of what is at stake *between* the melody and the tone will prove to be anything but incidental, as we will see).

A temporal object is one whose quality as passing in time is fundamental to our apprehension of it: when we listen to a melody, we have no choice but to listen to it *in* the time of its passing into the past – we cannot *stop* its passing in its tracks in order to contemplate a *moment* (unless we have a 'pause button', but in that case we are no longer considering the temporal object *as* a temporal object but as, for example, a 'freeze frame' that continues to pass from the present to the past even while the image remains unchanging). The reason to focus on a temporal object of this kind is that 'the perception of a temporal object itself has temporality, [...] the perception of duration itself presupposes the duration of perception'.[242] In other words, the perception of a temporal object is the perception of a flow in time perceived by a consciousness that is itself a flow in time within which this object's flow flows. To the objection that there is such a thing as 'objective time', that is, the time indicated, measured and recorded by the clock (such as a pendulum clock, invented in 1656 and using a harmonic oscillator and escapement mechanism; a quartz watch utilizing an electronic resonator vibrating at 8192 Hz, first unveiled in 1969, or an atomic clock based on the caesium standard, that is, 9162631770 Hz), Husserl responds that the very possibility of such objectivity is only ever phenomenologically constituted, and hence that the question of phenomenological temporality precedes the question of objective time. The *perception of duration* is in this way something quite different from, for example, the passage of time on which the functioning of a computer depends.[243]

For this reason, the analysis of temporality must suspend all reference to objective time and instead focus on clarifying how time is phenomenologically constituted in those intentional objects that exist *as* temporal: not just objects that *persist* in time as presenting a unity (as in any ordinary object, from a stone to a bust cast in stone) but rather objects whose fundamental character consists in their own flow through the *passage* of time (like a tone or melody). In so doing, what first becomes apparent is the difference between apprehending those phenomena that are presented in a temporal object and apprehending the durational quality itself as it is presented through the temporal object:

> By *temporal objects in the specific sense* we understand objects that are not only unities in time but that also contain temporal extension in themselves. When a tone sounds, my

objectivating apprehension can make the tone itself, which endures and fades away, into an object and yet not make the duration of the tone or the tone in its duration into an object. The latter – the tone in its duration – is a temporal object. The same is true of a melody, of any change whatsoever, but also of any persistence without change, considered as such.[244]

The function of the analysis of the temporal object (the tone, the melody, the recited poem) is to elucidate the phenomenon of time that is something other than the 'objectivity' of an instantaneous 'now': if time were but an endless series of now-points, there would be no perception of duration, and, by extension, no enduring perception whatsoever. Stiegler describes what it is that Husserl revealed through this analysis:

> Husserl discovered that the now is what passes, and that it is always already and immediately passing and past: still present, it is already past (i.e., retention). And at the same time already future (i.e., protention). This is the evidence, the phenomenological *datum* produced by the analysis of time in the temporal object's phenomenality.[245]

With this we arrive at Husserl's concepts of retention and protention, which as we have seen did not in fact appear in the lectures of 1905 but were fed back into them retrospectively, so to speak, by Edith Stein in 1917. The now itself, which is nothing but the flow of temporal passage, itself possesses retentional and protentional aspects, that is, it is already the retention of what has just passed by into the past and the protention of what is about to come: it must retain the just past and portend the immediate future, if there is to be any possibility of apprehending a melody *as* a melody, or even any tone *as* a tone.

The question, then, is the status of this retention of the just-past in the now, in comparison to that 'ordinary' retention that consists in the everyday fact that we can recollect not just the preceding moment of a note of a melody to which we are presently listening, but also the melody to which we listened yesterday, or a year ago. Husserl differentiates between them with the terms 'primary retention' and 'secondary retention'. He characterizes primary retention as something like 'a comet's tail that attaches itself to the perception of the moment',[246] while Gérard Granel will describe this retentional and protentional extension of the present moment as a 'large now'.[247] Secondary retention, memory as such, is on the contrary, for Husserl, *detached* from the moment: it is a re-presentation or re-production of a present that has now gone past, operating through the imagination with which, for example, we can 'run through' in our minds a symphony that we listened to at a concert the previous evening, privileging an imaginary now-point as our recollection moves along,[248] *just as if* it was back listening to the earlier evening's concert.[249]

Hence for Husserl, primary retention and secondary retention are fundamentally distinct phenomena, just as they are distinct from 'image-consciousness', that is, materialized re-presentations of the past ('paintings, busts, and the like'[250]): image-consciousness does not involve the actual re-presentation of the thing but, precisely, only its exteriorized image. Secondary retention, on the other hand, does in fact re-present the object, but it does so via the living imagination, whereas primary retention, for Husserl, involves no use of the imagination at all but only the apprehension of the durational character of the passing of the present into the past. Were we somehow to complicate this distinction between primary retention and secondary retention, this would inevitably entail what would for Husserl be the wholly undesirable consequence that an element of imagination would be introduced into perception. For Husserl, this would amount to an untenable denial of the 'real content' of perception *as* perception, even though *primary* retention is already a kind of inclusion of the past in the present that Husserl himself can describe only in terms of a process of *modification* of present perception *as* it passes into the past, a modification that alone makes the perception of duration possible. But if the past is already *past*, no matter how *just* past it may be, then what *is* this modification that occurs in the passing from present to past, if not a movement *from* perception to imagination, even if it is one that occurs *within* the comet's tail of a large now of primary retention?

This question may seem obvious, but it is not, in fact, the most fundamental question that must be addressed to this account of the relationship between primary retention and secondary retention. We must, according to Stiegler, 'revisit the entire question of the temporal object from a dynamic point of view',[251] where what is dynamic will prove to be the complex, looping play between primary retention and secondary retention, but also, and fundamentally, image-consciousness, or what Stiegler calls tertiary retention. In the very dynamism of this play, the terms by which Husserl intends to keep the primary, the secondary and the tertiary *apart* from one another will find themselves ruined, even while the distinctions themselves will continue to persist, and to persist as profoundly *necessary*.

The tone, the note and the selection involved in perception

We will now attempt to outline *three steps* that are necessary in order to 'revisit the question of temporal objects from a dynamic point of view'. The first of these steps concerns the *reciprocal* relationship between primary and secondary retention, and how this reciprocity relates to tertiary retention. More specifically, it is a question of recognizing that primary retention is always a *selection*, and that the criteria for such a selection can come only from one's accumulated stock of secondary retentions.

When discussing the paradigmatic temporal object, Husserl refers to a tone or a melody, but, in the details of his analysis of the consciousness of time, he really only takes the former into account: the phenomenological temporality of a *melody* tends to be regarded as only an unimportant *extension* of the temporality of the single tone. But what is lost in this assimilation of the melody to the tone? What, for example, is at stake in the fact that, as an intentional object, a tone can function *as* a tone or, on the contrary, as a *note*? What difference is in play between the (sonic) tone and the (musical) note? Might it even be that the noetic ear is musical *before* it learns to perceive a tone (just as we might also ask whether the voice was already singing before it learned what it is to speak, or the foot was already dancing before knowing what it means to walk)?

Hearing a tone as a note means apprehending it as irreducibly *belonging* to a piece of music, which is to say, functionally and aesthetically attached to other tones: 'melody can be composed as a unity only in this extension that always already transcends the elementary unity of a tone'.[252] Hence one could say that whereas one *hears* a tone, one *listens* to a melody, which is possible because we *already* know other melodies, we know in what it is that a melody consists, which is to say, we *know how* to listen to it *as* a melody. And so, when we listen to a melody, it is not at all unusual to call up secondary retentions of other melodies, given that such recollections and recurrences are the very condition of possibility of such listening in the first place:

> This *recurrence*, this dynamic, is inscribed into a flow to which it is *linked*, and *through which it connects to other temporal objects that are already-there in the secondary mode* of no-longer-being-there, and which enable it to *itself continue on*. We refer here to a melody and not, as Husserl ultimately suggests, to *a* tone. A melody is composed of notes, and a *tone* can become a *note* only in tying itself to other *tone-notes* with relations similar to those by which verses constitute a poem.[253]

By focusing analysis only on the tone, Husserl avoids asking about the implication this contains: that secondary retention makes a difference, or a différance, to primary retention itself. One might think that he allows for this possibility via the concept of *protention*, assuming that the anticipatory aspect of the way in which a tone is expected affects the very constitution of what is perceived, but Husserl sticks narrowly to the idea that protention is just the *minimal* expectation that when listening to a melody that has not yet reached an end, for example, one expects the arrival of notes left to come. This narrow concept of protention thus mirrors the limited notion of modification that Husserl applies to retention, as merely the immediate effect of passing itself, by which what is primarily retained ceases to be present even as it is retained in the comet's tail of the 'large now'. Husserl may thus be accused of 'a failure to think *modification* as recurrence: as the return of the modification of retentions onto the constitution of presentation itself'.[254]

How should we characterize this step, this modification that operates *within* primary retention itself? The phonograph was first invented by Thomas Edison in 1877, the commercialization of the graphophone started a decade later, the first commercially produced disc records, for Emile Berliner's gramophone, appeared in 1892, and better quality ten-inch records were produced for the Victor Talking Machine Company starting in 1901. Does this historical sequence of early sound-recording have any bearing upon the lectures that Husserl gave four years after this sequence, in 1905? Firstly, we can by no means exclude the possibility that it was exposure to this new technology, and the possibility it afforded of easy access to recorded melodies in domestic space, that prompted Husserl to reflect on the phenomenological constitution of the temporal object, with the melody as his exemplary case. But secondly, it may be that he was *aware* of these sound-recording inventions, and possibly provoked to think about the temporality of hearing and listening as a result, but had himself only limited *experience* of their use (the Victrola, for example, was not released until 1906, and it would still be a few more years before such devices became a widely diffused consumer item present in most middle-class homes).

This last possibility is significant, given that the capacity to record sound meant that, *for the first time in history*, it was possible for a listener to know that a sequence of sounds to which they were aurally exposed could be repeated identically on a second occasion (by replaying a recording), something that would be true neither of a melody whistled or hummed nor of a symphony performed by an orchestra. Today this is even truer: if I sit at home, put on an album (or select a playlist), close my eyes, and listen to the music that is electronically communicated from my device to my noise-cancelling headphones, and if I then do so once again, I can fairly know that the *datum* produced on the second occasion is an exact repetition of the first. But from such a process of exact repetition, only one phenomenological conclusion is possible: the flow of this *industrial* temporal object may be identical on both occasions, but the flow of my consciousness is *not*. What I hear, and what I listen to, in that recording, is not the same, and in fact what I *hear* is not the same, even though it *is* a recording: primary retention is *always and fundamentally a selection* (I can pay attention to the woodwind instruments or the brass, the melody or the bass line, different memories or associations may be voluntarily recalled or involuntarily evoked, and so on):

> Yet the role of secondary retentions as selection criteria in primary retention, and therefore as a horizon of expectation overdetermining the construction of a musical phenomenon while listening to a musical temporal object, only becomes obvious with the arrival of the phonograph. [...] The phonograph allowed one for the first time to repeat a temporal object – and obliged one to consider that when the same object is produced many times, different phenomena are produced every time.[255]

What the invention of sound recording shows is that between the first and the second occasion on which I listen to a recording, something must have happened to have altered the conditions on the basis of which that selection occurs – and in the first place *what* has happened is that the listener has retained the memory (the secondary retention) of having *already* listened to the recording: what has changed is the listener *as* a temporal consciousness whose primary retentions are constantly adding to a store of secondary retentions, of accumulated experience.[256] Between the first and the second time listening to a temporal object, the listener has accumulated a slightly different store of accumulated experience, and these accumulated secondary retentions function as slightly different *filters* meaning that slightly different selections are made, producing slightly different primary retentions.

If perception itself involves a *selection*, and if in fact no two encounters with temporal objects are ever precisely the same, *even where these objects provide identical 'givens', identical 'data', identical 'real content'*, then it is strictly speaking impossible to distinguish primary retention and secondary retention on the basis of presence and non-presence. Derrida had already reached a similar conclusion in *Speech and Phenomena* with respect to the very possibility of distinguishing the presence or otherwise of primary retention *in* perception. In other words, it becomes extraordinarily difficult for Husserl to clarify the status of primary retention with respect to perception, because in spite of everything, he cannot ultimately let go of the metaphysics of presence:

> Thus, in retention, the presentation that enables us to see gives a nonpresent, a past and unreal present. [...] As soon as we admit this continuity of the now and the not-now, perception and nonperception, in the zone of primordiality common to primordial impression and primordial retention, we admit the other into the self-identity of the *Augenblick*; nonpresence and nonevidence are admitted into the *blink of the instant*. [...] This alterity is in fact the condition for presence, presentation, and thus for *Vorstellung* in general [...]. The difference between retention and reproduction, between primary and secondary memory, is not the radical difference Husserl wanted between perception and nonperception. Whatever the phenomenological difference between these two modifications may be, [...] it only serves to separate two ways of relating to the irreducible nonpresence of another now.[257]

Hence Derrida is not saying only that Husserl, in trying to introduce the non-presence of primary retention into the presence of perception, gets lost in confusion. He is not just saying that with respect to primary retention, Husserl is having it both ways: present and non-present at the same time, or present in one passage of the text and non-present in another. While such accusations may be *justifiable*, Derrida is not ultimately attempting to refute the necessity of the concept: rather, he is arguing that alterity, non-presence, is the *condition* of presence, that the possibility of presence arises from out of absence, for otherwise the now would have no 'room', so to speak, for the *inclusion* of the *other* presence/nonpresence that is primary *retention*.

We find the echo of this argument in Stiegler, as for instance here:

> When does *perception* cease, since retention lasts beyond sensation?
>
> In the case of primary memory, it is no longer possible to speak about simple perception, in the strictest sense, since retention always already inhabits the large now: perceptual presence extends to the black hole of retentional absence, a

kind of im-perceptibility already being at work in the being-perceived of the temporal object, as its modification.[258]

There is no perception that is not always already retentional: there is, in this sense, *only* retention. Is Stiegler, here, merely repeating the Derridian argument? Is he listening to Derrida, and, hearing what *he*, Stiegler, hears in what Derrida says, and not what Derrida himself hears in what he himself says, nevertheless finds himself moving towards a position that is ultimately asymptotically highly similar to Derrida's? Here we should resist the temptation to fast forward too quickly through the respective flows of thinking of the two (or three, or more) thinkers, because, in this repetition of the question of différance, we may well think that it is in some sense the whole direction of the future flow of philosophy that is at stake.

Derrida takes note of Husserl's *broadening* of the present (Granel's 'large now'), and then draws attention to the strict impossibility of the inclusion of non-presence in presence. He then pushes that argument further, towards the conclusion that *both* purely immediate perception and primary retention must somehow include *non*-presence:

> The frontier must pass not between the pure present and the nonpresent, i.e., between the actuality and inactuality of a living now, but rather between two forms of the re-turn or re-stitution of the present: re-tention and re-presentation.[259]

As Stiegler observes, the two steps of Derrida's deconstruction, here, consist in 'first reflection upon, then the inversion (*le renversement*) of, the Husserlian expansion of the present to the "large now" of the temporal object'.[260] It is this manoeuvre that ultimately leads Derrida to conceive the trace and différance, and even the movement of différance qua history of life – including the bifurcation in or the continuity of that history that would consist in life's becoming conscious:

> Without reducing the abyss which may indeed separate retention from re-presentation, without hiding the fact that the problem of their relationship is none other than that of the history of 'life' and of life's becoming conscious, we should be able to say *a priori* that their common root – the possibility of re-petition [of the now that is first repeated in primary retention and then in secondary retention] in its most general form, that is, the constitution of a trace in the most universal sense – is a possibility which not only must inhabit the pure actuality of the now but must constitute it through the very movement of differance it introduces. Such

a trace is [...] more 'primordial' than what is phenomenologically primordial.²⁶¹

Derrida here inscribes the very problem of retention, and of the repetition as re-presentation it contains, into the history of life that in *Of Grammatology* extends from the amoeba to electronic card indexes – as the question of retention and protention extended far beyond intentional consciousness. And he does so in terms of an originary différance, or what Stiegler will call a default of origin, a trace that *precedes* the phenomenological opening itself. Stiegler, however, wishes to clearly emphasize that something remains *missing* from Derrida's deconstruction of the Husserlian metaphysics of presence with respect to the distinction between primary retention and secondary retention: like Derrida, Stiegler thinks that

> the *difference* between primary and secondary retention is not a *radical* difference insofar as primary retention is unceasingly composed *with* secondary retention, that is to say, insofar as perception is always projected *by, upon,* and *in* imagination.²⁶²

What, then, is the point of difference? For Derrida, it is the trace that is constitutive, but he does not tend to see the *distinction* between primary and secondary retention as *itself* productive: the deconstruction of the difference between them is the neutralization of any constitutive potential as the distinction falls into the familiar Derridian aporia. For Stiegler, however, it is the distinction between primary retention and secondary retention itself that is Husserl's real 'breakthrough' with respect to temporality, because in fact, and contra Derrida's reading of Husserl, and despite Husserl himself, what they form together is something other than an opposition:

> But it is no less the case that the *difference* remains and *constitutes* a distinction that is not an *op-position,* but precisely what I have called a *com-position.* Now this constitutive character of composition – that is, *the woof of time* – constructed by the difference between primary and secondary is a distinctive philosophical discovery on Husserl's part. At the end of his career, he supplements it with the discovery of retentional finitude and its primordial technicity in geometry. Neither of these advances were, in the end, fully acknowledged or explored in Derrida's thought.²⁶³

Stiegler here refers to two things: (1) the compositional character of the relationship between primary retention and secondary retention that weaves the fabric of temporality; (2) primordial technicity, that is, the technological genesis (image-consciousness in Husserl's terms, tertiary retention in Stiegler's) that ultimately lies behind the very opening of the distinction between primary and secondary, and also the possibility of its closing. These will be the second and third steps that are necessary in revisiting the question of the temporal object from a dynamic point of view. We will need to consider them in turn.

The stereotypical and the traumatypical

We can know for sure that primary retention composes with secondary retention because listening to an identical recording twice produces two different perceptual experiences. This difference between the first time and the second time can be due only to the difference that has occurred in the listener, which is to say the difference that has occurred in the accumulation of secondary retentions *between* the first time and the second time. What this shows is that primary retention is a *selection*, and this selection must operate according to criteria. Let us now pursue the *second* step of this dynamic reconsideration of the temporal object, which will consider the characteristics of this selective process.

Let us say that I listen to a poem read aloud that I have never before heard: I experience in this temporal object, as we have said, primary retentions that are themselves *selections*, where these selections are made on the basis of *prior* primary retentions that have now become secondary. What I hear in the poem, I hear on the basis of selections made from that 'real content', and these selections occur on the basis of secondary retentions, which are always *my* secondary retentions. This is why what *I* hear in the poem is not what *you* hear, because your secondary retentions are different from mine, because you have experienced primary retentions of your own that have now become secondary. (It is through recognizing this that it becomes possible to articulate Husserl's phenomenology of time-consciousness with Simondon's account of psychic and collective individuation.)

But this is not *all* that happens when I listen to a poem (or have any temporal experience whatsoever). This new poem that I have never before heard, in being added to the store of secondary retentions I have of poems I have previously listened to, *also recontextualizes* all those previous experiences of listening to poems. All of my secondary retentions, all of my memories, have the possibility of being recontextualized on the basis of new primary retentions. New primary retentions that I experience (and all primary retentions are new primary retentions) will sometimes conform to the understandings I have already acquired on the basis of previous experience, in which case these easily comprehended retentions will tend to *reinforce* the *arrangement* of these secondary retentions within my consciousness or unconscious. Other primary retentions – for example, a poem that is utterly unlike any poem that I have ever previously heard – will *confound* my anticipations (my protentions) of what can be *expected* in poetry, or by one or another poet, and, surprising me, will thus recontextualize my set of secondary retentions in a transformational way, upsetting their arrangement.

When, in the second volume of *Symbolic Misery*, Stiegler brings psychoanalytic considerations more directly to bear upon phenomenological questions, he will describe the difference between these two possibilities in terms of a distinction between stereotypical primary retentions and traumatypical primary retentions.[264] Whether they are stereotypical or traumatypical, however, is not a matter of the 'real content' of these retentions as such: they are stereotypical or traumatypical *only in relation to* the protentions and expectations that have formed within my psychic apparatus on the basis of the set of secondary retentions that I have accumulated. Where a primary retention tends to conform to the arrangement of the set of secondary retentions I have accumulated, that is, to be able to fit itself into that arrangement without disruption, which is also to say, where this primary retention functions protentionally in a way that fits in with the secondary protentions (accumulated desires and expectations) that are arranged within my psyche on the basis of these secondary retentions, then we can say that the primary retention is stereotypical; where it tends *not* to fit, and where it tends to therefore lead to the disruption and rearrangement of my secondary retentions and protentions, then we can say that it is traumatypical.

This will in turn affect the protentional selection process involved in my apprehension of primary retention itself, forming a recursive spiral that greatly exceeds in complexity the linear relationship that Husserl wishes to sketch out between primary and secondary. Hence irrespective of whether a new primary retention, in becoming secondary, reinforces or upsets the arrangement of my secondary retentions, what unfolds can be described only as a *play* between the primary and secondary that *works in both directions*, secondary retentions forming the selection criteria for primary retentions, and primary retentions, becoming secondary, recontextualizing existing secondary retentions and rearranging them, in a process of *continuous* modification.

The absolute separation between perception and imagination that Husserl wants to maintain cannot survive the recognition of this complex, compositional play. If the selection involved in primary retention amounts to a kind of in-camera editing (not limited to visual perception), so to speak, in fact every aspect of montage and post-production comes into play:

> But since there is a *difference* in each hearing of the identical, as is clear in phono-grammatic experience, *this montage is what (re)constitutes the Living Present itself, always already dying, as if it were only a plane linked to another plane (a secondary retention), which in turn precedes a plane to come (a secondary protention).*[265]

Stiegler notes Paul Ricoeur's observation that there is a large degree of freedom with respect to the way in which the past can be reproduced and reiterated when secondary retentions are reactivated, and himself concludes:

> Only an originary, 'cinematographic' possibility enables this pausing over the images of life, of epochs, frees these special effects such as slow motion, fast motion, condensation – *idealizations* by which something new occurs in a transcendental history.[266]

The 'exactness' of the repetition of the 'real content' in cinematic recording is not quite the same as in sound recording, but this is due less to the difference in technological apparatus than to the difference in the receptor organs it involves: my eyeball can always swivel its attention from one part of a screen to another, for example, in a way that is not possible for the listening ear. The fabric of cinematographic experience is in this way closer to the complexity of noetic consciousness than is the case for purely aural recording. Hence it remains the case that, in order to demonstrate that the repetition of the same *datum* does not produce the same experience, a sound recording is still a clearer exemplary temporal object than a film. Nevertheless, despite this greater level of complexity involved in the play between primary and secondary with respect to visual media, the *conclusions* drawn from the recorded melody about the singularity of all primary retentional experience remain entirely valid for the experience of cinematographic recording, and vice versa.

It is to this constitutively cinematographic possibility that Stiegler will turn in *Technics and Time, 3*, and to the possibilities this possibility opens up. What is the source of this 'freedom'? From where do these cinematographic possibilities arise? With this question of 'where', it is once again a matter of turning back to the question asked at the beginning of this lecture, 'Where are the idealities?', and to the question of primordial technicity that forms the *third step* in the dynamic revisitation of the question of the temporal object.

Ubiquitous image-consciousness and the question of protention

As we have seen, phenomenology pursues the constitution of these idealities by seeking their genesis: how is it that we ever manage to pass from intentional relations between flows of consciousness and flows of temporal objects to, for example, the purportedly non-temporal or omni-temporal foundations that are the transcendental objects of logical, mathematical and scientific knowledge? In pursuit of this question, Husserlian phenomenology wends its way through its own epochs and modifications, like a default of origin that constantly leads to the metastabilization of new philosophical systems but also to their eventual critical destabilization. It is in the unfolding of this history of transcendental genetics that Husserl is ultimately brought to the question of transcendental history, via the question of the 'origin of geometry', which will be less the culmination of these epochs than the suspension of their unfolding.

In the texts on the consciousness of internal time, as we have seen, image-consciousness (along with all the artefacts of objective time) is rendered phenomenologically incidental, derivative or trivial. And why? Because the imperative dictating the method always privileges lived experience over the non-lived, the already there:

> What is not in question is a re-presentation by means of a resembling object, as in the case of conscious depiction (paintings, busts, and the like). In contrast to such image-consciousness, reproductions have the character of the re-presentation of something itself. [...] The present memory is a phenomenon wholly analogous to perception. It has the appearance of the object in common with the corresponding perception, except that the appearance has a modified character.[267]

As with *Weltgeschichtlichkeit* in Heidegger, Husserl would *prefer* to discount or minimize the *specific* significance of 'image-consciousness', that is, tertiary retention, the already-there. But in Husserl's case, when it comes to the question of 'transcendental history', he in the end has the *courage* to acknowledge the necessity of suspending the privilege he has always accorded to lived experience in the constitution of idealities:

> When Husserl addresses the question of transcendental history, he locates the possibility of originary geometric

intuition within the possibility of cumulative science as intuition of re-actualization of invention's present. He can no longer relegate tertiary retention to a place outside it: the large now then becomes a *very* large now, an archi-now, and its composition a (re)composition.[268]

In other words, the constitution of the ideal objects of geometry may operate through a transcendental dynamic, but that dynamic is less and less focused on the ego, transcendental or otherwise, and increasingly on a collectivity that is irreducible to the individual, and on technological conditions that make possible the cumulative character of 'intersubjective' knowledge due to 'reactivation' and the stabilization of its 'objectivities', and where these technological conditions possess *their own* dynamic.[269]

Husserl's profound shift with respect to the fundamental assumptions of phenomenology will eventually lead Derrida to the notions of the trace and archi-writing, but this will happen only after a long *delay*. At the time of his dissertation in 1953, Derrida found this radical Husserlian reversal, this 'technicist explanation' of the origin of geometry, to be a 'rather laughable' hypothesis founded in 'prephilosophical empiricism'.[270] Derrida will himself, therefore, engage in a radical reversal with respect to Husserl, first revealed as such when in 1962 he comes to write the introduction to Husserl's text on geometry – and it will be by doing so that he *becomes* 'Derrida'. By that time, he will have come to understand that the finitude of retentional power is the very thing that necessitates the preservation of significations, values and the past as such in habitualities and sedimentations,[271] that the implications of the transcendental We are that 'it is the *we* that makes possible the reduction of the empirical *ego*',[272] that 'there is not first a subjective geometrical evidence which would then become objective',[273] that Husserl is not falling into historical empiricism because such possibilities of a geometric origin have 'always conditioned the existence of the ideal objects of a pure science', and hence these 'are *nothing but* the possibilities *of* the appearance *of* history *as such*',[274] that such possibilities depend on (as Husserl says) 'the broadest concept of literature', and that it is thus (the technics of) writing, 'as the place of absolutely permanent ideal objectivities', that opens the possibility of what Jean Hyppolite will call a 'subjectless transcendental field'.[275]

As Stiegler points out, however,

> the technological question posed by *The Origin of Geometry* is not limited to writing in the current sense [for example, it also consists in 'polishing', which Derrida had in 1953

described as a 'purely technical' origin], which leads to the question of what that signifies for the concept of archi-writing, and for the thoughts of the trace and of différance.[276]

And as was the case with regard to the relationship of différance to technical life, here Stiegler diagnoses 'a hesitation [...] as to the "technicity" of writing and arche-writing'.[277] Whether it is by polishing, or by inscribing a point, a line or a shape in the sand, producing geometrical figures that illustrate what does not *exist* but on the basis of which we can *think* geometry, these modes of inscription may be gestural or graphic without firstly or immediately being 'writing'. The origin of geometry would thus lie in the necessity of *both* figuration and the conceptual recording of the significance of this figuration: it requires *both* writing and *drawing*.

The price of this Derridian hesitation is an inability to think about the epochality not just of writing, but of tertiary retention in general, technics insofar as, beyond writing in its current sense, it is (always) a kind of memory. And this leads to a deficiency of actually existing Derridian deconstruction considered as a tool or a weapon with which to analyse and critique the most recent of those epochs – that is, beyond the popularity of the Victrola or the rise of electronic card indexes, the becoming-temporal-object of everything.

In fact, despite this late-blooming account of the technical genesis of ideal objectivity, this deficiency is also Husserl's, even though the distinction between primary and secondary retention and protention is absolutely necessary to any such analysis or critique. On the one hand, when he comes to write 'The Origin of Geometry', he grasps the constitutive role of tertiary retention as a technical retentional supplement for retentional finitude, opening the possibility of a dynamic of knowledge accumulation, condensation and reactivation that fundamentally displaces the *I* or the *who* as origin. On the other hand, however, not only does the focus on the tone come at the expense of the note, but the insistence in the earlier lectures that image-consciousness is incidental, and the subsequent failure to weigh the significance of the mass retentional supports that were then just emerging (radio and cinema), means that he *never* manages to apply the question of the historical dynamic by which the ideal objectivities of science are constituted to the ideal objectivities of perception and consciousness that had been his phenomenological focus in the lectures on time. Nor, then, can he deal with the fact that the play of the primary, the secondary and the tertiary bears the possibility not just of being *constitutive* with respect to knowledge, perception and consciousness, but also *destitutive*.

When looking at a photograph depicting an event to which I have borne witness, for Husserl it is only that 'I remember the latter *in* the former',[278] never that this exteriorized memory, supplementing retentional finitude, is what opens the very possibility of 'running through' the event again, with all the cinematographic special effects through which this secondary retention may be post-produced (which is the case, irrespective of whether this 'image' is *visual*). Furthermore, the becoming-temporal-object of everything, which had yet to occur in Husserl's time, depended on the *industrialization* of temporal objects, from the gramophone to the radio, cinema, television, YouTube, Skype, Zoom and beyond. Not only does this lead to a tertiary retentional system that enables mass broadcast, but it also does so at the speed of electromagnetic communication, that is, effectively without delay, 'live' across the globe, on screens that are ubiquitous and that take up an ever-increasing proportion of conscious time. The *third step* of this dynamic reconsideration of the temporal object thus consists in asking what difference it makes when there is no longer any way of separating the primary from the tertiary because the former is always and immediately apprehended via the latter:

> How is it then possible to distinguish, in the temporal objects that *are* news and current events, between *primary memory* – the 'just-having-been' – and *image-consciousness*, since what happens happens im-mediately *through* image-consciousness? The *lived experience* of these events is a temporal object *that is irreducibly an image-consciousness*, while the present *tends only to be the present as temporal object* (listening to radio, watching television).[279]

My lived experience thus becomes *absolutely inseparable* from image-consciousness. Such a technical system of mass broadcast without delay of ubiquitous industrial temporal objects enables the *exploitation* of the play of primary, secondary and tertiary retention in order to *condition and standardize protention*. The analysis and critique of such a mnemotechnical retentional system absolutely *requires* the Husserlian distinction between primary and secondary retention, because the very foundation of that system lies in the technological possibility of *conditioning* the play between them. But in addition to tertiary retention being that which opens this possibility of technological control, it will also be necessary to clarify other elements: (1) the relationship between protention and desire; (2) the relationship between this 'intersubjective' dynamic constitutive of knowledge and the Simondonian notion of 'transindividuation'; (3) the basis of the epochal character of mnemotechnical systems; and (4) the ways in which all of this demands a political economy of the production and destruction of knowledge. It is to these questions that Stiegler will turn in the second phase of his work, after September 2001, in which he elaborates a 'general organology' that will also be a 'pharmacology', and where the crucial analytical concept will prove to be 'grammatization' and the correspondingly crucial political concept will prove to be that of 'proletarianization'.[280]

4 The Question of Elon Musk and the Aporia of Sustainability

We Are Allowing the Mainspring of Humanity to Run Down

> History discloses two main tendencies in the course of events. One tendency is exemplified in the slow decay of physical nature. With stealthy inevitableness, there is degradation of energy. The sources of activity sink downward and downward. Their very matter wastes. The other tendency is exemplified by the yearly renewal of nature in the spring, and by the upward course of biological evolution. In these pages I consider Reason in its relation to these contrasted aspects of history. Reason is the self-discipline of the originative element in history. Apart from the operations of Reason, this element is anarchic.
>
> Alfred North Whitehead, *The Function of Reason.*

The question and the problem

What's Elon Musk got to do with us?[281] If we're going to use Musk as a prism through which to understand not just our contemporary existence but a possible fruitful future world, however improbable, how should we go about it? Should we take Musk as someone with the perspicacity not just to see problems but to initiate projects capable of opening new pathways to solutions, or should we see him as a figure whose extreme inventive cleverness with respect to *some* aspects of present or future systemic crises (climate change, AI, congestion) comes at the expense of a truly systemic approach based on a truly critical analysis? Musk's strategy, whether we look at Tesla, SpaceX, the Boring Company or Neuralink, is to use innovative product design to *induce* technological acceleration with the goal of producing a kind of widespread industrial-economic stimulus amounting to a *positive disruption*, with the intended outcome being to bifurcate away from a dangerous pathway for humanity and towards a more hopeful future.

The question for 'us', then, is whether we can believe that the Muskian model of acceleration, disruption and bifurcation sufficiently grasps the depths of the largely *negative disruption* that is currently unfolding at high speed due to the very same process of accelerated innovation. Should we accept at face value Musk's claim that he is a 'pro-human', pro-Earth proponent of biospheric transformation and *positive anthropogenic forcing*, or does such a claim obfuscate the reality that he is just a less unsympathetic libertarian ideologue of Silicon Valley computational, engineering and transhumanist 'solutionism'? Is he the wizard we are looking for or just one more salesman selling us the dream of a magic wizard hat and leading us down his own particular Yellow Brick Road?

A variation on the theme of this question would consist in asking: *is Elon Musk an artist?* Are his electric cars, rocket ships and wizard hats the artefacts of a new kind of rational magic, the incantatory objects of the positive bifurcation we are seeking today? But what is an artist, if we conceive this in 'social' or 'anthropological' terms? What is the *function* of art, and what is the function of art *today*? If we say that our species has from the outset co-existed with the material and technological artefacts and prostheses it produces, and that this production, which is *constitutive* for this species, and which for millennia occurred imperceptibly slowly but today operates extremely rapidly, requires forms of social organization in order to be used *well*, and then, through the changing of these technical systems, *destitutes* and disrupts social organization and so requires the invention of new forms of social organization, in turn requiring new instruments, and new ways of using these instruments – if all this is true, then is the function of art, which is itself a production of and by instruments and artefacts, to provide ways of *negotiating and facilitating* these disruptions, these problems, these questions, by providing ways of navigating the relationship between the known and the unknown, and so of *overcoming* these problems (until the next problems arrive with the next technical disruptions)? And if so, what is the function of art in a world where the perpetual and rapid acceleration of technological innovation has produced an immense set of problems that synergistically and antagonistically combine in a manner that seems to have set the course of the world system on an apocalyptic path?[282]

Is it conceivable that Elon Musk is (to put it in the terms of Joseph Beuys) *socially sculpting* Silicon Valley billionaires and, more generally, *capital*, through a corporate artistry conducted so as to affirmatively respond, and as quickly as possible, to the large set of grave problems and disruptions with which we are presently afflicted? And if we say no, this is not conceivable, if we wish to reject such a conclusion, as we are surely inclined to do, then is it enough just to smugly bemoan the hubris of this modern-day Icarus: would not the responsibility to think better and care better, and so to respond better, *with greater artistry, greater inventiveness and greater genius,* then *fall upon us?*

In raising this question – the question of Elon Musk – we are opening a path that will prove, in what follows, to be both elliptical and circuitous. But with regard to the conclusion to which it leads, we are obliged to be absolutely clear. Macroeconomic critique has long been concerned with the contradictions of capitalism, and rightly so: the antagonistic battle of tendency and counter-tendency within the hyper-globalized capitalist technosphere is undoubtedly thrusting the latter headlong to a limit point that ultimately threatens to 'clog the economic arteries and increase the dangers of a political stroke' that may well prove to be fatal.[283]

But in addition to these contradictions, there are also contradictions *within critical macroeconomic discourse itself.* On the one hand, the most clear-sighted discourses on environmental sustainability in the age of climate change understand full well that desperately needed 'dramatic reductions in emissions at current high levels of consumption are very challenging', to say the least: hyper-consumption profoundly threatens environmental sustainability and solvency in the age of the Anthropocene.[284] On the other hand, the most clear-sighted discourses on macroeconomic sustainability understand full well that this hyper-globalization, fuelled by financial deregulation and subsequent debt-driven bubbles, has led to 'more inequality, underconsumption, debt and, consequently, macroeconomic vulnerability'. Take note: what profoundly threatens macroeconomic sustainability and solvency in the age of hyper-globalization *is also under-consumption.*

This problem amounts to a dual contradiction, both of capitalism itself and of its critique: global ecological sustainability absolutely requires addressing the risks brought by hyper-consumption, while global economic sustainability cannot avoid addressing the risks brought by under-consumption. The depths of this dual contradiction justify referring to it as an *aporia of sustainability,* and the failure to resolve this macroeconomic aporia gives rise to the significant threat of a global economic insolvency and a global political stroke of a magnitude sufficient to expose human civilization to a level of danger that is best described in terms of 'extinction risk'.

Opening digression on the function of art, via Whitehead

Today, we think of art as a thing, as an object offered for sale at a gallery or maintained as a relic in a museum, or perhaps as an 'installation' or even an 'event', but in the prehistoric past, art was fundamentally a part of ritual. Hence Whitehead argues, for instance, that for the emotional beings that we are, ritual was the

> primitive outcome of superfluous energy and leisure. [...] Mankind became artists in ritual.[285]

If ritual is a function, then it is so as a divergence and diversification from biology, a differentiation from the aesthetic function in endosomatic life. For Whitehead, what matters with the advent of ritual is that what begins by having 'no direct relevance to the preservation of the physical organisms of the actors' comes to establish a new non-organic function precisely by this divorce from the organic, or as the aesthetic composition of the organic and the organological:

> It was a tremendous discovery how to excite emotions for their own *sake*, apart from some imperious biological necessity. But emotions sensitize the organism. Thus the unintended effect was produced of sensitizing the human organism in a variety of ways diverse from what would have been produced by the necessary work of life.[286]

Whitehead's use of this term, 'work', as that which is made necessary by our biological conditions of subsistence, must be understood in relation to his tripartite division in *The Function of Reason* between living, living well and living better. As a question of living well, we might say that the function of ritual is the artistic use of repetition to achieve the transformation of a situation: in the tribal dance, the diffuse collection of individuals who make up the tribe, with their disagreements and their disputes, are brought together into a higher unity, the unity of the tribe itself, *against the 'downwards tendency' to fall into disunity*; in the war dance, they do the same thing, but in order to galvanize that unity into the strength and the will to fight against another collective group; in the courtship ritual, two separate individuals are brought together and conjoined so that they will be raised into a unity that would be a subunit within the tribe, with the possibility of having children according to the law of the tribe and so on.

In every case, ritual is a 'way of artificially stimulating emotion',[287] the function of which is to generate artificial affective automatisms in order to transform a situation, and to transform it in terms of the relationship between different scales or orders of magnitude: the individual, the couple, the family, the tribe, the ethnic group, and so on. But how is this transformation possible? It is possible, and it is *only* possible, if the practitioners *know how to do it*, if they know how to carry out the ritual, if they know how to use the artistic objects that are sacred objects in a way that *achieves* and *performs* this ritual. It is through the practice of these art objects that *access* is gained to some higher value, beyond values, which supplies the criterion for the determination of value by which the arrangement of higher and lower levels can be organized. The transformation this involves is therefore *performative* in John Austin's sense: by doing something 'correctly', that is, in the right context and in the right way, that is, with knowledge, an *operation* occurs through which a transformation is effected. This transformation is the work art does in the ritual.

When we think about this 'right way', about the 'institutional context' that means a priest can *perform* the act of marrying a couple, it sounds as if the rule precedes the ritual: does this not imply that ritual is always 'conservative'? No doubt this is very often the case, because the function of art in such rituals is to transform a situation but to transform it in order to *maintain* the continuity of the relationship between these different orders of magnitude. But at the same time, at some point in time, a particular ritual *begins*. Rituals are *invented*. And rituals are constantly changing, even if this happens slowly and it may be that nobody is consciously deciding *what* to change. The fact is that the knowledge of what it means to perform a ritual 'properly' itself changes, as the world changes, as the individuals who compose that world change, and, most importantly, as the products of our technics change, giving rise to crises of performance and thus to challenges to old ways of doing things, that is, old ways of transforming situations, old ways of negotiating the relationship between the different orders of magnitude within a particular locality, and so on.

What is this 'knowledge' that makes it possible for art and ritual to transform a situation? It is the knowledge of how to make the objects of artistic production, and the knowledge of how to *use* them, how to practise them. But it is also a matter of a kind of 'cosmological' knowledge, of something *higher*, something that, in Stiegler's terms, does not exist but consists, something to be aimed at or something that orients how to negotiate this transformation of the relationship between orders of magnitude, and that does so by bestowing *meaning and value*.

This last kind of knowledge is of a very strange kind, because we, latecomers, we very often tend to think: but all these tribes, all these ethnicities, all these little localities, all these 'minor differences' (and their narcissism, as Freud said), each one of them 'knows' something different than all the others, and all these differing knowledges of higher beings and deities and so on are all incompatible with each other, if not simply (therefore) *false*. So surely this is not knowledge at all, we tend to think, but its very antithesis. Yet in fact, knowledge *always* has this very structure: it always aims at things that do not *exist*, like the point and the line that are the foundation of Euclidean geometry, but that *consist* – we need them, and we aim at them through our knowledgeable desire. Even in science, the aim is not to discover facts, but laws: which do not exist but consist.

Given all this, the function of art would then be to cultivate, to uncover and to utilize knowledge in the broadest possible sense in order to negotiate and renegotiate the transformation of situations existing between varying orders of magnitude, that is, varying scales of locality. And this is the case in a situation where, however apparently stable, new problems always eventually arise in this negotiation between orders of magnitude, in turn requiring the transformation of art itself, and of its knowledge. As Whitehead also understood (in relation to the rise of 'religion' as progenitor of living better), this then becomes a question not just of generating artificial automatisms, but, *on the basis* of those automatisms, of generating new knowledge enabling the autonomy of *thinking*:

> For just as ritual encouraged *emotion* beyond the mere response to practical necessities, so religion in this further stage begets *thoughts* divorced from the mere battling with the pressure of circumstances. Imagination secured in it a machinery for its development; thought has been thereby led beyond the immediate objects of sight. Its concepts may in these early stages be crude and horrible; but they have the supreme virtue of being concepts of objects beyond immediate sense and perception.[288]

Over the course of its history, this function of art (via ritual and religion), a function that is explicitly non-organic in the way it fosters first emotion and then thought, has undergone at least two fundamental divorces. First, the divorce of art from ritual itself: this is what produces the notion of the artist as producer of the art object. It appeals, like the ritual object, to something higher, but this 'something higher' that does not exist but consists is no longer necessarily theological, transformed gradually into the notion of beauty. The art object thereby becomes an aesthetic object in the classical sense, that is, in the sense that *emerges* from out of the ritual culture that ancient Greece still was, as tragic culture.

The second divorce occurs when artistic production is confronted with another kind of production: industrial production. Through this encounter, the art object becomes or resists becoming itself industrial, and, even more so, art becomes or resists becoming a *market*. In becoming industrial, in becoming a market, and even in its way of *resisting* becoming industrial or a market, art gets caught up in that commensurability of all things that is the *calculation* of the market, of the *art market*. And so it is forced to abandon that notion of 'something higher' that would be *beyond value* and hence able to *bestow value*, or in other words, it is forced to accept the market as value of values: the problem of modern art thereby becomes the constant problem of knowing what art is, *why* it is, why it matters – whether it has a function. Instead of beauty, it becomes the question and the necessity of the new – of some new *surprise*, or of at least being 'interesting'.

In this way, the 'knowledge' with which art becomes preoccupied is, a little like philosophy, more and more insular, internalized, a matter of rejecting past notions of art's function and of proclaiming new ones, through constant reiterations of this function that prove to very often be more or less calculated strategies on that very market, even at the moment when something is celebrated for 'raising questions' or 'changing perceptions' or just being abstractly 'radical'.

In this way, art comes to think of itself increasingly in terms of a war with itself, within the greater economic war that defines the global market. But in fact, art in this industrial age that continues today has, especially since the twentieth century, been involved in *another* war, with another kind of production – art *versus* what Adorno and Horkheimer called the 'culture industry'. And in this war, 'art' has found itself constantly losing ground, retreating further and further into a walled garden while the culture industry expands to a planetary scale, absorbing the 'art industry' that succumbs to marketing.

What fundamentally is the difference between this modern art and the culture industry? If there is a difference, it is surely not fundamental. If this is a war, it is not a war between two enemies, but between two *tendencies*. The first is the tendency that sees that the question of art ultimately cannot be divorced from the question of function, but that the question of function is always *open*, and for that reason involves a question of knowledge, where knowledge is always a matter of a desire for the knowledge of what does not exist, yet consists, and where this must therefore be constantly cultivated and practised and transformed. The second is the tendency that dissolves all of that into calculability, into the market, and into speculation on that market. This second tendency aims as far as possible at the destruction of localized knowledge, even as it more and more comes to value 'information' – because information, unlike knowledge, can be calculated.

Record of a living being who lives in fear

Is art in this open functional sense possible today, and if so, in what would it consist?

In 1954, the Japanese composer Fumio Hayasaka told Akira Kurosawa that he felt that someone who is in danger of dying is not capable of working well,[289] by which he was referring, in Whiteheadian terms, not to the necessary work of life, nor just to *living* well, but working in the transformational sense of responding to increasing entropy by struggling for ways of living *better*. Since Hayasaka was himself suffering from tuberculosis at the time (he would die from this disease the following year), Kurosawa thought that the composer was describing his own plight. In fact, however, Hayasaka was referring to something much more general, less than a decade after Hiroshima and in the wake of the hydrogen bomb testing that commenced on the Bikini Atoll on 1 March 1954 with the detonation of Castle Bravo, which was a thousand times more powerful than Hiroshima's Little Boy.

In addition to the general threat to Japan of radiation fallout brought by the series of hydrogen bomb tests, the first of this series, Castle Bravo, was also well known in Japan because of the radioactive contamination to which the crew of the fishing vessel *Daigo Fukuryū Maru* (*Lucky Dragon 5*) were exposed, leading to the death of one crewman, Aikichi Kuboyama, on 23 September 1954. Edward Teller, the nuclear physicist and 'father of the hydrogen bomb' (who would later become the inspiration for the character of Dr. Strangelove in Stanley Kubrick's eponymous film), reportedly said of this death, 'It's unreasonable to make such a big deal over the death of a fisherman'.[290]

Kurosawa decided to make a film on the subject raised by Hayasaka, which was released the following year, in November 1955, a month after Hayasaka's death (it would be his last movie soundtrack): its Japanese title means *Record of a Living Being*, but it is better known in English as *I Live in Fear*. The movie tells the story of a character who has started worrying and hates this remarkable innovation known as 'the bomb'. It is structured as an intergenerational dispute between an elderly man and his adult children: the latter ask the courts to declare their father incompetent because of his wish to sell the foundry he owns in order to finance the family's relocation to Brazil, where, he thinks, they will be safer, at least from this threat. (Apart from anything else, this is personally interesting to me, because in 1961 my father – who had himself unwittingly contributed to the Manhattan Project during the Second World War[291] – permanently moved from the United States to Australia, partly for this very reason.)

Despite the title of the film, the protagonist played by Toshiro Mifune claims that, in fact, he does *not* live in fear: on the contrary, all those who continue to live their lives as if this threat did not exist... *they* are the ones who are afraid. To be afraid is to run away from the knowledge one has of a problem, to deny that one is in possession of *problematic* knowledge, rather than to face it and respond. And to deny that of which one is in possession is to be possessed – that is, to be haunted by what one refuses to see. In short, this character is presented as a kind of parrhesiast, as someone with the *courage of truth*, but he is taken by those around him for mad: *he* is taken by his peers as the one who is possessed, which is *always* the fate of the parrhesiast, because the parrhesiast *is* mad – he is mad because, as is said to him in the film, this technological problem that so concerns him is 'too big for the individual'.

When he loses the court case, and can no longer pursue his plan, this presumptive madman *does* become afraid, very afraid, and, out of desperation, he sets fire to his own foundry in order to destroy his family's incentive to remain in Japan. When his workers ask him, 'does this mean that you do not care about *us*?', he recognizes his error: he needs a solution to this problem, not just for himself, not just for his family, but for everyone – which means, at another *scale*. And then he really does sink into madness. Arrested for the arson, a cellmate in jail says to him, mockingly (as if to Musk), 'If you're so worried, why don't you just leave earth?', and when he finds himself sent to a mental hospital, under the delusion that he is indeed on another planet, his psychiatrist states:

> Whenever I see this patient, I become melancholic. [...] All lunatics are melancholic, however this patient makes *me* melancholic. Maybe *I'm* not sane, although I believe I am. I'm often obliged to wonder, 'Is he a lunatic, or am I the lunatic?'

This is a film, in other words, about the relationship between fear and melancholy, but more fundamentally about the relationship between truth and denial. It is not just that the protagonist is a parrhesiast: the film itself is a kind of parrhesia, which is why Kurosawa and his co-writers felt that they were 'making the kind of picture with which, after it was all over and the last judgment was upon us, [they] could stand up and account for [their] past lives by saying' that at least they had made *this* film.[292] *I Live in Fear* is an attempt to dis-cover, to uncover, the knowledge of a dangerous situation, knowledge that is in everyone's possession, but of which they cannot manage to *take* possession in order to transform their situation, the *local* situation of the localized beings that are the citizens of Japan, collectively forming the people of Japan: Japanese society.

The film was a work of art in the genuine sense to the extent that it was an attempt to renegotiate the relationship between the orders of magnitude comprising this situation, and to do so from out of the need that arose from a new and unprecedented challenge, a new danger. In this sense, it is a work of art precisely because it is a question of responsibility, and of the responsibility of the artist. In fact, it turned out to be the celebrated director's greatest commercial failure: originally intended as a satire, it was anything but, and Kurosawa concluded that he had made it 'too soon'.[293] Or at least that is what he said nine years later, in 1964, the year of *Dr. Strangelove or: How I Learned to Stop Worrying and Love the Bomb*. (And it would also be worth comparing this to Sion Sono's post-Fukushima cinema, in particular *Land of Hope*, but also *Himizu*).

There is, of course, a long and entirely justified tradition of rejecting apocalyptic thinking, in the name of Enlightenment reason and progress, and there is good reason to remain wary of any trace of millenarianism. It is, however, now almost three quarters of a century since the 'dialectical' character of Enlightenment reason was first pointed out, in 1944, by Adorno and Horkheimer, for whom the 'rationalization' of this reason brought forth not just light but shade – darkness – as witnessed in the industrial revolution, at Auschwitz, and through the culture industry. Today we have reached another threshold, beyond this 'dialectic', where to overcome denial would seem to require the invention of a kind of 'rational apocalypticism', and one whose many facets have continued to proliferate. Yet the only *reason* to adopt such a rational apocalypticism is if, by doing so, a bifurcatory path can be opened up that, if it is not capable of leading us *away* from the apocalypse, at least has the potential to illuminate a possible way through it, however improbably.

Fear and denial today: on the biggest, dumbest experiment in history

Let us then state it for the record: I live in fear. And in melancholy. And also, most of the time, in denial. And so, probably, do you. All these, for all of us, are more or less unavoidable, at least intermittently, because we all know, in one way or another, that the scale of the problems we face is 'too big for the individual'. Today, it is not just one country and its citizens that live with this sense of danger. Today, the whole world exists with the sense that there is a danger to that whole world itself. And today, everyone in the whole world succumbs to the tendency to deny that sense, and to live as if they do not possess this knowledge, by which they are, accordingly, possessed. For art, as for everyone, this presents a threat, but art is already threatened, and firstly by its own dysfunctional counter-tendency, and so this threat is also a chance: a chance to rediscover and reinvent its function.

But art today – and everyone is an artist, as Joseph Beuys said, just as everyone is a philosopher, even if the vocation is not 'equally' actualized[294] – art must go beyond Kurosawa: we must not only uncover this knowledge and present it in order to transform the situation of this locality or that. Today, the problem is not just from one device, the hydrogen bomb, nor is it even from several devices, or many, but from an entire exospheric system that preys upon and destroys the entire biosphere, and does so in a situation where the culture industry has itself transformed, becoming global, networked and algorithmic, threatening every localization and hence every localized form of knowledge. The function of art today is not just to resist this destruction of localized knowledge: it is to invent new forms of localization and to cultivate forms of knowledge capable of making possible a genuinely solvent and sustainable global economic system – that is, a transformation giving rise to a new anti-entropic cosmological arrangement of those orders of magnitude comprising our planetary situation, situated as it is within an entropic universe. Making this highly improbable transformation possible is the true and only function of art today, however grandiose a claim this may seem to be on face value. A dream, what else?

Elon Musk, too, seems to feel these feelings of fear and melancholy. As far as it is possible to tell, his motivation for building Tesla does seem to really be the fear generated by what he calls the 'biggest and dumbest experiment in human history', the 'crazy game'[295] we are playing by pouring billions of tons of carbon into the atmosphere. To this we must add the possibility that this crazy experiment is approaching its endgame, the threshold at which even the reduction of carbon emissions to zero *may no longer be enough* to prevent catastrophe:

> Our analysis suggests that the Earth System may be approaching a planetary threshold that could lock in a continuing rapid pathway toward much hotter conditions – Hothouse Earth. This pathway would be propelled by strong, intrinsic, biogeophysical feedbacks difficult to influence by human actions, a pathway that could not be reversed, steered, or substantially slowed. [...] The impacts of a Hothouse Earth pathway on human societies would likely be massive, sometimes abrupt, and undoubtedly disruptive.[296]

Given that the leading scientists in the field feel compelled to present a hypothesis of such immense foreboding, contemplating the possibility of soon reaching a point where not only does disaster becomes unavoidable but it can barely be ameliorated, we can equally comprehend the mindset behind SpaceX: for Musk, the prime motivation behind his attempt to accelerate rocket engineering is the wish to construct an escape mechanism lest this big dumb experiment lead the planet to uninhabitability *with no way out*.[297]

But what we fear today, and what we *deny* today, is not just climate change or the anthropogenic (or 'anthropic') destruction of ecosystems: what we equally fear is the destruction of the only means we have of addressing these problems – our collective intelligence, collectively cultivated and applied to making collective decisions. What we are still most in denial about, what we are *still not thinking*, or that we have barely *begun* to think (barely has it ever become a political issue anywhere, for example), is how we have created computational, cybernetic and algorithmic systems that, in the name of commercial imperatives, produce individual and collective stupidity, madness, desperation, fear and, *therefore*, denial. Ex-President Obama was undoubtedly right when he said recently that Donald Trump must be treated not as a cause, not as a disease, but as a symptom: it is indeed a great mistake and stupidity of the 'resistance' to Trump to fail to grasp this fundamental fact, which, by denying it, is bound to produce even greater stupidity and madness, and on all sides. And Obama is right to say that Trump, with whom the world has become *possessed*, was elected by capitalizing on *resentments* whose flames have been fanned by politicians for years.[298] But if we agree with his thesis that Trump is a symptom, then it becomes all the more important to ask *by what means* those flames were and continue to be fanned – fanned with what *fans?* – and what *to do* about them.

Neuralink in the age of 'our id writ large'

From this angle, more significant than Tesla or SpaceX, more interesting than the Boring Company, is Neuralink, Musk's most fantastical if not science fictional entrepreneurial venture, devoted to developing so-called 'direct' means of interaction between the brain and the computer. No doubt we have every reason to be sceptical about his proclamations of imminent progress in this field, and he does seem to buy rather too readily into the cognitivist fable according to which the brain can survive its somatic death by 'uploading' its informational contents to some or other device, apparatus or cloud. Nevertheless, it is also obvious that Musk is no fool: he understands very well, for example, that we have *always* been co-existent beings. An individual is an individual *with* his or her tools, today his or her smartphone, and a collective is the same: a company, for example, is for Musk just a 'cybernetic collective of people and machines'.[299] We are technical beings through and through, both individually and collectively, and Musk's integrated perspective is not so far removed from what Stiegler calls *simple exorganisms* ('I and my tools', 'I and my house', 'I and my phone') in their relationship to *complex exorganisms* (which he divides into *lower* complex exorganisms, such as companies, cities, galleries, geographical societies, and *higher* complex exorganisms such as states and nations). The question would then be to know exactly what Musk means by cybernetic, and of knowing whether he thinks these individual and collective organisms, and their relationship to their machines, are *reducible* to cybernetics understood as the science of systems of control and communication *via the calculation of information.*

Another way of saying that humanity has always been co-originary and co-existent with technics is to say that what matters is not the demarcation of 'the human' but rather the advent of an organism in possession of what Musk calls a 'tertiary layer'. In relation to what primary and secondary layers would this layer be tertiary? For Musk, it is a question of the structure of the brain and nervous system. The primary and secondary layers are endosomatic: they are, respectively the *limbic system*, which, moving too quickly (as we shall see), is something like the animalian brain, and the *cerebral cortex* (or the neocortex), which is the cogitating brain, more or less. The latter is still, as Musk puts it, 'mostly in service to the limbic system':[300] behind the abstract uses we may make of our cortex, there almost always lies, in some way, an attempt to satisfy the finite and affective dictates of the limbic system – which we might well relate to what Freud called the drives.

Nevertheless, this secondary layer can achieve *relative* independence from the primary layer that is the limbic system, and this relative autonomy of the cortical is achievable in a situation where, furthermore, these two layers have, for the kinds of beings that we are, *always* existed alongside what Musk refers to as the tertiary layer. The latter is akin to a prosthetic envelope *through which* the individual brain relates to other brains, to tools, and to *itself.* It is the tertiary layer that opens up the relative independence of the secondary layer with respect to the primary layer, which is to say that it opens up what Simondon calls a transductive relationship between them. This is the very thing that Whitehead was describing when he claimed that ritual, which is a technique and as such a tertiary layer, a technical form of life, is the *source* of the sensitization that will lead to emotional life, and which in turn 'begets *thoughts* divorced from the mere battling with the pressure of circumstances'. Or in other words, it is a question of a divorce from circumstances inaugurating a regime of individuation divergent from what Simondon called vital individuation, characteristic of the history of life up until the advent of this tertiary layer.

Musk doesn't quite say this himself, but, from a Stieglerian perspective, it is only *through* the transductive relationship between the secondary and tertiary layers that this relative independence from the primary layer is achievable (either in human evolution or in the life of the infant equipped with Winnicott's transitional object). And, paradoxically, it is only *because* of the tertiary layer that the primary layer is *not just* and *not quite* an 'animal brain', precisely because it is divorced from biological exigencies – composed of *detachable* psychic organs – and through that *available* for the sensitization and noetization processes that constitute the very possibility of the secondary and tertiary layers themselves. It is a question of co-origination from out of an originary default, as Stiegler says.

With smartphones, computers and the internet, we find ourselves living today with what Musk calls a *'digital* tertiary layer', but, throughout the history of civilization (which for Musk is the history that begins with *writing*), what is crucial is that this interface between the brain and the tertiary layer has always been *indirect*, requiring a circuit of exchange operating through a medium (a support) that can be, in this history of civilization, language, painting, writing, sculpture, cinema, radio, television and so on: the Neuralink project[301] is to facilitate the emergence of a *direct* interface between these three layers that would amount to a neurotechnological bifurcation from what Simondon calls psychic and collective individuation and towards, again, yet another *new regime* of individuation, that is, a fundamentally new relationship between what Stiegler calls *endosomatization* and *exosomatization*.[302]

Musk is also no fool when confronted with the anti-social misery and unhappiness produced by social networks. When asked about it, he can perfectly clearly and from his own experience see that today's AI is, 'in large part, our id writ large'[303] – that is, in his terms, the limbic system writ large, at the expense of the cerebral cortex, and in that sense a *regression* from the relative independence necessary for the begetting of thought (and care). Or to put this once again in Stiegler's language, these anti-social networks systematically, algorithmically and performatively target the drives, inscribing themselves into the limbic layer and at the expense of desire (in the broadest possible sense as referring to the anticipatory and protentional aspects of the *conjunction* of the primary and secondary layers via the tertiary layer), ultimately destroying our capacity for reason (itself fundamentally tied to desire in the form of *reasons*). Musk, then, has a sense of the *pharmacological* character of the digital tertiary layer and of the dangers it *already* brings for psychic and collective life.

In terms of the *future* dangers he sees associated with advances in the digital tertiary layer, his great fear is that the slow speed of *indirect* data flow and data transfer between brain and machine suggests that when superintelligent AI appears, it will acquire an unbeatable advantage over these brains, hindered by their slow connections to the tertiary layer. For Musk, it is therefore this problem of 'bandwidth' between brain and digital tertiary layer that urgently needs to be resolved.

What seems odd, if not contradictory, is that Musk can see perfectly clearly that the AI we have right now is inscribing itself *into* the limbic system, *targeting* it, and that this gives rise to the crowd psychology and herd-like politics of scapegoats and post-truth characteristic of the 'id writ large' – he can see this, and yet he has not one real word to say about how and why some more *direct interface* with our desires and drives would get around the problem of these connected brains being targeted and hijacked in an even more intense and accelerated way. He does not seem to see that this id writ large is the *direct* result of the attempt by Facebook, Twitter et al. (not to mention Pornhub et al.) to use their *indirect but still powerful* connections to these brains not just to control individual psychic apparatuses but to undermine the local and singular relationships *between* these apparatuses. The paradoxical and dangerous result is a kind of hyper-synchronization that no longer resonates at an individual level yet produces seismic disruptions at the collective level.

Limbic resonance, regulation and revision

Given Musk's fondness for conceiving his Neuralink project on the basis of the tripartite division between the primary (limbic), secondary (neocortical) and tertiary (technical) layers, one might be inclined to suggest he reflect on the work of Thomas Lewis, Fari Amini and Richard Lannon, as set out in *A General Theory of Love*, and the trio of concepts they name *limbic resonance*, *limbic regulation* and *limbic revision*.[304] When Musk describes the limbic system, and refers to the id writ large, he seems to invoke a sense of the 'primitive' drives of the animal brain. For Lewis, Amini and Lannon, however, it is crucial to understand the limbic brain in its specificity as the *mammalian* brain, built upon the prior structures of the reptilian brain, and on which will be built the subsequent structures of the neocortical brain. In this conceptualization of the evolution of the brain and nervous system, therefore, Musk's 'primary layer' (the limbic brain) envelops a *pre*-primary layer, so to speak, and is already, in this way, quite far indeed from anything 'primitive' or 'reptilian'.

What differentiates the limbic brain from its precursors is the different relationship to offspring that is generally characteristic of mammals as compared to reptiles, a relationship we could characterize as the evolution of endosomatic forms of *care*, in terms of both parental concern and the response of young to the *absence* of a parent, and where these forms of care are also associated with increasingly complex forms of 'social' care. (But here it is necessary to recall that these forms of 'care' – and of sociality – are the result of selection pressures resulting from biological evolution, and therefore are not the same thing as the noetic and idiomatic forms of care made possible by artificial selection when life becomes exosomatic, where the latter forms arise from the composition of the secondary and tertiary layers, even if they are undoubtedly built on limbic foundations, and where, for *Homo sapiens*, even our limbic and reptilian layers have likely been reshaped by millennia of exosomatic evolution.)

Whereas the reptile's brain would consist of limited action sequences relating the interior milieu to the exterior milieu more or less directly, in the sense of being largely 'pre-programmed' for the individual organism, the limbic brain is composed of 'open loops' that can be formed only in relation to others, and this *openness* consists firstly in the possibility of being attuned to other interior milieus:

> With the effulgence of their new brain, mammals developed a capacity we call *limbic resonance* – a symphony of mutual exchange and internal adaptation whereby two mammals become attuned to each other's inner states. [...] To the animals capable of bridging the gap between minds, limbic resonance is the door to communal connection.[305]

Noting Konrad Lorenz's notion of *imprinting* to describe 'the tendency of birds and mammals to lock on to an early object',[306] and John Bowlby's *attachment theory* that 'theorized that human infants are born with a brain system that promotes safety by establishing an instinctive behavioral bond with their mothers',[307] the authors of *A General Theory of Love* formulate the idea of *open loop* systems that *cannot survive* without stabilizing themselves via processes of 'synchronization with nearby attachment figures', through which mammals 'adjust and fortify one another's neural rhythms in the collaborative dance of love'.[308] In short, the capacity for limbic resonance makes possible 'this mutually synchronizing exchange', effected through open loops between organisms, which they call *limbic regulation*, and where, as mentioned, these processes are not just definitional, but indispensable: 'A baby's physiology is maximally open-loop: without limbic regulation, his vital rhythms collapse, and he will die.'[309]

The therapeutic aspect of the 'general theory' argues that the therapist takes advantage of the mutual capacity for limbic resonance, that is, for reading and responding to the 'radiant aura of limbic tones'[310] expressed and written in a manifold of forms, so as to reset limbic dysregulation. This is not just a matter of filling in for deficiencies of limbic regulation, such as compensating for failures of attachment stemming from early life. To this necessity of synchronization must be added diachronic processes that *rewrite*, so to speak, the open loops of psychic and collective life, and do so both in the grey matter of the limbic brain itself and in the circuits of social existence. Such diachronizations are a matter of *limbic revision*:

> Overhauling emotional knowledge is no spectator sport; it demands the messy experience of yanking and tinkering that comes from a limbic bond. If someone's relationships today bear a troubled imprint, they do so because an influential relationship left its mark on a child's mind. When a limbic connection has established a neural pattern, it takes a limbic connection to revise it.[311]

When Lewis, Amini and Lannon refer to this 'messy experience' necessary for a therapeutics of limbic revision based on 'overhauling emotional knowledge', they mean that the knowledge required to undertake it can never be the merely abstract or cognitive information that might have been acquired in psychotherapeutic 'training', and that therapy can never *simply* be a one-way street:

> In the duet between minds, each has its own harmonies and the tendency to draw others into a compatible key. [...] Coming close to a patient's limbic world evokes genuine emotional responses in the therapist – he finds parts of himself stirring in response to the particular magnetism of the emotional mind across from him. His mission is neither to deny those responses in himself, nor to let them run their course.[312]

A therapist without this knowledge, without the ability to sense with their limbic brain, open to its necessity but curbing their own tendency towards excessiveness, is bound to go astray, which means: to 'substitute inference for resonance', to 'offer cookie-cutter solutions'.[313] In other words, the capacities made possible by the primary layer that is the limbic brain can be externalized and understood via the knowledge opened up by the arrangement coordinated between the secondary and tertiary layers that are the neocortical brain and exosomatic memory, but where these are subject to regressive or entropic tendencies. For this reason, a pharmacology is required, and specifically a pharmacology conceived in a tragic key and concerned with the ways in which this 'tertiary layer' promotes or impedes the anti-entropic and anti-anthropic possibilities of limbic resonance, regulation and revision:

> The evolution of the limbic brain a hundred million years ago created animals with luminescent powers of emotionality and relatedness, their nervous systems designed to intertwine and support each other like supple strands of a vine [and which later become the supple strands of the vine of psychic, collective and technical individuation]. But in life, as on the Greek stage, every attribute confers a matching vulnerability; each heroic strength finds its mirror image in a tragic flaw. [...] The limbic brain bestows experiential riches denied simpler creatures, but it also opens mammals up to torment and destruction. [...] The giant reptiles vanished when the skies darkened and temperatures fell. Our downfall is equally assured if we push our living conditions beyond the limits our emotional heritage decrees.[314]

For the authors of *A General Theory of Love*, the pharmacology of these limits consists firstly in noting that instead of 'protecting us from the frailties of the limbic brain, American culture magnifies them by obscuring the nature and need for love'.[315] More pointedly, they argue that 'we cherish individual freedoms more than any society, but we do not respect the process whereby autonomy develops'.[316] The condition of possibility of independence is the dependence that forms through limbic resonance; the condition of possibility of autonomy lies in the forms of regulation (all the synchronic automatisms of education) and revision (all the diachronic accumulations of education) that can thereby be cultivated and, in being cultivated, transformed.

Such conditions of possibility themselves have technical and technological conditions, but such technologies are always also themselves pharmacological. This is particularly so for the young: those for whom transitional objects are essential to the formation of bonds and attachments (which form not just attachments to others, but to every object of desire, including all the objects of knowledge). The authors of *A General Theory of Love* write as follows in 2000, that is, at least half a decade before the rise of smartphones and algorithmic social networks:

> A spectrum of surrogates occupy modern babies and toddlers: relatives, live-in *au pairs*, regular or revolving nannies, neighbors, institutional day care workers, television shows, Disney videos, interactive computer games. [...] These questions revolve around an inconvenient center of gravity: the specificity of a child's limbic needs. [...] But decades of attachment research endorse the conclusion that children form elaborate, individualized relationships with special, irreplaceable others. [...] A child's electronic stewards – television, videos, computer games – are the emotional equivalent of bran; they occupy attention and mental space without nourishing. [...] Today's machines deliver not a limbic connection but imprecise simulations. Small wonder that Internet use in adults actually *causes* depression and loneliness. 'We were surprised to find that what is a social technology actually has anti-social consequences', said that study's author.[317]

If such psychic disruptions were evidently recognizable in 2000, produced through the *indirect* means of targeting the limbic layer, how much further has this tendency progressed in the two decades since, with the introduction of those mobile computers that are smartphones and 'social networks' operating through supercomputing and making use of vast amounts of user data to run highly powerful algorithms dedicated to systemically interfering with every relationship to 'special, irreplaceable others'? The consequence, as Musk knows full well, has been the id writ large – writ from the computer onto our limbic matter, even if still not quite directly, and debilitating the secondary layer. Why, then, would Musk not be concerned about the attention-destroying and hyper-synchronizing processes that could eventuate if ever *direct* communication between the tertiary layer and the primary and secondary layers should be achieved?

The cinesphere as electronic monster

The possibility of such an eventuality was to some extent anticipated in a little-known novel written in 1956, the year after *I Live in Fear* was released: the book, written by David McIlwain under the pseudonym Charles Eric Maine, is called *Escapement* (a horological term referring to a device that transfers energy to the timekeeping element in order to render time countable), published in the United States as

The Man Who Couldn't Sleep (the mediocre film version from 1958 is called *The Electronic Monster*).[318] It postulates precisely the kind of brain-machine-interface that Musk envisions for Neuralink: in the novel, the builders of this fantastical device conjoin millions of users to just the kind of headsets (or 'magic wizard hats', as Tim Urban calls them) that Musk envisions, and provide them an endless procession of artificial dreams, or automated tertiary protentions, distributed across a vast global network, which they consume in an artificially-induced somnolescent state.

In the novel, this corporation, Cinesphere, bears little resemblance to what Musk intends for Neuralink, but it is motivated by a kind of maniacal 'philosophy' built around the concept of 'unlife'.[319] According to the four-page treatise that forms the centrepiece of the book, written by the philosopher-queen who is the corporation's head, there are such things as 'absolute concepts', meaning elements of thought that are fundamental and indivisible. Among these absolute concepts, we are told, would be 'life', but the opposite of this concept is not 'death' but 'unlife', which is itself absolute: if life is 'the instinctive drive to survival', the author of the treatise contends, then unlife must be 'the instinctive drive to non-survival', a kind of amalgam of the death drive and escapism: consumption of and by unreality, and in that a form of entropy peculiar to the kinds of beings we ourselves are. 'Escapement' techniques operate via an 'entertainment medium', but 'complete absorption' would require the 'escape medium' to be 'injected directly into the brain', through which its 'reality-tone' might not just be indistinguishable from 'real life' but potentially exceed it (in an industrial process of the absolute becoming-temporal-object of everything).

In any case, reality is nothing but this co-production between brain and medium, and it is for this reason that the opposite of life is not death, but unlife. Given the choice, audiences may prefer to dwell within this unconscious unlife escape mechanism for years or generations or lifetimes:

> Might it not be the destiny of man, in the twilight of evolution, to apply his immense technical knowledge to the creation of synthetic life? To determine once and for all the pattern of his experience in the strange illusory world of the mind.[320]

It is to the conquest of the mastery of this 'direct' medium, and to making it available to all, that the Cinesphere corporation is devoted, just as is the case in 'real life' for Neuralink. And here, we should not forget that Musk, too, subscribes to the 'information is everything' notion that opens up the possibility of Nick Bostrom's argument[321] according to which it may be not just possible, but inevitable, that our whole reality will prove to in fact have always been just a simulation run by beings operating with some vast superintelligent AI, cybernetic organisms who wish to create a cosmos less 'boring' than 'reality', whatever and wherever that may be – precisely what is foretold in terms of synthetic life in the treatise on unlife, but at the scale of the universe as a whole. For its success in this pursuit, Cinesphere is accused of producing an 'escapement mechanism that is allowing the mainspring of humanity to run down',[322] to the point that it threatens to 'undermine every […] governmental structure'.[323]

The limbic *de*-regulation (the drives unbound) that we are presently pursuing is itself a 'crazy game' that we are playing right now, not just with the gaseous composition of our geophysical atmosphere but with the noetic composition of our civilizational atmosphere. This experiment in human history is equally big and equally dumb, because it systemically *produces* dumbness, and it does so both bigly and big league. And, in so doing, it systemically prevents us from finding the thought, the care and the will to invent solutions to large-scale systemic problems. We are becoming dumb and numb, or else wild and desperate. This systematic production of stupidity and madness ought to matter to everyone, but in particular to ecological political parties constantly faced with 'democratic' parliaments and constituencies lacking the will to pursue effective environmental policies, and an increasingly deficient understanding of or trust in science.[324] But it is *this* 'ecological issue', concerning the ecology of the production of stupidity and madness, that they mostly continue to deny, even as they descry the 'denialists'. As do we all.

Energy return on investment and the competition of self-propagating supersystems

An invited background paper entitled 'Governance of Economic Transition', published prior to the 2019 United Nations Global Sustainable Development Report, points to changes in energy return on investment (EROI) – that is, the increasing amount of energy that must be invested in order for a unit of exploitable energy to be produced or liberated – as a key factor shaping the geopolitical future. 'For the first time in human history', they argue, economies are 'shifting to energy sources that are less energy efficient',[325] that is, for the first time in human history, instead of it tending to become easier and cheaper to obtain energy, it is becoming more difficult and more costly.[326] Or in other words, and as Nicholas Georgescu-Roegen pointed out long ago with respect to our efforts to undo our vast production of waste and toxicity, we will eventually be forced to confront, in a manner akin to Freud's protists, the 'numberless generations of Maxwell's demons needed for the completion of the project'.[327] According to the Finnish authors, this will in all likelihood give rise to geopolitical conflicts, and necessitate a shift away from a macroeconomic model based on endless growth and towards a model where 'economic activity will gain *meaning* [...] by rebuilding infrastructure and practices toward a post-fossil fuel world with a radically smaller burden on natural ecosystems'.[328]

These biophysical economists are undoubtedly right to draw attention, like Georgescu-Roegen, to the fact that in an earlier world of cheap and abundant energy, economists could get away with ignoring the significance of the second law of thermodynamics for economic science in general, and macroeconomics in particular. They ought no longer be able to so deceive themselves. Yet after drawing this conclusion about the need to redefine 'meaningful' economic activity, they then immediately add, 'in rich countries, citizens would have less purchasing power than now':[329] while this may be undeniable, we can only wonder to what degree the authors have considered *all* the relevant and interrelated systemic questions and implications of this need to reduce consumption, and whether a touch of parrhesiatic madness needed to be added for them to have done so right through to the end.

For these biophysical economists, the last few decades point to the conclusion that market mechanisms, and even international agreements, have shown themselves to be thoroughly inadequate ways of reducing emissions and, more generally, of governing this transition. There is no doubt that this is the lesson of recent history thus far, and it is for these kinds of historical reasons that Theodore Kaczynski has long ceased to believe that it is possible to hope to govern today's globalized 'self-propagating supersystems' (Kaczynski's name for planetary-scale complex exorganisms).[330] For this contemporary madman, it has become clear that the adoption of long-term strategies by one such supersystem will only lead, because of competitive disadvantage, to its short-term decline with respect to the others. For this reason, he contends from his maximum-security cell, the global technosphere as a whole will prove, through the pressures of this competitive struggle, to be inevitably bound to abandon such considerations – incapable of begetting thoughts divorced from the immediate battle with the pressure of circumstances, even at the cost of the destruction of its own future prospects.

Less apocalyptically than the Unabomber, the Finnish biophysicists conclude that in all likelihood 'a group of progressive states' will have to 'take the lead'.[331] But even if this is 'factually' correct, can we not ultimately see in this pronouncement another species of denial: while they acknowledge that 'dramatic reductions in emissions at current high levels of consumption are very challenging', are the authors capable of confronting the degree to which the current global economic model is fundamentally *tied* to increasing consumption and sustained purchasing power, that is, to avoiding *under-consumption*? In short, if dramatic reductions in emissions are ecologically necessary, nevertheless the dramatic reductions in consumption required for emission-reduction themselves entail genuine economic and political risk. Hence if we are to avoid economic collapse and the misery and poverty that accompany it, the economic transition called for by the authors must be governed in a way that takes account of entropic considerations *beyond* these thermodynamic and biophysical questions. What the world lacks more than anything is a persuasive vision not just of economic transition, but of the transition to a profoundly new economic model.

Walls, borders, membranes

Niccolò Machiavelli dwelt in a world where the value of values supplying the archi-criterion by which simple and complex exorganisms (exorganisms at different orders of magnitude) are to be arranged was collapsing. For his prince, therefore, a crucial question followed from this collapse of economic meaning: whether or not to build a fortress – a question that, according to Machiavelli, proves to be a matter of knowing whether doing so is more likely to be useful or harmful. His conclusion is that it may be necessary under certain conditions, but that if the walls of such a fortress prevent the prince from understanding and influencing (communicating and controlling, as the science of cybernetics describes it) what his subjects are saying and thinking, then it may expose him to serious risk, or to what in a more recent terminology could be called 'existential risk', whereas the 'best fortress', the best protection for a prince, is simply 'not to be hated by the people'.[332] There are many ways of understanding this 'ethical' debate about the condition of possibility, the conditional possibility, or condition of impossibility of 'autonomy', but this question of fortresses and hatreds and peoples is ultimately a question of the informational porosity or otherwise of the walls, borders and membranes of all kinds that form the edges of localized systems at different orders of magnitude.

In Machiavelli's day, these walls and fortresses were 'physical' in the sense of being geographical, because value lay in the possession of the land whose division Carl Schmitt still (that is, even further along into the collapse of the notion of the 'highest' value, described by Nietzsche as the 'death of god') thought was the only genuine basis of *nomos*. In the nineteenth century, it was the knowledge of machines and how to use them and how to program them – knowledge extracted from those not-yet-proletarianized workers who were the craftsmen and artisans in possession of such knowledge thanks to intergenerational transmission – that became the information to be kept behind the legal walls of patent protection.

Today, all these earlier walls remain, and more than ever they remain political issues, possessing us, but they now exist in a world of rapidly shifting energy return on investment, and a world where completely new kinds of walls and borders are being erected. For Machiavelli's prince, the best solution is to both have and not have walls, that is, to have walls that are porous but guarded, controlled: it is a question of the 'interface' between localized systems at different orders of magnitude. It is a question, in other words, of both: (1) the *psychic* systems of the *simple* exorganisms that in the past were the citizen, or the subject, or the faithful, but that today are largely reduced to being *consumers*; and (2) the higher-order *complex* exorganisms that are not just cities, states, universities, art galleries and companies, but the *planetary-scale exorganisms* that are Alphabet, Apple, Facebook, Amazon, Microsoft, Tencent, Alibaba and so on.

For these vast electronic monsters, network behemoths forming a digital leviathan that is a technosphere incorporating both exosphere and cinesphere, what passes and does not pass through the new walls of their planetarily-localized cybernetic systems is, first and foremost, *data*, in a way that is *ultra-porous* and yet *ultra-protected*, collected and treated in the name of a growth model based on continuously increasing consumption, for which this data serves the primary purpose of enabling systematic and performative targeting of the limbic systems of simple exorganisms qua smartphone-equipped consumers, and to control the limbic resonance processes of those same exorganisms qua social network users.

The biophysical economists may be right to point out that twentieth-century economics largely ignored the second law of thermodynamics and the vast 'sink costs' (or negative externalities) that arise for the ecosystems that support these economies, but there is another question of EROI, the question of the computational effort spent on harvesting data so that it may be invested in exploiting the *libidinal* energy of these consumers – that is, on constructing a global digital tertiary layer designed to *bypass* the neocortical layer and directly target the limbic layer – and of the sink costs of *this* libidinal investment (but in the economic sense of investment: investing *in* the libido) that leaves all our psychic apparatuses deregulated and in want of 'limbic revision'. In this situation, we find it impossible to prevent the membranes of our exorganism from being polluted by the toxicity we ourselves generate (just like the protists confined within the closed system of the petri dish described by Freud), and this immunitary failure strikes us at the level of the simple exorganism and its three psychic layers, and at the level of the collective exorganisms that consequently find themselves incapable of cohering.

Privatized Keynesianism and the aporia of sustainability in consumerist capitalism

Keynesianism is a brand of historically-informed macroeconomics based on the idea that the boom-and-bust 'cycles' of the capitalist system are best ameliorated by mechanisms designed to keep such fluctuations within tolerable limits. The main instances of such mechanisms are: increasing state investment in down times (and, more politically difficult, reducing it in boom times), and maintaining consumer demand via the purchasing power derived from employment and a functioning welfare state. This was supposed to be capital's 'compromise' to ensure its own long-term solvency in the age of mass production: the ultimate goal of these Keynesian mechanisms is to minimize the likelihood of systemic crises reaching threshold levels by maintaining positive socio-economic conditions for the stable rise of mass consumption. The virtue and the necessity of such a compromise became belatedly apparent to capitalists themselves after their disastrous flirtation in the 1930s with the possibility of divorcing from representative democracy and embracing Nazism and fascism.

In the 1970s, however, Keynesianism itself encountered insuperable crises: the difficulty of reducing stimulus in boom times, especially in countries without a corporatist model (one enlisting business and trade unions in the compromises required for the struggle for economic 'stability'), led to irresistible inflationary pressures. Keynesianism thus proved to be an ineffective immune system for the global capitalist economy. 'Fortunately', another model, based on the rejection of the Keynesian compromise and the unfettering of the market, had been waiting quietly in the wings.

What followed the crisis of Keynesian economics was, broadly speaking, neoliberalism, which is usually understood, rightly enough, as a kind of market fundamentalism that wants as far as possible to remove these protective elements that are 'governmental structures' and social systems. Colin Crouch has argued, however, that the real if perhaps accidental *function* of neoliberal economics has not been well understood, for it *also* constituted a genuine response to the threats to the Keynesian growth model. Crouch contends that neoliberalism can be understood as a kind of '*privatized* Keynesianism' founded on a vast extension of credit made possible by the deregulation of financial institutions, the marketing of debt and the subordination of the production economy to the financial economy: the real function of neoliberalism is to keep the economic system more stably maintained, even in times of economic stagnation, and to do so via credit-fuelled consumption.[333] This vast extension of credit becomes the fuel added to this open system in order to try, desperately, to support 'stable growth'. Of course, the inadequacy and short-termism of this kind of privatized Keynesianism as a means of stabilization have become obvious to all, especially since 2008 – now already *ten years ago*, but also *only* ten years ago – but its accidental 'necessity' at the time lay in the real fear of economic collapse and resulting poverty if this consumption-engine was not prevented from stalling by the failure of its Keynesian-consumerist engines.

Not unrelated arguments can be found in the *Trade and Development Report 2018*, published by the secretariat of the United Nations Conference on Trade and Development, a profoundly critical and thoroughly reasoned macroeconomic document. After growth halved between 1973 and 1986,[334] there began a new period of hyper-globalization, stimulated by both supply side and demand side factors. Three months to the day after the global television broadcast of the events of 9/11 starkly revealed the contours, significance and geopolitical performativity made possible by the cinesphere,[335] there occurred another fundamental macroeconomic event: the accession of China to the World Trade Organization on 11 December 2001, 'which lowered the cost of labour by enlarging the globally available reserve army of workers', enabling Chinese exports to increase 'from less than 2 per cent of world trade in the mide-1980s to more than 13 per cent in 2016'.[336] And in terms of demand, the report concurs with Crouch that neoliberalism can ultimately be understood as a transformation of Keynesian mechanisms:

> On the demand side, the end of full employment and the growing deregulation of financial markets encouraged a shift from wage-driven to debt-driven aggregate demand in large advanced economies.[337]

What comes after the inevitable collapse of privatized Keynesianism? Crouch, a good social democrat, and one perspicacious enough to see before most others the rise of post-democracy, doesn't really have a good sense of how to 'transition' a global macroeconomic system in which neoliberalism, even in its 'strange non-death', can no longer contain the propensity for (and in fact systemically produces) bubbles and collapses. The *Trade and Development Report 2018*, too, points to the strong existing incentives for large corporations to seek to 'boost profitability through means other than raising productivity', despite the long-term implications of doing so:

> such strategies only make the broader economic system more fragile and vulnerable, since together they lead to more inequality, underconsumption, debt and, consequently, macroeconomic vulnerability.[338]

For the secretariat of the UN Conference on Trade and Development, the privatized Keynesianism of hyper-globalization is thus fundamentally exposed to macroeconomic risk by ongoing *under*-consumption. But it is impossible not to notice that the report's prescription of a revival of the focus on employment[339] is matched by a downplaying of the impact of automation,[340] an inability to distinguish employment from work, a belief that automation can *increase* both employment *and* income,[341] and an almost complete *silence* on the relationship between consumerist *hyper*-consumption and ecological sustainability (the last of these making this critical report on sustainability almost the mirror image of the equally critical 'Governance in Economic Transition' report, which is almost completely silent on the macroeconomic risks of under-consumption).

It is because of this *fundamental contradiction with respect to consumerism* that it is necessary to refer to an *aporia of sustainability*. And this aporia, of course, and today's potential for crisis, does not end there: what comes after privatized Keynesianism in a global economic system where automation may indeed be a significant threat to employment, with large-scale consequences both for jobs and purchasing power, where the EROI is becoming an increasingly expensive calculation, where the ecosystems and geosystems (and not just climate systems) that support all economic existence are themselves being anthropogenically forced to their limits, and where the libidinal economies of the simple exorganisms that we are and hope to be are mined and exploited by social networks in a way that produces an id writ large incapable of producing limbic resonance yet prone to mimetic contagion (Peter Thiel was perhaps the first to understand this and so to *speculate* on it, philosophically and economically, via René Girard, who is in a way Facebook's very own philosopher of unlife[342]), all of this together producing a vast propensity for entropic implosion and explosion?

Macroeconomic and civilizational extinction risk

How much significance should be attributed to this aporia of sustainability? If, as the subtitle of this chapter suggests through a quotation taken from McIlwain, we are witnessing the running-down of humanity's mainspring, then are we entitled to view this as a question of what Nick Bostrom – the probability-calculating shamanic philosopher from whom Musk acquired the notion that our entire existence may in fact be a 'simulation' – used to call 'existential risk', but now prefers to call 'extinction risk'? For Bostrom and Musk, immediate sources of existential risk can be found in catastrophic climate change and the possibility that superintelligent AI could effectively take all possibility of decision-making out of the hands of the human species. Does what we are arguing here make any difference to this kind of risk assessment?

In this regard, we can construct an analogy between the biological and the technical (that is, human) worlds. In the case of the destruction of ecological systems, there is a subspecies of ecological denial that consists in admitting the fact of anthropogenically-forced climate change but ignoring or minimizing other forms of ecological disruption such as habitat destruction and loss of biodiversity. It is only on the condition of practising this species of denial that it is possible to believe in the possibility of 'saving' human civilization through some vast geoengineering program: the latter essentially consists in the hope that it is possible to maintain terrestrial habitability for human beings while simultaneously allowing the anthropization of the planet to reach such a point of saturation that non-agricultural (non-anthropized) life would inevitably succumb to a mass extinction event. But in fact, it is highly likely that allowing the mainspring of biological evolution to run down will have profound consequences that in turn massively increase the existential risks to which humanity itself is exposed, because the complexity of the functional integration of the global ecosystem exceeds our ability to predict the consequences arising from its destruction. It is on this denial that the hubris of geoengineering solutionism is founded.

Analogously, the real questions of AI turn on another subspecies of denial with respect to, not biodiversity, but what Gerald Moore calls noodiversity.[343] All of the forms of knowledge that have arisen and declined, or that have been lost or transformed, are the ongoing product of a similar kind of noological (and artificial) evolution, producing forms of functional integration operating within and between the complex exorganisms that are tribes, ethnicities, cities, countries, religions, civilizations and so on. But we *already* live in a world where there exists exceedingly powerful computation dedicated to gathering so-called 'big data' (that is, data that is *too big* to be treated by anyone other than a few planetary-scale exorganisms such as Google, Amazon, Facebook and so on, and China[344]) and using it to influence and control behaviour. Influence and control of this kind are firstly assigned to the commercial imperatives associated with the consumerist economy, but they are also utilized for the purposes of political influence and control, as shown by the Cambridge Analytica scandal associated with the election of Donald Trump, which is symptomatic both of the power of big-data control and the potential it contains to lead to wild uncontrollability: the vast performativity that continues to unfold in this direction amounts to what can be described as both a *telecracy* and a *datacracy*.

The problem is that the performativity this involves (which is the entire aim of this algorithmic governmentality) depends on the *calculability* of the data acquired, that is, on the reduction of noodiverse knowledge to information that is susceptible to computational and probabilistic processing. And the circuit that runs from gathering this data to performatively feeding the computational results of its treatment back to the users and consumers who are its source (where this performativity ultimately stems from the enormous *speed* of this process compared to that of human neural circuits) has the effect of destroying these forms of knowledge, thereby systematically and systemically eliminating noodiversity even as increasingly orderly 'patterns' and correlations can potentially be discerned, maintained and exploited. As we are about to see in the next section, this is the distinction to which Robert Smithson drew attention in pointing out that processes of crystallization, while seemingly increasing 'order', are nevertheless entropic: this orderliness is anything but functional organization.

In short, this destruction of knowledge raises the possibility that extinction risk is to be found not just in the production of artificial intelligence, or superintelligence, but equally if not more so in the production of artificial stupidity on a vast scale that we might be tempted to call superstupidity. Inextricably entwined with this process is the influencing and control of affect (in order to control behaviour) through what Moore calls 'dopamining', necessitated by a consumption system that is fundamentally dependent on dependence, that is, on logics of addiction. Despite these forms of limbically-targeted control, the misery generated by the latter tends to lead to desperation, that is, to a generalized unsanity (to borrow a term from a recent movie by Steven Soderbergh) that ultimately increases the unpredictability and uncontrollability of the behaviour supposedly being 'controlled'.

This in turn is capable of being exploited by parties and movements founded on resentment, regression and the designation of scapegoats.

Actuaries of the future of humanity such as Bostrom seem oblivious to the aporia of sustainability and the intensification of the vicious circle to which it gives rise via the systemic and systematic artificial stimulation of unintelligence, de-emotion and unsanity. At the theoretical level, this is ultimately because they, like Musk, for all their dedicated futurism, are operating with a notion of the collective as the mechanistic sum of atomized logical individuals, that is, with a decidedly eighteenth-century social 'physics', subject to the first but not the second law of thermodynamics. Countering this theoretical deficiency requires not just the economics of endosomatic entropy and negentropy delineated by Georgescu-Roegen (and visible again in the ecological economics of the Finnish biophysical economists), but also an account of the entropic and anti-entropic tendencies of the noesis and noodiversity made possible by what Alfred Lotka called exosomatic processes. At the political and organizational level, such a theoretical deficiency is ultimately because the institutes concerned with these extinction risks are not 'authorized' to elaborate new macroeconomic models or new data architectural models. At the psychological level, it may well be that they, too, like Musk, like all of us, are afflicted with melancholic moods and a propensity for denial.

But if we assume that those who have their hands on the powerful hardware and software behind the operation of this production are not themselves so completely dumbed down and numbed down and blinded by their blind profit-making as to be incapable of seeing that their actions are now giving rise to this production of artificial stupidity and unsanity, then we must conclude that they believe that their systems are (or soon will be) *so* powerful as to enable even these problems to be 'solved' (in terms of their own immediate interests) through a kind of algorithmic geoengineering. In other words, the crystal palaces and fortresses these new princes (such as Peter Thiel) are building, whose walls will undoubtedly be inordinately thick, will, so they hope, be protected by an algorithmic, performative, telecratic and datacratic governance powerful enough to counter any existential risk to which they themselves would otherwise be exposed, including via the mass deployment of 'escapement mechanisms' in an automated post-work and post-labour world.

An 'optimist' among their number might say that, thus far, this strategy, which too is a kind of anti-social sculpture, has 'worked' in the sense that a global systemic collapse has yet to eventuate. But this vicious circle – where a vast project of data collection has the effect of destroying knowledge and producing stupidity on a planetary scale

– inevitably leads to recursive consequences that will rebound upon the macroeconomic, financial and technical systems on which this strategy ultimately depends: all these global crystal palaces will find themselves increasingly fragile and vulnerable, however superintelligent they may have in the meantime become. This algorithmic production of artificial stupidity and unsanity, combined with the aporia of sustainability for which the risks of hyper-consumption and underconsumption present a seemingly unsolvable macroeconomic and ecological conundrum, amounts to an entropic vortex: evidence that it introduces whole new levels and kinds of macroeconomic and civilizational extinction risk, rebounding upon the ability to address *other* kinds of extinction risk, is abundant.

Spirals, crystals, desolation

Robert Smithson's monument to entropy, *Spiral Jetty*, is no longer submerged beneath the waters of the Great Salt Lake that had long been subjecting it to the entropic forces of fluvial geomorphology: thanks to an extended drought in Utah, it has returned to visibility, sparking attempts to preserve this work of art from 1970, but where these counter-entropic efforts would seem to go against the wishes of the artist himself. Smithson's accidental death in a plane crash in 1973 was itself a great entropic loss for the attempt to think entropy in cosmological terms *beyond* the confines of the fields from which it emerges. In an interview conducted two months before his death, for example, Smithson, a reader of Georgescu-Roegen (he points out that for Georgescu-Roegen, Sadi Carnot could be called an econometrician), showed clearly that, long before the United Nations *Global Sustainable Development Report*, or the United Nations *Trade and Development Report*, he understood that economics, including Keynesianism (and now, privatized Keynesianism), is based on a fundamental evasion of the second law of thermodynamics:

> Economics seems to be isolated and self-contained and conceived of as cycles, so as to exclude the whole entropic process. [...] So that a kind of blindness ensues. I guess it's what we call blind profit making. And then suddenly they find themselves within a range of desolation and wonder how they got there. So it's a rather static way of looking at things. I don't think things go in cycles. I think things just change from one situation to the next, there's really no return.[345]

But beyond economics, Smithson also understood the general challenge of integrating and exceeding the question of entropy as it appears distributed across various disciplines. In a text from 1966, after noting the 'attempt to formulate an analog between "communication theory" and the ideas of physics' on this question, he immediately refers, not to Schrödinger or Wiener but to A. J. Ayer, who 'pointed out, not only do we communicate what is true, but also what is false', where 'often the false has a greater "reality" than the true'. Smithson concludes:

> Therefore, it seems that all information, and that includes anything that is visible, has its entropic side. Falseness, as an ultimate, is inextricably a part of entropy, and this falseness is devoid of moral implications.[346]

Here Smithson sees that the question of integrating and extending the question of entropy beyond the confines of physics and information exceeds the objectivity of science itself, leading to the necessity of a consideration of the true 'falseness' of what is almost a kind of unlife *beyond the pleasure principle*:

> There's a certain kind of pleasure principle that comes out of a preoccupation with waste. Like if we want a bigger and better car we are going to have bigger and better waste productions. So there's a kind of equation there between the enjoyment of life and waste. Probably the opposite of waste is luxury.[347]

We tend to associate entropy with the rather fuzzy concept of 'disorder', but Smithson, himself no fool, quotes the Nobel-prize winning physicist Percy Bridgman to show this may mislead us in our everyday judgments about what *counts* as entropic:

> But I think nevertheless, we do not feel altogether comfortable at being forced to say that the crystal is the seat of greater disorder than the parent liquid.[348]

Contemporary disruption is precisely this kind of entropic crystallization, not just in terms of the crystal palaces of nineteenth-century industrial capitalism but the digital crystal palaces that form the exospheric and cinespheric tertiary layers of twenty-first century algorithmic capitalism. If the latter do not make us totally insane, we nevertheless find all about us the evidence that the rationalized but irrational unlife of this strange non-death is at the very least turning us unsane. Diagnosing this entropic crystallization of contemporary life means bringing 'Descartes' cosmology [...] to a standstill', re-introducing 'delayed action, inadequate energy, general slowness' into a picture of existence capable of grasping that the instantaneity of pre-formatted protentions offers only the illusion of movement.[349] For Smithson, this requires the artist, the philosopher, or all of us, to construct new kinds of conceptual 'ready-mades', but through a kind of artistic practice whose condition of possibility lies within Bergson's account of the history of philosophy as clothed in 'ready-made garments of [...] ready-made concepts'. Yet at the same time, he argues, such ready-mades must be an-artistic in the Duchampian sense, which is their condition of *impossibility*, as monstrosities beyond the limits of conceptual idiomaticity, a material necessity and a necessary materialization, yet always bound to be off the mark, and thus 'definitely outside of Bergson's concept of creative evolution'.[350] A kind of madness of pre-formatting is required.

The exospheric and cinespheric digital tertiary layer seems to head off in advance the rise of any kind of positive bifurcation, whether it is a matter of the disruptive innovation of the Muskatel variety, or the transition to a new economic governance of the Finnish variety, or Crouch's recommendations of a renewed 'creative tension' between state, market, corporation and civil society.[351] Beyond all these approaches and analyses, *countering this vast negative disruption requires the large-scale implementation of a new macroeconomic model based on a new resolution of the aporia of sustainability*, taking account not just of the biophysical constraints of thermodynamic entropy and Schrödingerian negentropy but of the bio-techno-affective constraints of informational entropy (the entropy of falseness that in the 1970s Smithson identifies with both movies and printed matter[352]). Moreover, it is a question of going beyond the integration of these two entropies, which Smithson glimpsed as the new work of the new a-transcendental an-artist capable of inhabiting the highly improbable madness of planning for anything positive today,[353] and which Stiegler refers to in terms of the sur-real cosmology of a (theoretical and practical) neganthropology of what he calls 'anthropy' and 'neganthropy'.

As Musk says, the cortex is *not* completely independent of the limbic system: the former remains functionally tied to the latter, even if this *partially* independent cortex has *from the outset* existed only in relation to a tertiary layer with which it forms a circuit, and where what circulates along this circuit is the libidinal *energy* via which the drives are sublimated into desires that have not just detachable but infinite aims. All this means that, contrary to transhumanist ideology, reason is always ultimately a question not *just* of calculations or computations or cogitations but of *reasons*, and not just a question of the speed of calculation but of the slowness of thinking. It involves motives and decisions that are always singular, that is, never *completely* calculable, and always involving randomness, chance and accidentality, *in their positivity and paradoxical improbability* – it is a question of life, but of life lived noetically. This necessary accidentality is essential to biological evolution,[354] but also to the work of art:

> This *necessary accident* reveals itself in each work of art, as the jumping out of a singularity that is literally *improbable, unprovable*, and that goes much further than a *simple, provable universality* – provable as apodictic universality, which can in this respect be subsumed under the concept of a determinate judgment. That such a *singularity* opens up another dimension, another plane, means that this dimension, this plane, is that which spontaneously leaps forth from any desire – to the extent that desire *renders* its objects *infinite* as the object of a singularity [that does not exist but consists].[355]

What does not exist but consists, the infinite that lies beyond calculation and as object of desire, is that with which we can struggle against the entropic tendency, but, as Smithson seems to understand, we can do so only through a quasi-causal *twist* on the falseness that we are bound to produce through our circuits between the primary, secondary and tertiary layers (whether printed matter, movies or the directly-cortical magical wizard hats pursued by Neuralink), a twist that *adopts and realises* what is not true, what does not exist, that *makes* it real, however improbably. This is *why*, for Smithson, the entropic falseness we inevitably produce with these exosomatic instruments is never *just* entropic: in and of itself, it is 'devoid of moral implications'.

And this is why, for Whitehead, the function of reason is the promotion of the art of life, where this includes its transformation – not just to live, or to live well, but 'to live *better*'[356] (or in limbic terms: not just to *resonate*, not just to achieve healthy *regulation*, but perpetually open to unexpected limbic *revision*). Strange as it may seem, all this bears fundamentally upon the question of global sustainable development in a situation where such sustainability depends not just on regulation or transition but on transformation, that is, on a bifurcation through which we can live better. The aporia of sustainability, and the necessity of an affirmative bifurcation with respect to this aporia, thus *undeniably* lead (despite the proliferation of forms of denial) to an imperative to invent a new macroeconomic art of life on the basis of this 'neganthropological' question of entropy, but where entropy must be conceived *beyond* thermodynamics *and* information theory, or, at the very least, to prepare the grounds for such for those remaining after what seems to be an impending and perhaps inevitable global collapse. The sur-real function of 'art', today, can only be to foster, beyond the pre-formatted ready-mades of platform capitalism, a social sculpture capable of promoting the self-discipline of *this* originative element.

5 Carbon and Silicon: Contribution to an Elemental Critique of Political Economy

Introduction: aporia of sustainability and the blind-spot

We are confronted in the twenty-first century with an array of serious problems but among them two immense challenges stand out: on the one hand, those problems presented by *carbon technologies*, and, on the other hand, those posed by *silicon technologies*. While it may seem that nothing can trump the planetary threat of climate change, in fact both of these challenges involve existential threats and dangers amounting to what is sometimes called 'extinction risk', not least because these two challenges are absolutely inextricable.

What follows is an attempt to outline the stakes of this situation in an age that has come to be known as the Anthropocene. An idea of the conditions within which those stakes are unfolding can be illustrated by juxtaposing two recent official declarations:

1. On 8 October 2018, the Intergovernmental Panel on Climate Change (IPCC) published a special report on *Global Warming of 1.5°C*: the 'Summary for Policymakers' argues for the urgent necessity of aiming to limit global temperature increases to no more than 1.5°C, stating that keeping climate change at or near this limit can today be achieved only if global net anthropogenic CO_2 emissions are reduced by 45% (from 2010 levels) by 2030 and are reduced to zero by 2050, which can be achieved, according to the IPCC, only with rapid, far-reaching and unprecedented transitions in energy, land, urban, infrastructure and industry systems, far beyond what would be possible under the current nationally-stated mitigation ambitions.[357]

2. One month after this declaration by the IPCC, on 5 November 2018, President Xi Jinping of the People's Republic of China (PRC) spoke at the opening of the China International Import Expo in Shanghai, reportedly stating that 'China is a big market of over 1.3 billion people' and that he 'would turn his country of 1.3 billion into global consumers'[358] by increasing imports to USD$45 trillion over the next fifteen years, as well as continuing to pursue economic policies aimed at a correspondingly large increase

in the domestic consumption of *domestically* manufactured consumer products.

The IPCC claims with 'high confidence' that there are 'a wide range of adaptation options that can reduce the risks of climate change'. Furthermore, the PRC shows evidence of understanding the seriousness of global warming and at least some commitment to pursuing climate policies that encourage the development of renewable energy resources, the transition away from fossil fuel-based transport and so on.[359] Despite these positive signals and efforts, we nevertheless believe that throughout the world there is a fundamental disconnection between discourses and policies on *ecology* and discourses and politics on *economics*: can commitments to *large decreases in global carbon emissions* really be maintained while at the same time maintaining commitments to *large increases in global consumption and manufacturing?* We believe that the disconnection if not irreconcilable contradiction between these discourses and commitments ultimately reflects what could be called an *aporia of sustainability.*

In other words, contemporary geopolitics seems marked by the virtual impossibility of finding a viable macroeconomic pathway out of the contradiction between economic imperatives founded on the existing 'perpetual growth' global macroeconomic model and ecological imperatives founded on the discoveries by climate science about the effects of anthropogenic atmospheric emissions. More than that, we contend that the difficulties involved in the attempt to resolve this aporia are greatly exacerbated by technological processes of other kinds, processes presently giving rise to what Bernard Stiegler has recently termed an 'immense regression'.[360]

With respect to the last of these questions, we believe that there is a widespread intellectual and political *blind-spot* about the economic, political, psychological and sociological significance of the vast technological transformation that has unfurled across the past quarter of a century. More specifically, it is today crucial to understand the complex and fundamental ways in which the economic and ecological poles of this aporia of sustainability relate to and are compounded by the transformation of computation, information, network technologies, and the algorithmic technologies that link them all together.[361]

The elimination of this blind-spot should therefore be an urgent priority, and the combination of the aporia of sustainability and the unfolding of a process of immense regression incontestably amounts to a global crisis. If so, then this, like any crisis, calls for a critique, on the basis of which alone it is possible to make good decisions. In that light, what follows can be considered as a preliminary contribution to what we propose calling an 'elemental critique', that is, a new critique of political economy founded on the respective technologies of *carbon* and *silicon*.[362]

On the notion of an 'elemental' critique

Before attempting to identify the content of any such critique, some words concerning the term 'elemental' may be advisable.

1. The focus on 'carbon' and 'silicon' indicates that this is indeed a matter of the crucial place of the sixth and fourteenth atomic elements of the periodic table in the technological transformations of the nineteenth, twentieth and twenty-first centuries, the span of time covered by the so-called Anthropocene era. To this extent, the 'elemental' character of the critique we are proposing means that it does not forget the fundamentally 'material' character of these transformations, even if this is always and everywhere a question of what these materials can be *organized to do* and what they can organize *us to do, in terms of both supporting and undermining the possibility of individual and collective autonomy.*

    We could also relate this notion to Whitehead's account of mathematics as a 'primordial element' in the history of thought that, combined with today's physical understanding, suggests the possibility of 'some new doctrine of organism which may take the place of [...] scientific materialism'.[363] For us, however, this element is not just scientific but technical, and the 'organism' under the microscope is not just organic but, in Stiegler's terms, 'organological'.[364] In the case of silicon technologies, digital and computational technologies have also made it possible to analyse, isolate and manipulate the chemical elements of the periodic table, as well as the genetic elements of which DNA is composed, giving rise to new and powerful technologies combining and recombining these elemental materials in ways that can be both beneficial and monstrous.

2. More importantly, however, by 'elemental' is meant the Aristotelian notion that, for sensible beings, each of the senses has its own 'element'. The distant echo of this can be heard, for instance, in the quotidian English expression according to which those who find themselves in circumstances to which they are very well-suited can be defined as

being 'in their element' (a professional swimmer in a swimming pool, for instance, or a river[365]).

For Aristotle, the element is what suffuses the milieu of a sensible being, *through* which perception operates (in the case of vision, for example, it operates not through light but, more primordially still, through 'the transparent'[366]). This element itself, however, is very difficult for the sensible being to perceive: as Stiegler has often mentioned, Aristotle offers the example of the fish, which, according to Aristotle, 'would not notice that the things which touch one another in water have wet surfaces'.[367]

The element of the fish, water, is so *intimate* to its existence as to escape perceptibility (with the possible exception of the *flying* fish, who may have an *intermittent* experience of this element, in briefly *leaving* it). One of the most recent formulations of this idea by Stiegler is the following:

> A change of technical system always initially entails a disadjustment between this technical system and what Bertrand Gille called the social systems, which had hitherto been 'adjusted' to the preceding technical system, and which had therein formed, *along with it*, an 'epoch' – but where the technical system as such fades into the background, forgotten as it disappears into everydayness, just as, for a fish, what disappears from view, as its 'element', is water.[368]

In the case of the elemental critique being proposed here, this does not mean that we have no *awareness* of the suffusion of carbon and silicon technologies in our surroundings: the thick anthropotechnical film of automobiles, electrically-powered devices, smartphones and internet devices that covers the earth and surrounds our existence is *transparently* obvious to everyone. Rather, what is meant by the quasi-imperceptibility of the element is that there is something about our *entanglement* with these technologies, and in particular with silicon technologies, that we find very difficult either to pinpoint or to grasp.

This is so precisely *because* of this suffusion and because there is no positive prospect of any *disentanglement* (other than through a shift towards some *post*-silicon technologies, which are likely in any case to bear many of the same characteristics as silicon technologies in terms of being digital, networked, algorithmic and so on). Contemporary technologies, and especially silicon technologies, are so difficult to perceive because, although they consist in nothing but external devices (or the possibility of *internal* devices such as those of neurotechnology), they are nevertheless always and constantly *occupying us and within us*, almost *haunting us*. Technics is the spectral element that constitutes 'the transparent' for *noetic* beings: our attention perpetually operates *through* such technologies but is only intermittently attentive *to* such technologies.

3   'Elemental' has a third sense, indicated for instance in Sigmund Freud's description of the fate of microscopic organisms in a petri dish:

An infusorian, therefore, if it is left to itself, dies a natural death owing to its incomplete voidance of the products of its own metabolism. (It may be that the same incapacity is the ultimate cause of the death of all higher animals as well.)[369]

What Freud describes here amounts to the entropic consequences for any kind of being occupying a closed system in which it lacks the means to eradicate the toxicity brought by its own waste products, throwing the system into uncontrollable disequilibrium and ultimately leading to its collapse. In the case of the 'metabolism' with which we are dealing for the 'higher animal' that we ourselves form, a being that in Aristotle's terms is not just sensible but 'noetic', which is to say a *being that knows*, this 'metabolism' is not just biological but fundamentally and irreducibly psychological, sociological and technological.

The 'metabolic' productions of the technical, knowing beings that we ourselves are also contain the possibility of exposing our 'element' to potentially fatal toxicity, when we lose the intergenerationally transmitted capacities of knowledge and care required to take care of life in any particular technical system. But when this becomes a matter of our 'noetic element', the entropic consequences entailed by this 'self-poisoning' are no longer just thermodynamic or biological but psychic and social. All technical systems are localized, but the locality of today's technical system has reached the scale of the biosphere itself (producing what we can call the technosphere): in such circumstances, where there is effectively no 'outside', the risks of toxicity are that much greater.

The division of twenty-first century technologies

Some remarks are necessary about the attempt we are pursuing here to distinguish carbon technologies from silicon technologies. The first is that this is neither an absolute distinction nor an opposition: in the world in which we live today, almost every internal combustion engine that is manufactured for an automobile is also a computer, with the ICE powering the CPU and the CPU governing the rhythms of the pistons and so on. Even more obviously, every digital device is powered by electrical energy, a high proportion of which is produced through carbon combustion of one kind or another.

These specific examples point to a far more general characteristic: just as *we* are inextricably entangled with the technical milieu we have constructed across the entire biosphere, so too are the various kinds of technologies inextricably entangled with each other (and with us), thereby forming what Bertrand Gille called a technical system. It is a 'structural' or synchronic system in the sense that each technical artefact finds its possibility only in relation to a plurality of others which it cannot do without.

The second thing to say is that these names, carbon and silicon, are to some extent an abstraction in the sense that we are creating a very broad categorization that is in some way just a useful fiction. In practice, they could be construed in a more inclusive way as referring to technologies lying outside the strict (atomic) bounds of these 'elemental' characteristics. There exists a complicated relationship between the dominant technologies involved in the technical system of a particular epoch and the form of thinking that is possible in that epoch. Norbert Wiener, writing at the midpoint of the last century, argued that the 'thought of every age is reflected in its technique',[370] and he delineated the shifts of technical system from the eighteenth to the nineteenth to the twentieth centuries in a way that is congruent with the division we are proposing here:

> If the seventeenth and early eighteenth centuries are the age of clocks, and the later eighteenth and the nineteenth centuries constitute the age of steam engines, the present time is the age of communication and control.[371]

Wiener associates the first of these epochs, that of Newton and Huyghens, with the age of navigation made possible by precision instruments, opening up a new scale of maritime commerce based on 'the engineering of the mercantilists', while from the nineteenth century and 'almost to the present time', the Newcomen engine and its heirs would give rise to all those large-scale industries based on thermodynamics and irreversible processes, and most recently the communication age, based on a 'split between the technique of strong currents and the technique of weak currents', has led to a proliferation of electronic instruments opening onto the age of the 'automatic computing machine'.[372] The range of technologies included in each of the very broad categorizations we are describing here is thus quite large. Furthermore, it is always the result of local and historical processes that can both begin and end, where the end is not determined in any teleological way by the beginning, and where there is nothing permanent or eternal about this distinction.

Nevertheless, thirdly, our contention is that, in *this* epoch, an account of these particular abstractions can nevertheless be *fruitful*. In the technical system of the twenty-first century, or at least of its first few decades, it is indeed possible to *make* this distinction between two vast technological categories. For example, *a high proportion of the largest global companies measured by revenue are based on carbon technologies*,[373] while *a high proportion of the largest global companies measured by market capitalization are based on silicon technologies*[374] (these two facts also indicating something about the relationship between the present and the future, as perceived by investors). More than that, it is *necessary* to make this distinction in order to elucidate fundamental questions of political economy that have thus far tended to be avoided in most theoretical or policymaking considerations with respect to the consequences generated by our own metabolic products.

For these reasons, we will now outline what is intended by each of these categorizations respectively, in relation to their genesis, function and fate.

Carbon technologies

Hominims acquired the ability to create and use fire as early as the Lower Palaeolithic and the controlled use of carbon combustion became common in the Middle Palaeolithic. From that moment, the beings that would become ourselves found themselves within a fiery element defined by the capacity for artificial, controllable energy production and consumption founded on the flammability of organic materials. From the moment cooking was invented, this capacity was a matter of the potential to produce and consume energy in order to do work, thereby opening the possibility of 'ways of life', or what Marx called a 'mode of consumption':

the hunger that is satisfied by cooked meat eaten with knife and fork differs from hunger that devours raw meat with the help of hands, nails and teeth.[375]

Both dangerous and beneficial, controllable within the risks of being extinguished or turning wild, this first symbol of technics was also the first object of *care*, long before the Neolithic Revolution. In addition to warmth and cooking, the development of the controlled use of carbon combustion gave rise to other technologies, such as smelting, forging and gunpowder.[376]

But the *modern* history of carbon technologies obviously begins with the invention of heat engines powered by hydrocarbons derived from fossilized organic matter. More specifically, it begins with the external combustion engine, and more specifically still with the industrial (or thermodynamic) revolution that was set off by the steam engine envisaged by the University of Glasgow repairman James Watt, which he patented in 1781 and which was to transform manufacturing and rail and maritime transport throughout the nineteenth century.

In the twentieth century, fossil fuel power plants linked to electricity grids would further vastly transform both production and consumption, and automobiles equipped with internal combustion engines would transform road transport and make possible the rise of global aviation. The combustion of hydrocarbons, however, inevitably releases a significant level of 'metabolic products': while for the ten thousand years prior to the industrial revolution the global atmospheric CO_2 concentration was 280 parts per million, in 2018 it stood at 410 ppm, with annual emissions and concentrations continuing to increase.[377]

Silicon technologies

Turning to the history of silicon technologies, the first integrated circuit was produced in 1958, the first CPU in 1971, the Apple II and Commodore PET home computers entered the market in 1977, the Microsoft Windows 'operating environment' was first released in 1985, the World Wide Web was opened to the general public in April 1993, Amazon was founded in July 1994, the domain name google.com was registered in September 1997, the Tencent and Alibaba conglomerates were founded in 1998 and 1999 respectively, the Facebook social network was made universally open in September 2006 (with active users rising from 100 million in August 2008 to two billion in June 2017), the capacitive multi-touch smartphone known as the iPhone was launched in June 2007 and Uber's mobile app and transport services were officially launched in July 2009.

It is notable that this timeline of significant dates increasingly focuses on *consumer*-based silicon technologies, reflecting the vast entrance of these transformational technologies into the consumer market over the past forty years. It is also notable that we have chosen to end it in 2009, reflecting that the last decade has seen a period of *consolidation and monopolization* of the silicon economy in the hands of a small number of super-giant corporate players.

Today, it has become *transparently* clear to everyone that silicon technologies have transformed *every* aspect of production and consumption,[378] along with scientific and technological research of every kind, and this is especially so in the quarter of a century that has transpired since the internet became public and global. All of this amounts to a vast 'disruption' of the technical system, along with every other psychosocial and institutional system.

This history is obviously familiar, and its facts are moreover available to anyone anywhere with a smartphone and internet access. Compared with the history of carbon technologies, however, which have existed in one form or another for hundreds of thousands of years, the silicon technologies just listed have a history lasting just a few decades. On what basis can this amount to some vast and fundamental division, or does their rapid ascent and ubiquity generate a kind of illusion of exaggerated significance? In fact, silicon technologies must be inscribed into a much older genealogy, even if still not quite as long as the history of the acquisition and use of fire. But this is possible only if we consider these technologies not in terms of their atomic or molecular composition but in terms of their elemental function.

Retentional technologies and the industrial capitalism of production

If the elemental function of carbon technologies fundamentally consists in the production of chemical energy in order that it can then be transformed into mechanical or electrical energy and consumed as work, then the elemental function of silicon technologies fundamentally consists in the production of an artificial *memory* that, too, can be put to work in manifold ways. Silicon technologies are *retentional* technologies (to borrow a term from Husserlian phenomenology). In Stiegler's work, this very long history of retentional technologies (and especially of what he calls *hypomnesic* technologies, those technologies that are *purposely* rather than *accidentally* retentional) has been explored in detail and with respect to a wide variety of dimensions.

If we here prefer to refer to *silicon* technologies – while keeping in mind the mnemotechnical history that extends through cave painting, the invention of writing systems (including alphabetization, which remains an almost unchanged standard from the Roman Empire to the Digital Leviathan), the printing press, the phonograph, the radio, cinema, analogue television and the becoming-digital of everything that we now see unfolding with silicon technologies strictly speaking – if we refer to *silicon* technologies, therefore, it is only because the proliferation of uses, services and functions associated with this latest stage of memory technology seems so greatly to exceed the mere ability to 'record the past'. And yet, this is precisely the basis of all of them.[379]

The industrial revolution whose possibility we previously ascribed to Watt's steam engine could never have occurred without retentional technologies of a kind we have hitherto failed to mention: those technologies by which the complex and continuous gestures of workers of all kinds were broken down analytically into their discrete elements, in order to be then programmed back into machines powered by the heat engines of Watt and his successors: the paradigmatic case of such a machine is *Jacquard's loom*, but a thousand examples could no doubt be cited.

The basis of this analytical process is what Stiegler refers to as 'grammatization', the process of turning something temporal (like speech) into something spatial (like writing), by turning the continuous into the discrete, on the basis of which it can be analysed and reproduced. The noetic, political and economic consequences of grammatization can be to support new forms of knowledge, but grammatization can also lead to what Stiegler calls 'proletarianization' (drawing on Gilbert Simondon's reading of the *Grundrisse*'s 'fragment on machines'). If proletarianization has in traditional Marxist discourse been understood to refer to the systematic separation of workers from the means of production, Stiegler's use of the term draws attention to the way in which those means firstly consist in the *knowledge* possessed by workers and transmitted intergenerationally.

It is this knowledge that is literally removed from the minds of weavers and programmed into Jacquard's loom and a thousand other machines, dispossessing the workers of their knowledge and literally destroying the intergenerational transmission of all manner of skills and crafts. In addition to the ownership of the energy-production capacities of the heat engine, what in fact made the rapid acceleration of the industrial revolution possible was thus the ability of the capitalist to dispossess the worker of the knowledge of how to *make* things, knowledge that was then turned into information and recorded and exploited in the retentional technologies of machines: it is here that the history of industrial automation and artificial intelligence truly begins.

Industrial capitalism based on production thus arises from the concentration of carbon technologies in the hands of capital, but *equally* from the capitalist acquisition of retentional technologies through which workers, systematically dispossessed of knowledge, become labourers, that is, servants of the machine. From this vast process is born that great division between capital and proletarianized labour on the basis of which Marx and Engels would construct a revolutionary politics.

In fact, of course, this founding moment of the industrial revolution was only the first step of a history that would continue through many chapters, including ones that Marx could never have anticipated: one key way in which to understand this set of chapters is as the unfolding of the epochs of grammatization. To pursue this history in terms of the distinction between carbon and silicon, it is worthwhile returning to the recent proclamation by the Chinese president concerning his country's ambition to produce 1.3 billion 'global consumers'.

On the vision of a nation of 1.3 billion 'global consumers'

An issue that has been raised many times by many commentators, with potentially very significant global macroeconomic consequences, is the wage pressure in China that seems bound to result from the enormous rise of Chinese prosperity. This prosperity has been generated by clever and concerted development policies, and by the so-called 'opening up' of China to the world, but what was *primarily* made available through this opening up was the vast army of low-cost labour that China was able to supply to domestic and foreign manufacturers of all kinds. In this way, the consumers of the industrialized democracies became able to purchase low-cost consumer goods, corporations became able to inexpensively mass produce products and thus maintain profitable businesses, and China was able to attract an increasingly large proportion of the global manufacturing sector to the mainland, together driving an economic transformation not just of the economy and society of the PRC but of the whole global economy.

Increasingly of course, and by design, this is not a one-way street: exports *into* China are themselves increasingly profitable for foreign manufacturers, and likewise the enormous rise in Chinese prosperity opens up new opportunities for domestic producers. Hence President

Xi's declaration. His quantification of import levels is of course highly conditional upon global and Chinese economic conditions that could easily and unexpectedly shift (with the vagaries of what is wrongly called the economic 'cycle'). Beyond that, however, China's economic rise inevitably leads to pressure for the *redistribution* of the wealth that has been generated, ultimately including to the millions of subsistence labourers in Chinese factories. As this wage pressure becomes increasingly difficult to resist, even for an economy that is still subject to strong centralized control, the very basis of that *generation* of wealth is potentially threatened.

None of this would in any way count as news for President Xi. But if it is not news, then what is his strategy for dealing with this pressure? What are the implications of his statement that he wants to produce a country of 1.3 billion global consumers, especially given that he is also asserting the PRC's capacity for *long-term* planning, at least compared with the government of his American 'rival' (who could argue?)? It is hard to avoid the conclusion that behind such a pronouncement is the thought that the solution to this dilemma lies in a transformation of manufacturing through which a high proportion of these labourers will become dispensable. In other words, to build this market of global consumers, a very great number of these labourers will, in the medium term at most, need to be replaced, not by some *new* army of cheap human labourers, but by automation and AI, that is, by a process of robotization.

Such a transition obviously implies other questions concerning the need for a new *basis* for redistribution to replace the disrupted wage labour (and welfare) model that has been the engine of the Keynesian model for many decades. Such questions are difficult and fundamental, amounting to the question and the *challenge* of what Stiegler has called 'automatic society': in a world where *labour* requires fewer and fewer human beings to operate machines, what is the future of *work* (where we are thus *distinguishing* work from proletarianized labour, and where it is only the worker and not the labourer who has the possibility of transforming his or her conditions *through* such work) and what is the basis of the distribution of the *income* without which these 'consumers' will be unable to consume?[380] It is ultimately these questions that are implied by the declaration of an intention to create a market of 1.3 billion Chinese global consumers, along with those ecological questions implied by the aforementioned aporia of sustainability.

The vision that lies behind such a declaration, therefore, bears some resemblance to that described by Marx and Engels in *The German*

Ideology: a vision of a society that no longer forces me to constrain my existence to a fixed, limited role in order to subsist, and instead

> makes it possible for me to do one thing today and another tomorrow, to hunt in the morning, fish in the afternoon, rear cattle in the evening, criticise after dinner.[381]

For Herbert Marcuse in 1969, this 'early Marxian example' did indeed sound 'embarrassingly ridiculous', but only because the vision it offers in fact refers to merely 'a stage of the development of the productive forces which has been surpassed'.[382] With 'the development of the productive forces beyond their capitalist organization', he suggests, a transformation may well be accomplished in which the 'quantitative reduction of necessary labor could turn into quality (freedom)' and 'the stupefying, enervating, pseudo-automatic jobs of capitalist progress would be abolished'. But Marcuse argues that this will *also* require a transformation of the noetic beings that we ourselves are: it 'presupposes a type of man with a different sensitivity as well as consciousness'.[383]

Today, this vision might be reinterpreted as one in which the *revolutionary* expansion of automation and artificial intelligence opens up prospects for the emergence of new forms of autonomy (ignoring, for the moment, the question of what it would mean to go 'beyond capitalist organization'). In such an interpretation, it would be as if the technological system becomes a new kind of 'preindividual milieu' (in Simondon's terms), simply supplying the background conditions from out of which, liberated from the enervating toil of proletarianized labour, new noetic beings will crystallize.[384] But in 2018, President Xi's concern does not seem to be with how to produce new forms of autonomy or noesis: by this statement at least, he wants to create neither new kinds of workers nor new kinds of citizens but 'global consumers'. The possibility of raising the latter prospect without considering the former challenge, we argue, is symptomatic of a failure to address the real stakes of silicon technologies in the twenty-first century.

Rising prosperity may well be bound by economic law to lead to rising consumption, but the manner of the correlation is dependent on numerous other factors. In China and Asia generally, for example, there is a well-known tendency to save rather than spend (compared with Western consumers), with overall macroeconomic effects on investment and consumption, not to mention the 'global savings glut' diagnosed by Federal Reserve Chairman Ben Bernanke in 2005, which is to say, a potentially unstable tendency in which savings are favoured too greatly over investment (from the standpoint of the existing macroeconomic model). In short, 'global consumers' are artificial beings, not natural ones: *con*-sumers must be *pro*-duced – they must be *made*.

Protentional technologies and the hyper-industrial capitalism of consumption

The twentieth century can be understood as the age of the global *cinesphere*.[385] The pharmacological (which is to say, both entropic and negentropic) character of this cinesphere can be discerned by conjoining two statements that appear in the first episode of Jean-Luc Godard's *Histoire(s) du Cinéma*: first, that cinema replaces our gaze with a world that conforms with our desires, and second, that for fifty years, in the dark, we burned imagination (that is, libidinal energy) in order to heat up reality.[386]

That consumers must be produced through cinespherical means was precisely the realisation that came to capitalist producers at the beginning of the twentieth century. For Marx, the spread of machines (powered by carbon technologies and programmed by retentional technologies of mechanical grammatization) amongst the capitalist class was bound to make it increasingly difficult for any one capitalist to maintain an edge over others, leading to his diagnosis of a tendency of the rate of profit to fall. Economists ever since have disparaged this analysis, above all on the grounds that it is not what is observed in the economic history that has unfolded since it was described by Marx, 'natural' boom-and-bust 'cycles' notwithstanding. Indeed, this history does not seem to confirm Marx's analysis. But this may be the result less of analytical error than of a fundamental transformation of capitalism resulting *from* this tendency: in short, what Marx could not *imagine* was the development of a capitalist *imagination* capable of solving this dilemma, even if this solution is itself only a *postponement* of this tendency.

The essence of this 'solution' was the realisation that it is possible to create new markets, not just by geographical expansion, but through the possibility of manipulating consumer desire and therefore consumer behaviour. If capitalism is a perpetual economic competition giving rise to perpetual technoscientific innovation, this is not just a matter of R&D and production: it is also a matter of the socialization of that innovation – all those processes through which new products are taken up by consumers, by which they are *adopted*.

The shift to a *hyper-industrial capitalism of consumption* was in part a matter of the new organization of consumption that arose when Henry Ford realised that the wages he was paying to those employed on his assembly lines could in turn be used by them to purchase the very products they were producing. But the large-scale investment required to achieve the productivity gains to be realised from mass production was feasible only if consumer behaviour could be more or less reliably predicted, which is to say, *produced*: for this new consumer market in transport vehicles powered by internal combustion engines to succeed, it was necessary to invent public relations, or in other words, marketing.

As Stiegler has shown on many occasions, this invention was made possible not just by the discovery of this 'idea', but by the development of new forms of grammatization, and specifically the 'grammatization of the sensible' inaugurated with audiovisual technologies such as radio, cinema and television. It is not technological change as such that Marx could not anticipate, but the significance of the new analytical and programming possibilities opened up by these new retentional technologies (Guglielmo Marconi patented his wireless telegraphy system in 1896, Marx having died in 1883). With these powerful new tools that could be used to access and influence the minds of potential consumers on an *industrial scale*, it became possible to completely transform the basis of profit-making in industrial capitalism, by constantly *manufacturing the market* for the new products that could then be constantly introduced and updated.

By accessing consciousness and targeting the unconscious, marketing and its associated technologies and techniques have progressively learned how to make consumer behaviour *controllable*, by interpolating (in the literary sense) tertiary retentions into the stream of consciousness. The basis on which it can do so, however, depends on *reducing* desire as much as possible to a *calculable* phenomenon, which is to say, *grammatizing* the relationship to the future. In other words, this amounts to a grammatization of *protention*, Husserl's term for my immediate expectation, but expanded here to include every form of motive, reason, expectation, dream and desire.

This in turn involves a *detachment* of desire from everything *in*calculable, incomparable and *long*-term (including every form of education and intergenerational transmission), inducing a *regressive* tendency that aims instead only at the finite and short-term goals of the consumer behaviour required by the market. But this ultimately risks being self-destructive for the consumerist model itself, setting up a tendency for the *libidinal* economy (on which the macroeconomic 'perpetual growth model' fundamentally depends) to collapse, as libidinal *energy* is depleted: the ability to stimulate the perpetual increase in consumption required by the consumerist economy is thereby threatened. It is ultimately for this reason (along with the aporia of sustainability) that consumerist capitalism can be nothing but a postponement of Marx's diagnosis with regard to the rate of profit.

Silicon technologies and the ultra-industrial capitalism of algorithmic platforms

The protentional grammatization technologies of the twentieth century had only limited means of accessing the information and data that is necessary in order to calculate and predict the relationship between, firstly, *grammatized content* (for example, a television commercial that, in Husserl's terms, amounts to a kind of *industrial* temporal object), secondly, *protentional conditioning*, and thirdly, *consumer behaviour*: the clearest indicator was ultimately the success or otherwise of a marketing campaign. But with the introduction of silicon technologies that now dominate the twenty-first century, this question is fundamentally transformed, because the consumers of such grammatized content are ceaselessly and immediately sending data *back* to producers. On the basis of such data, producers can ever more finely calculate the relationship between particular content and particular responses from particular 'kinds' of users.

The extreme speeds at which these processes occur in contemporary algorithmic silicon systems means that it is also possible for these producers to *adjust* content in a very rapid and targeted way that was simply impossible in the twentieth century. This speed *exceeds* that of noetic processes themselves, and this rapid exchange and algorithmic control of vast amounts of user data gives rise to a kind of informational and protentional shock wave, analogous at the noetic level to the 'sonic boom' produced at flight speeds above Mach 1.[387]

Every major consumer platform today utilizes ultra-powerful algorithmic techniques of this kind in order to absolutely maximize their ability to performatively influence consumer behaviour. Furthermore, global 'platforms' such as Alphabet and Facebook are now among the largest corporations on the planet and have become so through the *new market* they have created for the vast amounts of data generated by their users.

If the capitalism of analogue audiovisual technologies was already hyper-industrial and performative (in Austin's sense), then the new market of platform capitalism based on silicon technologies, user profiling and social networking is *highly* performative and can thus be considered an *ultra-industrial capitalism of algorithmic platforms*.[388] But this only intensifies the deleterious effects of such processes on the libidinal economy of consumers. And this in turn is bound to intensify the self-destructive tendencies of the consumerist macroeconomy, since it ruins the very basis of its 'success': the control of desire.

The anti-politics of ultra-industrial populism in the Entropocene

Behind this highly paradoxical intention to *produce consumers* lies the even more paradoxical belief that this mass of consumers can continuously drive the engine of the global economy like a perpetual motion machine, and drive it to new heights. But perpetual motion is a myth based on the notion of an abstract machine that is *thermodynamically impossible*, and the 'heights' to be reached are in this case transparently at odds with the unambiguous imperatives declared by the IPCC. But in addition to that, the billions upon billions of bytes of data gathered from consumers by producers and platforms, fed into increasingly powerful and increasingly intelligent automated algorithms designed to calculate and control behaviour according to the imperatives not of the IPCC but *solely of the market*, has an extremely *ruinous* effect on the psyches of the individual consumers of whom this market is composed (who are today targeted almost from *birth*, if not from before birth), giving rise as it does to an infernal spiral of consumerist addiction.

Evidence abounds throughout the industrialized democracies of the political consequences towards which this ruination tends. And these consequences are intensified by the fact that all these performative techniques are applied also in the *political* realm. If, as Stiegler suggests, this entails the replacement of the adoptive performativity of 'democracy' with the adaptive performativity of 'telecracy',[389] where the *demos* no longer finds itself in possession of any *kratos*, then the algorithmicization of this telecracy via the silicon technologies of platform capitalism is already exposing the utter vulnerability of 'representational' political systems to a thoroughgoing disintegration at the hands of the 'owners' of this data and the manipulators of these algorithms.

This can be described as an *ultra-industrial political regression* (a new form of what is often called 'populism') to which ultra-industrial capitalism tends to give rise. But regardless of the degree to which the leading industrial populists imagine they can cynically keep hold of the reins of power as they exploit the fears and irrationality of the crowd, the enormous risk that they are precipitating is of hubristically engendering processes that will completely run out of all control. All of this is what first began to get going with the shift from an industrial capitalism of production to a hyper-industrial capitalism of consumption a century ago, for which the immensely destructive wars of the twentieth century stand as testament, and it is all this that *remains* at stake in the wish to create a society of global consumers in an ultra-industrial capitalism of algorithmic platforms.

On crystallization and crystal palaces

For Marcuse, as we have already mentioned, the reduction of the need for labour made possible by automation opens up the prospect of a new age of autonomy. Such autonomy, however, is by no means a guaranteed outcome: it 'presupposes a type of man with a different sensitivity as well as consciousness'. Marcuse himself describes what this means only rather abstractly as involving a 'union between causality by necessity and causality by freedom', which he problematically understands in terms of an 'instinctual transformation'.[390]

In Simondonian terms, we might say that, in the age of silicon technologies, the invention of a new noetic milieu is in principle *entirely* possible (and, what's more, that there is no future for knowledge, understood in the broadest possible sense, *other than through* silicon technologies, all knowledge always being a possibility for noetic beings that is only ever opened up *intermittently, technically, retentionally and protentionally*). But this possibility of a new noetic *element* is realisable only provided that the arrangement between the technical and the psychosocial is re-organized so as to *foster* (rather than undermine) psychic and collective individuation processes giving rise to the new sensitivity and consciousness (new noesis) for which Marcuse calls.

Simondon's first, 'physical' model for the emergence of individuation from out of a preindividual milieu is the way that crystals emerge from out of a parent liquid possessing just the right molecular composition for a process of crystallization to be catalysed by a germ. But as the artist Robert Smithson pointed out (via the work of the physicist Percy Bridgman), the crystals produced by this process run counter to the commonly-held layman's conception of entropy as always leading from states of order to states of disorder:

> But I think nevertheless, we do not feel altogether comfortable at being forced to say that the crystal is the seat of greater disorder than the parent liquid.[391]

The crystal *seems* to be *organized*, because it appears to our eyes to be order*ly*. In fact, as a perfectly ordinary thermodynamic process, it complies with the 'arrow of time' and corresponds to a lower state of potential energy: the *regularity* of the crystal gives rise to the *illusion* of what only seems to be counter-entropic organization.

Genuinely counter-entropic processes are possible at the biological and noetic levels – even if these counter-entropic tendencies, too, can only ever be *localized* and *temporary*. For exosomatic beings, such processes depend on the accumulation of past noetic wealth, the improbable memory of which they cultivate and transform in order to maintain the rich cohesion of a particular locality on a particular scale, and to produce new improbable futures.

Contemporary disruption and regression are, however, precisely a kind of illusion of counter-entropy of the sort produced at the molecular level by crystallization. This is not just a question of the crystal palaces of industrial capitalism but also of the silicon crystal palaces that form the exo-techno-cine-spherical tertiary layers of algorithmic and ultra-industrial capitalism. They may be highly ordered and regularized, but beneath this deceptive surface they are thoroughly entropic for noetic processes, precisely because they fail to cultivate and draw upon this wealth of knowledge, instead destroying it and replacing it with the dictates of the market of calculable information.

For Smithson, writing in the 1960s and 1970s, it was a question of thinking thermodynamic entropy beyond the pleasure principle:

> There's a certain kind of pleasure principle that comes out of a preoccupation with waste. Like if we want a bigger and better car we are going to have bigger and better waste productions. So there's a kind of equation there between the enjoyment of life and waste. Probably the opposite of waste is luxury.[392]

Smithson's raising of the question of entropy also extended beyond the relationship between thermodynamics and the death drive already suggested by Freud. Hence his call for an 'attempt to formulate an analog between "communication theory" and the ideas of physics'.[393] Unfortunately, how far he may have been led by these speculations will remain forever unknown, thanks to his untimely death in a plane crash in 1973.

Reinventing economics as the science of counter-entropic struggle in exosomatization

Carbon technologies are thermodynamic: their function is to contribute to the struggle of noetic, technical (that is, exosomatic) life against its irreducible entropic conditions. But in utilizing these technologies to pursue anti-entropic ends, and given that all negentropic systems are *localized* systems that are bound to remain entropic in an *overall* sense, we inevitably produce entropic consequences *elsewhere*. And when those systems have extended across the entire biosphere, cinesphere, technosphere and exosphere, then this 'elsewhere' remains precisely *here*, and the toxicity they produce is unavoidably self-poisoning, ruining its biospheric element just as does the infusorian in Freud's petri dish.

Silicon technologies are informational: their function, too, is to contribute to the struggle of exosomatic life against its irreducible entropic conditions. But in this case, the toxicity they produce pollutes not the biosphere but the noetic element of the knowing, technical beings who must nevertheless find the noetic *resources* to address *all* of these self-poisonings, whether carbonic or noetic, and to do so by *making good collective decisions*. It is this *division* between two kinds of entropic toxicity, and the necessity of recognizing the *gravity* of informational entropy, that we here seek to highlight.

Most economic theory (like most philosophy) has, to its detriment, remained rooted in a mechanistic physical conception that predates the discovery of the second law of thermodynamics, at least if we believe the economic historian Philip Mirowski.[394] This means that economic systems are not truly viewed as dynamic processes in perpetual struggle against entropic tendencies but are instead understood as involving one or another kind of static or cyclical equilibrium making possible the fantasy of perpetual growth.

From the work of the physicist Erwin Schrödinger, the mathematical biologist Alfred J. Lotka and the economist Nicholas Georgescu-Roegen, however, it becomes possible to see biological (endosomatic) evolution as precisely involving manifold processes amounting to so many struggles against entropy, where these struggles are always localized – at the scale of the cell, the organism, the species, the ecosystem or the biosphere. And it also becomes possible to see that *economic* processes are what replace these evolutionary tendencies when life becomes technical (exosomatic), still always localized – at the scale of the tribe, ethnic group, society, nation or global economic system.

Mirowski's work has focused largely on the history of economics in the twentieth and twenty-first centuries, and more specifically on the way in which the history of neoliberalism has interacted both with the notion of information and with the integration of computation into economic theory and practice.[395] From Hayek's argument in 1945 that the 'decentralized' market makes better use of knowledge in society than do 'centralized' authorities and bureaucracies, the history of neoliberalism has amounted to the history of the notion of 'the market' as a vast 'information processor'. In the unfolding of this history, the market-*qua*-information-processor is found by neoliberal economists to depend less and less on the 'rational agents' of neoclassical economics, as the concept of (economic) knowledge is reduced more and more to calculable information that may escape the level of the individual altogether.

In turn, economists take advantage of this conception by redefining their function less as scientists and advisers and more as engineers and designers of markets, whether the market is being designed to facilitate the sale of the electromagnetic spectrum, to mitigate carbon emissions or to find market-based solutions for the market-induced problems of the global financial crisis.[396] This, however, entails a contradiction: setting out from an idea of 'the Market' as the best and most efficient guarantor of correct outcomes, if not as a transcendental and universal processor of truth, neoliberal economists then start to manufacture diverse and specific markets. But the good outcomes promised by the purveyors of these markets (in competition with purveyors of other markets) absolutely depend on the initial conditions set by economists, who are able to do so, they claim, thanks to their 'expertise', which they then market to governments, institutions and other economic actors, including at the highest levels, arguing that this is the only way to ensure positive outcomes, since there is no such thing as the market *itself*.

The contradiction is thus between an absolutized, 'universal' conception of 'the Market' and a localized (but still informational and computational) conception of specific but highly artificial markets, where the assertion of this universality in fact ends up authorizing the elimination of the wealth of actual knowledge embodied in institutions of exchange of all kinds. Furthermore, the *consumer* market, as we have already seen, is *premised* upon *systemically* depriving these consumers of knowledge in a way absolutely at odds with the conception of an economy of 'rational actors' contributing to some market-based information processor. Mirowski's work makes clear that the dangerous turn of recent macroeconomic history – characterized by neoliberalism, financial crisis and proletarianization (in Stiegler's sense) – has everything to do with the failure of economic theory to incorporate an understanding of entropic and counter-entropic processes, at both the thermodynamic and informational levels. The implicit question it raises is how to reinvent economic theory and practice by incorporating such an understanding from its founding premises.

For a general theory of entropy

This in turn raises the question of the necessity of a *theory of general entropy*. Such a theory would on the one hand seek to juxtapose and articulate the thermodynamic notion of entropy with the informational notion, and to exceed the limitations especially of the latter.[397] And it would also be in this way an account of the relationship between every kind of counter-entropic system, which is to say every kind of *localization and de-localization* process that *works against* the tendency towards the elimination of improbabilities, which is to say the elimination of the past (as what, for any noetic system, opens the possibility of a *future*). But as Smithson's association of entropy with both waste and *luxury* already suggests, this also bears upon Georges Bataille's 'notion of expenditure' and 'general economy' (not forgetting that for Bataille, expenditure beyond subsistence is not a question merely of waste but of an irreducible necessity *of life*).

What this implies, ultimately, is that any such theory is compelled to integrate difficult mathematical, scientific, economic, anthropological and technological questions with others that exceed these divisions between fields of knowledge, in the first place because what is at stake is the counter-entropic function of knowledge itself. Stiegler has indeed begun a project to open up this question of entropy in terms of its thermodynamic, biological, informational and noetic dimensions (in all of its 'exorganological' dimensions, in Stiegler's recent terms), drawing on the work of Vernadsky, Georgescu-Roegen and Lotka, among others, and in discussion with scientists such as Giuseppe Longo, but in truth it is extraordinarily complex and requires large-scale transdisciplinary contributory research projects to be established involving scholars across a wide variety of fields. Despite this apparent daunting complexity, it is the conclusion of this 'elemental critique of political economy' that, in the context of the Anthropocene, such a theory of general entropy has today become an urgent necessity.

Why is such a theory necessary? Because what is ultimately at stake in the complex field that is unfolding between carbon technologies and silicon technologies in the *Entropocene* is the need to completely reinscribe old values in new terms, where values are what supply the criteria on the basis of which decisions are taken and resources invested in order to generate *wealth* (as distinct from narrowly calculable economic 'value' or 'prosperity'). Investment must here be understood in every sense and in a *general* sense as that 'putting in reserve' – that *work* – that alone is capable of opening the possibility of another future. Every question of investment is in this way a question of struggling to differ and defer entropy *in general*, in the movement of what Derrida called différance (but where this is also a differentiation beyond the limits of Derrida's formulation).

In a context in which the globalized systems of consumerist capitalism are reaching their limits, and in the process dragging many other systems past their limits, including geophysical systems such as the climate system, and also including the noetic systems through which alone good collective decisions can ever hope to be made – in such a context, where a cascade of catastrophic system failures seems entirely possible if not highly probable, it is solely on the basis of such a theory that counter-entropic investment prospects with the potential to bifurcate away from such a globally dangerous and monstrous situation can be identified, imagined, invented and *realised*. Such a bifurcation, and the general theory on which it can be established, will presuppose a reconsideration of the very basis and division of fields of knowledge, but it will also require a complete reorganization of silicon technologies at least as profound as the elimination of carbon technologies called for by the IPCC, and on a comparably short timespan.

For a new critique of global governance

Finally, for all the seeming 'straight talking' by the IPCC, it remains captive to the institutional conditions it is compelled to occupy. If the questions raised by this body concern not just scientific understanding but policy and action (in relation to which the term 'mitigation' is entirely inadequate), then this too is a question of the conditions of making good collective decisions. In truth, if the IPCC is to be something other than a diarist of the downfall, then it (or some related body) cannot avoid the question of the relationship between policy recommendations and the *conditions* of actual decision-making and actual transformation (or 'transition'), including the conditions of will, belief and expectation, or alternatively of apathy and nihilism. In that case, it is also obvious that the question of the future of the noetic element cannot avoid confronting the question of the future of international decision-making, and vice versa – the question, precisely, of the wealth and diversity of *elemental* conditions required for neganthropic choices to be made and actions to be taken.

The United Nations is a body composed of a General Assembly whose individual autonomous members have a commitment to addressing the issues of carbon technologies that can be described as patchy at best, and subject to a Security Council with even less resolve, not least because of the economic *fear* generated by the aporia of sustainability. This General Assembly and Security Council are themselves premised on the sovereignty of nation-states, whose political systems, whether representative or otherwise, are entirely subject to what we have called 'telecratic' tendencies. Furthermore, what ecologists and the IPCC must not avoid reckoning with, without denying the processes of psychosocial and economico-institutional denial that are also clearly operative, is the possibility that the fear generated by the aporia of sustainability is in many ways *legitimate*, and that this fear is itself a very significant threat in terms of the possibility of becoming a *panic*, even if it is also true that the paralysing consequences of such fear and panic in turn catastrophically seal the fate of the biosphere.

In short, it is a question of the possibility of dealing noetically with the aporia of sustainability. But the fact is that this society of nations is *also* composed of members almost *none* of whom have *any* effective analyses or policies with respect to silicon technologies that reflect any true weighing of the stakes of the immense transformations such technologies have wrought and are continuing to bring. Yet these technologies are well on the way to destroying the local conditions for the flourishing of noetic and exosomatic life (at all scales of locality), just as carbon technologies are well on the way to destroying the local conditions for the flourishing of biological and endosomatic life (at all scales of locality).

What this ultimately suggests is that a critique of the political economy of silicon technologies cannot avoid a critique of the character and institutions of decision-making at every level of locality from the sub-national to the international and global, as well as of the elemental conditions in which they operate. And the purpose of such a critique can only be the reformulation and reconstruction of these institutions and bodies on the basis of new values legitimating new criteria for investment to be derived from the kinds of considerations whose first steps we have tried to outline in this paper, and whose ultimate basis must lie in a theory of general entropy and counter-entropy. For in the case of international governing and advising bodies such as the IPCC and the United Nations, these organizations, too, form a sometimes almost imperceptible aspect of the global element.

6 Psychic and Collective Anaphylaxis: For an Organological Critique of Sovereignty

Prefatory remarks taking account of the current context

This chapter, like the others of which this book is comprised, was written prior to the SARS-CoV-2 pandemic that has brought a vast and rapid change to the entire global political and economic landscape. It has also exposed the enormous risk that has been run for decades by the unfettered progression of what Bernard Stiegler calls generalized proletarianization, leading to the so-called 'post-truth' era characterized by a loss of belief, faith and trust in every form of authority and knowledge, and afflicting populations, the news industry and governments. At the time of writing, the full cost of this risk remains unknown, but, a century after the flu pandemic and the efforts to form a league of nations that occurred in the aftermath of the First World War, the globalized technosphere is today vastly more complex and sophisticated, and perhaps therefore more *fragile and susceptible*, than was the case in 1918 or 1920. Suffice it to say that a concatenation of unpredictable events has every chance of unfolding in a descending spiral that could end in global economic catastrophe, leading the 'final and greatest bubble in history' to burst, and in turn making much more probable all manner of other catastrophes.

Hopefully such a spiral ending in global depression and war can be averted through collective efforts that draw upon the noetic and cultural resources that human civilizations have accumulated, maintained and transformed across millennia. What seems clear is *firstly* that this pandemic event amounts to the greatest ever test of those resources on a global scale, in a situation where the quality and speed of decision-making is paramount, and *secondly* that the industrial democracies of the West have proven themselves to suffer from a perpetual and underreactive lateness of reason and decision-making. Not only were the countries of Europe and North America slow to act, but the decisions they eventually made were less wise and less rational, it seems, than those made by Eastern nations, for reasons that have everything to do with the fact that the Western virtues of 'freedom' and 'democracy' have shown themselves over half a century to be highly vulnerable to corrosive infection by, firstly, the analogue mass media, and, secondly, algorithmic platform capitalism.

It is precisely such a constitutive lateness that is thematized in this chapter, which argues that for reasons more general than viral pandemics, the feverish speed and danger of contemporary technological transformation forces us to confront the fact that our models and institutions of collective decision-making are afflicted by a dangerous tendency to *lag*. What SARS-CoV-2 shows is both that viral formation operates more quickly than human transformation, and that viral transmission in the age of mass global transportation tends to (but does not necessarily) operate more quickly than the transmission of knowledge capable of taking care of the risks posed by that transmission, and that this exacerbates the dangers of both underreaction and overreaction. As economies collapse, and as overreactive and scapegoating resentments build between one civilization (or 'self-propagating supersystem') and another, then, in the absence of prophylactic treatments, this anaphylactic danger is bound to reach extreme levels.

Ultimately, all these problems stem from an inability of current models of decision-making and political economy to conceive the relationship between all scales of locality, from the individual organism to the family, the tribe, the ethnic region, the nation, the civilization and finally that global locality that is the anthropized (that is, technicized) biosphere – it is precisely this insufficiency that is exposed by the SARS-CoV-2 pandemic, which has shown beyond all doubt the irreducibility of the question of borders, their necessity and their necessary *porosity*. For that reason, despite the fact that the animating questions here concern the significance of the (only slightly) longer-term ecological crisis with which the planet remains confronted, and despite the fact that it has not been rewritten to take into account more recent developments, it turns out that the 'biological' themes of immunity, auto-immunity and anaphylaxis pursued in this chapter have a more than metaphorical significance with respect to the global crisis that is currently unfolding.

What we are up against

As ever, it is worth knowing what we are up against before deciding which assumptions to keep and which to challenge, which forms of 'common sense' or orthodoxy to throw out or reinforce, or which scale of problems to try to think through. For that, a necessary if not sufficient starting point is a cursory examination of the progression of the rate of carbon dioxide emissions into the atmosphere,[398] of the distribution of those emissions by region of the world,[399] and by type of fuel.[400] What such an examination makes apparent is that, whatever strategies are being adopted, whatever claims are being made that the climate problem is eminently solvable, whatever reassurances are being given about future progress, the fundamental fact is that emissions have continued to increase at an accelerating rate, where the only real – albeit brief – deceleration was the result not of any rational amelioration strategy but of the unplanned and nearly catastrophic global financial crisis of 2008. The recent claims by the UK to be planning to adopt a 'net zero' emissions policy to be achieved by 2050 are the latest in this series of non-claims and non-solutions.

What we are confronted with, therefore, amounts to a *constitutive and systemic underreaction to a real emergency*. The more or less continuous acceleration of the rate of CO_2 emissions, in the context of the increasingly dire predictions of the IPCC and the short deadline they insist is necessary if we are to prevent the worst case scenarios, should be enough to give pause to those intellectuals and academics who would like to dismiss, as either 'utopian' or 'apocalyptic' – that is, as 'unrealistic' – attempts to face this crisis by considering the necessity for systemic transformation at the planetary scale...that is, a real dream of revolutionary transformation (the question being what 'realism' and 'revolution' really mean today and in this context).

To open the question of planetary-scale transformation, not just of the use of energy technologies but politically, culturally and so on, is to enter into a kind of madness, since it seems to be entering the zone of some absolute impossibility. But if continuing the current path without changing direction inevitably heads towards catastrophe, then it itself depends on the rise and persistence of new forms of unreason and insanity, amounting to a situation that Leo Strauss described as 'retail sanity and wholesale madness'.[401] And it becomes crazy *not* to open alternatives, however highly improbable they may appear or be (within the limits of our protentional finitude): there is no alternative but to consider alternatives that seem to be impossible, and therefore mad. It is for this reason that I asked in the second chapter:

> Is there a madman who, by dint of an uncommon willingness to peer more deeply into the shadowy parts of our collective souls, can illuminate these tenebrous sources [of rising madness], and so aid in re-orienting our disorientation?[402]

I then discussed two madmen who try to propose another response to the current apocalyptic path, and we can both recapitulate and extend that discussion a little further now.

Theodore Kaczynski, who since his capture and conviction has continued to write from his prison cell, does not doubt that 'modern society is heading for disaster', and he conceives the nations and civilizations of which it is composed as 'self-propagating systems' engaged in perpetual competition. But he concludes that, faced with planetary systemic limits, these self-propagating systems, which have now formed into massive supersystems that tend to eliminate smaller systems, will fail to ensure their own survival, for two reasons: (1) in this perpetual competition at the limit of the global system, short-term exigencies will conflict with long-term strategies, and so such supersystems will tend to 'rationally' decide to act against their own long-term survival interests; (2) all attempts at 'rational human control' of such self-propagating systems have failed, to a significant extent simply because of the great difficulty of anticipating future developments of complex systems, whether internally or in external relation to other complex systems. The terrorist's ultimate conclusion from these arguments is thus strictly logical: if all life depends on the biosphere, and the technosphere that now lies across its entire surface is bound to lead to its destruction, then there is no choice but to destroy this global technical system, even at the cost of destroying human collective decision-making systems as a whole.[403]

On 29 January 2008, which means, after the first indications of the coming global financial crisis but before it became 'full blown', Peter Thiel, member of the PayPal mafia, Facebook investor, and devotee of René Girard's theory of mimetic desire, responded to the feeling of wholesale madness from the perspective of the investor, or the speculator, that is, one who purports to calculate risk in relation to the economic future. While he acknowledged the great risks and injuries that accompany globalization and its hegemony of calculation, he argued that 'the real alternative to good globalization is world war', and that 'all versions of anti-globalization are incoherent'. Hence he concludes that there are 'no good investments in a twenty-first century where globalization fails', and therefore that 'investors have no choice but to bet on globalization'.[404] This is so, even though 'the line between good and bad (or no) globalization is very thin', and hence 'catastrophic approximations abound', and even though 'the competition close to the core of "globalization" may become military' and 'may run into a version of the apocalypse'.

Thiel thus argues in January 2008 that the great financial bubbles of recent times (the 'China bubble', the 'technology bubble', the 'hedge fund bubble') may be less irrational than they at first appear. On the one hand, bubbles involve a 'serious miscalculation about the true probability of successful globalization', because, like Kaczynski, he sees the limits of the ability to forecast or control the unfolding of highly complex processes: 'the greatest uncertainties about the future of the world have involved questions about the rate and the nature of globalization'. On the other hand, futures in which globalization fails end badly for all investments, and from this fact a 'rational' tendency forms, which is rational despite and because it consists in *over-investing* in possible futures where globalization succeeds, and thus Polanyi's great transformation (which Thiel calls the Great Boom) is either 'not a bubble at all' or 'it is the final and greatest bubble in history'. But by April 2009, by which time the bubble had definitively burst, Thiel perceives a world in which financial crisis is 'facilitated by a government that insured against all sorts of moral hazards', a government that had forgotten the invigorating and dynamic effect of real 'Schumpeterian "creative destruction"', leading Thiel to a conclusion regarding the powerlessness of politics that is identical to the Unabomber's, even if reached by a diametrically opposed path:

> I no longer believe that politics encompasses all possible futures of our world. In our time, the great task for libertarians is to find an escape from politics in all its forms – from the totalitarian and fundamentalist catastrophes to the unthinking demos that guides so-called 'social democracy'.[405]

It is on this basis that Thiel goes on to declare his faith in the transhumanist solutionism of *cyberspace disruption*, outer space *colonization* and the legal and political vacuums opened up by *seasteading*, intensifying the power of the technosphere against the uselessness of the political and especially 'democratic' realms. Like Kaczynski, then, Thiel has lost all faith in modern collective decision-making processes as a means of stabilizing systemic relationships, but the prescription he ultimately favours, which consists in maximizing globalization and minimizing its governance, is diametrically opposed to the Unabomber's willingness to eliminate both.

In the madness of globalized ecotechnics, can anyone but a madman avoid denial?

Why these two figures? Because neither of them are in denial about (1) the scale of today's problems and the planetary character of the risks they entail, (2) the systemic character of these problems and risks, or (3) the fact that the *question* raised by these planetary-scale problems and risks concerns a globalized technical system inseparably tied to a globalized economic system. In other words, they understand, more or less, the scale of the problem raised by what, in 1993, which is to say prior to the opening of the World Wide Web that would vastly deepen and transform this process, Jean-Luc Nancy had already called 'ecotechnics':

> The economy can no longer be represented as an 'infrastructure'. There is no longer an economy. Rather, there is *ecotechnics*, the global structuration of the world as the reticulated space of an essentially capitalist, globalist, and monopolist organization that is monopolizing the world.[406]

Globalization can thus be characterized as the inextricably economic and technological (ecotechnical) unfolding of a planetary process of monopolization, today (after 1993) including those functional monopolies that are also the 'functional sovereignties'[407] of platform capitalism (where we can in fact define functional sovereignty as a destruction of the function of the sovereignty of what Stiegler calls higher complex exorganisms).

If we do not wish to participate in the dismissals and denials of ordinary madness, and if we do not wish to resort to the extraordinary madness that would simply *accelerate* destruction, either in the name of *globalized anti-ecotech terrorism* or in the name of *globalized pro-ecotech disruption*, then the issue at stake can only be to find another relationship to these globalizing ecotechnical processes, which is to say their transformation. It then becomes a question of what systems need to be transformed for today's global crises to be able to be addressed, in what way they need to be transformed, and how it is possible to set out in a direction that increases the likelihood of such a transformation.

The systems that *most* obviously need to be transformed are the economic and industrial systems, given their direct responsibility for so many elements of contemporary crisis by virtue of the consumerist perpetual growth model that virtually guarantees a constant rise in energy production and the pollutants associated with that production. But when we observe the worldwide failure of will, at all levels of the population, in the face of this 'extinction risk', and the corresponding rise of suspicion about *all* claims to knowledge, authority and reason that has come to be called the 'post-truth age', we are drawn to a less obvious but perhaps more fundamental answer: what needs to be transformed are the systems influencing and undermining individual and collective motivation and belief. Despite their open acknowledgment of the scale of risk we currently face, what neither Kaczynski nor Thiel can offer is any insight into the existential character of our contemporary crisis, which is also to say the degree to which it is precisely a matter of the destruction of the possibility of 'ek-sistence' as such.

Today, it is the global system of digital networks that plays the greatest systematic role in this influencing, this undermining and this destruction. Digital networks form the engine of the consumerist perpetual growth model by making possible the algorithmic exploitation of the libidinal economy of every individual in order to drive ever more intensive consumer behaviour. In the pursuit of the aims of this consumerist perpetual growth model, these networks are depleting the capacities for long-term thinking and caring required for dealing with *any* systemic crisis, which is reflected in the fact that, in their *current* form, they are leading to the reign of suspicion, doubt and uncertainty in all areas of knowledge and decision-making. If it is true that Thiel and Kaczynski are not in denial about the scale of these ecotechnical challenges, nevertheless they both fail to address these *existential* and *systemic* questions of the relationship between always *localized* systems and the function of knowledge and desire in the operation of those systems.

The internation from 1920 to 2020

In other words, what must be addressed are the entropic characteristics of the industrial-economic system, and the entropic characteristics of the systems of desire and knowledge – these latter systems, *too*, being wholly industrial. These are the conclusions that follow from Stiegler's philosophy, and it is for this reason that he has far more to tell us about the character of our present predicament than the pro-ecotech and anti-ecotech madmen we have examined thus far, who are above all *symptoms* of this globalized ecotechnical process. Ecotechnics, taken as a general convergent tendency, can neither be simply denounced nor celebrated, and to do either is already to begin to seek a scapegoat: what matters is how well we socialize or fail to socialize the relationship between technics and economics.

In recent works, this concern with localized systems at the planetary and sub-planetary scale has led Stiegler to call for a revival and reinterpretation of a concept introduced by Marcel Mauss in 1920: the *internation*. In 'The Internation and Internationalism', a title that refers to Mauss's own 'La nation et l'internationlisme',[408] Stiegler has argued that Mauss's neologism is a precise articulation of these issues concerning locality and globalization, framed in terms of the future of the relationship between the national scale and the international scale:

> What in Mauss barely amounts to a thesis, outlined in a paragraph entitled 'L'internationalisme' in which he makes the case for an internation where nations would co-individuate and transindividuate (if we can consider it in Simondonian terms), must be reconsidered starting from the question of what we should apprehend as constituting this neganthropy

> [...]. It then becomes possible to imagine the program of a new critique of political economy that would be based above all on a reconsideration of work as insoluble into labour or employment, inasmuch as work projects itself *beyond the fact of proletarianization* leading to the automation described in the *Grundrisse* as the constitution of vast automatons. The latter are, however, condemned to become *closed systems*, [...] to contribute further to the increase in the rate of entropy (by anthropization), an increase that lies at the root of the problem of the Anthropocene era.
>
> Such a reconsideration of economics [...] obviously poses a major problem for Marxist-style proletarian internationalism, given that negative entropy, as well as negative anthropy, or neganthropy, can occur only within localities.[409]

But to take up Mauss's concept of the 'internation' as referring to the necessity of producing, through a new critique of political economy, a new neganthropic relationship between the national level and the international level, is also to acknowledge that there is an unavoidable need to address transformational questions at the political level and the institutional level, or in other words at the level of political institutions, and more particularly still, *sovereign* institutions. What then did Mauss himself intend with this idea, how should we interpret Stiegler's call to revive it, and to what problem can it constitute a response today?

Internation, then, is the name Mauss gives to a new way of conceiving the relationship between different scales of political institution – the national scale and the international scale – implying some 'third way' beyond either a nationalist 'localism' or an internationalist 'universalism', preserving the notion of locality while acknowledging that no process of territorialization exists without a corresponding process of deterritorialization, with the consequence that, today, localization can be strongly delocalized. And Mauss seems to combine the *socialist's future-oriented interest in reinventing the apparatus of collective decision-making* with the *anthropologist's past-oriented interest in the wealth of cultural life* (Mauss being both an anthropologist and a socialist), that is, with the functional richness of localized knowledge, and the possibility of either strengthening or weakening this noetic soil, grounded in what Stiegler will call the noetic necromass.

In a set of texts on the nation and internationalism dating from around 1920, then, Mauss was preoccupied with the relationship between scales of localities and the consequences of this relationship for the future of international relations after the First World War.

For Mauss, not all localities are the same, and those 'institutions of institutions' whose tasks include 'establishing and enforcing social norms' (as Jean Terrier puts it) are what he mostly calls 'states', but where the ability to establish and enforce these norms derives from an 'extrinsic' relationship to an exteriority such as a religious or cosmic order.[410] We can thus understand 'states' in Mauss as more or less corresponding to what Stiegler calls higher complex exorganisms, as distinct from lower complex exorganisms such as a factory or an institution, which rely upon a higher complex exorganism for access to the criteria through which such norms are formed and maintained. Only such higher complex exorganisms possess the character of being able to access such criteria directly, through a directly extrinsic relationship, so to speak.

But at the same time, this extrinsic relationship is also the basis for a differentiation between states and nations, or societies and nations: for Mauss, not all states or all societies rise to the level of nations, and in his estimation, in fact, very few have done so throughout history. A nation necessarily entails a 'system of legislation and administration', as well as the notion of rights and duties of the citizen and of the *patrie*, but these 'beautiful flowers' of human civilization and progress remain rare and fragile, as he puts it in 'La nation et l'internationalisme'.[411] For nations, the in principle applicability of these rights and duties to all is established, which presupposes the formalization of law – the writing of the law and the literacy of a public capable of reading it, of interpreting it, and, when necessary, of transforming it. But for this, formalization is a necessary but not a sufficient condition. Hence in a contemporaneous text, Mauss defines the nation as a

> society materially and morally integrated, with a stable and permanent central power, with determinate borders, whose inhabitants possess a relative moral, mental and cultural unity and consciously adhere to the state and its laws.[412]

Terrier highlights that with this understanding of the nation, Mauss is contesting two other ways in which the nation could be and has been conceived. For nationalists, the nation is a cultural phenomenon, a set of existing traditions transmitted from the past, leading to the fetishization of national culture and legitimating a politics based on defending against threats to cultural identity.[413] For others, the nation tends to be conflated with the state itself, that is, with its apparatus and institutions, a conception that Mauss argued amounts to '"hypostasising" and "divinising" the state instead of the nation'.[414] For Mauss, both the 'cultural' and the 'formal' aspects of the nation, both the set of traditions and understandings and the apparatus of law and administration, are fundamental to the specific character of the nation, which we might also describe as its 'localist' and 'universalist' tendencies. But this is more than just a balancing act on Mauss's part. What makes it possible for Mauss to hypostasize neither the state nor the nation is also the fact that what defines them is not just how they *exist*, the facticity of national cultures and state mechanisms, but how they are themselves nothing but orientations towards a possible future, objects of desire in which we invest, on the basis not that they exist but that they *con*sist (as Stiegler would say). As Terrier states:

> There is one further aspect which makes Mauss's understanding of the nation a fundamentally political one. In his reflection, the nation appears primarily as an object of the future, as an object of desire, yet to be attained.[415]

For this reason, Terrier concludes that Mauss was 'trying to offer a sociological analysis of a social organisation that was still in the making', and hence that it was 'a declaration of hope that the *future* of politics would see the triumph of the national principle' thus understood, a 'political intervention, disguised as a sociological treatise'. Mauss's hope was that the lessons of the First World War would be learned by nations, making it possible to 'move away from false notions of nationhood which nurtured hatred and violence'.[416]

This account of what Mauss means by the nation is necessary for an understanding of his position with respect to internationalism. The wealth of the nation, for Mauss, we could say, lies in the future-oriented neganthropic potential of the relationship between its cultural richness and its decision-making apparatus, both of which are in fact historically singular. Cosmopolitanism, for Mauss, was the name of those species of internationalism that ignored this relational source of wealth and advocated the dissolution of the national into the international. Such a universalist cosmopolitanism, Mauss argues, denies the virtuous singularity embodied in the nation. Against such cosmopolitan internationalism, the aim of a reinvented internationalism should be to forge greater interdependence between nations, firstly in order to render military conflict an increasingly unpalatable and impossible way of resolving international tensions.

Even though Mauss rejects any 'idealist' conception of cosmopolitanism (idealist because assuming an abstract humanness that would transcend the material concreteness of social life) based on some or other notion of global citizenship, his appreciation of the role of borrowing and cross-cultural transmission means that his understanding of this transnational interdependence is not just a question of aligning common interests, signing treaties or founding international administrative bodies. Mauss recognizes genuine interdependence as that which opens the possibility, not of the desirability of world government, but of the advent of 'global human civilisation', a 'hypersocial system of social systems', which is to say a genuine process of transindividuation operating at a scale above that of the nation.[417] If, in the life of the nation (or the higher complex exorganism), the selection criteria are fundamentally *extrinsic*, that is, related to an order of magnitude exceeding the national level, then so too must we conclude, as Terrier puts it, that 'the social is a function of the intersocial',[418] or as Mauss puts it, that

> it is an abstraction to believe that the internal life of a nation is not for a large part conditioned by that which is external to it, and vice versa.[419]

Here, finally, we can get a sense of what Stiegler means when he describes the internation, Mauss's name for this reconsideration of internationalism, as the site of the co-individuation and transindividuation of nations. If it is possible that this process of the internation could ultimately lead to one planetary-scale civilization, then, as Terrier concludes, the paradoxical result must nevertheless be understood as a 'global civilisation of interdependent nations [...] accompanied not by a diminution, but by an increase of the individuality of each composing part', a 'more fortuitous diversity of nations' that 'will transform them into *collective individuals*'.[420] It is with all this in mind that we can understand what is 'barely a thesis' in 'La nation et l'internationalisme':

> The second stream of ideas [about internationalism] is beginning to be clarified [...] due to the proximity of the utopias and cosmopolitanism from which it was born. We propose to keep for this the name of 'internationalism'. It is the movement that tends to unite nations and not to destroy them. Inter-nation is the opposite of a-nation. Internationalism is, if we agree to grant this definition, the set of ideas, feelings, rules and *collective groupings that aim to conceive and govern the relations between nations and between societies in general*. Here, we are no longer in the realm of utopia but in that of facts, at least in that of anticipations of the immediate future. In reality, there is a whole movement of social forces that tends to practically and morally regulate the life of the relations between societies.[421]

The internation in the age of proletarianization and carbonization

The relevance of Mauss's analysis is clear and indisputable. Currently we are living through a time in which there is an increasing split between those who, in Mauss's terms, hypostasize the nation and those who hypostasize the state. That is, there is an increasing split between those who see the role of politics today as defending against threats to cultural identity and those for whom no geopolitics is conceivable outside the framework of cosmopolitan globalization. In fact, it is the vigour with which the latter is pursued, eliminating the 'whole movement of social forces that tends to practically and morally regulate the life of the relations between societies', that produces the former as a counter-reaction, both poles thus missing the lesson taught by Mauss that the social is a function of what he calls the inter-social. The invention of the printing press that led to the printing of the Bible in national languages rather than transnational Latin, thereby giving birth to a new deterritorializing spirit, would also, and by the very same act, contribute to the rise of the nationalist spirit. In this way, the very poles that Mauss hoped to transcend with the notion of the internation may be thought to have formed into an oppositional schema precisely because of the pharmacological character of literal tertiary retention.

In any case, the contemporary version of the problem first identified by Mauss was already identified by Arnold Toynbee in *Mankind and Mother Earth*, published posthumously in 1976:

> Mention has already been made of the discrepancy between the political partition of the Oikoumenê into local sovereign states and the global unification of the Oikoumenê on the technological and economic planes. This misfit is the crux of mankind's present plight. Some form of global government is now needed for keeping the peace between one local human community and another and for re-establishing the balance between Man and the rest of the biosphere, now that this balance has been upset by Man's enormous augmentation of human material power as a result of the Industrial Revolution.[422]

It might seem from Toynbee's invocation of 'global government' as if he is arguing for the necessity of the elimination of the local in favour of the global, on the grounds that only by overcoming 'political partition' will it be possible to match the vast processes unfolding as technological and economic 'global unification'. In fact, however,

Toynbee's position is more complex: sovereign states, he argues, are far too large to be able to take advantage of the psychic and collective processes that depend on scales of locality in which interpersonal relations can form the basis of processes of trust and confidence; at the same time, they are too small to be able to take care of the biosphere, because the competition between them produces short-term interests leading to war and empire (a position echoed more or less by Kaczynski). He therefore advocates the strengthening of locality at the microcosmic level of the town or village, combined with a kind of global sovereignty based on networks of communication:

> The present-day global set of local sovereign states is not capable of keeping the peace, and it is also not capable of saving the biosphere from man-made pollution or of conserving the biosphere's non-replaceable natural resources. […] What has been needed for the last 5,000 years, and has been feasible technologically, though not yet politically, for the last hundred years, is a global body politic composed of cells on the scale of the Neolithic-Age village-community – a scale on which the participants could be personally acquainted with each other, while each of them would also be a citizen of the world-state.[423]

The problem he identifies is that this realignment of scales of locality, made possible by the speed and breadth of technological communication achieved over the past century, cannot be won by military conquest in an age that has also given rise to nuclear technologies capable of global-scale destruction. But nor can we count on global communications to be sufficient to produce the will or wisdom for such a realignment, leading Toynbee to a stark conclusion that seems all the more probable today, almost half a century later:

> In the age in which mankind has acquired the command over nuclear power, political unification can be accomplished only voluntarily, and, since it is evidently going to be accepted only reluctantly, it seems probable that it will be delayed until mankind has brought upon itself further disasters of a magnitude that will induce it to acquiesce at last in global political union as being the lesser evil.[424]

It is because of the current intensification of such pharmacological threats that Stiegler has argued for a 'new wealth of the nation', which wealth is fundamentally and very broadly conceived as knowledge – of every kind. Today, the consequences of this elimination are evidenced by the depths of what Stiegler calls proletarianization (understood as this destruction of knowledge, which is also to say, of the ability to work, live, care and so on), and it is for this reason that, for example, he has argued that the problem of decarbonization is inseparable from the problem of deproletarianization. But if we raise this question of carbon, that is, of climate change and the Anthropocene in general, then we cannot also avoid the question of time limits.

From this perspective, the problem of the internation, if we wish to retain this word, has a character absent from Mauss's reflections a century ago. We live in a paradoxical if not aporetic time, in which the necessity of thinking and the urgency of decision-making are both equally undeniable, however much they are denied. We cannot possibly 'choose' one of these imperatives over the other, even though one depends on taking our time and the other on absolutely refusing to do so any longer. The impossibility of resolving this contradiction has thus far produced a kind of stalemate between thought and action, a vacuum that functions as a form of paralysis.

But if we cannot resolve this contradiction, our problem can only be to inhabit it in another way, to make this apparent impossibility the source of the dynamism of a new process. This is precisely what Stiegler knows and understands, and for him the internation signifies the need to foster a new wealth of nations that opens up the conditions of knowledge and belief that alone make good decisions possible. With this we cannot but agree, but the question remains of whether the tireless energy he expends and encourages us to expend on the work of the internation *in fact* does justice to the imperative of urgency. To weigh this question, we require a critique of political economy focused not only on those aspects that Mauss attributes to the nation, but equally to those he attributes to the state, that is, the apparatus of decision-making (law, politics, administration and so on).

What we must undertake is therefore an exorganological critique of *sovereignty* at all scales of locality, and we aim to sketch out the stakes of such a critique in what follows. As an opening statement, what we propose is that this macro-institutional question of a critique of national and international sovereignty is (1) necessary, and (2) something that extends beyond the concepts of (a) 'digital sovereignty', or (b) some form of, let's say, 'counter-institution' (the opening of a counter-globalization, say). Both of these, it seems to me, are necessary questions, but, as we have tried to suggest, they tend to try to address the anthropologist's concern for the noetic verdancy of locality (by reconceiving both wealth and locality) while tending to leave unaddressed the socialist's question of a reinvention of the most fundamental mechanisms of deliberation and decision-making operating at these macro-institutional scales.

The necessity of such a critique is obvious when one considers the *current* relationship between the national and international levels of political institution given that the founding principle that made the United Nations possible (without which it would never have been agreed to by the founding nations) is that the principle of national sovereignty must be guaranteed, and thus that international sovereignty is essentially just the name of a mechanism for peacefully resolving problems at the supra-national level. Nevertheless these resolutions are the result of collective processes that take the sovereignty of the nation-states of which these collectives are composed as sacrosanct and inviolable (in theory, if not in practice). If a supra-national sovereignty is thereby constituted at the international level, it is only as the sum of these national sovereignties, and it has always been beholden to the collective will as embodied in this sum of national wills represented in the General Assembly or the Security Council (the latter being the embodiment of the other condition without which the United Nations could never have formed: the condition that assured the hegemony of the major powers).

Wherever new international sovereign elements are instituted, it is only through a ratification premised on national sovereign bodies as the only legitimate deciders. The problems and impossibilities of this system are theoretically, practically and historically obvious. The question is: what *other way* of relating the national and the international, beyond just a rearrangement of various actually existing powers (that is, deckchairs, and ones that are increasingly clearly steering *towards* the iceberg that they can already *see*), could be contained in the resources made available by the concept of the internation?

Elements of an exorganological conception of sovereignty

So as to pursue this question further, let us begin to inquire about the elements required in order to subject the concept of sovereignty to an exorganological analysis. What exorganological understanding can we offer of the concept of sovereignty and what implications can we draw from it? The first point it is necessary to make in this regard is that sovereignty, especially in the modern world, involves a *double spatialization*.

The first spatialization entailed by sovereignty is the delimitation of a zone of applicability, a territorialization of law, which is to say a localization. It is this with which Alain Supiot is concerned in 'The Territorial Inscription of Laws', where he draws attention to the historical contingency and future uncertainty of what came to be a strongly-defined association between a particular legal regime and a specific territory in the so-called nation-state: there was a time before this association, and we seem today to be headed towards its dissolution.[425] In terms of a time before law was strictly associated with a determinate bordered area, there were, for instance, epochs during which it was possible for different legal regimes to apply to different individuals within the same space of land.[426] Like Mauss, Supiot understands that the strict territorial sovereignty of the nation-state was an outcome centuries in the making and involving multidimensional factors that may both strengthen or weaken the social cohesion underlying sovereign institution.

Mauss's notion of a new internationalism, involving an increasingly interdependent 'internation', was motivated by the horror of an unprecedented war of nations that seemed to demand reflections on how to truly establish the conditions of a lasting peace, so that it may be possible to avoid the repetition of destruction on such a scale. What Mauss could not have anticipated in 1920, but which Supiot can see clearly in 2009, is that the territorializing trajectory that gave right to the strong association between territory and sovereign law can also be *weakened* by the intensification of interdependence, and, more specifically, by the intensification of the *economic* interdependence that results from ecotechnical globalization. The new ideology of 'universal laws' does not exactly correspond to the kind of political 'cosmopolitanism' that Mauss had feared would become the dominant form of internationalism, but rather involves those economic pseudo-laws propagated by the doctrine of the 'Total Market'.[427]

This 'dissolution of the singularity of territories into an abstract, measurable and negotiable space' is accomplished by processes such as 'law shopping', or by 'scoring' each country in terms of how favourable it is for business investment (where the highest score is given to the country with the lowest taxes, the least stringent regulatory regime, and so on), as the World Bank does, forcing all the nations of the world to 'vie with each other in "territorial competitiveness"'.[428] What Mauss could not see, therefore, was that interdependence, which he hoped would foster the conditions of a new peace, would, when it took the form of processes of economic interdependence operating according to the ideology of the universal market, lead both to a deterritorializing dissolution of the very sovereignty of the nation itself, and at the same time to a vast *economic* war. The consequences of a war of this kind, in which we find ourselves thoroughly enmeshed today – where the 'legal supports [...] established at the national level [...] are being eroded by the process of globalisation' and thus 'the rules of the free market are no longer subtended by anything' – can be as devastating as any military conflict, given that, as Supiot concludes, these conditions 'will ineluctably generate insanity and violence' and 'can only lead to ecological, social or monetary catastrophe'.[429]

Supiot's analysis is undeniably perspicacious. At the same time, this dissolution of sovereignty has what seems to amount to a kind of limit, which Supiot describes but perhaps without drawing out all its implications (especially since it is with the mention of this limit that he *concludes* the first part of his analysis, on the 'institution of territories', and does not return to this question in the second part, on globalization and the 'deterritorialization of law'). As Supiot rightly points out, the basis of all these processes is the law of property, which itself has a long and complicated history. But whatever the *philosophical* basis of any supposed right to property, such as Locke's argument that it lies in the ability to work the land with the instrumented hand and thereby make it fruitful, the *juridical* basis cannot be anything but a framework of localized laws ultimately dependent on a claim of sovereignty. Hence whatever the tendency towards the erosion of legal supports due to globalization, there is *also* a kind of *limit* to that erosion, as Supiot acknowledges:

> The *dominium eminens* of the State has not disappeared completely, however. [...] More generally, the right to property must operate in conformity with the law. Exercising this right even supposes the existence of a sovereign State to ensure that the property of each is respected by all.[430]

This might be framed as a tension between territorialization and deterritorialization in the making of a globalized animal with the right to make promises (to put it in the terms of Nietzsche's *On the Genealogy of Morality*).

It is also, however, a question of the relationship between this *first* spatialization that Supiot describes in terms of the territorial inscription of laws, and the *second* spatialization to which we have referred, which concerns the space of *literal* inscription, and which, unlike those tribes and societies based on customary rules, necessarily involves *writing down* the law.[431] In addition to territorial spatialization, then, modern sovereignty is also a matter of the spatial materialization of laws in the form of literal tertiary retention – of writing. All political sovereignty in the contemporary world is based on a foundational document, an artefact printed on paper and signed in ink by pen-equipped hands, whose declaratory and performative characteristics are taken as marking the commencement of a bordered locality and the foundation of a sovereignty lasting in perpetuity. It is probable that there is no lawful constitution of political locality and sovereignty anywhere on this planet, on the scale of the nation-state, that does not take the form, ultimately, of a written document (and it is almost a tautology to say so, since to refer to something as lawful essentially means, today, that it has reference to *written* law). To say this is to make a statement about the tertiary retentional basis, which is also to say the technical and exosomatic basis, of the enduring nature of what, in 'Critique of Violence', Walter Benjamin called 'law-making violence' (or 'law-positing violence', a translation that better emphasizes the 'autotelic' character of this violence, although it correspondingly de-emphasizes the fact that such violence is a doing-that-makes *and* a *making*-that-does, a fabrication that *performs*, as the performance of an *institution*), one of the two kinds of violence that Benjamin argues circumscribe the entire field of what he calls 'violence as a means'.

In that essay from 1921 (which is to say, at almost the same time that Mauss was barely elaborating his thesis on the internation), Benjamin argues that the two kinds of violence-as-a-means are law-making violence and law-preserving violence. To what does the word 'violence' refer here? We can say, firstly, that it has to be understood in relation to the kinds of considerations that Nietzsche associates with 'the animal who can make promises', that is, the being who is capable of entering into contracts, because Benjamin is explicit that no matter how 'peacefully it may have been entered into by the parties', a legal contract always 'leads finally to possible violence', and thus that 'the origin of every contract also points toward violence'.[432] For Benjamin as for Nietzsche, the origin of law lies in the possibility of enforcing contracts – it is primarily for this reason that it constitutes a 'means', and why it is ultimately a question of the means of violence: the promise involved in a contract always contains, as its *basis*, the implication of a threat.

But if what Benjamin is concerned with here is violence as a means, then, in the case of law-making violence that *institutes* and *constitutes*, we can also understand this 'as a means' as referring to the ability to break open a path in existence as Heidegger describes it in 1935, which leads Rudolf Boehm to describe Heidegger's logic as follows:

> That the being of man is *tekhnē* means that he is violent. That man is violent means that his being is *tekhnē*. What, then, is the meaning of this word [*tekhnē*]?[433]

For Heidegger, this violence of the violence-doer who is 'man' (as Heidegger says here, rather than Dasein) is what comes out of, runs up against, and breaks into the violence of the overwhelming that we have every reason to read (despite Heidegger's own understanding) as referring to the entropic character of the universe, one sign of which is the following statement:

> There is only *one* thing against which all violence-doing directly shatters. That is death.[434]

The violence of man that is *tekhnē* could then be interpreted as referring to that anti-entropic, or rather anti-anthropic possibility which is that of man-the-law-maker (or positer), which, in his turn, Heidegger indicates in 1935 by describing the *polis* not just as the Greek name for the state, but as 'the site of history' that can be called political only

> insofar as, for example, the poets are *only* poets, but then are actually poets, the thinkers are *only* thinkers, but then are actually thinkers, the priests are *only* priests, but then are actually priests, the rulers are *only* rulers, but then are actually rulers [...] because they *as* creators must first ground all this in each case.[435]

In other words, they are *only* an emergence from an originary default of origin, but one that must *actually* quasi-causally and neganthropically adopt that default so as to be worthy of what happens to themselves and their institutions. There is thus an affinity here between what Heidegger is talking about and what Benjamin is talking about: violence-as-a-means means violence-as-*tekhnē*, as long as we hear 'as a means' in this fundamental sense of the enigma or the mystery of *tekhnē*. Violence then means an irruptive possibility, the inscribing of a future into becoming by the self-positing of a new law: the 'autonomous' character of all sovereignty relates to its capacity for violence in this sense, and the weakness of the Weimar Republic was for Benjamin the sign of the loss of the consciousness of this character:

> When the consciousness of the latent presence of violence in a legal institution disappears, the institution falls into decay. In our time, parliaments provide an example of this. They offer the familiar, woeful spectacle because they have not remained conscious of the revolutionary forces to which they owe their existence. [...] They lack the sense that they represent a lawmaking violence; no wonder they cannot achieve decrees worthy of this violence.[436]

What Benjamin is describing here (which might well also be taken for a description of the nascent League of Nations, if not the United Nations) is the decay of representative democracy *from* the *autonomous* law-making violence that is the 'revolutionary' foundation of any constitutional sovereignty and *to* the *automatisms* of a law-preserving violence unworthy of the name, that is, an empty vessel of power unworthy of our collective *effort*. And this decay from the *autonomous* to the *automatic*, from sovereign law-making violence to merely its preservation, is also what is perceived, rightly or wrongly (but often enough rightly), by those who see national sovereignty being dissolved into international institutions or economic globalization, in both cases seeing the larger locality into which this dissolution occurs as amounting to a kind of non-localized machine or leviathan that operates purely by calculation, that is, automatically – a sovereign without sovereignty, or a functional pseudo-sovereignty: a sovereign automaton.

Power and knowledge, care and control, locality and journeying

It is not at all difficult to see that Benjamin's account of violence-as-a-means can be reinscribed into an account of the irreducibly localized character of exorganic and noetic life, which, as Stiegler has pointed out, always involves a primordial opening and a deterritorialization. This forms the heart of political life

> inasmuch as, essentially, it negotiates a compromise between power, which tends to *synchronize* locally, but always in excess of its own locality […], and knowledge, which tends to *diachronize* locally, but always in excess of its own locality.[437]

In these terms, which also relate to and deepen the Maussian idea that the social is a function of the intersocial, *local diachronization qua knowledge* corresponds to Benjamin's law-making violence, while law-preserving violence amounts to what Stiegler calls *local synchronization qua power*. In relation to these correspondences, two points are worth making in passing, although we will not have time to go into either of them in detail here.

1. This pair, knowledge/power, associated here with the diachronic/synchronic couple and, we are suggesting, with Benjamin's law-making/law-preserving distinction, can also be written as *care*/power: conceived functionally (in Stiegler's Whiteheadian sense, where reason is a fundamental and essential characteristic of exosomatization), knowledge is always a form of care, such as for example the therapeutics required by any transformation of the technical system, through the practices of which, alone, the shocks

produced by a new technical development can be fruitfully adopted thanks to a metastabilizing 'second moment'. What we would like to insist upon is that this knowledge-as-care is always also a question of control: all culture, as a form of care and cultivation, is a form of control – *in a positive sense*.

In associating control with diachrony rather than synchrony (rather than power), therefore, we do not mean 'control' in the sense that Deleuze deploys it in his discussion of 'control society'. *And yet*: such a control society, which is to say the performative modulation of behaviour through the desire technologies of the analogico-digital apparatus, is possible only because of the prior and irreducible fact that all culture is, *as* knowledge-and-care, a kind of control, which is to say, a kind of technically-mediated behavioural performativity (in Austin's sense) operating through processes of adoption, involving rituals, games, festivals, calendars, laws, rules and work, a performativity that arranges expectations and motivations (that is, behaviour) in time and space. This primordial form of control has a relationship to power, we could say, that is akin to the relationship of justice to law, or of ethics to morality: control is performative in an infinite way in the sense that it does not itself exist (only power exists), but it orientates behaviour by knowledgeably aiming it at improbable consistencies that do not themselves exist except asymptotically – at infinity.

2   It was the *Antigone* chorus that allowed Heidegger to think the being of man in terms of violence-as-*tekhnē*, and he *returns* to this reading in 1942. If he again takes up the Sophoclean 'ode to man', it is to press this analysis into the service of a reading of Hölderlin's hymn 'The Ister', a poem concerned with flows and counter-flows between East and West, home and foreign, 'ancient' and 'modern', past and future, space and time. More particularly, Heidegger inscribes this analysis of violence-as-*tekhnē* into a very elaborated account of the relationship between locality and journeying, or in other words into a relationship between territorialization and deterritorialization, that is, between locality and the excess *over* locality that, according to Stiegler, conditions the relationships between the synchronic and the diachronic. It is only at and as the first step of his account that Heidegger makes the following claim:

> Our claim is this: the river is the locality of the dwelling of human beings as historical upon this earth. The river is the journeying of a historical coming to be at home at the locale of this locality. The river is locality and journeying.[438]

The stakes involved in Heidegger's decision to *once again* take up the *Antigone* chorus in this context and in this year have yet to be weighed, and have yet to be weighed in particular in the context of the twenty-first century, but, we would argue, this forms a crucial hinge between the existential analytic and the question concerning *Gestell* in the post-truth Anthropocene.

Poetic revolution and the deconstruction of sovereignty

Let us return to Benjamin's argument that the loss of the knowledge of the violence latent in legal *institution* leads to institutional decadence, or in other words to a regression of sovereignty from the autonomous to the automatic, or again, to an elimination of the diachronic under the hegemony of the synchronic. Benjamin's criticism is typical of many arguments about the fate of sovereignty under technocracy, ecotechnics or *Gestell*, as the leviathan of politics succumbs to a calculating automaton that *eliminates in advance* the very function of sovereignty: collective deliberation and decision on the basis of reason. Such arguments, however, ultimately rest on *opposing* autonomy and automatism: if they must indeed be distinguished, nevertheless the automatic is the *condition* of the autonomous – or, rather, of disautomatization (just as one cannot become a great, that is, autonomous, pianist without first and for a long time practising one's scales).[439] With this thought, we can reinterpret Benjamin's lament about contemporary politics not in terms of an opposition between the automatic and the autonomous, but in terms of what Benjamin actually says: this woeful spectacle concerns a loss of consciousness, that is, a process of forgetting, which threatens every institution. It is a question not of opposition but of composition, because the same thing that opens the possibility of autonomy (the consciousness of possibility) is the same thing that closes it off in forgetting: its tertiary retentional basis.

It is with all this compositional thought in mind that we should interpret how Derrida deconstructs sovereignty in early-twenty-first century (post-9/11) texts such as *Rogues* and *The Beast and the Sovereign* (and see also a recent article by Mauro Senatore in relation to Derrida's 'deconstruction of the Freudian *Trieb*'[440]). In 'The Reason of the Strongest (Are There Rogue States?)', delivered on 15 July 2002, Derrida strives to describe the performativity involved in the law-making violence of 'sovereign self-determination', that is, 'the power that *gives itself* its own law, its force of law', in terms of a 'desire' for 'autotelic' self-institution.[441] The presupposition of sovereignty, in order for it *to be* sovereign, then, is, as Derrida says, that it be 'indivisible', 'ahistorical' and 'a force that is stronger than all the other forces in the world', hence rooted in what must always be one species or another of political theology, but where this then becomes the *condition* of something like democracy but *also* its perpetual threat, which Derrida calls its risk of 'autoimmunity'. We can hear a faint echo and a complication of Mauss's rejection of the 'idealism' of cosmopolitan universalism in Derrida's conclusion that

> sovereignty is incompatible with universality even though it is called for by every concept of international, and thus universal or universalizable, and thus, democratic, law.[442]

Derrida gives the example of the Universal Declaration of Human Rights, which is not opposed to and does not limit the sovereignty of the nation-state: rather, it is an instance of performative law-making violence that institutes *another* sovereignty, that of the human being. His conclusion: 'it thus reveals the autoimmunity of sovereignty in general'.[443] Or taking the concept of the 'rogue state' as an example, it can be considered a compensatory fantasy by which states try to boost their own *national* sovereign legitimacy by associating themselves with an *international* sovereignty in relation to which they say some *other* nation-state is deficient, thereby exposing, he thinks, that there is no pure sovereignty: sovereignty can only ever be a desire that *tends*, and a tendency that, *as* a tendency, may always succumb to a counter-tendency (which is how Derrida interprets the actions of the United States after 9/11).[444]

Related questions had already been discussed by Derrida four months earlier, on 13 March 2002. On that day, Derrida took up his argument from earlier in the course that became *The Beast and the Sovereign*, according to which

> a political revolution without a poetic revolution of the political is never more than a transfer of sovereignty and a handing over of power[445]

(but we would immediately want to add that it is *also* necessary to consider the converse: that a poetic revolution without a political revolution, or, let's say, without an organological revolution of the mechanisms of power or the technics of sovereignty, risks becoming only an epiphenomenal 'resistance' within a sovereign context that remains untouched, because unreinvented).

In other words, Derrida is arguing that a real revolution is always more than just a transfer of sovereignty: it is a revolution of sovereignty itself, which is also to say, a revolution of the political itself, a 'poetic' revolution in the sense that it 'breaks into' existence as a transformation of the conditions of singular, idiomatic locality itself. It is here that it would be necessary to really enter into the questions that Heidegger raises about Hölderlin in relation to 'locality' and 'journeying', his assertion that the rivers *are* the poets,[446] and his reading of the opening lines of the Ister hymn, 'Now come, fire! / Eager are we / To see the day', and what they mean for the advent of the *Ereignis*.[447] But it is also here that Derrida's argument that a political revolution must also be a poetic revolution is highly reminiscent of Heidegger's stance in 1935 that the *polis* is the site of history only if it contains *actual* poets (1935: when Heidegger seems to want to say, after the failure of the rectorate that had already taken place, that the 'revolution' of 1933 will not *actually* be a revolution unless it is redoubled with a poetic revolution, raising highly complex and difficult questions not just about Heidegger's discourse and politics at this time but about the way it is mirrored in Derrida's in 2002 – the only meaningful point being that this difficulty is *ours*, and we must *make* it ours, as Derrida well knew[448]).

In short, the *problem* of sovereignty can never be reduced to a *political* question founded on an *opposition* between, for example, legitimate and illegitimate violence. This leads Derrida to seek a new kind of language with which to describe this problem of sovereignty, that is, a non-oppositional language no longer based on 'pure' or 'indivisible' sovereignty, or on an *opposition* of the autonomous and the automatic, but on a *compositional struggle* that needs to be described with different kinds of concepts – those of the *complications and co-implications of economy and desire*. If what is at stake in politics, he argues,

> is not only an alternative between sovereignty and nonsovereignty but also a struggle *for* sovereignty, transfers and displacements or even divisions of sovereignty, then one must begin not from the pure concepts of sovereignty but from concepts such as drive, transference, transition, translation, passage, division. Which also means inheritance, transmission, and along with that the division, distribution, and therefore the economy of sovereignty. [...] For in fact, as we know well, wherever – today more than ever but for a long time now – wherever we think we are up against problems of sovereignty, [...] the question is not that of sovereignty or nonsovereignty but that of the modalities of transfer and

division of a sovereignty said to be indivisible – said and supposed to be indivisible but always divisible.[449]

And the way we need to view this deconstruction of sovereignty, first of all, is as a *critique* that we must interpret through what *we* know well, in *our* today: that this compositional struggle *for* sovereignty is also a struggle *against* the *de-composition of sovereignty*, that is, the decomposition of politics itself, a *destitution* of political constitution that today seems to be unfolding before our every eyes, and precisely in those sovereign localities where constitutionality had seemed to be most firmly established. And this is so, despite and because of the need for a poetico-political revolution of sovereignty itself (which is nothing other than the question of the *Ereignis* – provided that we reinterpret this question neganthropologically).

Canguilhem's immunology of propulsive and repulsive constants

Derrida in this way translates the discourse of sovereignty into the language of psychoanalysis. Or, it would be better to say, the question of the sovereignty of the higher complex exorganism is translated by Derrida into the psychic language of the noetic soul, or, in other words, the simple exorganism. For in addition to the (psychoanalytic) relationship of desire and drive that it implies (or: does not *quite* imply, but which we can interpret in these terms, Derrida himself, I think, leaving some confusion here about the relationship of desire and drive), what is at stake is the compositional relationship of physiology and pathology, in Canguilhem's sense in *The Normal and the Pathological*.

Having defined the *object* of physiology as the exosomatic being who can extend its organs but who can also succumb to the temptation to fall sick, and who thus exceeds its biological constants, Canguilhem defines physiology as 'the *science of the stabilized modes of life*',[450] or, we would say after Simondon, the metastabilized modes of life, that is, a threshold of stability always on the way to an instability requiring a *new stabilization*:

> There are two kinds of original modes of life. There are those which are stabilized in new constants but whose stability will not keep them from being eventually transcended again. These are normal constants with propulsive value. They are truly normal by virtue of their normativity. And there are those which will be stabilized in the form of constants, which the living being's every anxious effort will tend to preserve from every eventual disturbance. These

are still normal constants but with repulsive value expressing the death of normativity in them. In this they are pathological, although they are normal as long as the living being is alive.[451]

New modes of life, new metastabilizations, however, 'can be established only after having been put to the test by disrupting an earlier stability'.[452] Canguilhem identifies two such modes of life, associated with two kinds of constants:

- there are those modes that are associated with constants that do not prevent, and in fact enable, their own 'transcendence', that is, adjustments based on an encounter with disruption, leading to the stabilization of a new mode with new constants – these constants being in this way 'propulsive', or, we can say, associated with the regularization of diachronic processes;
- there are modes that are associated with constants that try only to conserve themselves *at all costs*, without any leeway for any disturbance, holding to a normal state without any passage to a new normativity (hence containing the 'death of normativity') – these constants being in this way 'repulsive', or, we can say, associated with a hyper-synchronization leading to unbound hyper-diachronic pathologies.[453]

In other words, in no way are Canguilhem's notions of propulsive and repulsive constants a question of an opposition between states defined as normal/healthy and abnormal/pathological. Rather, these are tendencies and counter-tendencies within the dynamic of the unfolding of a disruption that provokes a crisis, tendencies that expose the physiological or pathological character of an existing 'normal' *in relation to* that unfolding critical situation.

Hence Canguilhem compares *immunity* and *anaphylaxis*, both of which are cases of immunological reaction, where the former leaves the organism 'insensible' to an intrusion, while the latter is an 'acquired supersensitivity' that provokes an *over*reaction. Anaphylaxis involves a *shock overreaction* that can in fact be so *disruptive* of the metastability of the systems of the organism that it can quite easily prove to be fatal. Immunity, on the other hand, represents the immune system's normal functioning, maintaining its resilience and cohesion by neutralizing pathological elements.

> The presence of antibodies in the blood is common to both forms of reactivity. But while immunity makes the organism

insensible to an intrusion of microbes or toxins in the inner environment, anaphylaxis is an acquired *supersensitivity* [...]. After a first modification (by infection, injection or intoxication) of the inner environment, a second break-in is ignored by the immunized organism, while in the case of anaphylaxis, it provokes a shock reaction of extreme gravity, very often fatal.[454]

Canguilhem's primary point, however, is that *both* immunity *and* anaphylaxis must be considered 'normal': they are both forms of reactivity producing antibodies. It is simply that, in the case of anaphylaxis, that reactivity *over*reacts to a 'second break-in' in a way that proves to be harmful to the organism:

> The presence of antibodies in blood serum is thus always normal, the organism having reacted by modifying its constants to a first aggression of the environment and being regulated by it, but in one case the normality is physiological, in the other, pathological.[455]

Political constitution, constitutive slowness and anaphylactic risk

How does this bear upon Derrida's question: the problem of impure sovereignty and the discourse required to describe it? More importantly, how does it bear upon the organological critique of sovereignty insofar as the internation is the name of the problem of locality and political constitution at the scale of the national, the international, and the relation between them? How does it do so in the context of the Anthropocene as a systemic terminus calling for a transformational (that is, revolutionary) reinvention of economics, industry, knowledge and desire?

What we are arguing here is that the organological critique of political institution we outlined above needs to be inscribed into the kind of physiological/pathological standpoint we have just seen via Derrida and Canguilhem (which is really to say, an exorganological or neganthropological standpoint, in Stiegler's terms). *If temporalization means the organized processualization of space, and, more specifically, the presentation and proliferation of diverse improbabilities against the repulsive entropic tendency towards the probable and the average, then sovereignty refers to the default of origin that always forms the more or less violent basis of the propulsive regularization of these improbability-producing diversifications in a locality whose singularity is defined and preserved less by this default of origin than by what it opens up: the possibility of a collective belief in the future of the sovereign process*. What that means, specifically, is that it is a question of understanding how the tertiary retentional basis of sovereignty that exists throughout the modern world as the prime artefactual foundation of political constitution requires a critique of the ways in which it functions propulsively or repulsively in relation to the transformation of the Anthropocene called for by the IPCC in the space of a single generation of human life, and in which it seems so disastrously impossible for any of us today to truly believe, or to find the will to truly effect.

If we can say that economics has tended to remain within an eighteenth-century 'Newtonian' social physics, in the sense that it is based on the notion of psychic atoms who make individual decisions, or rather purchasing 'choices', motivated by 'individual' reasons and interests, and who do so in a market context conceived in pre-entropological terms, then precisely the same claim can be made about political conceptions: modern 'representative democracy' is premised on the notion of psychic atoms who make individual decisions, or rather electoral 'choices', motivated by 'individual' reasons and interests, and who do so in a political context conceived in pre-entropological terms. Today, these psychic atoms, whether economic or political, have been fused into audiences.

Unlike the economic conception of the *consumer*, however, perpetually propelled to make increasingly *rapid* choices about the acquisition of consumer products to which this consumer must continuously adapt, the conception of the *citizen* on which representative democracy is *initially* founded (before this atomic fusion based on turning citizens *into* consumers), there is an in-built *slowness*: the diachronization towards which representative democracy aims is built on the idea that there must be time for deliberation and reflection, both at the level of citizens and at the level of their representatives. Parliament, congress, assembly, council: such bodies aim towards a spacing of the time of decision by relying on the propulsive constants of regulated deliberative processes based on written laws enacted on the foundation of political constitutions that are artefactual and artificial (defaults of) origins of new localized, singular collective processes (and to which can also be added the cumulative character of common law mechanisms of legal evolution, which as we will see below have a particular status in relation to biological metaphors).

This constitutive slowness is a fundamental notion informing the literal tertiary retentions that are the law-making documents of political constitution (such as the 'Declaration of Independence' leading to the 'United States Constitution', or the 'Declaration of the United

Nations' leading to the 'Charter of the United Nations': the default of origin, which as Benjamin and Heidegger argued is always a kind of violence, always also and necessarily involves a *tekhnē*, and is as such *complicated*). Such documents aim to inaugurate new localized, singular collective processes *not only* by opening a mechanism for law-preserving processes of deliberation and legislation, but *also* by *instituting* the diachronization of their own reproduction across time in the form of processes of constitutional change or amendment. But these anti-anthropic processes (in Stiegler's sense) changing or amending the foundational document, processes that we could describe as the negotiation and arrangement of the diachronic and the synchronic, or of the autonomous (or the *dis*-automatized) and the automatic, are always intentionally *difficult*: they are always framed in order to favour a certain *inflexibility*, which is to say, to guarantee that constitutional evolution operates *slowly* (the US Constitution has been amended a total of 27 times in two centuries, the 27th Amendment being ratified 27 years ago in 1992, with this particular amendment having been first *proposed* for ratification in 1789, while the UN Charter has *never* received *any* substantive amendments other than to facilitate the inclusion of new members).

The reason for this principle is clear enough: the framing and founding of a political constitution is or should be a careful (or care-filled) process, because such a document is an extreme kind of *pharmakon*: potentially highly beneficial (that is, negentropic) but also highly dangerous (that is, entropic), and the risks brought by any change, and especially by rapid and hastily-considered change, always contain the threat of becoming a *mutation* that may send political diachrony into a self-destructive vicious spiral. History is littered with examples where a constitution too easily amended (or, if not 'too easily', then as the result of deliberate interference and manipulation, that is, corruption by power) leads to a distortion and perversion of the political process, and is one prime mechanism by which 'democracy' regresses to 'demagoguery'. Better too slow than too fast, better too difficult than too easy: this is the conservative thought, favouring synchrony over diachrony, taking care of subsistence (survival) before existence (transformation in the name of what does not exist but consists), that lies behind the tendency towards 'repulsion' contained in most of the 'propulsive constants' embedded in the foundational documents of constitutional sovereignty. What this implies is that, if there is a pharmacology of speed, then this cannot be divorced from a pharmacology of slowness.

But if this is the outcome of an eighteenth-century, pre-entropological political conception based on the notion of individualized social atoms, it is nevertheless *also* the case that there is a strong parallel between this conception of constitutional *reproduction* and the reproduction involved in biological evolution. The reproduction of the genetic molecule that is the retentional diachronic mechanism of life functions, and must function, *almost* perfectly, which is also to say, *automatically.* This 'almost' perfect automatic reproduction is the key to the proliferation of life through biological evolution: were there *no* copying errors, a kind of perfect automation of biological reproduction, then the form of life would be frozen in time, hyper-synchronized, and species would be unable to adapt to changes in the local ecosystem. But if there are just a few too many copying errors, then this failure and inadequacy of the automatisms of reproduction produces a preponderance of hyper-diachronic mutations inevitably leading to fatal distortions and perversions, to unviable monstrosities.[456]

By keeping such errors to a small but essential minimum, the process of reproduction operating via selection and mutation is capable of producing a transformation and proliferation, a deferral of entropy via the diversification of organs and species, operating at a *very slow rhythm*. What does 'fast' or 'slow', which are relative rather than absolute concepts of speed, mean in this context? Firstly, it could mean compared to the length of a generation or the lifespan of an individual: evolutionary change necessarily occurs at a rate far slower than that of the succession of generations. More fundamentally though, it is a question of the relationship to the rhythm of the change of the ecosystem itself, where an ecosystem is above all a milieu or a niche consisting, primarily, in the co-existence of species in perpetual struggle, against each other and against entropy, within a localized geographical and geological environment that itself mostly changes extremely slowly relative to the pace of biological evolution.

Extrapolating from this sense, we can see that the biological organism and the constitutional organism *are* both, in a way, negentropically conceived: they are both founded on a necessarily slow, multi-generational process of self-transformation, where this 'engineered' slowness is the very basis of propulsive survival against the entropic tendency, which is thus *presupposed*. In this sense, political constitution has always been founded on an intuitive or unconscious recognition of entropic risk, in spite of the fact that it has remained within a Newtonian conception lacking any awareness of the concept of entropy.

But this principle of slowness is itself founded on one fundamental assumption: that the rhythm of change of the milieu itself remains slow. In the context of the 1930s with which we have been occupied here, this is reflected in origins of neoliberalism. As Barbara Stiegler has shown, these origins lie in Walter Lippmann's conception of political economy as a response to the 'lag' of the human species, the discrepancy in rhythms between human inclinations that have resulted from a long evolutionary history and the demands of a rapidly changing environment arising much more recently from the great acceleration that is the industrial (or thermodynamic) revolution. Hayek, too, as we will see in the next chapter, wishes to root his conception of political economy in an understanding of biological evolution and its consequences, and in both cases, Lippmann and Hayek, this *attempt* will prove to be somewhat more complex, and thus more of a *challenge*, than their critics are willing to acknowledge. For Lippmann, this lag, this constitutive slowness of the human species compared with the perpetual flux of industrial life, produces a tension between flux and a more desirable and liveable 'stasis', and the political problem to which it leads, and which for Lippmann is the problem *legitimating* the questions of neoliberalism, is that this divorce, this disadjustment of rhythms, will give rise to nationalisms, fascisms and all those isolationisms that amount to so many reactions and overreactions to the instability of a world dominated by endless flux.[457]

That Lippmann (like Hayek) is an originator of neoliberalism[458] does not in and of itself invalidate the *problem* to which he draws attention – that the relationship between the rhythms of life and industrial rhythms can lead to dangerous oscillations – and, as Barbara Stiegler concludes, simply *avoiding* the questions of biology and politics only ends up conceding the ground to the most reductive characterizations of this relationship.[459] A derisory condemnation of Lippmann's 'naturalism' in the name of some superior 'constructivism' denuded of any biological connection is likely only to end up introducing and relying upon a metaphysical opposition that is philosophically regressive and politically impotent (and where, what's more, Hayek himself relies on just such an opposition, but with the polarities reversed when he distinguishes the spontaneous ordering of *kosmos* from the artificial orders of *taxis*). Here, we will not attempt to redraw the contours of the relationship between biology and politics in any detail, even if we agree about the necessity of the project, but we will nevertheless suggest that Lippmann's *question* remains ours, now more than ever, and in multiple ways, and above all as the question of a new politics and philosophy of locality that, precisely, exceeds the metaphysical opposition of naturalism and constructivism.

Hence, for example, we wish to affirm that if it is true that what defines the biological milieu is, firstly and most importantly, all those *other* species occupying a locality and with which the organism interacts or avoids interacting, then one fundamental distinction between species from this perspective is their generational timespan, which is also to say, correlatively, their mutation rates. The lifespan of a bacterium before division, for example, is infinitesimally short compared to the lifespan of a human being or any animal, which means that productive mutations in bacterial forms can occur much more rapidly than the ability of animal life to adapt to it through the mechanisms of accidental mutation and natural selection. Likewise, the success of a virus is a function of the conjunction of the speed of transmission between individual hosts and the speed of mutation, opening up the possibility, for example, of a *seasonal* transformation of the milieu of a species completely at odds with the pace of its own evolutionary adaptive mechanisms. Hence the rapidity of this reproduction and mutation mean that these changes have the potential to introduce new disease phenomena that may rapidly affect the survival chances of more slowly adapting species (and, we can add, this dangerous potential can easily be exacerbated when it comes into contact with, and combines with, the rhythms of industrialization and consumerism that contain the possibility of precipitating and transporting pandemics).

The function of the *immune system* is precisely to make it possible for the organism or the species to cope with these rapid evolutionary changes affecting its milieu and thus affecting the chances of its existence: the immune system is an adaptive mechanism operating *within* the individual organism but with prophylactic effects for the species as a whole. But we must immediately add that *every immune system is, strictly speaking, a retentional system*, one completely disconnected from the nervous system, operating behind the back of consciousness but retaining the past in the present in order to recognize the return of past threats and neutralize their entropic risk. It is for this reason that one cannot (within limits) catch the same cold twice, and this is how a perpetual war is set up between the organism and its milieu, but fought 'internally' and with a different retentional apparatus than that utilized in its 'external' war. Yet *like* the psychic apparatus, it is a retentional system evolutionarily set up precisely in order to cope with evolutionary rhythms that exceed that of the organism and its species. Antibiotics and vaccines amount to the exosomatization of the means with which this war is conducted, and antibiotic resistance stands as testament to the ferocity with which it is conducted and the potential consequences of losing ground. And, again, it is quite possible to see common law as the exosomatic equivalent of this kind of immune system at the level of the nation (in Mauss's terms), common law being a retentional apparatus that adapts to changing circumstances without constitutional or legislative change but by remembering the lessons learnt from past cases in order to facilitate future judgments, that is, decisions.

The conception of modern sovereignty ultimately remains pre-entropological, however, to the extent that it fails to take account of the possibility of disruptions to the milieu occurring more rapidly than the ability of constitutional or common law mechanisms to adapt to these disruptions – or, rather, to *adopt* them. Political sovereignty remains an eighteenth-century concept because it was only in the nineteenth century that rapid changes in the socio-technical milieu began to occur (with productivist industrialization founded on heat engines and the grammatization of gesture), it was only in the twentieth century that highly rapid psycho-socio-technical changes began to occur (with consumerist marketing and the grammatization of the audiovisual), and only in the twenty-first century that these mutations of the milieu took the form of that ultra-rapid destabilization of 'everything' that we now call 'disruption' (with platform capitalism and the digital grammatization of 'everything'). When change in the surrounding environment begins to hasten to this extent, however, the pharmacological virtue of slowness turns into an absolute vice, as the governing mechanism built on these longstanding propulsive constants can no longer keep pace with the rhythm of environmental change, and thus progressively finds that the constitutional and immuno-logical mechanisms designed to cope with these intrusive disturbances instead give rise to shock reactions that, more than just instances of autoimmunity, prove increasingly to be catastrophically *anaphylactic*.

In relation to endosomatic evolution, one way in which we can define the Anthropocene is as the *suspension of the basis for this fundamental fact of biological life that the milieu will, in general terms, always change slowly*. The Anthropocene is precisely a question of the inability of the propulsive mechanisms of genetic diachrony to cope with the vast *acceleration* of the change of the local milieu that is the biosphere-cum-technosphere. The many-generational processes required for species adaptation simply cannot cope with an environment that is completely transformed at the rhythm of centuries, let alone decades. Faced with this vast differential of speed between exosomatic différance and endosomatic différance, the propulsive constants governing the evolution of life themselves become pathological in the sense that what *was* a synchronized metastability comes to *function* as a hyper-synchronic rigidity, inflexibility and non-adaptability.

Yet this is precisely the same situation in which we ourselves, as exosomatic beings, find ourselves in this Anthropocene of which we ourselves are the authors (however complex a proposition this 'we ourselves' may be): the propulsive constants of the institutions with which we hope to respond to the vast acceleration of technospheric change, constants that hitherto had been the prophylactic mechanisms preventing the regression of democracy, find themselves powerless – *because too slow* – to any longer deliberate and decide about such reactions. This in-built slowness that was hitherto conceived as a guarantor against the slide from democracy to tyranny thereby turns into the very lumbering and *underreacting* inefficacy that precipitates this slide, as normative immunological processes, faced with disruption, succumb to shock reactions leading not just to 'autoimmunity' but to the risk of catastrophic *political anaphylaxis* on the largest possible scale. Political anaphylaxis: that is, *suicidal overreactions on the civilizational scale*, if not the planetary scale.

Furthermore, as we know well today, this is not just a question of the growth of technology in general but of the consequences of the introduction of those specific technologies that are *new tertiary retentional systems*, firstly analogue and then digital: the risk of psychic and collective anaphylaxis is today greatly exacerbated by the vast *speed* of the algorithmic mechanisms producing proletarianization and denoetization relative to the speed of the cultivation and transformation of knowledge. In endosomatic life, the evolution of nervous tissue and the brain was the elaboration of an entirely new retentional system (as was the immune system, as we have seen), one whose advantages meant that those species lacking the memory and therefore adaptability made possible by the brain found themselves in a completely changed milieu, but one in which their own survival still depended on change that could occur only at the pace of genetic drift. The political organisms of constitutional sovereignty in *exosomatic* life largely find themselves, with respect to these new *tertiary* retentional systems of what is now called 'platform capitalism', in the same position as plants did in the world into which animals arose: *at their mercy*.

Constitutional political systems are stuck with propulsive constants deliberately and with good reason set to a metronomic pace completely at odds with the rhythms of the tertiary retentional systems of the twentieth and twenty-first centuries, and in particular the system of global digital networks. And when we refer to the 'speed' at which these operate, what this means, first and foremost, at least as far as the systems of political sovereignty are concerned, is that the *performativity* of (essentially consumerist) behavioural control made possible by these systems is vastly greater than the adoptive performativity of citizenship, vastly greater than the engineered speed of deliberation and decision-making on which political constitutions are premised. 'Choice', for the consumer, the citizen and the representative, becomes an illusion, and a *delusion or a hallucination* itself engineered by the very mechanisms that destroy the possibility of *actual* decision, which is to say, the possibility of making (a) différance.

It goes without saying that this is not an easy problem to solve. As mentioned, this constitutive slowness is well-founded, because the mortal risks of rapid constitutional change are real. Is it a question, then, of *increasing the pace* and *loosening the bonds* of constitutional 'adaptability', which courts these risks, or of *insisting* on remembering the continuing virtuousness of institutional slowness, which courts the risk of a perpetual lag translating into permanent political impotence? If we (somehow) change mechanisms of political constitution so that they can 'keep pace' with technological change, if we (somehow) shift the basis of sovereignty from a written document to some more easily malleable tertiary retentional basis, on the grounds that we *must* move at the pace of disruption, so that we can *keep up*, then is this not almost certainly a recipe for anaphylactic disaster of one kind or another?

Yet the reality of the Anthropocene is that the technosphere *is* changing at the pace of disruption, and catastrophically so, requiring transformation at a speed greater than that enabled by the propulsive mechanisms and institutions of the sovereignties of literal tertiary retention. This means that such mechanisms and institutions *underreact*, lagging further and further and further behind in their attempts to deliberate and decide with respect to this transforming environment: hence the graph of carbon emissions continues its unabated upward trend. And the symptoms of this lag, combined with the hyper-performativity of algorithmic behavioural manipulation, themselves produce a vast pathology of *overreactive* madness and stupidity and an immense regression from democracy and towards unprecedented and perhaps unimaginable forms of tyranny, within a 'post-truth' age that in turn destroys the capacity for deliberation and rational decision-making, neutralizing in advance any possibility of a 'poetic revolution' and precipitating a headlong rush into a political anaphylaxis that could itself easily prove fatal – at a civilizational and biospheric scale.

To propose some genuine reinvention of the notion of sovereignty itself, at the level of the nation and at the level of the relations between nations, is obviously to raise a vast problem, since, in Derrida's terms, it would be to raise the question of a planetary-scale revolution, not just political but poetic, that is, idiomatic, localized, knowledgeable, desiring, desirable and singular. To raise such a question is surely to enter into another kind of madness that consists in gesturing to the absolutely impossible. But if the Neganthropocene is the name of a necessity of reinvention of macroeconomics, of industry, of data systems and of knowledge and desire themselves, at a profound level and on a planetary scale, as the only way of addressing the crisis that has come to be known by the name of the Anthropocene, then the ability or inability of current decision-making macro-institutions to effect transformation is an unavoidable question. The function of this chapter has been to draw attention to this unavoidability, by conducting an exorganological critique of the tertiary retentional basis of the speed of those institutions, founded as they all are on artefactual and artificial written documents designed to *regulate the pace* of deliberation and decision-making at the national and international levels. Our contention is that the internation is, or should be, or must become, *also* the name of the problem this raises in terms of the *mismatch* between the rhythms of change at the levels of different tertiary retentional systems and in the context of the anaphylactic risk we face today at *every* level.

7 For a Neganthropology of Markets

> Robbed of the protective covering of cultural institutions, human beings would perish from the effects of social exposure; they would die as the victims of acute social dislocation through vice, perversion, crime, and starvation. Nature would be reduced to its elements, neighborhoods and landscapes defiled, rivers polluted, military safety jeopardized, the power to produce food and raw materials destroyed. Finally, the market administration of purchasing power would periodically liquidate business enterprise, for shortages and surfeits of money would prove as disastrous to business as floods and droughts in primitive society.
> Karl Polanyi, *The Great Transformation*.

Introduction

What is usually called globalization can be understood as a simultaneously and inextricably economic and technological process through which the singular character of human localities is ever-increasingly undermined and destroyed by the effort to make every aspect of existence a 'standing reserve' for the extraction of profit. Human localities are defined by all kinds of rules and systems that amount to ways of life, forms of culture and political processes, and it is all these that are progressively eradicated as globalization continues to produce what might well be considered as the universalization and absolutization of the market. Nevertheless, it is crucial not to start any analysis of these processes by making the error that would consist in *opposing* 'technology' and 'culture', because culture, politics and ways of life themselves all have technical conditions – for example, the technics of writing, and all the forms of knowledge of *how* to read and write that it entails.

If culture consists of rules and systems, ways of programming the relationship to the future, then these always rely, in one way or another, on memory supports. In exosomatic life, it is no longer possible for the rules of genetic or instinctive behaviour to navigate the dangerous currents that arrive in the course of an evolution that is no longer just biological but technological, and it becomes unavoidably *necessary* to rely on these memory supports and the possibilities they offer for retaining, accumulating, transmitting and transforming the lessons that are learned about how to subsist and exist within technical systems. All of the rules and laws and systems and cultures that have arisen in human collectivities amount to localized ways of intervening in or stabilizing the process of exosomatic evolution that has been ongoing for two or three million years, adding up to so many ways of *selecting* from among exosomatic possibilities, where the criteria for such selections consist in forms of *knowledge* (understood in a very broad sense). It is all these forms of knowledge, and the education and transmission systems that support them, that, too, are destroyed by the relentless advance of globalized exosomatization, including in its most technologically developed and accelerated stage, for which various names have been offered, such as platform capitalism, algorithmic governmentality, and disruption.

One significant consequence of this progressive destruction of localities and local specificities has been the counter-production of all manner of *reactive* symptoms, through which individuals and groups of one kind or another express and act out their feelings of frustration, powerlessness and resentment about this seemingly inevitable process of technologization devoid of socialization. But these attempts to in one way or another *resist* the onslaught of unsocialized and delocalized globalization inevitably *remain* reactive precisely in the sense that these individuals and groups have been dispossessed of forms of knowledge that would make it possible to take action, that is, to effectively imagine and realize positive alternatives, which is also to say, alternative selections from among exosomatic possibilities and new ways of relating to and exchanging these exosomatic possibilities. If politics remains a possibility of human existence today, it cannot consist in the reactive attempt to resist the deterritorialization of globalization without addressing the loss of knowledge that is the very condition of possibility of locality; politics can consist only in the struggle *against* those tendencies undermining knowledge and *for* new tendencies likely to re-engage forms of knowledge and to generate the desire to live well, *both* locally *and* de-locally (that is, globally, because the latter *also* has the perpetual possibility of opening up *new* localities and forms of locality).

It is important to recognize that these reactive symptoms, which try to hold back the tide of the destruction of localities without leading to new knowledge-able and reason-able and desire-able possibilities, are not limited to the politics of nationalism or xenophobia found in reactionary forms of right-wing politics or religious fundamentalism or terrorism. They are also common in forms of left-wing politics fixated on questions of identity, resistance to power or spectacles of protest unaccompanied by meaningful visions of a pathway towards a deproletarianized future. Whether right-wing reactions are more dangerous than left-wing reactions is beside the point: what makes this situation *most* dangerous is the way all of these poisonous reactions *combine and reinforce each other*. In *all* of these symptoms, there is *something* that is right, which is to say that all of them reflect one or another form of real suffering, one or another form of real proletarianization, one or another form of injustice, but there is always also something wrong, because they are based on a distorted pictured since they are not founded on any critique capable of shifting from resistance to invention, that is, to the possibility of inventively bifurcating towards an alternative future.

At the same time, globalization and disruption have led to the destruction not just of human localities but of biological ones, that is, ecosystems, including the planetary-scale ecosystem that is the biosphere. In particular, the continued extensive use of fossil fuels as the means of powering these global processes, ever since the thermodynamic revolution that began in the nineteenth century, has proven to have disastrous consequences for climatic systems, and consequently for all those ecosystems whose sustainable functioning depends on the more or less stable continuation of similar climatic conditions. But fundamental to the *continuation* of this biospheric crisis is that destruction of all the rules, systems and knowledge that hitherto had been the very basis for struggling against the dangerous possibilities *always* brought by technological evolution (but previously always on smaller scales): the destruction of human localities is thus *also* the destruction of the possibility of responding positively and inventively to the destruction of ecosystemic localities and the biospheric locality itself.

Without doubt, this very dangerous situation risks both macroeconomic crisis and what we have referred to in the previous chapter as political anaphylaxis, and as such demands a new critique of political economy, as Bernard Stiegler has argued.[460] Karl Polanyi argued that it was the very rise of the self-regulating market, which is to say the *automation* of economic exchange processes, that necessitated 'the institutional separation of society into an economic and a political sphere',[461] so that the latter might curtail the absolute character of the former. For Mauss, the notion of the internation examined in the previous chapter had to address *both* these dimensions of the political and the economic. It would necessarily entail a reinvention of the national that, as Jean Terrier describes, implies 'the extension of popular control to the economic sphere, i.e. the development of social property in the form of cooperatives'.[462] For Stiegler, whatever the internation names, it must be accompanied by and is inseparable from a new economic approach, which he refers to as the 'economy of contribution' or the 'contributory economy'. Despite this acknowledgment, and the significant work undertaken to reinvent forms of accounting and certification, especially at the microeconomic and mesoeconomic levels, Stiegler's neganthropological account has yet to delineate a vision of how this new economy, taking the struggle against entropy and anthropy as its fundamental criterion and value, could be scaled up to the global macroeconomic level evoked with the concept of the internation. This chapter aims to sketch out elements of this problem by turning to some key economic thinkers of the past and present.

The contributory economy and the market

The essence of the idea behind the contributory economy consists in acknowledging that the disembedded, absolutized and computational market, as the destroyer of localities and knowledge, must be replaced by new economic models that facilitate and encourage the creation of localities and knowledge, including *new kinds* of localities and *new kinds* of knowledge, through a reinvention of work conceived as knowledgeable economic action (as opposed to proletarianized labour, itself increasingly replaced by automation and robotization). The internation, at least as Mauss sees it, amounts to a call for the invention of a new geopolitical process, distinct from the 'universalized' internationalism of globalization but also from the reactive 'particularism' of nationalism. Only such a political reinvention, enriching the wealth of nations while simultaneously intensifying their mutual interdependence, combined with the widespread introduction of local contributory economies, so the argument goes, would be capable of producing political processes capable of making good collective decisions with respect to the highly urgent and large-scale problems with which we are currently faced, not just in terms of the toxicity being unleashed on the biosphere but equally the toxicity we are introducing into our political, cultural and social atmosphere.

One virtue of this two-pronged response consists in the fact that, contrary to most defences of the local against the global, the cosmopolitan or the universal, it conceives human locality on a basis *other than* the *opposition* of 'culture' (or 'society' or 'nation') to 'technology'. Behind the notions of contributory economy and internation is the thought that *every* kind of locality stems from the irreducibly local character of the endosomatic or exosomatic struggle against entropy, that is, against the tendency towards the flattening out of difference and diversity brought by the tendency towards the probable and the average. And it recognizes that, in the case of *human* localities, this struggle against entropy, a struggle conducted *for* and *with* the means of knowledge, is never *opposed* to technology but rather always occurs in technological conditions, that is, exosomatic conditions, and more precisely in mnemotechnological conditions, that is, in hypomnesic conditions. Economics always involves forms of knowledge concerned with what to do with, how to deal with, and how to exchange the products of exosomatization in a particular epoch, within a locality and between localities (whether adjacent localities or between scales of locality).

One potential problem with this approach, however, consists in the possibility that the economic and political elements of this response may not have been drawn deeply enough from the critique of political economy that forms their basis. This critique asserts not *just* that globalization, disruption, algorithmic governmentality and platform capitalism destroy localities, knowledge and the biosphere, but that they do so for *systemic reasons* connected to the character of the *global macroeconomic model*. But *more than that*, it argues, as far as I understand it, that this model *destroys itself*, by asserting:

1. that the basis of this model lies in the entropy-denying fantasy of perpetual growth;

2. that the basis of this perpetual-growth model lies in the fantasy that consumption can perpetually increase;

3. that in the twentieth century capitalists learned that to invest in mass production and conquer new markets they must capture the desire of consumers in order to influence their behaviour, which, they discovered, it is possible to do on a mass basis through the calculated use of audiovisual technologies;

4. that what fuels the attempt to perpetually increase consumption *today* is the exploitation of desire and libidinal energy by algorithmic marketing exploiting both audiovisual technologies and digital, network technologies;

5. that this exploitation of libidinal energy has the self-defeating tendency to deplete the energy of those consumers on which it depends, by undermining long-term desire and exploiting the drives;

6. that this consumerist perpetual-growth model also drives a shift towards a large new wave of automation and robotization;

7 that this drive to automate has the self-defeating tendency to undermine the employment base on which this post-Keynesian consumerist model also ultimately depends in order to ensure the purchasing power and confidence necessary for the continuous increase of consumption.

The contributory economy responds to this final point – the destruction of employment – by introducing new forms of local economic activity conducive to new forms of work, that is, new forms of individual economic behaviour capable of producing knowledge rather than destroying it. It is also an attempt to reverse the depletion of libidinal energy by introducing mechanisms that will have the effect of stimulating ways of life and fostering long-term desire. The way it does so is by experimenting with and elaborating new economic models based on the possibility of either remunerating non-market activity (outside employment) or forming anti-entropic local markets.

It is less clear, however, how these mechanisms (contributory economy and internation) can respond to *all* the elements of the critique from which they emerge: if the cause of the current urgent biospheric crisis lies in the very foundations of the consumerist perpetual-growth macroeconomic model, then how can the contributory economy in fact *replace* that model with *another* macroeconomic model on the scale of the whole planet? If such a thing *were* imaginable, would it be a matter of (a) *applying* the contributory model to the whole global technosphere, or would it on the contrary be a matter of (b) somehow scrapping the global system altogether and replacing it with a diverse set of medium-scale contributory economies, each related according to some principles other than those of the market? If (a), then the question is: but how can an entire planet function according to a contributory model? If (b), then the question is: but how can a planetary network of local economies sustainably interact according to principles other than those of the market? The simple and naïve answer would be: through the recognition that however much short-term national interests may differ between nations, they share the same long-term interest of ensuring the sustainability of their common biospheric locality, and therefore ought to be capable of negotiating principles of exchange founded on anti-entropic criteria. But if this then implies that the answer to either (a) or (b) is, 'through the formation of new global regulatory institutions', then a further political question becomes: what is the basis of the legitimacy or sovereignty of such institutions? And the economic question becomes: what are the mechanisms by which such institutions either control or replace the global market?

One reason for this dilemma is ambiguity about the concept of 'market'. As mentioned, Stiegler's work makes clear that the fundamental question of economics is the generation of selection criteria for exosomatic possibilities and impossibilities, and that these criteria changed in the Anthropocene age: from spiritual, religious and also *scientific* criteria to those of the hegemonic market – calculation and rationalization applied at every level and in every dimension and field. It thus makes clear that the *problem* is not economics but the market, or rather, a *shift in the nature, extent and function of markets*. Nevertheless, the relationship between the contributory economy and the market still seems somewhat unclear, and this lack of clarity lies at the root of the problem of relating the small-scale notion of the contributory economy (producing new kinds of markets on non-consumerist foundations) to the very large-scale problem of the consumerist perpetual-growth macroeconomic model itself (on which all smaller scale markets currently ultimately depend).

Stiegler on information, knowledge and the market

Stiegler's article, 'The New Conflict of the Faculties and Functions: Quasi-Causality and Serendipity in the Anthropocene', published in *Qui Parle* in 2017, is a version of a text that will be published the following year in another version as the afterword of the French re-publication of the three volumes of *Technics and Time*, intended as a bridge to subsequent volumes. It begins by making a connection between the concept of negentropy and the Derridian notion of différance (given that both of these name deferrals that produce differentiations), and by noting the numerous attempts to take account of the concepts of entropy and negentropy in other scientific fields. In another text, he notes that, as far as 'conceptual transfers' of the concepts of entropy, negentropy and anti-entropy into the human and social sciences are concerned, the results have all been 'more or less disastrous', and mostly ceased after the publication of an article by René Thom in 1980.[463] Yet he argues that these failures do not justify the abandonment of these questions, and to pretend otherwise amounts to 'a regression and a denial'.[464]

Stiegler then takes specific note of the work of Nicholas Georgescu-Roegen, for whom our economic behaviour involves negentropic processes associated no longer with the biological beings that evolve through endosomatization but with the technical beings associated with what Alfred Lotka called 'exosomatic evolution', a key difference of the latter being that behaviour is conditioned no longer by instinct but by desire and knowledge, both of which are *irreducible* to instinct. Such knowledge is acquired and contained not on the scale of the species, but on the territorial scale of the tribe or the ethnicity or the society, a singularization and idiomatization always also on the way to becoming deterritorialized. Stiegler argues that the processes whereby knowledge is now deterritorialized, industrialized and automated on a planetary scale – processes whose common names are globalization and the Anthropocene – call for a new approach to knowledge in general, and in terms of its faculties and functions in particular. More pointedly, he argues that these processes, which are *also* equivalent to the furthest, *computational* development of what in the *Grundrisse* Marx called 'fixed capital', are ultimately entropically self-destructive and thus require a 'new economy [...] based on the constant critique of the limits of exosomatization insofar as it is pharmacological'.[465]

From there, Stiegler returns to an argument put forward in *Technics and Time, 2* concerning the difference between knowledge and information, and with the way this distinction arose in the nineteenth century with the development of newspapers, advertising and telecommunication networks. Despite the seeming difficulty that these notions have produced in the history of, for example, information theory (as well as in economics), Stiegler's distinction between them is perhaps surprisingly straightforward: whereas information tends to lose value over time, this is not the case for knowledge, which can continue to rise in value and for unpredictable reasons. What causes this loss of value of information? In these terms, value means the difference a bit of information makes or can make *to me*, in the sense of an advantage I can have that others don't have. If so, then the spread of information that occurs when it is broadcast (for example, in newspapers, on television, over the internet) decreases that difference as this information becomes a difference held in common (which is to say, no longer a significant difference).

Yet this is so only because information is then also a commodity and because the space in which it is diffused is also a *market*, 'a *computational milieu* that turns behaviors into *inherently* calculable objects'.[466] On this market that has developed since the nineteenth century, knowledge is more and more turned into information, which is to say turned into calculable value for particular interests. Since this general spread of information depends on eliminating everything incalculable, however, it ultimately leads to the evaporation of its value, which is to say that it succumbs to informational entropy. It is *also* to say that it undermines psychosocial negentropy, because, as irreducibly singular, local and idiomatic, knowledge and desire *always exceed* the calculable, aiming at idealities that exist only at infinity, or in other words that do not exist, but consist. Even the geometrical point, for example, does not exist, and is even defined by its inexistence, but it is starting from this consistent but non-existent point that geometry has extended a chain of knowledge lasting more than two and a half millennia.

Stiegler's conception of knowledge, then, is grounded in the thought that philosophical questions about, for instance, the division of faculties, cannot be separated from economic or bioeconomic questions about the *function* of knowledge, where the latter provides the localized criteria for selections among individual and collective behavioural possibilities. Before it is understood in relation to information, knowledge must be conceived as an evolutionary process for forms of life that are no longer just endosomatic, in which the struggle for the continuation of this evolution is no longer just biological, but economic. Because epistemological concepts therefore possess an economic dimension, and vice versa, Stiegler argues that the 'new economy' must be 'founded on a neganthropology', that is, on a form of thought that is also a form of care, in which the critique of the limits of exosomatization implies the need not just for concepts of entropy and negentropy, but 'anthropy' and 'neganthropy' – addressing the absolutely irreducibly 'pharmacological' character of exosomatization as a form of life that is dependent upon artificial and technical (organized but inorganic) forms of memory (which Stiegler calls 'tertiary retention' and more particularly *hypomnesic* tertiary retention).

It is the circuits of these retentional forms that open up the possibility of the accumulation of knowledge, but it is these same retentional forms that make it possible to turn knowledge into calculable information, and then computationally calculable information. More generally, this pharmacological character of the tertiary retentional systems of exosomatic evolution means that the processes involved in exosomatic evolution, which are not just biological but economic, can, if we are insufficiently careful, lead to increases of entropy and anthropy at the expense of negentropy and neganthropy. Thus far, we, exosomatic beings, have not been careful enough, especially as the absolutized market extends its reach to every corner of the planet and every field of existence. The aim of any 'new economy' capable of responding to the limits of the Anthropocene must therefore be to maximize negentropy and neganthropy while minimizing entropy and anthropy, within that 'locality' whose dimensions are today those of a thoroughly anthropized biosphere. Essential to a new neganthropic macroeconomic system, therefore, is the cultivation of forms of knowledge and desire capable of engaging in the perpetual struggle to take care of contemporary exosomatic evolution.

Individuation, disindividuation and the market

Stiegler thus presents an account of the Anthropocene as essentially involving the rise of a form of economic organization in which the market becomes increasingly 'absolutized' and 'hegemonic', with the consequence that knowledge is increasingly turned into information within the locality of a market that is itself increasingly de-localized, that is, globa-loca-lized. But do *all* markets contain this tendency towards absolutization insofar as calculation forms an irreducible *element* of market behaviour, in which case the problem of the absolutized market is simply what arises with the exacerbation of this tendency as markets extend beyond sustainable limits? Or does this absolutization stem from a *transformation* of the very notion of the market, so that it stops being one kind of thing and instead becomes another kind of thing, implying that there could be or have been markets that are not founded on calculability at all, or for which this element remains inessential? What is a market?

Stiegler's 'general organology', or more recently his 'exorganology', is describable in modified Simondonian terms as involving three strands of individuation – psychic, collective and technical individuation. None of these three unfinished and ongoing individuation processes can be extricated from the other two without collapsing, which does not mean that the unfolding of this collapse cannot last a long time. The opening of exosomatization (or what Leroi-Gourhan called exteriorization) leads to the advent of a technical individuation process that is both cause and consequence of hominization. The latter is irreducibly psychosocial in the sense that the individuation of the individual is not possible outside of the individuation of the group, while the individuation of the group is possible only insofar as it is composed of *different* individuals, each individuating singularly, this separation and connection of psychic and collective individuation (via technical individuation) being in contrast to the vital individuation processes characteristic of endosomatic evolution, which defers entropy by differentiating itself into organs and species within the possibilities that arise within a niche or an ecosystem.

From such a perspective, should we conclude that a market is a collective individuation process, such as, for example, the village market in which farmers, artisans and other locals would congregate to exchange goods, whether by barter, truck, exchange or sale, but also to exchange knowledge about many things directly related to those goods but also about many things only indirectly related to them? Are such markets – which are, precisely, *local* in the sense of forming more or less centralized meeting points of exchange, inhabiting a localized system of multi-dimensional knowledge – of a completely different type from *the* market (or the *M*arket), or does the latter just amount to the accentuation of the negative pharmacological characteristics of the technical aspect of *any* such market?

Would what we today call 'the market' then amount to a *disindividuation* process resulting from these negative pharmacological characteristics, where this form of the market doesn't truly catch hold until the nineteenth century (even if the enclosure of the commons and the extension of global trade through colonial enterprise set the conditions for the rise of this market), and which has now become computational, premised on the 'general equivalence of everything' (that is, on the calculability of information, to some extent no longer premised on money but on data 'itself') and thus on its 'universality' (that is, its absolute delocalizability)? Or could it be that what happens in the twentieth and twenty-first centuries is that the market disindividuates itself as a *collective* individuation process and hypostasizes itself as a *technical* individuation process, and a highly pharmacological one at that, with the power to unravel from, and undermine, all forms of collective individuation? But under what conditions and through what mechanism could a collective individuation process find itself transformed into a purely technical individuation process? And if so, is this transformation reversible: is it possible for the market to once again become a collective individuation process, even at a planetary scale, and under what conditions? Or must we look towards some new dream in which the market assumes some form never hitherto seen, in which case what?

The neganthropological *purpose* of such questions would be to enable us to begin forming an idea of: (1) how the Stieglerian presentation of markets and information relates to the way these are conceived in economics; (2) what role the market or markets would then play in the 'new economy' called for by Stiegler; and (3) how this new neganthropic economy of contribution can possibly be scaled up to replace the *global* market responsible for the vastly anthropic character of the so-called Anthropocene.

Polanyi and the disembedding of the market

Michel Bauwens has a conception of a possible economic future that is quite closely related to Stiegler's, although the two are far from identical. In an introduction to a report on *P2P Accounting for Planetary Survival*, he argues that new economic tools are required in order to respond to our increasing recognition of 'systemic crisis and its relation to ecology'.[467] For Bauwens, the idea of the 'commons' amounts to a 'third dimension' beyond the two poles represented by Friedrich von Hayek and Karl Polanyi in the so-called 'calculation debates' concerning the relative merits of the free market economy and the centrally planned economy. By taking up the tools of mutual coordination, shared logistics and shared accounting, new ethical exchange mechanisms, and a new planning framework in which economic choices are embedded in an understanding of the needs of the biosphere, Bauwens argues in favour of what he calls 'cosmo-local production', where knowledge will be shared globally but production will be as local as possible, so as to optimize the reduction of the so-called human footprint.

Bauwens thus wants to transcend an opposition between two economic poles, understood in terms of planning versus freedom and corresponding politically to the positions of socialism and liberalism. The planned economy that lies behind the scenes of this picture is that of the Soviet Union and the free market referred to here is that of Hayek, understood as the father or the grandfather of the free market absolutism that has come to be commonly known as neoliberalism. Yet neither of these positions characterized the global ecotechnical system that dominated the second half of the twentieth century, based on Keynesianism, the welfare state and consumerism, and whose vestiges remain even today, even if greatly modified. Insofar as the Keynesian economic model whose seeds were planted after the Great Depression and which bore fruit until the 1970s was neither a socialist planned economy nor the naked neoliberalism that would not take hold until the 1980s (by taking advantage of the opportunity presented by the crisis of Keynesianism), was this not already a matter of transcending these two poles?

This Keynesian model, which formed the macroeconomic *basis* of consumerist capitalism, arose only when it became clear that the economics of capitalism could dismiss the politics of representative democracy only at its peril. That is, it arose from out of a power struggle in which centralized planning and brutal but empty 'freedom' were *already* framed as the opposition to be overcome, even if this was only *after* the capitalist 'flirtation' with extreme authoritarianism, a context described well by Colin Crouch:

> But equally, and increasingly during the course of the 19th century, property owners sought defence from interference in their rights by the property-less, the great mass of the population. Democracy was the potential enemy of the capitalist economy. As political movements representing the industrial working class gravitated towards Marxist ideas,

these fears became very real. Often property owners decided that, if forced to choose between an anti-liberal regime that would still defend property rights and a liberalism that was sliding towards democracy, they would prefer the former. During the 1920s and 1930s this led many to make a further compromise, preferring the demotic anti-liberalism of fascism and Nazism, antithesis though that was to 19th-century liberalism, to a democracy that increasingly seemed to imply Bolshevism.[468]

Polanyi offered a similar analysis in 1932, and in addition made clear how this situation gives rise to what Benjamin called the decay of political institutions when the consciousness of their latent violence is lost. He also clarified the way in which this decay is virtually bound to be expressed in two forms: on the one hand, the 'woeful spectacle' that Benjamin observes when politics forgets its origins and is thereby left barren, and which Mauss calls cosmopolitanism; on the other hand, the reactionary authoritarianism of the local politics of nationalism, fascism and so on. Here, Gareth Dale summarizes Polanyi's position, after discussing the latter's notion of *Übersicht*, a capacity for oversight without which, for Polanyi, a rational economy is impossible, which is to say an economy that knows how to form prices neganthropically:

> The loss of overview, Polanyi concluded, is 'the deepest cause of the chasm between democracy and economy'.
>
> Polanyi wrote those words in 1932, and the chasm to which he refers was to become a central element in his explanation of the interwar crisis. Capitalism and democracy, he argued, had once been bedfellows. But now they had entered a condition of permanent conflict, in which liberalism had rallied to the interests of capital, tossing aside the flame of democracy. Once a tribune of democracy and competition, liberalism had since the 1870s been 'barren'; it now kowtowed to monopoly capital and supported either 'neo-democracy', a pale and derivative reflection of the real thing, or out-and-out authoritarian reaction.[469]

The difference in these portrayals is only that the turn to an authoritarianism willing to guarantee property rights is presented by Crouch as a turn *away from* bourgeois liberalism and by Polanyi via Dale as a turn *of* that liberalism. In any case, pale, barren, sterile pseudo-democracy or out-and-out authoritarian reaction are the political poles that seemed to appear in the interwar period as a consequence of the historical divorce of capitalist economics and representative democracy.

If for Benjamin this distribution of outcomes stems from the forgetting of the revolutionary violence of political institution, for Polanyi it is much more directly a long-term consequence of a particular revolution – the Industrial Revolution – whose fundamental characteristic was the shift from markets to a 'market economy'. Polanyi recognized, however, that this shift 'cannot be fully grasped unless the impact of the machine on a commercial society is realized',[470] which in Stieglerian terms we would express as the fact that this market economy was made possible by the thermodynamic revolution of the steam engine and the revolution of grammatization exemplified in Jacquard's loom. For Polanyi, a market is simply 'a meeting place for the purpose of barter or buying and selling'.[471] What's more, markets originate to a large extent as meeting places for the transacting of long distance trade, that is, trade between localities, and, for this reason, in 'primitive society [...] local markets are of little consequence' for an understanding of the economic cohesion and functioning of the locality itself.[472] It is only as society becomes more complex, and especially with the introduction of the industrial machine, that the 'market pattern' begins to assume a larger role conditioning the character of local economies, because the greater the complexity of an economy, the more necessary it is to ensure that the elements of that complexity are arranged and supplied in a highly coordinated way, for which prices become the regulatory mechanism.

Even so, such market relations continued to be *embedded* in what Polanyi calls social relations, where the latter served as an *external* regulatory mechanism, through which, for example, 'the peace of the market was secured at the price of rituals and ceremonies which restricted its scope while ensuring its ability to function within the given narrow limits'.[473] Only with a great phase-shift in complexity did this situation change to one in which social relations would be embedded in the 'economic system', as the functional character of *the* market shifted to become a *self*-regulating system directed by prices and nothing but prices:

> The step which makes isolated markets into a market economy, regulated markets into a self-regulating market, is indeed crucial. The nineteenth century [...] naïvely imagined that such a development was the natural outcome of the spreading of markets. It was not realized that the gearing of markets into a self-regulating system of tremendous power was not the result of any inherent tendency of markets

toward excrescence, but rather the effect of highly artificial stimulants administered to the body social in order to meet a situation which was created by the no less artificial phenomenon of the machine.[474]

What Polanyi here describes is an *automation* of market functioning, through the introduction of artifices in the form of new automatisms. This came at the expense of social autonomy, ultimately giving rise, through being unrestricted, unlimited and disembedded, to the alternative between the 'woeful spectacle' of political automation and the anaphylactic reaction to it represented by those authoritarian crystallizations that sacrificed psychic autonomy to the automatisms of the crowd.

The shift from markets to 'One Big Market'[475] involves more than just an agglomeration of markets, for Polanyi, because these 'highly artificial stimulants' transform non-commodities into commodities. While a commodity is something *made* for the purpose of being sold on the market, the vast complexity of the machine-based economy means that *all* elements necessary for the functioning of that economy must be treated according to the *fiction* that they *are* commodities when they are not. More specifically, it was necessary to create new markets 'for labor, land, and money, their prices being called respectively [...] wages, rent, and interest'.[476] Neither labour, nor land, nor money, Polanyi insists, are so made, and thus their commodification as wages, rent and interest count precisely as the introduction of processes based on such highly artificial stimulants.

What necessitates the introduction of these particular stimulants is the advent of 'more complicated industrial production'. In societies based on industrial production, capitalists must ensure a ready supply of labour, land and money, but these three elements could only be adequately guaranteed by liberating them from the constraints of social embedding. For that reason, industrial society depended on these non-commodities 'being made available for purchase', an 'extension of the market mechanism' that was 'the inevitable consequence of the introduction of the factory system in a commercial society'.[477]

Now this consequence is for Polanyi based on something false; these artificial stimulants are essentially fictitious:

> But labor, land, and money are obviously not commodities; the postulate that anything that is bought and sold must have been produced for sale is emphatically untrue in regard to them. In other words, according to the empirical definition of a commodity they are not commodities. Labor is only another name for a human activity which goes with

> life itself, which in its turn is not produced for sale but for entirely different reasons, nor can that activity be detached from the rest of life, be stored or mobilized; land is only another name for nature, which is not produced by man; actual money, finally, is merely a token of purchasing power which, as a rule, is not produced at all, but comes into being through the mechanism of banking or state finance. None of them is produced for sale. The commodity description of labor, land, and money is entirely fictitious.[478]

This commodification of labour, money and land can be reinterpreted today as describing the processes referred to as proletarianization, financialization (including and enabling Crouch's privatized Keynesianism) and the anthropization by which the biosphere becomes a thoroughgoing technosphere. For Polanyi, all of these are symptoms of that great disembedding by which the market was able to continue the unfettered pursuit of self-regulation, via 'highly artificial stimulants' and 'fictitious commodities', and to do so beyond all limits.

Hayek and the two sources of order

As we have seen, Michel Bauwens argues for a 'cosmo-local' approach to the economics of production, in which knowledge is shared globally but production is kept as local as possible. Without wishing at all to challenge this idea, we would like however to draw attention to the complexity of the concept, which Bauwens frames as a matter of transcending the classical economic opposition between *planning* and *freedom*, represented respectively by Polanyi and Hayek. But is Hayek a *straightforward* enemy of the cosmic or local character of knowledge? It's complicated. Given Polanyi's position as the economist who thinks the great transformation that we now call the Anthropocene in terms of the *disembedding* of the economy, that is, as the distillation of the market considered as an abstract machine divorced from all localized knowledge and social relations, we might well assume that Hayek, as the patron saint of what Philip Mirowski calls the Neoliberal Thought Collective, simply *endorses* this disembedding from local conditions and unequivocally advocates adapting to those purportedly 'universal' rules embodied in market calculations. But while it is no doubt the case that this is the historical *effect* of Hayek's work concerning the use of knowledge in society, nevertheless the *form* of his argument does not fit at all neatly into an opposition between the universality of market calculations and the singularity of local knowledge. Quite to the contrary.

Hayek's position in 1945 is of course well known, but let us restate that his starting point for the evaluation of economic systems is the existence of two different kinds of knowledge. He wants to redress what he perceives as a tendency in economic planning to overvalue expert or scientific knowledge and undervalue other forms of knowledge. What are these other forms of knowledge? Hayek is explicit that he means knowledge of *locality*, in both senses of the genitive:

> Today it is almost heresy to suggest that scientific knowledge is not the sum of all knowledge. But a little reflection will show that there is beyond question a body of very important but unorganized knowledge which cannot possibly be called scientific in the sense of knowledge of general rules: *the knowledge of the particular circumstances of time and place.*[479]

In Hayek's view, such localized forms of knowledge of the circumstances of time and place tend to be downplayed. He wants to argue that if there is such a thing as economic truth, then it is something generated through the collective and combined *interaction* of all these localized knowledges, in a manner that exceeds each of these local knowledges and, *in total*, exceeds the capacities of so-called expert knowledge. The market operates through the delocalization of local knowledge but *on the essential basis* of local knowledge, and the latter may often be of a kind that resists formalization, that is, a kind that is 'very important but unorganized'. The odd thing here is that by 'unorganized' Hayek does not at all mean that it is not *organic*, quite the contrary, if by organic we mean arising from processes of 'natural' growth (in his terms, and as we shall see). Rather, this unorganized knowledge is, precisely because of its *being* organic in its origins, of a kind that cannot easily be reduced to calculable processes – or more specifically, in his view, the calculability necessary for a so-called *planned* economy.

His argument is thus that *what a market does* is itself *not* reducible to calculation: its work consists in this mutualizing delocalization. This is the basis of his most famous and most fundamental claim: that the market must, as far as possible, be left *to its own devices*, so to speak, without interference from those who arrogantly imagine that their technical expertise trumps what the market unconsciously and collectively 'knows'. Central planning, on the other hand, without the benefit of this mutual interaction of localized knowledge, will always be forced to rely on other forms of information, such as statistical aggregation, which is to say, calculations of probabilities on the basis of accumulated information.[480] It is precisely the universality of calculation, then, turned into aggregations of statistical information, that Hayek *rejects* as a basis for economic organization, because of the *hubris* implied in the belief that, divorced from local knowledge, it becomes possible to calculate everything.

To more fully understand Hayek's theoretical conception, however, and notwithstanding Edward Nik-Khah and Philip Mirowski's no doubt correct assertion that 'Hayek changes his mind',[481] it is necessary to examine Hayek's work of political economy dating from almost thirty years after 'The Use of Knowledge in Society', that is, his three-volume work, *Law, Legislation and Liberty* (1973).

Hayek's organizing concept, as set out in the first volume, is not negentropy, but *order*. Order is defined by Hayek in terms of a strong interdependence of elements, which together form a dynamic driving a path towards future states of those elements and future states of their interdependence. While there are many forms of order found in biological life, Hayek distinguishes the order found among the kinds of beings that we ourselves are by the degree to which it depends on 'co-operation with others', which means, he immediately adds, that it depends on the *predictability* of others as the basis for coordinated action:

> we depend for the effective pursuit of our aims clearly on the correspondence of the expectations concerning the actions of others on which our plans are based with what they really do.[482]

Hayek does not ask *why* our species is distinguished by the kind and extent of its cooperative behaviour, or why it is that human beings are capable of such a wide variety of *improbable* behaviour, and yet remain capable of producing this *correspondence* between what we expect others to do and what we anticipate for our own future. Had he reflected on the fact that what opens this infinite behavioural field is tertiary retention and especially *hypomnesic* tertiary retention, then he may not have fallen so easily into the metaphysical trap of opposing culture and technics, as we shall see.

For Hayek, it is this potential correspondence of the behaviour of others with my own expectations that defines the forms of order possible for our species, or for what he calls 'social life'. At bottom, this is a question of asking how 'culture' always involves (techniques and technics of) control, but we might well also relate this to the Nietzschean question of the production of an animal with the ability to make promises, that is, as we have said in the previous chapter, to sign contracts. But for Hayek, and even though we might think that the rule of the promise and the law of contracts are the very basis of *market* behaviour, this kind of *deliberate* production of order, which Nietzsche argues always has its origins in violence, thus leading to the association between order, command and obedience, and therefore with authoritarianism and totalitarianism, is only *one* way in which order arises in social life. The economist argues that there are, on the contrary, *two* sources of order: *exogenous* and *endogenous* sources.

In other words, the authoritarian form of order, based on command and obedience, would be exogenous, because, to put it in Aristotelian terms, the principle of the movement of this form of ordered system lies outside itself, having been *introduced* and *constructed*. Not having the principle of its movement arising from within itself, endogenously, it therefore lacks a soul moved by desire (in the Aristotelian sense), being instead a kind of hybrid being, an 'artificial order' that would be a 'directed social order' – directed, that is, *from the outside*.[483] An *endogenous* order, for Hayek, is a 'grown order', self-generating, a *'spontaneous order'* whose movement arises from its own internally localized source.

This distinction between exogenous order and endogenous order is an attempt by Hayek to deepen his 1945 distinction between systems in which the assumption of expert knowledge justified the command and obedience of central planning, and systems in which local knowledge of the circumstances of time and place operate according to other rules, 'orderly structures which are the product of the action of many men but are not the result of human design'.[484] In other words, these 'grown', 'spontaneous' endogenous structures are the product of the interaction of many localized forms of knowledge, 'unorganized' in the sense that they arise without predetermined purpose or teleology, while order of the exogenous kind is applied and constructed from the outside, and designed with specific purposes in mind, *like a machine*.

Kosmos and taxis

The names that Hayek gives to these two kinds of order are drawn from ancient Greek: for the 'made order', *taxis*, and for the 'grown order', *kosmos*. Hayek defines cosmic order, which we can understand as a kind of *transindividuation of local collective knowledge*, in terms that *oppose* it to what he sees as the artifices of command and calculation. From 1945 until 1973, Hayek will continuously associate 'the Market' *entirely* with this endogenous form of order. His argument for doing so rests essentially on the claim that markets are nothing technical, that they do not ultimately reflect processes of technical individuation. Instead, they are just the sum total of the transindividuation of economic knowledge within and between processes of psychic and collective individuation.

This is so because the market arises *spontaneously*, he thinks, in this way 'comprising more particular facts than any brain could ascertain or manipulate',[485] that is, calculate or compute. Yet the market still somehow generates 'purposive action' that tends to 'secure the preservation or restoration of that order', which is to say that 'the elements have acquired regularities of conduct conducive to the maintenance of the order'.[486] Since purposiveness can easily be heard to imply teleology or design, Hayek, reasonably enough, prefers to describe this kind of conduct in terms of 'function', and it is these functional recursive patterns that produce negentropic metastability.

In endosomatic life, the forces that produce biological endogenous orders are the selection pressures associated with biological evolution. The endogenous orders of noetic souls, however, necessarily involve another kind of behavioural selection process, producing not the laws of biology but the rules of society:

> Society can thus exist only if by a process of selection rules have evolved which lead individuals to behave in a manner which makes social life possible.[487]

Despite this admission, Hayek never acknowledges that this *other* selection process, producing not scientific laws but social 'rules', has anything to do with anything *artificial*. For Hayek, unlike for Polanyi, the market *never* involves the introduction of 'highly artificial stimulants', because it is *always* the expression of that diversity of knowledge and behaviour that conforms to psychosocial human *nature*. Hayek wants to insist that the non-biological selection processes played out on the market nonetheless operates *like* biological selection, with a *spontaneity* that is neither exogenous nor biological.

A *taxis*, on the other hand, is purely exogenous, while a *kosmos* is purely endogenous, even though both are the result of spontaneous but non-biological selections. Here we can see the roots of a form of social Darwinism, based on the notion that the superiority of one set of 'rules' rather than another lies precisely in their having arisen spontaneously, that is, endogenously, through a kind of *blurring* of the distinction between these two forms of selection. The question remains: what is the source of this 'spontaneity'?

What Hayek's distinction between *kosmos* and *taxis* really describes is a metaphysical *opposition* between culture and technics. In the case of *endogenous* order, the knowledge animating its dynamic is itself endogenous, product of a particular time and place, where the epistemological guarantee of the validity of that knowledge lies in the degree to which it serves non-teleological but functional ends. In the case of *exogenous* order, the knowledge dictating events is itself exogenous, which is to say, at perpetual risk of proving to be an inadequate set of (technical) instructions, because they have not arisen from out of a true, which is to say spontaneously generated, relationship to the function of reason (if we may use Whitehead's terms).

It is for this reason that, for Hayek, only an endogenous order can be described as a *kosmos*. Exogenous orders are simply the external products of a mechanistic universe, and are thus more *vulnerable* to the entropic tendency. Only endogenous orders are capable of achieving the autonomy and resilience required for dealing spontaneously with the shocks of existence. For Hayek, the function of an exogenous organization such as *government* is indeed like 'the maintenance squad of a factory', best limited to ensuring 'that the mechanism which regulates the production of [...] goods and services is kept in working order'.[488]

Yet a *taxis*, wherever it forms the basis of systems of highly-developed exogenous orders such as forms of government, is inevitably encumbered, Hayek argues, by

> the problem which any attempt to bring order into complex human activities meets: the organizer must wish the individuals who are to co-operate to make use of knowledge that he himself does not possess.[489]

The great difficulty of government, then, even in terms of this limited function, is the inability to engineer command and control structures (themselves 'highly artificial stimulants') *capable* of maintaining the production mechanism in working order.

Government is on the side of exogenous *taxis* (that is, technics) and the local knowledge arranged by market operations is on the side of endogenous *kosmos* (that is, culture). This surprising logic perhaps becomes more comprehensible when we consider it in relation to Canguilhem's attempt, undertaken for completely different purposes, to distinguish the machine from the living organism:

> In a machine, its construction is foreign and presupposes the ingenuity of the mechanic; conservation demands the constant surveillance and vigilance of the machinist, and we know how irreparably certain complicated machines can be damaged through lack of attention or surveillance.[490]

This maintenance – requiring attention and vigilance in the face of the degradation of entropy and the disruption of shocks, which Hayek sees as possible only for the endogenous orders of a *kosmos* – is really the question of the *care* necessary to maintain negentropic tendencies or facilitate anti-entropic novelty.

If it is not maintained, cleaned or even occupied, even a house (and not just a 'complicated machine') will before long succumb to entropic tendencies. How a house is built, and how it must be kept, are thus a question of the negentropic resilience made possible by the knowledge of life, and this knowledge might seem to arise 'spontaneously', that is, transgenerationally through the transindividuation of knowledge, but it is nevertheless strictly *exosomatic*, not 'endogenous' or 'natural' in any way that could oppose the organic and the organological. In other words, what is at stake, here, is the *knowledge of care* that processes of technical individuation always require, if they are not to fall apart or become dangerous. It is thus a question of the second moment of the doubly epokhal redoubling, which Hayek excludes as a possibility for the exogenous orders of *taxis*. And, of course, he never asks about the conditions of the production of a political economy of attention or vigilance capable of keeping its mechanisms in working order.

The cybernetic kosmos

If Hayek would nevertheless be right to think that care is necessarily and essentially a question of localized knowledge that cannot be *reduced* to the statistical aggregations of computation, what is then very odd is that the science to which he ascribes the possibility of elucidating endogenous order is precisely that science of control that Heidegger would see as characteristic specifically of *Gestell*:

> The study of spontaneous orders has long been the peculiar task of economic theory, although, of course, biology has from its beginning been concerned with that special kind of spontaneous order which we call an organism. Only recently has there arisen within the physical sciences under the name of cybernetics a special discipline which is also concerned with what are called self-organizing or self-generating systems.[491]

Hence for Hayek, this 'special discipline', cybernetics, does indeed seem to replace both biology and economics (the sciences of endosomatic and exosomatic selection) as *the* science of *phusis*, which is to say, of every form of endogenous order, and especially the market. It is in this manoeuvre that the computational turn is opened up, through which economics *authorizes* its own disassembly, *even though* his basis for doing so can be seen to consist in a defence of local knowledge *against* the notion of universal calculation or computability.

On the one hand, the market is associated with the natural world, with the wealth arising from the rich soil of (naturally human) localities, the particular circumstances of places and times, forms of spontaneously generated knowledge exceeding the narrow understandings of technical hierarchies. The market would then amount to a device that arises in complex societies, which are always based on exchange, but a device that arises in a way that is somehow both spontaneous and yet non-biological. And the *function* of this market device would then be nothing other than to *amplify the combined effects* of microcosmic *kosmoses*, scaling them up macroeconomically.

But on the other hand, the form of knowledge capable of *knowing* the endogenous order of a *kosmos* is the *highly* technical (not to say *technological*) and very *recent* science of cybernetics. So: the market is assigned by Hayek to *phusis*, precisely because of the locally cosmic character of the knowledge that *operates* the market, but, in the same gesture, the knowledge of *phusis* is then itself assigned to that 'new fundamental science which is called cybernetics', in which, as Heidegger said in 1964 (nine years before *Law, Legislation and Liberty* and twenty years after 'The Use of Knowledge in Society'), the 'operational and model character of representational-calculative thinking becomes dominant'.[492] Is there not a kind of parallel here between the *use* Hayek makes of cybernetics and the role Simondon wants to give to his so-called 'mechanology'?

(It would also be possible to relate Hayek's distinction between two forms of order, exogenous and endogenous, to Edgar Morin's distinction between two forms of causality, *endo-causality* and *exo-causality*.[493] Exo-causality, for Morin, refers to the causality of the physical universe, which simply concerns statistical probability and the 'general' possibilities of equilibrium and disequilibrium that exist for states of matter and energy. Endo-causality, on the other hand, is 'circular', 'local' and 'temporary', that is, the causality of negentropic life, involving retroactive loops that improbably 'repel external causality from the looped zone'.[494] Hayek's gesture with regard to the respective endogenous and exogenous orders of *kosmos* and *taxis* mirror's Morin's distinction between two causalities, where exogenous orders alone participate in exo-causality, that is, thermodynamic entropy, as if the mechanical artifices of machines and institutions are not *part of* retroactive loops that *also* involve endo-causal forms of life, and as if markets are simply endo-causal *expressions* of life that involve no artifice. It is for this reason that we can conclude that Hayek's distinction *functions* in a classically metaphysical way, which also means that it functions to *eliminate* the question of the *pharmacology* of *all* of those 'orders' that are formed precisely from the complex relationships of exorganic life, a form of life whose condition of possibility *is* its relationship to its prostheses.)

It might well be thought that Hayek's underlying manoeuvre is to conceive the localized knowledge of a *kosmos* essentially as the kind of knowledge involved in running a firm, that is, *microeconomic* knowledge. It would then be possible to argue that what Hayek is actually undertaking *is* a reduction of local cosmic knowledge to the calculability of cybernetics, with no *actual* concern for the destruction of localized forms of the knowledge of how to make and do, the knowledge of how to live, and so on. No doubt this is not false: if endogenous knowledge is amenable to being elucidated by cybernetics, it is surely because it is for Hayek above all the *organizational* knowledge required for running a business that is at stake. Yet the hierarchies and command structures of a business, which more than anything are what are open to cybernetic reduction, but which are not themselves examples of the 'use of knowledge in society' that happens on a *market*, are surely a question of *taxis* rather than *kosmos*. But the *kosmos*, for Hayek, is *not* the firm, but the market itself.

More than anything else, Hayek's argument is about the limits of control. In a *taxis*, we might have a considerable ability to fashion or tailor a system according to the dictates of specific requirements, but, in the case of a *kosmos*, 'the degree of power of control over the extended and more complex order will be much smaller'.[495] To illustrate this point he offers the example of a crystal or complex organic compound, which we can never produce by arranging individual atoms one at a time, he says *in 1973*, but what we *can* do is create the conditions in which the atoms will by the action of their own forces begin to produce these complex forms.[496] Likewise, we cannot mechanically engineer endogenous orders to guarantee expected outcomes, given the dispersal of actors and the specificity of their local knowledge, and, for Hayek, there can be no better process than the endogenous *market* for sifting and ordering this diversity and specificity, even if it can do no more than secure 'a certain probability that the expected relations will prevail'.[497]

Attempts to 'intervene' in the economic universe by trying to 'supplement the rules governing' the market order, therefore, 'can never improve but must disrupt that order', because it will always be the case that the directing authority itself only possesses localized (that is, partial) knowledge, and thus acts in ignorance of the functional role played by knowledge held by other actors.[498] Hence he concludes about any such attempt:

> What it overlooks is that the growth of that mind which can direct an organization, and of the more comprehensive order within which organizations function, rests on adaptations to the unforeseeable, and that the only possibility of transcending the capacity of individual minds is to rely on those super-personal 'self-organizing' forces which create spontaneous orders.[499]

For Hayek, this 'transcendence' of individual minds means that the localized knowledge of a *kosmos* may be *embodied* in each of its members, but at the same time exceeds and thus eludes those members. It is thus a quite peculiar kind of knowledge that may very often not be known as such by those in whom it is, precisely, embedded. For this reason, efforts to artificially *engineer* the endogenous market order by adding exogenous command structures (laws and regulations beyond those arising 'endogenously') are bound to tip the balance from the side of liberty and towards authoritarianism: exogenous command is *necessarily* weaker because it is not based on a *relationship* between the local and its delocalization.

The metaphor by which Hayek defines this risk is that of physical systems, that is, thermodynamic systems, entropic systems that tend to 'perfect disorder'. It is evident, he says, 'that in society some perfectly regular behaviour of the individuals could produce only disorder'. What Hayek thus seems to gesture towards, here, is the near contemporaneous observation made by Robert Smithson: that a perfect crystalline structure *seems* highly ordered but is *in fact* entropic compared with the mother liquid from which it emerges, no matter how subtly the conditions may have been arranged at the outset. Likewise, a society of perfectly regulated individuals would be similarly entropic, because, we might add, a degree of irregularity (that is, diversity) is fundamental to the immune function, but where this is a question, not just of thermodynamic entropy, but of informational entropy – of that 'fascist ant-state with human material'[500] about which we were warned by Norbert Wiener. For Hayek, however, the threat of such a fascist ant-state falls purely on the side of the statistical aggregations of 'central planning': it does not seem to occur to him that such a threat might be entailed by the (taxical) *application* of cybernetics to that endogenous order that he understands market operations to be, let alone by applying cybernetics in the manner of today's performative algorithmics (a 'soft' *taxis*, we could say).

Hayek can *indeed* be understood as a perverse and metaphysical *champion* of the 'cosmo-local' and its knowledge, *against* the control society built on the 'statistical aggregations' of forms of *taxis*. But the assumption that lies behind all of his work is that the endogenous, non-teleological *but unconsciously cybernetic* ends of the market order will always be less entropic than any exogenous, and presumably *non*-cybernetic, form of conscious-but-*artificial* control. Hayek's version of the cosmo-local is therefore fundamentally based on a *denial* of Stiegler's demonstration that the *condition* of all neganthropic order *is* artificial, and that the function of neganthropic reason arises and can arise only from processes of artificial selection, where shifts in these processes *disrupt* existing systems and existing forms of knowledge, and therefore present a *problem* requiring the *care-ful reinvention of knowledge* and not just the *assumption* that existing knowledge guarantees successful adjustment to changed economico-technological conditions.

What Hayek *wants* to argue, by distinguishing and indeed opposing *kosmos* and *taxis*, is that care is only ever really a property of *microcosms* (simple exorganisms and lower complex exorganisms, that is, microeconomic exorganisms), and hence that *macrocosms* (higher complex exorganisms that authorize or legitimize forms of *taxis*, that is, macroeconomic rules and laws) are only capable of being taken care of through the market-produced *amplification effects* of microeconomic care. But there is another way of stating this conclusion: it is to claim that society, and in particular a society regulated 'endogenously' by market operations, should not be understood on the basis of the metaphor of a nervous system, that is, of a *central* nervous system, because there is no centralized regulatory mechanism capable of taking care of all its dimensions. Rather, the systems of a society more closely resemble an immune system, where it is microcosmic encounters, occurring at very small localities but very widely dispersed throughout the social organism, that produce the greatest general systemic benefit, and do so without coordination, and precisely without any *awareness*, and with barely any need for a *taxis* of any kind. Hayek's epistemology could be construed as fundamentally immuno-logical in this sense.

But for those coming after Hayek, the lesson from his work is *also* that there is little point in invoking the cosmic or the local unless we know *very clearly* what we mean by these terms, what they have to tell us about the relationship between the biological and the technological, and how they relate to conceptions of entropy, negentropy and anti-entropy. What Philip Mirowski and Edward Nik-Khah will show, in *The Knowledge We Have Lost in Information,* is that the crystal palaces of neoliberal capitalism emerge in a complex and symptomatic way from their contradictory Hayekian provenance, taking the cybernetic cue as a basis for 'taxically' transforming economic systems, but in so doing progressively eliminating from their argument the Hayekian *faith* in the localized knowledge of endogenous orders.

It is the Hayekian fact that individuals do not necessarily know what they know that will become the basis for the progressive elimination of knowledge from economic ideology in favour of forms of calculable and computable information available only to economists themselves, or, ultimately, only to the machines themselves. The *effect* is played out across the last fifty years of efforts to exogenize the endogenous by *forgetting* Hayek's suspicion of the engineering of rules. Mirowski details how economists themselves will become entrepreneurs engineering new markets, building these supposedly pure crystalline structures atom by atom, and progressively liberating themselves from the vaguely-remembered shadow of the notion of the market as a locus of endogenous and localized knowledge. What will thus be gradually but relentlessly expunged from the economic theory of the Neoclassical Thought Collective is any remnant of the virtue of knowledge, local or otherwise.

Philip Mirowski, the stabilizing archi-criterion and the war against reflection

Philip Mirowski is an economic historian and philosopher whose perspective may be far from that of most economists but where this may prove to be the very thing that opens the way to a critique of the last half-century of economic theory in terms of the kinds of questions that underlie Stiegler's analysis. Mirowski's first major work, for example, *More Heat Than Light. Economics as Social Physics: Physics as Nature's Economics*, is dedicated to 'the most profound economic philosophers of the 20th century: Thorstein Veblen and Nicholas Georgescu-Roegen', that is, respectively, the economic philosopher of consumerism and the economic philosopher of entropy.

After paying his respects to these two saints, Mirowski proceeds to unfold a work devoted to the way in which economists have suffered from 'physics envy'. By this, he means (as he summarizes it in a reply to critics) that 'neoclassical economics was born of the inept imitation of early nineteenth-century classical mechanics'.[501] Neoclassical economists, in other words, longingly admired the billiard-ball precision of classical mechanics: he would later summarize the book by stating that it described these as aspiring to imitate a

> physics prior to the Second Law of Thermodynamics, a science most assuredly innocent of the intellectual upheavals beginning at the turn of the century and culminating

in the theories of quantum mechanics and statistical thermodynamics.[502]

Had they paid attention to the question of entropy, they would not have been able to persist in fantasies of 'natural cycles' and 'perpetual growth', and they may, especially if they had also read Schrödinger, have had a way of reflecting on how behavioural decisions in the biological world of endosomatic evolution are a function of the localized systems formed by organisms and species in their improbable struggle to persist against the entropic tendency. They may then also have had a way of reflecting on how, in *exosomatic* evolution, the capacities for making those decisions are furnished by criteria that are no longer just biological but economic. Such criteria are therefore essentially historical, but they are also *pharmacological*, which is to say, a locus of struggle to ensure that a transformed economico-technological system functions positively within the limits of its operation.

The criteria by which selections are made from among behavioural possibilities in exosomatic evolution are commonly called *values*: these are first and foremost the orienting principles according to which care is taken of life within the technical systems of this or that epoch of exosomatization. Values are the orienting principles through which care is taken of these technical systems via the social systems that arrange these technical systems with the individuals living within any particular locality, and through which care is taken of the social systems themselves and the individuals of which they are composed. Abandoning the standpoint of 'early nineteenth-century classical mechanics' might have led to a way of reinterpreting John Locke, for whom the source of value was the work done upon a milieu by the instrumented hand of man in order to extract utility. But without such a revised social physics, Mirowski finds that the basis for this or that economic approach, the way of divining those first orienting principles, always seems to turn out to be based on some or other metaphor, where these metaphors are mostly more or less false ideas about equilibrium and invariance – or in other words on an *acknowledgment* of the necessity of some kind of account of so-called 'feedback loops', but at the same time a *denial* of the fact that such loops exist only in localized dynamic systems still subject to the overall tendency.

When Mirowski himself asks about this need of economists to grab onto one founding metaphor or another, he turns for illumination to the anthropologist Mary Douglas, and to the following quotation from her book, *How Institutions Think*:

> Equilibrium cannot be assumed; it must be demonstrated and with a different demonstration for each type of society…

> Before it can perform its entropy-reducing work, the incipient institution needs some stabilizing principle to stop its premature demise. That stabilizing principle is the naturalization of social classifications. There needs to be an analogy by which the future structure of a crucial set of social relations is found in the physical world, or in the supernatural world, or in eternity, anywhere, so long as it is not seen as a socially contrived arrangement.[503]

With this consideration of the need for a founding analogy or metaphor, for a stabilizing principle by which to 'naturalize social classifications', Douglas and Mirowski are addressing fundamental issues lying at the base of any economic science, past, present or future: (1) the fact that there is a need for an archi-criterion to function as the value of values; (2) the fact that this archi-criterion can be bestowed only by what Stiegler calls a higher complex exorganism and as a local and historical expression of the struggle against entropy; and (3) that, *as* an archi-criterion, it cannot be something 'real', and thus its relationship to the 'supernatural world' or 'eternity' is *always* a kind of 'sur-real' and 'cosmic' analogy or metaphor, a de-spatialization or de-temporalization concealing that the higher complex exorganism is itself only ever local and temporary. What we might also add to Douglas's and Mirowski's economico-anthropological diagnosis is that, *prior* to the naturalization of social classifications, societies are characterized by the *naturalization of technical existence,* one of the consequences of which is to obscure that economics and economic values are a socially *and technically* contrived (or highly artificial) arrangement whose function is to perform the entropy-reducing work required to prevent any technical system from destroying the society it ostensibly serves.

As for the sur-reality of the cosmic metaphor or analogy underlying these processes of arrangement, the difficulty lies in the fact that such a founding metaphor is scarcely capable of deriving an adequate 'theory of moral sentiments' from any kind of *mechanistic* physics. With hindsight, we can see that Newtonian physics is itself nothing other than a kind of de-localizing conception founded in a placeless universal space. The struggle against entropy conducted by those exosomatic beings who are also noetic beings is not just a question of *information* about the 'particular circumstances of time and space' within an abstract mechanistic universe or perfectly balanced cosmos, through which some fantasy of a permanently stable existence can be maintained. Rather, it is a question of the localized and differentiated knowledge that *takes care* of a locality that is not just a space but a place and not just a time but an epoch, and that does so by always striving to rise above the anthropy that this dynamic situation always also produces. This is what Stiegler argues in 'The New Conflict of the Faculties and Functions':

> These forms of knowledge [*savoirs*] produce tastes [*saveurs*], differences, noodiversified nuances through which the exosomatic being constantly raises itself toward a noesis that is more than human, which is always sur-human (just as the cosmos is always sur-realist: the cosmos, which is not just the universe, is composed of places within which improbable possibilities – sur-real possibilities – well up).[504]

Within these new perspectives, the *duty* of the economic beings that we must be is no longer just moral: it is cosmic. Based on the noetic power of dreaming (and of realizing our dreams, which is the condition of exosomatization), we must, using every means at our disposal, make this duty serve a sur-realist and serendipitous cosmology, a quasi-causal cosmology.[505]

On the genealogy of cyborgian economics

In *Machine Dreams: Economics Becomes a Cyborg Science*, Mirowski argues that these founding and orienting metaphors shifted in the history of twentieth-century economic theory: whereas neoclassical economics was based on the notion of the 'rational individual' as the atom of social physics, in neoliberal economics this individual tends to become, instead, an elementary cog within a giant machine, one that may not need any longer to be presumed to be 'rational', and one that, eventually, may almost be dispensed with altogether, at least for the purposes of calculation. But this cannot be understood simply as a *fall* from a humanistic economics to an inhuman one, or from a critical sense (in Kantian terms) to an a-critical one. Mirowski argues that the deficiencies of the original models – the fact that they *implied* some kind of full psychology or anthropology but never elaborated either, and hence that this economics cannot even *truly* be considered 'Newtonian' because it never defined the character of the billiard balls that would be its social atoms – helped to make this change possible:

> the 'methodological individualism' to which neoclassicals pledge their troth is an empty creed, for there are no full-blooded individual humans in their models. Hence all those methodologists who whine about the 'atomistic' character of orthodox economics mistake the promotional verbiage for

substantive content. I would add that the models are not so much atomistic as 'machinic', and that once one meets that conceptual requirement, then all other ontological commitments go flying out the window.[506]

This abandoning of 'ontological commitments' in favour of an already-implied machinic conception reaches its culmination, according to Mirowski, when economics turns computational, that is, informational. Economics becomes a 'cyborg science' when it possesses the following characteristics, or rather, when it begins to be possessed by them:

1. it makes use of the computer as a primary metaphor and reference point, especially the fact that it *apparently* 'straddles the divide between the animate and the inanimate, the live and the lifelike, the biological and the inert, the Natural and the Social, and makes use of this fact in order to blur those same boundaries in its target area of expertise';[507]

2. from this blurring of boundaries, it begins to attribute machine-like or computer-like attributes to biological or human functioning, and to construct approaches based on assemblages of these likened elements: 'it agglomerates a heterogeneous assemblage of humans and machines, the living and the dead, the active and the inert, meaning and symbol, intention and teleology'[508]

3. as the distinction between the biological and the social becomes vague, the 'sharp distinction between "reality" and simulacra'[509] is also weakened, with the consequence that cyborg science increasingly operates in the field of simulations;

4. questions of 'order' and 'disorder' become 'veritable obsessions',[510] relating these in various ways to thermodynamic entropy but even more to concepts such as noise, signal degradation and chaos;

5. concepts such as 'information', 'memory' and 'computation' come to be seen as *physical*, the first then tending to be conceived 'as an entity that has ontologically stable properties';[511]

6. the genealogy of these sciences does not arise from the discovery of new facts or the genius of a new idea but from a planned exercise, usually techno-scientific and

techno-economic but also often military, or in other words they are themselves products of what Hayek would call exogenous rather than endogenous design – the *'new cyborg sciences did not simply spontaneously arise; they were consciously made'* – and their 'blurred ontology' arose from similarly 'exogenous' concerns, given that it 'derives from the need to subject heterogeneous agglomerations of actors, machines, messages, and (let it not be forgotten) opponents to a hierarchical real-time regime of surveillance and control'.[512]

It is not that any one of these notions is inherently wrong, and in fact they mostly have origins in intuitions about the necessity of overcoming previous limits that are rooted in something true and necessary. The relationship between the animate and the inanimate, the living and the dead, the biological and the social, and the relationship between these relationships (as Heidegger would say), are all unavoidable questions that arise over the course of the twentieth century. Similarly, the meaning of order and disorder in various scientific fields (in both the 'life sciences' and 'human sciences'), the function of simulation and modelling in science (which is also to say, of prediction), and the relationship of information and memory to matter, are all absolutely crucial to a reinvention not just of economics but of science and philosophy in general. But under the influence of a confluence of forces, these notions all tended to be interpreted and conjoined in a confused manner that proved incapable of lifting their underlying significance from the veil of ideological obfuscation. In this way, they ultimately served to *legitimate the concept of the absolute market while simultaneously undermining the Hayekian defence of that concept on the grounds of its endogenously-produced distributed knowledge.*

The rise of neoliberalism and the market as an information processor

Mirowski and Nik-Khah turn again to the fate of this raft of questions in *The Knowledge We Have Lost in Information: The History of Information in Modern Economics*, to a large extent dating this turn from the 'The Use of Knowledge in Society', which is also to say, from one of the key moments of the inception of what would become neoliberalism. In other words, the shift to a machinic conception of economics begins when the question of the knowledge held by the formerly-conceived 'rational' economic agents of neoclassical economics begins to be re-conceived as a question of computable information. Mirowski shows that this information will be increasingly understood as lying somewhere *other* than in the heads of agents. For Hayek, and in one way or another for almost *all* mainstream economists thereafter, the values of things and hence the basis of their distribution do not lie in something known to the individuals of a society, but something that exists only in 'the Market' itself, and from this thought arises the notion that the true function of any market is to operate as a giant 'information processor'. In this sense, we can say that the fundamental premise of neoliberalism is that the market *itself* becomes the stabilizing principle, the naturalization of social classifications, the archi-criterion.

For Mirowski and Nik-Khah, following on from the former's work in *Machine Dreams*, it is thus strictly impossible to separate the informational and computational concept of 'the Market' from neoliberalism. They identify six important tenets of the latter:

1. As stated, the neoliberal market is to a large extent '*posited to be an information processor more powerful than any human brain, but essentially patterned upon brain/computation metaphors*'.[513]

2. The meaning of being a 'human person' is fundamentally revised: no longer a producer who through his or her works produces value, but instead a repository of 'human capital' (according to Gary Becker, whose significance was seen clearly and early by Michel Foucault) from whom value can be extracted.

3. 'Freedom' is conceived as value of values, but the conception of freedom to which neoliberals are willing to commit is mostly limited to choices *within* a society rather than extending to questions about the use of knowledge as an anti-anthropic means of social transformation, and this is so because 'contemplation of how market signals create some forms of knowledge and squelch others'[514] would pose a threat to the conception of the Market as a transcendental (that is, non-pharmacological, independent of its supports) information processor.

4. 'Inequality' is considered not as an unfortunate by-product of the operation of the capitalist market but as a functional necessity and a source of the dynamism of the Market as a motor force.

5 If indeed it turns out that 'the Market' causes problems, then such problems will always turn out, for neoliberals, to themselves require market solutions (whether those problems are a decline of education, a rise in greenhouse gases, or the global financial crisis itself).

6 While their dedication to 'freedom' means that neoliberals oppose 'regulation' as a fetter on economic behaviour (which Stiegler would say is their opposition to the regulation of the technical system in general by the social systems in general), they make an exception for criminal law. As Richard Posner put it, the 'function of criminal sanction in a capitalist market economy, then, is to prevent individuals from bypassing the efficient market'.[515]

Neoliberal market fundamentalism would thus consist in the twofold claim that the 'freedom' of the market is what guarantees its capacity to function as an efficient information processor, and that its ability to function as an information processor is what demands that it remain 'unfettered'. From this standpoint, it is impossible to separate the rise of neoliberalism from the rise of the computer as information processor. Nevertheless, according to Mirowski and Nik-Khah, the notion of the market 'as such', as 'something that has always existed in a quasi-natural state, much like gravity',[516] faces a challenge when two things begin to occur: (1) the computer itself changes, from a device for making calculations to a network of 'distributed all-purpose communication devices [...] culminating with the spread of the Internet';[517] (2) regulators begin to intervene in economic affairs, making efforts 'to improve or otherwise reconfigure specific markets'.[518] In other words, the neoliberal notion of the market-qua-information processor *as* archi-(non)criterion of the most efficient truth (the 'truth' of *Gestell*) *both* establishes itself through *and* is challenged by the transformations in computational technics and economic institutions.

We can have no trouble understanding how 'the Computer' is in fact a process of technical individuation that has been vastly defunctionalized and refunctionalized over the past several decades: even beyond Mirowski's point, it has been transformed from a machine for making calculations to the prime interface between the noetic soul and its milieu, via which every possibility of information and knowledge is opened up and closed off, within a network of networks that is increasingly enslaved to consumerist ends pursued through the harvesting of 'big data'. But it is necessary to offer some examples to elucidate how 'the Market', too, can be defunctionalized and refunctionalized, manufactured, engineered and sold as a product. Does not this fundamentally conflict with the Hayekian notion of markets as endogenous repositories of cosmo-local knowledge, which, if tampered with according to exogenous imperatives, are bound to become dangerously unbalanced? What does it mean to say that there were efforts to improve or reconfigure markets, how could Hayek's work possibly lead to such efforts, and what has been the impact on the notion of 'the Market' qua information processor that has formed the perverse archi-criterion of the non-necessity of the truth?

The first example of such intervention given by Mirowski and Nik-Khah concerns the effort of the United States government across the second half of the twentieth century to promote the growth of the national mortgage market. After the privatization of Fannie Mae in 1968, the foundations were laid for the securitization of mortgages, and over time this gave rise to numerous other forms of 'financial innovation'. This trajectory, which forms a key part of the shift towards what Colin Crouch calls 'privatized Keynesianism',[519] through which the role of Keynesian mechanisms for maintaining stable levels of consumption were replaced by the invention and growth of consumer credit, leads to the proliferation of new instruments that produce new markets (the market is the *product* of the inventing and sanctioning of such instruments). What Mirowski and Nik-Khah describe in this way is the evolution of all of these kinds of financial instruments, which are also new and strange markets, and which would eventually culminate in the global financial crisis that would reveal the self-poisoning toxicity lurking within these instruments and markets.[520]

A second example offered by Mirowski and Nik-Khah is the set of electromagnetic spectrum auctions run by the Federal Communications Commission (FCC) starting in 1993.[521] This centrally-conceived example of the creation of a new market was premised on the ideas:

- that 'the Market' can most efficiently reconcile political, scientific and economic considerations;
- that this implies that 'market design' engineered by economic experts can thus serve public policy;
- that the best measure of the quality of this service is the revenue brought by the auctions themselves.

What became clear in the lead-up to these auctions, however, is that it is not 'the Market' that would determine these outcomes, but the set of rules determined for the *particular* form of auction or market algorithm chosen by the regulatory body. Furthermore, the *participants* in these FCC auctions themselves hired their own game theorists in order to influence the *initial choice* of form and algorithm (not only in order to 'win', but in order to increase the likelihood of the auctions generating lower revenues generally). The most important outcome of the purported 'success' of these spectrum auctions was the evolution of a market in market design itself, with numerous economists taking out patents on various 'made-to-order' market forms, along with the software and other elements necessary to create a full market 'package' with which to compete for government and other contracts.

The final example they offer is the attempt to find market solutions to the global financial crisis itself, whose causes can to a significant extent be traced precisely to the earlier attempts at market creation and design. In the face of the undeniable reality of that crisis, and the risk it posed to the entire global economic system, key figures of economic governance in the United States attempted to fashion the Troubled Asset Relief Program (TARP) into a market solution for a market problem. The crucial moment in the unfolding of that crisis, in which it became absolutely necessary for action to be taken, was the moment when the extent and spread of the toxicity of securitization became undeniable, because it was at this moment that banks and investors suddenly understood that there was nowhere that could be considered immune from catastrophic risk. And it was this understanding, this moment of *economic anaphylaxis*, that threatened to freeze the entire financial system, as banks and investors recoiled in fear and desperation from the possibility of increasing their exposure any further.

Treasury Secretary Hank Paulson and Federal Reserve Chairman Ben Bernanke had the idea, or were given the idea by 'experts' in market engineering, that market designers could resolve this crisis through the design and implementation of a TARP market whose auction system would successfully *differentiate* between toxic assets and genuine assets. The highly dubious assumption behind this idea was that, in all these bundles and packages of loans and securities, there must be some that were still worth something, and the problem was thus not value but information about its location. Through the information-processing characteristics of such a market, the idea went, the government would come to discern where true value lay, and would be able to offer fair prices for these assets, lubricating and unfreezing the financial system.

The *most* perverse aspect of this scheme lay in the fact that it had to aim at a *particular* threshold of value: too low, and it would confirm the essentially worthless character of all these assets in general, inevitably leading to a crash; too high, and it would seem like a wasteful and politically indefensible throwing of government money in the direction of those responsible for the crisis in the first place. In short, the 'real value' of the assets such a market was supposedly there to divine was really a question of engineering the *right* value for the (economic *and* political) circumstances. In practice, it turned out that the difference between, on the one hand, the ideological notion that *the* Market functions as the most *neutral* and efficient information processor and, on the other hand, the *competition* between economists about which *particular* market design would deliver the right outcome, rendered the solution unworkable (especially given the crisis timeframe faced by governments and regulators), and was abandoned by Paulson and Bernanke.

The overall lesson of these examples for Mirowski and Nik-Khah is threefold:

1. There is a progressive elimination of the noetic role of the psychic individual (or the simple exorganism) from the conception of the market qua information processor, an elimination that occurs as economists strive to reduce markets to calculable and programmable elements, as 'the profession came to hold that its task was to build markets in such a way that agent cognition should be irrelevant to their successful operation',[522] a situation the authors describe as the production of 'artificial ignorance';

2. There is a contradiction between, on the one hand, the neoliberal ideology of the Market as most efficient information processor, and, on the other hand, the plurality of actual markets, a contradiction that is brought to an extreme when economists become designers and engineers of markets, even if this is a *plurality of the calculable*, so to speak, rather than genuine neganthropic diversity, and where the *possibility* and the *necessity* of *maintaining* this contradiction arises *because* knowledge has been systematically eliminated from the agents of the market as well as from governments and institutions, and hence the 'god's-eye knowledge'[523] required to sculpt market outcomes must be ascribed *solely* to those experts who will then become the economist-sophists selling markets designed and marketed as 'boutique' solutions rather than 'universal' information processors;

3 All of this unfolds not just as an inevitable tendency of knowledge to regress to information, or as if an inevitable effect of the rise of computation is to eliminate psychic and collective individuation, but rather as an ideological economico-political *program* in which neoliberalism 'influenced the way computational themes would enter economics',[524] a neoliberalism whose battle cry might be freedom but whose fundamental goal remained power, to be obtained by the *means* of power.

From cybernetic neoliberalism to platform capitalism

Some questions, problems and conclusions suggest themselves on the basis of Mirowski's work:

- In addition to exposing the notion of the universal market qua information processor as an ideological fantasy, it also shows that all of those diverse, engineered, idiomatically-calculable (so to speak) markets are themselves based on models of the relationship between information and economics that are largely *performative fictions*, informational prostheses whose function is to serve *particular* aims (favour particular selections) while still *partaking* in and *taking advantage of* the fantasy of the universal, neutral and efficient information-processing market.

- While Mirowski exposes the failure of economics to incorporate the question of thermodynamics, and is thus concerned with the way in which economic phenomena are subject to entropy, he *also* has a notion that markets 'reproduce' in an essentially negentropic way, 'by extruding copies of themselves', which are 'then "selected" for persistence by the human beings who make use of them and constitute the environment in which they grow and reproduce'. It is the irreducibly non-mathematizable character of the goals of these human beings that means that markets can never converge to a single form, but where there is, nevertheless, a negentropic 'arrow of time' in 'market evolution', a tendency towards increased complexity according to principles of 'von Neumann (*not* Darwinian) evolution'.[525] But is this so-called market evolution process really capable of being characterized as negentropic or neganthropic, whether according to biological or informational metaphors? To what extent does the answer to this question depend on whether the effect of these markets on psychosocial individuation is to foster the latter or undermine it, and to what extent is it possible to engineer markets to these neganthropic ends?

- According to Mirowski, the source of the dynamic but pharmacological *mutation* of these evolving markets lies in attempts to '"bend" or "break" the rules; this source of randomness [is] beneficial for the evolutionary process, if kept within certain bounds'.[526] But is the notion that the dynamism of this evolutionary process comes from the hubris of the rule-breakers (who want to take advantage of the constraints and limits of existing markets) not rather too close to the very ideology of the libertarian disruptors, who are no longer merely neoliberal precisely to the extent that they are even more likely to conceive criminal sanction as itself a brake on market efficiency, and who for that reason prefer to engineer and occupy legal vacuums by always being *in advance* of the law, whether criminal or otherwise?

- If Mirowski's goal is to describe the 'history of information in modern economics', and if for that reason he focuses on the shift whereby economists become not just scientists but purveyors of market design, then in the twenty-first century isn't it necessary to recall some other kinds of examples too? Did not platforms such as Amazon and eBay create new markets with specific sets of rules designed to serve particular goals and objectives? More importantly still, did not Google and then Facebook design new algorithmic markets that have enabled them to dominate global advertising, by taking advantage of the vast bi-directional flow of information occurring on their search engines and social networks? In short, are not the platforms of platform capitalism nothing other than new forms of market design resulting from new kinds of collaboration between computational and economic engineers, but forms whose goal is to eliminate the economists themselves in favour of a *purely* automatic information processor?

A fundamental lesson from Mirowski's work is, as mentioned, that governments and institutions have been proletarianized *by* economists *with respect to* economic knowledge itself. It is this economic proletarianization that subsequently *forces* these governments to turn *back* to economists in order to find market-informational solutions (purportedly useful performative fictions) to problems caused by markets themselves, including the problem of climate change, but where this 'turning back' simply introduces new chances for new problems. On the other hand, the engineered algorithmic markets of platform capitalism operate *automatically* to disrupt other markets, in the name of freedom but according to imperatives that would seem to exceed Mirowski's notion that neoliberalism is concerned only with freedom *within* society rather than *about* it. It is hard not to conclude that this dual process of market evolution does indeed evince an 'arrow of time', but one that seems thoroughly entropic, a complexification of markets, perhaps, but one that is also the creation of a new, standardized hegemony, in a shift that seems to define the Anthropocene as a period across which markets of every kind cease to have anything to do with collective individuation processes and are ever-increasingly-automatic technical individuation processes. But a technical individuation process that is not transductively entwined with psychic and collective individuation processes is itself unsustainable...

There is also, obviously, a great *practical* contradiction involved in this Hayekian and post-Hayekian position: on the one hand, the claim that all interventions into the operational mechanisms of endogenous markets are forms of *taxis* that 'can never improve but must disrupt that order'; on the other hand, through the Mont Pelerin Society and a thousand other ways, being engaged precisely in a concerted effort to intervene in how those mechanisms are organized and to disrupt the rules that govern them, and eventually in the engineering of new markets with highly artificial rules, from Fannie Mae and Freddy Mac, and the FCC's electromagnetic spectrum license auctions, to Amazon, Alibaba, Facebook and Google, via the Troubled Asset Relief Program that tried to ameliorate the 2008 financial crisis. In yet another book, *Never Let a Serious Crisis Go to Waste*, Mirowski highlights this practical contradiction between what Hayek claims and what he does, which is, precisely, an *ideological* contradiction:

> All this taxonimizing was fine; but the question that was motivating Hayek, even if he never adequately addressed it directly, was: What sort of 'order' was the MPS, and what sort of order was the Neoliberal Thought Collective dedicated to bringing about? [...] Here he elided acknowledgment that the MPS and the larger NTC did not themselves qualify as a spontaneous order [...]. When you unpacked all the shells of the Russian doll, it was just another elaborate hierarchical movement. [...] Either the dividing line between kosmos and taxis was bright and clear, and the MPS was an example of a taxis, which was thus illegitimate by his own

lights, or else kosmos and taxis were hopelessly intertwined, but then there was no dependable way in his system to separate 'government' from 'market', and the politics of the NTC would threaten to become unintelligible. The Hayekian wing of the thought collective has never been able to square this circle, so it has to resort to double-truth tactics.[527]

That to which Hayek gave birth, that of which he was the patron saint, or the godfather, was fundamentally a political program whose teleological objective is to promote a very particular ideology. And the great ideological contradiction on which this program rests is that it starts from the *valuation* and *necessity* of localized knowledge, but only in order to wage a war *against* local knowledge, *against* education – and *against* reflection:

> Though it sounds paradoxical to say that *in order to make ourselves act rationally we often find it necessary to be guided by habit rather than reflection*, [...] we all know that this is often necessary in practice if we are to achieve our long-range aims.[528]

The glue that binds all the open cracks in this political ideology masked as economic wisdom is the notion that information is independent of its supports. Even if we conceive of localized knowledge as forms not just of neganthropy but of immunity, always potentially anthropic and auto-immune, we can do so *only on the condition* that we conceive what circulates through such an immuno-logical system as being *retentional*, not informational.[529] Retentionality (and, correspondingly, protentionality) can *never* be thought independently of its supports, and this means that it can never be abstracted from the functions it serves, poorly or well, where these functions include that of reason as the path not just to living or living well, but to living better, that is, the path that leads to the possibility of a transition from one metastable state to another. The consequence is that today, when such a transition is more crucial than ever before, and specifically at the macroeconomic and biospheric scale, the path towards such a transition is fundamentally impeded by the computerized automation of all forms of knowledge and the subsequent proletarianization of politicians, citizens, the media *and* experts – all layers of the population.

The contributory economy and the global macrocosm

Let's return to the question of the contributory economy. It has the explicit aim of reversing the neoliberal tendency identified by Mirowski through which the psychic individual is reduced to 'human capital' and ceases to be the producer of value by his or her works. By re-establishing the possibility of work, by remunerating it, and by measuring its value according to the ultimately incalculable archi-criterion of neganthropy, the individual (worker) again becomes a generator of knowledge in a way that can then be shared and in this way a contributor to genuine local wealth.

Beyond the level of individual work and its social effects within a city or even a country, however, the necessity of a new economic model is established by a critique of the global economic system that shows this system is reaching its limits – in terms of the destruction of its own basis in the conditions of the biosphere, the destruction of its own basis in terms of the exploitation of libidinal energy (and the belief in knowledge it makes possible), and the destruction of its own basis in terms of the elimination by automation of the post-Keynesian distribution mechanism necessary for a consumption-based model. As stated, the potential problem with the contributory economy is that it seems at first glance to be a model applicable to the scale of the local community, and perhaps even to the national scale, but it is more difficult to see how it can be scaled up to a planetary-scale locality, *even though* that is the scale that ultimately necessitates a new model. The problem is that, *unless* this upscaling occurs, the contributory economy risks remaining an epiphenomenal half-solution, akin, despite all its virtues, to a kind of grand, and in itself very worthwhile, tending of one's own garden.

What we can see by reading Mirowski is that this is not just a question of the hegemony of *the* Market, but of the combined unfolding of: (1) the history of computation; (2) the economic problem of the role of information and markets in society; and (3) a neoliberal economics that *drives* the reduction of (economic) knowledge to information, but where this unfolding history nevertheless *in fact* leads to a proliferation of variegated markets rather than a truly *universal* market. It is markets that become universal, rather than *the* Market, but this apparent *diversity* of markets is also an *industrialization of the market itself*, as markets become products bought and sold by economists, and, precisely, *marketed* by them – yet one more 'highly artificial' process of commodification, as Polanyi would say.

What we can see by going *beyond* Mirowski is that platform capitalism is the attempt to exceed *all these scales* and dispense with economists themselves, except as in-house engineers dedicated to ceaselessly improving the algorithms that function automatically within these platforms, without need for the 'selections of the human beings who make use of them'. Economists may have been drivers of proletarianization, including the proletarianization of political representatives who thereby become dependent on their for-sale expertise, but the *overtaking* of such schemes by platform capitalism demonstrates the *degree* to which this ends up rebounding upon them as the proletarianization of economics itself.

In the universe of algorithmic platforms, it is not individuals who 'bend' or 'break' these rules in order to drive market evolution but the platforms themselves that are designed to operate as far as possible outside of *all* rules by being in advance of all rule-makers, and where these platforms *are* markets. They do so in order to generate addictive processes for the human beings who are still necessary for the system as producers of clicks and ultimately so that they will click the 'buy' button as frequently as possible. At the same time, energy markets and carbon market mechanisms continue to be formed or proposed, as market solutions utilizing different indicators but still devised by economists as a way of solving problems caused by global markets themselves. If, as seems to be the case, such solutions prove to be fantastical, then does the internation name a non-market mechanism that would amount to a global institution operating according to qualitative neganthropic criteria rather than calculable economic indicators? Does it name a *more-than*-market solution that *incorporates* global markets into a broader transformation of the conditions of globalization? Or might it, considered in relation to macroeconomics, amount to a placeholder name in lieu of an upscalable remedy?

It seems indubitable that Stiegler is right to argue that decarbonization is impossible without deproletarianization. The neganthropic economy of contribution aims precisely at renovating new knowledge, locally and on the basis of a 'cosmic' conception of the difference between knowledge and information, which is precisely lacking from other attempts to reimagine the function of the market in relation to the contemporary crisis. In this way, it hopes to generate not just 'awareness' of the necessity of fundamental transformation, but the will required for the shift to a new model and on a short timescale.

Yet the fact remains that today, seven of the ten largest corporations in the world *by revenue* remain fossil fuel energy companies (and the largest of all is the emblem of consumerism that is Walmart), and seven of the ten largest corporations in the world *by market capitalization* are the leading companies of platform capitalism. By whatever measure of their size, these planetary giants are not just *expressions* of a universal market: they *define and engineer* the markets in which they operate. At the same time, they are the leading drivers of climate change, addictive consumerism and automation – that is, they are fundamental agents of the headlong rush towards limits. There no longer seems to be any doubt that merely tinkering with the mechanisms operating at the microcosmic levels of this macrocosmic global economy will not make a difference to its overall operation sufficient to alter its fundamental and fatal trajectory.

It is thus strictly impossible to deal with the question of what it means to reinvent economic processes without paying close and specific attention to the details of the mechanisms operating on the largest scale of this entropic and anthropic reality. To pay attention to this entropic reality implies asking what macroeconomic model cannot just ameliorate but replace the consumerist perpetual-growth model, and this in turn implies asking what function markets fulfil in such a model and at every scale, including the largest. It means knowing whether those markets need to be re-engineered by knowledgeable economists, and whether and how the role of markets would no longer be to computationally process 'correct' information about calculable 'exchange values' and instead be to generate real but incalculable knowledge defined according to neganthropic values in order to generate real but incalculable neganthropic wealth. What would it mean for a *global* market to be a generator of such knowledge, and how is such a thing even conceivable, let alone achievable?

Wolfgang Streeck and the interregnum

In his diagnosis of the current state and prognosis of the coming end of capitalism, Wolfgang Streeck shows that before it 'will go to hell', capitalism will 'for the foreseeable future hang in limbo, dead or about to die from an overdose of itself', which is to say that it will 'issue, not in another order, but in disorder, or entropy'.[530] He neatly sums up the absence of epoch brought about by the efforts of the post-Hayekian Neoliberal Thought Collective:

> As long as the capitalist dynamism continues to outrun collective order-making and the building of non-market institutions, as it has for several decades now, it disempowers both capitalism's government and its opposition, with the result that capitalism can neither be reborn nor replaced.[531]

Streeck characterizes this *interregnum* as an 'age of entropy' dominated by an ideology of *disruption* and *resilience*. Beyond Schumpeter's creative destruction, disruption is the ideology of the 'Darwinian battlefield of global capitalism'.[532] Resilience is its counterpart: 'adaptive adjustment', whose function is to make the inevitably individualistic characteristics of an 'under-institutionalized' and 'de-socialized' society survivable, and thus:

> The more resilience individuals manage to develop at the micro-level of everyday life, the less demand will there be for collective action at the macro-level to contain the uncertainties produced by market forces – a demand that neoliberalism could not and would not fill.[533]

Streeck explains in perfectly clear terms where this age of entropy, dominated by a disruption that is anything but anti-anthropic and a resilience that is anything but immunizing, leaves those who remain within its localities, and who are effectively no longer citizens, but users:

> The de-socialized capitalism of the interregnum hinges on the improvised performances of structurally self-centered, socially disorganized and politically disempowered individuals. Four broad types of behaviours are required of the 'users' of post-capitalist social networks for the precarious reproduction of their entropic social life, bestowing resilience both on themselves and on an otherwise unsustainable neoliberal capitalism, summarily and provisionally to be identified as *coping, hoping, doping* and *shopping*.[534]

Today, in the midst of the economic fear brought by the pandemic, we see the immense dangers to which Streeck points coming to fruition at lightning speed. But we are also bearing witness to the return of the idea that government and centralization are fundamental to economic operations, along with the idea that the market *absolutely cannot survive* without massive exogenous (in Hayek's terms) intervention, in the form of 'stimulus packages' on an unprecedented scale. But these vast centralized fiscal operations are today being organized around repulsive constants that are premised on the desperate wish to maintain the *current* state of the system (that is, to freeze the fascist ant-state in place, so as to keep the rich rich and lessen the risk to that crystallized state posed by the threat of the poor revolting), which may be utterly understandable in an emergency, but is bound to be ultimately highly entropic, given that this under-institutionalized and de-socialized system is undeniably (however frequently denied) reaching its threshold limits.

The consequences of pursuing such repulsive constants while the cosmos collapses will inevitably be to intensify auto-immune, if not anaphylactic, tendencies, but the *question* of the economic immune function of centralized higher complex exorganisms is at least thereby raised. If, as Modern Monetary Theory insists, money is nothing other than a form of grease held by currency-issuing governments in limitless supply, through which the contours and flows of the production-consumption dynamic can be shaped, then what other possibilities might such an approach offer for vastly and rapidly reshaping the Anthropocene?

Do such ideas make it possible to conceive a way of escaping from an interregnum that is ultimately doomed by the aporia of sustainability? Is it possible to replace the current environmental paradigm, which consists in the fanciful notion of decoupling the consumption of matter and energy from the existing macroeconomic system, with a real conception of macroeconomic reinvention, founded on the functional, perpetual, temporary and local struggle against all forms of entropy, whether thermodynamic, biological or informational? A great part of the challenge of economic transition is to rethink this economic function in relation to propulsive constants, which is to say, in a way that might prove capable of taking care of all scales and dimensions of our cosmic sur-reality. A dream, what else?

Postscript: Bernard Stiegler on the future of economics and information

This chapter has tended to focus on the difficulties and improbabilities of shifting from one global economic model to another, however certain it seems that without such a shift the current system is bound to collapse. For Bernard Stiegler, the questions raised by this situation cannot be addressed without rethinking the very foundations of the notion or the concept of information lying at the heart of the computational systems powering that model in today's algorithmic and platform capitalism. This is not at all a question of wanting to eliminate algorithms or any other form of the applied mathematics utilized by such platforms in their treatment of 'big data'.

But it *is* a question of the necessity of providing a critique, not just of the *use* of algorithms and so on, but of the *basis* underlying them, so as to go beyond a use of algorithmic technology premised on eliminating everything incalculable. It is for this reason that Stiegler refers to the necessity of a 'refoundation' of *informatique théorique*.[535] Such a refoundation raises questions that exceed the discussion undertaken in this chapter (even if they are at least implied), but those questions seem at once highly necessary, very complex and a little obscure. On 10 May 2020, Stiegler wrote to the author about these questions, and it seems right and just to reproduce his words in this context, so as to leave these questions open, as a building site for further reflection, critique and construction, if not at the centre of our macroeconomic problem, then at the edges, where tolerable variabilities may have the chance to germinate, flourish and eventually transform the whole, provided that we learn how to cultivate and care for an anti-anthropic planetary garden.

Bernard Stiegler, Communication to Daniel Ross, 10 May 2020

To refound [*refonder*] is probably one of the weightiest verbs imaginable. Yet it is necessary to refound: we need foundations. The question is: how long should they last?

For a Sahara nomad, his stay is based on sand, and although it is only for a short time, he does not pitch his tent just anywhere. For the Dakota Indian, it is different, but the tepee, too, needs a ground [*sol*], less shifting, but still temporary. The question is: what is the ground when it comes to computer science [*informatique*]? Whether it is granite, even steel, or basalt, in any case this ground will disappear in the ineluctably growing chaos. What constitutes metaphysics is what is blind to this fate. But to struggle against metaphysics is to *refound while expecting to have to refound once again* – still one more effort! The question is then also: what is the scale of time, and therefore: what is the extent [*circonscription*] of its locality?

This having been said, I absolutely do not want to use the verb '*refonder*', and if I have used it, it is also for strategic reasons.

On the other hand, the theoretical computer science [*informatique théorique*] that underlies the whole of today's exploitation of information is based on what claims to be a foundation, and one that would purport to be eternal: Turing's theory of calculability. It is therefore a matter of causing this to collapse so as to refound something else.

What is computer science, *informatique*? It is a stage of grammatization, which is itself a dimension of exosomatization.

What is *theoretical* computer science, *informatique théorique*? It is what claims to state the foundations of this grammatization *like* Aristotle's theory of categories claims to found the grammatization of the *glossa* (here, I consider that Derrida is a bit too quick to dismiss Benveniste's questions), and, through that, of *logos*. 'Like' means here: just like Aristotle, it ignores what grammatization is, and rationalizes it, beyond all reason.

Computer science is not just a theory of calculability, it is also a theory of mathematical logic – one that keeps all the metaphysical attributes of logic in general. It establishes the functions of what it claims to be a rational calculation, that is, an automatic system of the production of truth. To 'refound' computer science is therefore to reconsider the meaning of 'rational' and 'true'.

The metaphysical attributes of theoretical computer science currently consist in:

- not seeing that in any grammatization there are technological physical conditions, and that this involves the hyper-material;
- the fact that truth is a processual function (of which the vicissitudes of sociology and anthropology, along with economics, are avatars);
- the fact that in this process, truth is pharmacological and never finally established.

What could a 'refounded theoretical computer science' be? It would:

- be a computer science that takes entropy into account through and through, in its three forms;
- aim to produce information in order to put it at the service of knowledge, and by convoking such knowledge;
- for this purpose, define the new basic functions, no longer of calculability or of mathematical logic, but of an automatic and networked system for reactivating Kant's lower functions and everything that has since been added to such functions (for example, the transitional dimension of the imagination, the unconscious content of reason, the retentional content of the schematism, and so on);
- do so, where these functions are implementable on networks accessible through interfaces themselves conceived in relation to these functions.

It would therefore be a computer science that would start from Kant's critique of Leibniz's failure to differentiate understanding and reason, Leibniz being himself the starting point of what will lead to computerized grammatization.

I do not think that it is the economists who functionalize information technology in order to find a solid basis: it is *capitalism* that has the imperative need to calculate everything, which the economists rationalize instead of critiquing (including the so-called Marxist economists who understand absolutely nothing about all of this, even though it was something that Marx understood so well). Theoretical computer science has served as an ideology amounting to a hyper-rationalization (in Adorno's sense of rationalization) well beyond economists: everyone, every day, tells themselves that calculation is still more efficient than anything else, and everyone bows to this fact – which is the fact of the market having become computational through and through.

In this context, theoretical computer science claims to be able to impose itself as the law of all exchange. It has done so by 'hypertrophying' the function of the understanding, which is irrational. And if it is irrational, it is not for Kantian metaphysical reasons (the kingdom of ends, and the freedom that is attached to it, etc.), but because of entropy (from which the kingdom of ends *flows as a counter-current*).

What I therefore call 'new theoretical computer science' designates nothing other than the hyper-critical theory of the exorganogenesis of perpetually pharmacological noesis (in the absence of such a hyper-critique, negatively pharmacological), where mathematics is a dimension of the world in concrescence, and which, as soon as it is instrumentalized as 'applied mathematics', loses all its privilege of being an 'eternal foundation', which it is only on the condition that it is useless: as soon as it is used, this 'foundation' collapses [*ef-fondre*], that is, accelerates entropy.

You ask, 'what is the real basis of the connection between information and economics in exosomatization?', and you add: 'the starting point has to be the idea of "exchange", where what is exchanged is always some kind of hyper-material object and its significance'.

I was delighted to see you raise this question because at the time I sent you this text, I wrote another one, which I have not finished, to answer a question from a high school girl of the Thunberg generation about automation, employment, etc. – an unfinished response that I reproduce below:

> The economy is above all a system – in this instance, a system of exchange. And a human society cannot do without such an economy. What is exchanged? Above all, products of exosomatization, or products obtained thanks to exosomatization (raw materials, subsistence products, services, etc.).
>
> As exosomatization transforms – during exosomatic evolution – the conditions of such exchanges vary, sometimes very profoundly: the objects or services exchanged evolve, and the types of exchanges themselves evolve (through the division of labour, social hierarchies, juridical relations, the nature of the knowledge required, etc.).
>
> The anthropological theory of exchange is very important: we could say that it founds anthropology as a science – and it is generally related to the system of kinship in 'ethnic cells' (if we can use the terminology of Leroi-Gourhan, who

himself is interested in the technical exchanges made possible by the detachability of organs).

When Georgescu-Roegen posits that we must read Schumpeter with Lotka, this means that we must put back, at the centre of observation, the conceptualization and organization of the economy, the *fact of exchange*, inasmuch as it is *required by the exosomatic form of life*.

Every economy is therefore a system of exchange, and, in the economies before history (in Lévi-Strauss's sense, in the sense that there are societies with 'slow history', which are also the economies organized by the clan, the tribe or the ethnic group), symbolic exchange, sexual exchange and the exchange of material goods (resulting from exosomatization) are inseparable. There is no 'economic system' outside of the 'symbolic system' that governs exchanges in their totality.

As social organizations become differentiated, and of course, in particular, starting from the moment when sedentarization leads beyond the hunter-gatherer economy, this differentiation gives rise to what Georges Dumézil called the 'three functions'[536] (today highly contested, in particular by Jean-Paul Demoule, who shows that this theory has fed into the discourse of the 'new right' and the far right in general, and even into anti-Semitism).

The differentiation of social organizations is inseparable from the transition from the predatory economy (hunting, gathering, war) to the economy of inter-ethnic and international trade and exchange. There are, however, overlaps between dominant forms of predation, on the one hand, and forms of peaceful trade, and peaceful economico-political entities can indeed shift to a war-predation economy when their peaceful economy weakens, or when they covet access to new resources, including as the practice of slavery. On all of this, we should read Kojin Karatani.

There are stages in exosomatization that correspond more or less directly to changes in social organizations and their economic and political systems. I will not recall them here, except to point out that over the last six centuries (since the late fifteenth century, which means both the discovery of America and the printing press), very clear-cut stages of exosomatic evolution correspond to very clear-cut stages of economic systems.

The fifteenth century saw the beginning of the movement of the planetarization of exchange that will lead – starting from slavery and 'triangular trade' – to what is today called globalization. The latter amounts to the stage in which, *de facto* if not *de jure*, the economy becomes planetary, in the sense that between North America, Europe and Asia (including the Middle East), constant, more or less contractual relations are established, organizing a planetary division of labour, and intensifying the quantity, quality and speed of flow, to a point that would have been unimaginable even fifty years earlier – all of this systemically mobilizing automated financial flow management systems, 'agile' design, production and distribution processes, new tracking and transport systems such as containerization, etc.

What has been called interdependence has thus crossed a major and undoubtedly irreversible threshold, which presupposes exospheric infrastructure and infrasomatization, that is, the concentration and synchronization on a planetary scale of all types of flows by means of statistical calculation algorithms, and which, as I have tried to show elsewhere in various contexts and analyses, is absolutely toxic and unsustainable.

That being said, whoever claims to act to change this *literally infernal becoming* (hell being the *absolute destruction of all grounds for hope*, and what generates this destruction – in the form of fires, hurricanes, pandemics, addictions, denoetization, economic ruin, etc.) has the obligation to take into account the fact that *the economy is firstly a system*, and, more precisely, a system of exchange, and therefore to take into account the fact that if it is indeed a question of changing this system, this can be done only by cultivating new dynamics within the system (first of all, on its edges), and in no circumstances outside it.

This is why, as I told you, if a proletarian consumes more energy than a robot, which is often the case, it is more rational to use the robot than the proletarian. This is all the more the case, given that the proletarian can then deproletarianize himself or herself, that is, decarbonize himself or herself, and in so doing decarbonize the economy (political as well as libidinal) as a whole.

We are now in a situation of possible short-term global collapse. This is undeniable, even if we can have lengthy and even interminable discussions of the meaning of this 'possibility'. In this situation, the first obligation is to guarantee subsistence. It is a moral obligation, but it is also a political one: without such a guarantee, the ultra-violent explosion of social bodies is assured. And along with it, the *total* domination of the far right.

This means, for example, that if we take the question of the dependence of urban centres on food producers into account, but also the dependence on food distributors, which forms a highly complex and tangled network, then we cannot ignore the issue that the conditions of exchange between these urban centres and across these networks, both to reduce dependence and vulnerability and to assure day-to-day subsistence, will be dictated *according to the dominant exchange system*.

Under these constraints and many others that I will not mention here, it is a question of ensuring that the inventive and creative edges of the system (which are fed by it), which I call transitional edges in a sense that I will specify later, allow *tolerable variabilities* to proliferate – if not by this or that dimension of the system (for example, purely speculative shareholders who control what no longer amounts to investment but to speculation, itself based on strategic marketing that is fully subject to the constraints and canons of a total economic war), then at least by the central dimensions of the generation of utility as well as knowledge – insofar as these alone can contribute to limiting anthropy and generating, via neganthropy, anti-anthropic, inventive, creative and transitional bifurcations, such that they make the global system of exchange percolate and transindividuate in a new way.

To do so, it is necessary:

- to have a reality principle that is well-tested in the various features that make up the global system of exchange in which we find ourselves;
- to have critical concepts that make it possible to identify and overcome internal and external limits;
- to have a method for concretizing such concepts in such a way as to constitute platforms for the negotiation of new collective agreements within the global exchange system, but by differentiating such agreements on various scales, whose diversity must be reconstituted;

- to define clear objectives, based on rigorous concepts and in-depth analyses, in order to initiate *'on the edge' actions that converge from these various edges*, and, in so doing, come closer to what, within the system, constitutes its dominant and toxic aspects 'at the centre';
- to pose the question of a new public power that would make it possible to implement this method and these objectives through a cooperation based on a capacitation of various actors, not just in terms of knowledge that would make it possible to critique and overcome a state of fact, but in terms of their relational practices within transitional existential territories, which must be constituted, leading to forms of cooperation operating according to new criteria of wealth and value, and of the production of this value, the latter being understood as what makes it possible to transform wealth (knowledge) into organizations.

It is by integrating these factors that we must ask ourselves the question of automation, of employment, of work, of energy costs, but also of the energy gains that can be generated.

8 Towards an Exergue on the Future of Différance

Introduction: Leroi-Gourhan, Derrida, Stiegler

We must repeat what Derrida says, go back to his text and say again what we find there, which we will, of course, find unchanged, because it will *never* change, remaining exactly the same for as long as paper or digital copies remain. We must do so, not *in order* to repeat it but so as *not* to repeat it, or to repeat it *differently*, to find the play of a different interpretation and to discover what it *could* say and what it could *not* say, and even to discover, if we dare, what it *might have said* and *should have said*, even if, in such circumstances, perpetrating violence to the letter of the text is not just an irreducible possibility but a vital necessity. Only in this way can Derrida's work live on, in a perpetual struggle against the entropic but probable fate that would consist in closing in upon itself and closing off new improbabilities until 'there will be nothing left', as he said himself while pondering the fate of his work on the cusp of his own becoming-a-ghost.[537]

Bernard Stiegler attempts to do just this in *Technics and Time, 1*, by pointing to 'something of an indecision around différance'.[538] Before describing this indecision, it is worthwhile reminding ourselves of the epochal significance that Derrida ascribes to what is 'neither a word nor a concept' but a term that is 'the most proper in order to think, if not to master [...] what is most irreducible about our "epoch"'. The starting point for thinking différance, then, is

> the place and the time in which 'we' are, even though [...] it is only on the basis of *différance* and its 'history' that we can allegedly know who and where 'we' are, and what the limits of an 'epoch' might be.[539]

In relation to those limits, *Of Grammatology* already famously stated that, with respect to a future that can present itself only as a kind of monstrosity in which the values of sign, speech and writing will be made to tremble, and with respect to that which will guide us towards this future, 'there is still no exergue'.[540]

It is no doubt the case that différance should be thought as the origin-without-origin of the play of difference, signifying that there is no sign whose meaning does not refer to other signs, no signified that is not itself a kind of signifier, signalling the inscriptive detour necessary for language or speech of any kind to arise. Différance thus forms a significant part of the arsenal of Derrida's critique of the structuralist tendency to neutralize time and history, and to 'totalize' structure, that is, to close the system. Nevertheless, it is *also* a matter for *us*, the 'we' of this epoch that has come to be called the Anthropocene (and which Stiegler takes as the new name for what Heidegger was trying to describe in terms of *Gestell*), of rethinking what it means that différance and its 'history' are the sole basis on which it would be possible to know who and where 'we' are. And it is a matter of doing so *together with* what Derrida *also* says in *Of Grammatology*: 'the history of life – of what I have called differance'.[541] It is in the elucidation of this topography that seems to map différance onto the history of life that Derrida refers to the work of André Leroi-Gourhan, and it is the character of this elucidation that will lead Stiegler to pinpoint what seems to him to be Derrida's indecision.

Here we will not replay all of the intricacies of Stiegler's delineation of this Derridian moment,[542] nor draw out the consequences of Stiegler's account of how the Anthropocene reaches the very limits of the possibility of epochality. But we should at least recollect some of what is contained on that single page of *Of Grammatology*:

- différance is conjoined with the history of life at the moment when Derrida introduces Leroi-Gourhan in order to think 'man and the human adventure' no longer in opposition to nature, but as simply a stage in a history of life that would be 'the history of the *grammè*';[543]
- this history is thus that of forms of 'inscription' and a 'liberation of memory' that runs from 'elementary programs of so-called "instinctive" behavior up to the constitution of electronic card-indexes and reading machines' and that thus 'enlarges differance';[544]
- Derrida draws this into the question of the 'program', referring to cybernetics but expanding this to a larger 'history of the possibilities of the trace as the unity of a double movement of protention and retention' that 'goes far beyond the possibilities of the "intentional consciousness"';[545]
- this relationship of memory and program, retention and protention beyond intentional consciousness, is thus an epochal history through which we can begin to know who and where we are, not just by tracing the emergence of writing back to the history of *Homo sapiens* but, as Francesco Vitale says, by conceiving différance as 'a genetico-structural condition of the life of the living and of its evolution'.[546]

Derrida recognizes that this succession, from the amoeba to the 'passage beyond alphabetic writing', 'structures the movement of its history according to rigorously original levels, types, and rhythms'.[547]

Leroi-Gourhan divides the evolution of instinct and intelligence into the lower invertebrates possessing very short action sequences, social insects that seem capable of a good deal of complexity in terms of behavioural programs, the vertebrates, with an increasing ability to vary behaviour according to what is retained in a 'potential' memory recording past experience in increasingly detailed ways, and the higher vertebrates that alone possess the possibility of choosing between action sequences.[548] In terms of 'the criteria of humanity', Leroi-Gourhan shows that the process of hominization (which by definition *predates Homo sapiens sapiens*, and by a long way) required the freeing of the hand and is thus 'conditioned by erect posture':

> Freedom of the hand almost necessarily implies a technical activity different from that of apes, and a hand that is free during locomotion, together with a short face and the absence of fangs, commands the use of artificial organs, that is, of implements.[549]

Leroi-Gourhan refers to the process of the increasing use of artificial organs (which Alfred Lotka calls exosomatic organs) as exteriorization, because it opens up new vistas of the relationship between hand, face and brain, but also because it simultaneously and *accidentally* opens up the realm of a new kind of memory not possessed by other species – an exterior, non-living memory – giving rise to all the related but separate possibilities of gesture, language and graphic representation (long before writing in the strict sense):

> In this book the term 'memory' is used in a very broad sense. It is not a property of the intelligence, but any kind of support or medium for action sequences. That being so, we can speak of a 'species-related memory' to define the fixing of behaviour patterns in animal species, of an 'ethnic' memory that ensures the reproduction of behaviour in human societies, and in the same way of an 'artificial' memory, which in its most recent form is electronic, which, without recourse to either instinct or reflection, ensures the reproduction of mechanical action sequences.[550]

This rupture between species and memory results in the creation of a potential memory 'whose entire contents belong to society', so that, at birth, individuals are 'faced with a body of traditions', that is, an ethnic past they have not lived but which they must adopt.[551] Hence Leroi-Gourhan understands the kind of beings that we ourselves are in terms of the tripartite division between 'species-related memory, social memory, and "mechanical memory"',[552] where the last of these, ensuring the reproduction of sequences of mechanical actions such as those formerly manual gestures programmed into the factory machines of the industrial revolution, refers to that passage beyond alphabetic writing described by Derrida.

Here we must make two points:

1 Some confusion remains in Leroi-Gourhan, because the 'social memory' possessed by *Homo sapiens already* has artificial conditions, mediated by technical artefacts. It is to clarify this relationship between social memory and technical memory that Stiegler will turn from Leroi-Gourhan to the Simondonian account of individuation, insisting (beyond Simondon) on the inextricability of its psychic, social *and technical* strands. Hence 'mechanical memory' is certainly not the *beginning* of exteriorized memory but its fate, threatening to *displace* social memory (as an-epochal *Gestell*).

2 Although Leroi-Gourhan refers to the 'criteria of humanity' and to 'the uniquely human phenomenon of exteriorization of the organs involved in the carrying out of technics',[553] this *in fact* amounts to a displacement of the animal/human distinction and a rejection of anthropocentrism. It is not at all a question of metaphysical essences but of epochs of inscription, leading to the *extended co-causal co-origination* of technics and the expanding brain as each forms the condition of the other in the initially very slow (no longer genetic) evolution of exteriorization.

But in general, what Stiegler gains by going back from Derrida to Leroi-Gourhan is first the realization that it is necessary to think what Jacques Derrida calls différance – which constitutes *the process of the production of traces*, which he also calls supplements – precisely *as* a process.[554] And second, it is the thought that it is necessary to distinguish, within différance that is the history of life, a new age of this process: from the moment there appears what Georges Canguilhem calls the technical form of life, différance must *also* be understood as the advent of the process of *exteriorization*, that is, a change begins when organisms begin to put themselves outside themselves, and therefore to inaugurate a new form of *memory*.

While Stiegler acknowledges the complex history of rigorously original levels, types, and rhythms, his own reading of *Gesture and Speech* thus more clearly delineates *three great epochs of memory*:

genetic memory; memory of the central nervous system (epigenetic); and techno-logical memory (language and technics are here amalgamated in the process of exteriorization).⁵⁵⁵

But Derrida himself pays little attention to the epochs of this succession, despite the *very reason* for him turning to *Gesture and Speech* in the aid of a deconstruction of the metaphysical opposition of human/animal (or culture/nature) lying precisely in the fact that it is *through* this *consideration of kinds of memory* that the question is shifted *from* 'the human' and *to* the adventure that begins when life starts to produce organized inorganic material things. With the advent of exteriorization, the lessons of experience can be conserved and transmitted between the generations, starting from the earliest flint tool. With the advent of forms of exteriorization *dedicated* to this conservation, it becomes possible to systematically *accumulate* such lessons – becoming the history of knowledge, that is, of noesis as a function of life, or what Stiegler calls a différance of différance.

Derrida's indecision and the uninterestingness of the question of the human

Derrida's gesture with respect to Leroi-Gourhan consists neither in making différance 'scientific' nor in deconstructing Leroi-Gourhan's scientific discourse: it is a question of allowing a kind of mutual exposure with the aim of opening up the possibility of 'a new logic of *repetition* and the *trace*' giving rise to new 'histories *different* in their type, rhythm, mode of inscription'.⁵⁵⁶ What Stiegler suggests is that Derrida did not quite take the full measure of this exposure to Leroi-Gourhan, not quite seeing that this history of life as modes of inscription is firstly that of the passage from the genetic to the nervous to the technical, and so never managed to open up these new and different histories.⁵⁵⁷

It is with this in mind that we should conceive Stiegler's account of Derrida's 'indecision'. In brief, if différance is the genetico-structural condition of life and evolution, that is, if it refers to the trace and the putting in reserve that together open the possibility of the proliferation of life in general, then how are we to understand that Derrida *also* seems to ascribe différance to that which opens up *after* life introduces the *new* economy of retention and protention that will arise with technical memory?

> *The trace is the differance* which opens appearance [*l'apparaître*] and signification. Articulating the living upon the nonliving in general,…⁵⁵⁸

> culture as nature different and deferred, differing-deferring; all the others of *phusis* – *tekhnē, nomos, thesis,* society, freedom, history, mind, etc. – as *phusis* different and deferred, or as phusis differing and deferring. *Phusis in différance.*⁵⁵⁹

For suggesting that the break in différance is at least as important as its continuity from *physis* to *nomos,* Stiegler has periodically suffered the rebuke of anthropocentrism.⁵⁶⁰ In fact, Stiegler:

- learns from Leroi-Gourhan the lesson that what matters is not the human but the rupture of the link between species and memory (a rupture that predates the human) brought by artifices;
- responds to Derrida's call for histories different in their type, rhythm and *mode of inscription,* understanding that this is firstly the question of artificial exteriorization as the advent of *new retentional forms;*
- recognizes that these new histories also open a history of new kinds of protentions, that is, expectations, anticipations and desires.

Stiegler has *no* investment in 'the human', nor in any positivist or empiricist metaphysics.

> General organology posits that the *organological* – understood in the sense of the *technical and technological supplement* – is what modifies the *organic,* that is, the process of its *différance*: of its differentiation and its delay [*temporisation*], its spacing and its temporalization, and in such a way that a *new process of individuation emerges,* that is, a new form of life. [...] And in this regard, I must say that I myself do not relate the technical form of life to the human: it is a subject I do not wish to debate because, from a philosophical perspective, the question of the human has never seemed to me to be of any great interest.⁵⁶¹

Stiegler has *no* investment in 'the human', nor in any positivist or empiricist metaphysics. If, for Derrida, retention and protention already go far beyond intentional consciousness, it is because he sees retentionality and protentionality as characteristics of the whole history of life qua différance, prior to the evolution of any intentional consciousness. What is crucial for Stiegler, however, is that the 'living present' of any organism possessing something that Husserl could come to call intentional consciousness necessarily passes through the non-living, and for this reason he completely agrees with Derrida that the relationship of spacing and temporalization must therefore be understood grammatologically before it is understood phenomenologically. What continues to be at stake in Stiegler's work is this life-death of retention and protention, but conceived explicitly in terms of the succession of retentional-protentional forms that have emerged and tend to persist: persist *against what?*

Even if it seems obvious that life is a process that temporarily defers entropy by differentiating itself through the flourishing of species, the answer to this question was not something made as clear as it could have been, either in *Of Grammatology* or in *Technics and Time, 1*. This is in part because the *earliest* of these forms – the genetic molecule that has persisted, differently, ever since the dawn of biological evolution – was insufficiently theorized in its relation to subsequent retentional forms.

Derrida, Jacob and retentional confusion

In what follows, therefore, we will follow out a line of consequences that can be seen to flow from the Derridian indecision diagnosed by Stiegler, and we will ask whether these consequences led to further deficiencies and ultimately to an inability to conceive a new logic of the trace and repetition. For what has plagued Derridian thought is the threat of sterility: an inability to reproduce *differently*. Our contention is that these consequences begin to be played out in a seminar series that was given in 1975–76 but not published in French in its entirety until 2019. We will then see that this leads to another step not being taken: the translation of this problematic of différance, the trace and modes of inscription, retention and protention *into* the problematic of entropy and what struggles to counter it, and the relationship of these struggles to the question of information.

That Derrida entitles this seminar *Life Death* [*La vie la mort*] with no conjunctive 'and' or 'is (not)' serves to indicate that 'this alterity or this difference was not of the order of what philosophy calls opposition'[562] but instead involves another logic, or another 'topos' [*topique*] – some uncertainty seems to remain here.[563] The issue at stake with this deconstruction of the opposition of life and death is precisely that of the future of the question of différance qua history of life opened up in 1967, but eight years later the interlocutor is no longer Leroi-Gourhan but the geneticist François Jacob. Derrida wants to deconstruct what he sees as an oppositional logic set up by Jacob between two kinds of memory, but, as we will see, Derrida tends to project into Jacob's text that which he already expects to find, seemingly without memory of what he should have learned from his earlier reading of Leroi-Gourhan.

It is worth noting that a large portion of what Derrida tries to do in this seminar consists in showing (and in trying to 'deconstruct') the way that Jacob both undoes the logic of metaphysical opposition through the very discoveries of genetic science *and* falls back into such oppositions, in particular through the 'models' and 'analogies' he uses to describe these discoveries. But what is the status of these models and analogies: does their importance for Jacob really go to the heart of his research or do they merely facilitate the task of popularizing scientific knowledge for an untrained audience? These deconstructions, in particular of Jacob's assertions about the origin of sexual reproduction or the origin of death 'in the proper sense', that is, about the evolutionary introduction of these new *distinctions* into the history of life, themselves tend to raise metaphorical eyebrows about Derrida's *judgment* about *what* to deconstruct and how.

The opening lines of *La logique du vivant* (1970) introduce the scientific question of life in terms of reproduction, that is, 'the begetting of like by like'.[564] It is not that molecules produce identical copies of themselves but that the macro-molecules of life shape the slightly *different* molecules that will then be produced: the repetitive begetting of like from like is *also and necessarily* the begetting of difference. Jacob notes that this process, heredity, is now described 'in terms of information, messages and code'.[565] The organism is thus 'the realization of a programme' in which 'the intention of a psyche has been replaced by the transmission of a message'.[566]

With this conception of message transmission, Jacob wants to replace the obsolete notion that evidence of design implies evidence of intention, that is, of a designer. His scientific goal is to conceive the organism in a radically dynamic way as itself only a mediation between past and present, 'a transition, a stage between what was and what will be', emphasizing that it is *reproduction itself* that is the only actor on this stage in the theatre of life, bearing witness to the final disappearance of a whole set of 'antitheses': 'finality and mechanism, necessity and contingency, stability and variation'.[567] The organism is but an eddy in the process of biophysical becoming, through which run rivers of matter and energy, carried along by currents whose understanding requires a new concept: the program.

> The concept of programme blends two notions which had always been intuitively associated with living beings: memory and project.[568]

Derrida notes that with this concept Jacob does not rely on the reference to inscription or to the graphic, or to phonetic writing or non-phonetic writing.[569] But having noted it, he immediately adds that he will come back to it later, and we are immediately led to wonder whether this acknowledgment will prove to be limited or conditional. Jacob wants to emphasize the way in which genetics overcomes a confusion surrounding reproduction that has existed for centuries: the belief that environment influences heredity. As Derrida says, this confusion consists in confounding what must be distinguished (epochally): two memories, 'genetic and nervous (cerebral)'.[570] Two terms marked with three words, one in parentheses: will these signs need to be made to tremble? Derrida is referring to the following passage in *The Logic of Life*:

> For modern biology, the special character of living beings resides in their ability to retain and transmit past experience. The two turning-points in evolution – first the emergence of life, later the emergence of thought and language – each corresponds to the appearance of a mechanism of memory, that of heredity and that of the brain. There are certain analogies between the two systems. Both were selected for accumulating and transmitting past experience, and in both, the recorded information is maintained only insofar as it is reproduced in each generation. But the two systems differ with respect to their nature and to the logic of their operations. The suppleness of mental memory makes it particularly apt for the transmission of acquired characters. The rigidity of genetic memory prevents such transmission.[571]

In writing 'nervous (cerebral)', Derrida is thus following Jacob, who describes this *second* emergence firstly in terms of the brain and secondly in terms of 'thought and language' – even though the emergence of the brain predates the emergence of 'thought and language' by hundreds of millions of years. A reader of Leroi-Gourhan would surely know that this is a question of the second *and third* emergences, as we have seen, but it seems impossible at this point to decide exactly what the geneticist intends. Derrida's 'nervous (cerebral)' almost seems like the emergence of a repressed memory of having read *Gesture and Speech*, but where the rigidity of the archaeologist's printed text may not have fixed itself strongly enough in the philosopher's supple brain.

Jacob exacerbates this confusion by characterizing these memories as respectively rigid and supple (which will be a key part of Derrida's 'deconstruction' here), *on that basis* describing them as variously preventing or allowing the transmission of acquired characteristics.

'Rigid' means that what happens to the individual organism in the course of its existence makes no difference to what it transmits genetically to the next generation; 'supple' means that the individual organism learns lessons from experience with the potential to alter its behaviour. But these lessons retained by an individual are lost with the death of the organism: only with the third emergence, with exteriorization, can these lessons be acquired, transmitted and *accumulated*, through the *re-*interiorization of what has been exteriorized, *thereby* leading in return to the possible emergence of the noetic processes of 'thought and language'. But exteriorized memory has this characteristic precisely *because* it possesses a technical 'rigidity' that nervous memory lacks: forms of artificial memory such as writing have the potential to retain their structure rigidly (exactly) over the course of many generations, precisely because they are *not* living but the articulation 'of the living upon the nonliving'.

How do we explain this confusion? In Jacob's case, his primary concern is with the 'first emergence', that is, genetic heredity: he is a geneticist concerned with human reproduction and those emergences that followed and led to the *distinction* of the technical living thing are merely of tangential or analogical interest. He can allow himself to forget the succession of epochs that he seems to collapse into the 'second emergence' because his reason for raising this division of emergences is only to elucidate that the scientific discovery of the genetic molecule as the basis of the first emergence enabled a correction of the Lamarckian error.

In Derrida's case, this confusion of memories (and of memory) threatens more significant consequences. Perhaps Derrida is just following Jacob's text in order to allow the oppositions it contains to 'undo themselves'. But Derrida never does allow this confusion to be brought to light. What he *does* do is try to undermine this 'opposition' between two kinds of memory and therefore the analogy between them, by describing the relationship between rigidity and suppleness as 'economic' or 'quantitative', on this basis concluding that it is not a question of analogy but of resemblance:

> If, therefore, within the analogy, rigorous criteria are lacking to oppose the two systems, so that one can today also describe institutional memory, the institutional program [...] in the same terms as the genetic program, then the analogy is no longer simply an analogy between different things but a resemblance within the element of homogeneity.[572]

It is as if institutional memory were simply the expression or extension of cerebral memory. But if 'institutional memory' can be described as resembling genetic memory by a certain character of rigidity and yet *also* possesses an ability to transmit acquired characteristics across generations, is this not precisely because institutional memory is not the expression of *a* memory but the coalescence of *two* memories, nervous memory and technical memory, and is this not precisely what Leroi-Gourhan means by socio-technical memory?

'Rigidity', in this case of institutional memory, means that its evolution operates according to a dynamic that exceeds the knowledge of its members, who are largely ignorant of the consequences that will follow from changes introduced into the system. Hence Derrida himself will refer to 'cerebral-institutional programs (psychic, social, cultural, institutional, politico-economic, etc.)' as evincing a causality that 'Jacob seems to want to reserve for genetic programs'. All these strange qualifications and hyphenations of the psychic and the technical, from the 'nervous (cerebral)' to the 'cerebral-institutional', ultimately lead Derrida, when he wants to point to Jacob's error in imagining that institutional programs are changed deliberately, to *introduce his own* rigid opposition between two memories, now termed with misleading simplicity the genetic and the non-genetic:

> Similarly, the heterogeneity between causes and effects [...] characterizes the non-genetic program as well as the genetic program. Where does Jacob get the notion that, outside the genetic system and the genetic programs, changes in program are deliberate, essentially deliberate? Where does he get this notion if not from an ideologico-metaphysical opposition that determines superior or symbolic programs (with humanity at the very summit of these) on the basis of meaning, consciousness, freedom, knowledge of the limit between the inside and the outside, objectivity and non-objectivity, etc.?[573]

For Derrida, Jacob's suggestion that non-genetic programs (such as institutions) are subject to *deliberate* change stems from his having blindly adopted a set of metaphysical oppositions, essentially those of the natural and the human. But is this overly general and simple but peripheral claim by Jacob really enough to justify Derrida's accusation of 'ideologico-metaphysical opposition'? Isn't it rather Derrida who effects a conflation of the psychic and the technical in order to *form* an opposition between the genetic and the non-genetic?

It is at this point that Derrida's reading of Jacob's description of genetic science meets up with the structuralism of the social sciences. Derrida points out that the singular achievement of structuralist science is to have shown that the systems linked to language, the symbolic, cerebral memory and so on, function through an internal regulation that, *like* the genetic program, *escapes deliberation and consciousness*, so that there can be no rigorous opposition between these two programs. Hence Derrida calls for a *general* notion of program, in the absence of which any 'philosophy of life' is bound to fall into a logocentric teleology and a humanist semantics.[574] But this call is founded on an opposition of the genetic and the non-genetic, itself arising from the conflation of the psychic and the technical. Such a conflation, however, is possible only by forgetting Leroi-Gourhan's focus on the emergence of different kinds of memory, forming different epochs, ages and eras of différance qua history of life, and this forgetting is precisely what Lévi-Straussian structuralism *authorizes* through its tendency towards the exclusion of the diachronic.

According to Derrida, the absence of such a general notion of program means that Jacob inevitably falls into logocentrism because his use of analogy brings into play the 'whole conceptual machine of *logos*' in order to describe what amounts to a form of non-phonetic writing. Derrida's own chapter on 'The Program' in *Of Grammatology*, by contrast, exists precisely so as not to avoid the necessity of the deconstruction of this logocentric machine.[575] Yet if Jacob's approach to the general reconstruction of the program in this work of popular science is not 'deconstructive' in the strict sense, nevertheless we have also seen that *Derrida's* opposition of the genetic and the non-genetic in relation to forms of memory is itself a reduction *to* oppositional terms of the retentional aspect of any such general programmatics.

Life-death and the illusory isomorphism of energy and information

The price to be paid for this confusion is the inability to pursue as far as possible the notion of différance as the history of life-death, the risk being that it leads to the sterilization of the Derridian project. In fact, Jacob's 'memory and project' might have been conceived in terms of such a general notion of program, and thus in relation to a history of retention-protection, but where this is conceived less in grammatological terms as the arche-writing of life than, more dynamically, as the arche-cinema of life: *anima* being always already cinema.[576] On this basis, a genuine encounter might have been staged between the phenomenological, the scientific and the deconstructive – exceeding all three terms while tying them together inextricably. It is possible to see the inklings of such a project in the remainder of *Life Death*, but we can also see how and why it stalls.

In the fifth session, Derrida's reading of Jacob brings him to the question of the difference between what the bacterium does and what Dasein does, or in other words to the question of 'world' and the Heideggerian problematic of beings that are with or without world (or poor in world), and more pointedly to the question of the world in which it is possible to raise the question of this difference of worlds. This world within which the world of Dasein can be considered together with the bacterium's *Umwelt* would be, he argues, a world without homogeneity or totality, operating according to a logic neither of the *is* nor of the *and*, neither of *identity* nor of *opposition*, but, precisely, of différance.[577] We can interpret this *question* – of the world in which we could think the bacteriological (non)world together with the noetic world of Dasein – as the question of the open system of knowledge with which it would be possible to think this *difference* that bifurcates the history of différance.

The 1975–76 seminar is the one in which this bifurcation *could* have been thought because it is here that there *almost* arises the questions:

- of how the deferral that makes a difference is ultimately the question of life *as that which struggles against the entropic tendency*;
- of how *this* question is *not just* a question of deconstructing the relationship between *the animal and the human* but *also* the relationship between *the animal and the machine*;
- of how this implies the necessity of *re*constructing a general programmatics on the basis of new distinctions, requiring new terms with which to consider the counter-entropic character of endosomatic and exosomatic systems.

Our contention is that the entire issue of *life-death* lies here, in these questions that remain just below the visible horizon of Derrida's discourse, provided that we take them as gesturing towards the monstrosity in which consists *our epochal problem*.

If the organism is an eddy in becoming, it is because what it emerges from, and what then irrigates all of its genetic tributaries, rearranging the contours of the counter-flow that is its functioning, behaviour and reproduction, are rivers of energy and matter (without opposing these terms) that both turn against and contribute to the entropic current, as Edgar Morin describes:

> living organization [...] succeeds, once constituted, in emerging and perpetuating its improbability, that is to say in creating islets and networks of probability in the ocean of disorder and noise. And it is the idea of negentropic organization,

which bears in itself this idea of re-ascent against the current of entropy, but also, and this is the complicity of the concept of negentropy, in following and feeding this very current.[578]

The formation of these memorious and projective contours is what shapes the flow of the becoming-space of time and the becoming-time of space. But what guides this formation of temporalization and spacing that appears in the course of disappearing is also open to being conceived as *informational* (without initially presuming to know what this word means). It is this informational aspect that leads Jacob from the analogy of animal and human to the analogy of animal and machine, and to the basis of such an analogy in the fact that both of them may be considered as localized and temporary counter-entropic systems: 'Animal and machine, each system then becomes a model for the other.'[579] Jacob is thus led to a conjoined reading of Schrödinger on the genetic organism as negentropic and Wiener on the computational machine as anti-entropic, both of these being systems enabling a temporary and local reversal of entropy through the 'messages' circulating along and between sensorimotor systems and feedback loops.

Derrida's primary question in the *sixth* session is the reciprocal character of these models and analogies. Establishing the informational character of the messages of such counter-entropic systems is possible only via informational systems that themselves arise *from* these systems, and this would indicate both the technico-phenomenological basis of the scientific investigation of these systems and the limits of the entangled objectivity of such a scientific project.[580] The scientific 'world' in which there can be an analogy between the counter-entropic character of (1) the bacterium, (2) Dasein and (3) the computer *is* a world but is bound to be *only* a world: knowledge itself has the character of an open, local and temporary system, something Derrida himself indicated from the beginning of the seminar when he described the process of life in terms of (that which defines access to) knowledge.[581] If we seem to be able to detect an echo of Canguilhem here, it also seems to point us to Whitehead's reflections on the function of reason in the struggle between the upward and downward trends.

Yet as Derrida points out, the risk implied by this kind of 'isomorphism' indifferently linking energy and information with respect to any kind of 'system' consists in concluding that the basis for this co-modelling of diverse systems lies in the analogous character of 'exchange'. Such a conclusion makes it easier and easier to shift focus from exchange to 'communication', and to privilege 'information' as the *what* being exchanged, so that the 'content without content' of exchange as matter and energy are abstracted away, since they are merely variables between different kinds of systems.[582] But in so doing, the matter and energy of this *what* are hypertrophied into non-existence:

> The circulating, circular model is at once informatic [*informatique*] (if information is only a formal message) and energetic. That which one might have wanted – and can always still want – to eliminate surreptitiously by privileging the message or communication or form, namely, the energetic, does not let itself be reduced.[583]

It is for this reason that it is strictly impossible, as Derrida himself knew, to conceive différance and the trace as if they have nothing to do with the material or the energetic, and therefore with the scientific approach to these questions, even if it can never be *reducible* to science. And therefore, he adds, 'whenever one speaks of textuality, the value of relations of force, of a difference of force, an economic agonistics, will be just as irreducible', just as, he concludes, every textual system opens onto an outside (which is also to say, arises from out of the complicated origin of a différance).[584]

Here, Derrida is engaged with considerable foresight in what amounts to a critique of the tendency of the contemporary age to view all systems through a narrowly-conceived cybernetic lens, in which 'information' would be the universal element. With this thought of the irreducibility of energy and of an economic agonistics that never forms a closed system (including textual systems, or systems of knowledge), Derrida might well have been on the way to reinscribing différance into a history of life-*death*, that is, of *more than one* kind of struggle against entropy (or the struggle against more than one kind of entropy), in a way that opens up a programmatics founded on a critique of both structuralism and cognitivism. Hence, he does go on in this session to recognize that it is not possible to separate the message as such from the feedback loop or regulation system with which it is involved:

> we do not have two concepts here (message plus energy regulation): in the message there was selection or sorting, and the principle of this selection that is constitutive of the very operation of the message had to obey certain economic laws.[585]

A message is 'informatic' to the precise extent that it is an improbable selection from among a set of possibilities, and this selection must occur according to criteria, which are supplied by the energetic and biological and economic functionality of the recursivity of the system. This recursivity consists in reintroducing into the system (and this is the very thing that *makes* it a 'system' in a sense that is not true of a purely 'physical' system such as a hurricane or some other meteorological 'system') the results of past action ('already, in one form or another, a memory or an archive of messages') in order to 'redress' the tendency of the mechanism towards disorganization. Derrida is explicit that this produces, 'locally and temporarily, a reversal of the tendency or the direction of entropy':

> Regulation thus consists in compensating for each local deterioration by means of a certain work or energy that comes from elsewhere within the organism or from outside the organism. This work or this local supplementary energy is itself then subjected to the same law, the same tendency, as will each one that follows, each loss being compensated by a gain, though in such a way that, if the system were closed, and according to the second law of thermodynamics, the disorder and the deterioration would go on increasing. The living being, insofar as it tends to reestablish the prior order or maintain the preexisting order, can thus never be a closed system.[586]

Derrida might then have asked about the relationship between the difference and deferral of différance and the local and temporary redressing of the second law of thermodynamics that is always in some way a question of an archive or a memory. He might then have reflected on the *different* (and *différant*) character of the 'economic laws' operating on the selection involved in exosomatic versus endosomatic diachrony, given the degree to which the former involves the *continuation* of biological evolution via the *suspension* of its selection criteria.[587]

To do so, however, would have required recollecting Leroi-Gourhan's argument that exteriorization *always* constitutes a kind of memory *because* it is an archive. It would then have been a matter of asking what forms the criterion for selection when these feedback loops involve a circuit that passes through exteriorization qua artificial memory, and what kind of energy circulates along such circuits, where this energy is what makes possible the protentional, performative or 'procursive' aspects of 'work'. It is possible to ask such a question, for example, by giving a critique of Lévi-Strauss's rejection of Mauss's use of *hau* to describe the energetics of gift exchange: contra Lévi-Strauss, the question is not whether this energy can be said to 'exist objectively', but rather of what existence means when it does not involve the 'objectivity' of physical science.[588]

Instead of that, Derrida takes the 'structural openness of every living system' as a way of quasi-deconstructing Jacob's claims about sexuality and death: for Derrida, this openness means that reproduction and death have always involved a relation to the outside, to however minimal an extent, and to ascribe this contamination of the inside by the outside to accidentality is to remain within an opposition between them that would still be metaphysical. In addition to acknowledging that the cybernetic notion of feedback that Jacob takes from Wiener 'displaces' the opposition of animal and machine, Derrida attends at length to the limit of the analogy by which each 'becomes a model for the other', focusing on the relationship between the notion of analogy, the notion of model and the notion of reproduction that underlies and breaks with these quasi-analogous models. We are unable to provide a treatment of all this here, which is at times interesting but rather tangential to what seems to this author to be the key outstanding questions implied by the notion of 'life-death'. Suffice it to say that Derrida seems to want to say that Jacob has become too invested in the analogous character of information, message, text and code in these various systems, and yet the last lines of Jacob's book make apparent that Jacob understands the world he is creating through his scientific work as involving systems of knowledge that are inevitably locally-inflected and temporary.[589]

The problems posed by the energetic model in psychoanalysis and its deconstruction

1. How the process of *exteriorization* amounts to an artificialization of memory giving rise to the technical and noetic life of mortal souls who thereby enter into a co-emergence of interior and exterior...

2. How this technical life implies, especially after the advent of *hypomnesic* forms of retention deliberately designed to store memories and project dreams (rupestrally, literally, mechanically, cinematographically or digitally, each temporalizing and spacing in rigorously original ways and thus making new différances), the *pharmacological* (that is, simultaneously and irreducibly distributed between poisonous and curative possibilities) artificialization of desire through the circulation of libidinal energy in circuits running through and between noetic souls and their retentional systems...

3 How this libidinal energy locally produced by exosomatic beings can be exploited and degraded by a consumerist perpetual growth macroeconomic model that leads to the *entropic* exploitation and degradation of all the matter and energy on which the biosphere depends, and to the nihilistic destitution of the diversity of 'social memory' and the noetic procursivity it makes possible and on which it depends...

...these three questions (exteriorization, pharmacology, entropy) roughly correspond to the three phases of Stiegler's work.[590] It is undoubtedly through his intimate familiarity with the 'fascinating inheritance'[591] of his master and supervisor that Stiegler was able to engage on this path of care-ful thinking. But Derrida himself was prevented, or prevented himself, from seeing the possibility of such a path, seemingly by failing to remember what he should have read in Leroi-Gourhan and failing to see how Leroi-Gourhan should have informed his reading of Jacob. We will now see that he also failed to see how the questions of thermodynamic and cybernetic entropy raised in that seminar ought to have recurred in his reading of Freud on the life and death drives. The upshot is that after 1976 Derrida withdraws from the question of the relationship between deconstruction and the sciences, at the precise moment when he might have taken further steps in that direction: a chance was thereby missed to elaborate and constitute the question of the relationship between retention, entropy, desire and technics.

The symptom of the withdrawal occurs in the eleventh session, where Derrida considers Freud's decision to privilege 'the economic point of view' and the *sources* of that view of energy and its circulation. After noting that the Freudian distinction between free and bound energy refers back to Hermann von Helmholtz and 'the principles of Carnot-Clausius and of the degradation of energy', Derrida simply decides to 'leave aside, at least for the moment, this tricky question of borrowing an energetic model'.[592] He thus retreats from any engaged reading of Jean Laplanche's chapter on the death drive in *Life and Death in Psychoanalysis*, despite this being (as he adds in a footnote in the version of this text that appears in *The Post Card*) 'a chapter which I presume to be read here'.[593]

Laplanche begins that chapter by considering the 'economic problem of masochism', then turning to the account of the death drive in *Beyond the Pleasure Principle* and the ambiguity contained in Freud's statement that the pleasure principle 'endeavours to keep the quantity of excitation present in it as low as possible or at least to keep it constant'.[594] Freud thus repeats what he said in the *Project for a Scientific*

Psychology, where he writes that 'the nervous system is obliged to abandon its original trend to inertia (that is, to bringing the level [of $Q\eta$] to zero)' and 'put up with [maintaining] a store of $Q\eta$ sufficient to meet the demand for a specific action'.[595] Laplanche asks whether we can really conjoin, as Freud seems to want to do, the notion of keeping excitation as 'low as possible', at 'zero', to the notion of maintaining it at a level that is 'constant' or 'sufficient'.

Laplanche notes that the issue of excitation and its circulation concerns what amounts to a 'homeostatic system', but in that case *zero* and *constant* are hardly equivalent: the first refers to the final inert equilibrium of a closed system receiving no additional energy whereas the second refers to the *metastable* equilibrium of an open system that both receives and expends energy. It is we who introduce this Simondonian term, metastability, into Laplanche's argument: limited stability at the limit of instability. Hence metastability refers to a composition, a play or a tension between equilibrium and disequilibrium, which is to say between synchrony and diachrony, *tending* to synchronize but also to desynchronize, that is, to diachronize.

One would surely think that the functioning of an organism, an open system fed with rivers of matter and energy, involves a (dis)equilibrium that is irreducibly limited to achieving no more than such metastability, always on the way to becoming unstable, and that the drives, of whatever kind, are, as a product of aeons of evolution, ultimately premised on the struggle for such synchronic maintenance and, where necessary, diachronic transformation. This is what one would be inclined to think, given what it also implies: that when the synchronic and diachronic tendencies composed within an organism begin on the contrary to *decompose*, the organic systems it contains find themselves stretched beyond their limits and the organism succumbs – to the inert state of entropic 'equilibrium' otherwise known as death. But with the focus on the death drive as a fundamental tendency of the biological organism, it is not 'constancy' but this entropic 'zero' that Freud finds himself increasingly unwilling to discard from life:

> And it is quite true that with *Beyond the Pleasure Principle*, it is the same priority of zero which, under the name of Nirvana, is being reaffirmed. The displacement of the term 'pleasure principle' should not mislead us: the pleasure principle, insofar as, throughout the text, it is posited as being of a piece with 'its modification' as the reality principle, is henceforth situated on the side of constancy. It is 'its most radical form' or its *'beyond'* which, as the Nirvana principle,

reasserts the priority of the tendency towards absolute zero or the 'death drive'.[596]

It is at this point that Laplanche introduces the link to the Helmholtz school (via Ernst Brücke) and Helmholtz's distinction, based on Carnot and Clausius, between 'free energy' and 'bound energy'. Helmholtz – who among other things is responsible for the popular dissemination of the idea of the heat death of the universe (by considering it as a closed system subject to the second law of thermodynamics) – understood the 'freedom' of free energy to refer to its availability for use, whereas bound energy would be that *unavailable* energy uselessly dissipated by the system. As Derrida notes, what Laplanche shows is that, in *borrowing* this energetic model to describe the free and bound energy of the psyche, in creating a 'certain analogy'[597] between mechanical energy and libidinal energy, Freud in fact reverses its terms:

> Freud takes up terms charged by Helmholtz with the meaning of the second law of thermodynamics; he more or less reverses their meaning, interpreting the adjective 'free' in the sense of 'freely mobile' and no longer 'freely usable'.[598]

Whereas in engineering free energy is what can be used, that is, 'invested' in work (as for instance in a combustion engine, converting chemical energy into mechanical energy and in the process making the latter freely available for work, but also inevitably giving off heat, that is, unusable energy), for Freud, energy that has been invested (in objects of desire, in the aims and work of psychosocial life) is *bound* energy. It is at this precise and delicate point that Derrida decides to 'leave aside, at least for the moment, this tricky question of borrowing an energetic model'.

Laplanche explains how these problems arise from the 'naïve model' that Freud deploys in order to understand the energy circulating around the nervous system, 'as if what were under consideration were a hydraulic draining system' controlling bodily movement and evacuating its energy. It is this death-driven tendency towards energetic evacuation, hypothesized on the basis of an obsolete 'mechanistic' understanding of biological functioning, that leads Freud to the notion of a 'reserve of energy' that the system must 'learn to tolerate' but that it also, Freud thinks, wants to keep as low as possible. What then makes it possible for this minimal constancy of excitation kept in reserve to be nervously triggered in appropriate directions are the 'exigences of life', or in other words the functional pressures of an existence that Freud still considered to be mechanically biophysical, so to speak:

> Thus, in the transition from a mechanism regulated only by the death drive to an organization subject to the constancy principle, it is the *very idea of life* that would serve as mediator and catalyst. And on every occasion on which Freud refers to the 'biological standpoint' in the *Project for a Scientific Psychology*, he does so in order to bridge the gaping discontinuity in the 'mechanistic' argument.[599]

In other words, although the Freudian conception of the organism, premised on a hydraulic mechanics, wishes to see this drive for the entropic zero as lying behind all observed behaviour, Freud must nevertheless account for the différance that seems evidently to be expressed by all those efforts to maintain the constancy of life – to keep it going – yet he has no way of accounting for such efforts other than by contradictorily invoking the 'exigencies of life' as such. Ultimately, these 'exigencies' amount less to the invocation of some teleological 'final cause'[600] than to the long-term and as such virtually automatic consequences of the evolutionary pressures of selection.[601]

Beyond Laplanche, however, it is necessary to point out that Freud has at his disposal *only* Helmholtz: unlike Laplanche, unlike Jacob and unlike Derrida, he is writing several decades before Schrödinger's Dublin lectures. In other words, Freud is trying to conceive the 'mechanical' functioning of the psychic organism at a time when the problem of the biological standpoint with respect to the second law of thermodynamics was far from being clearly elucidated. It is Helmholtz, after all, who first speculated that *chemical* processes, too, must be analogous to physical ones in terms of the relationship between free and bound energy: the question of *biological* processes remained a step yet to be taken.

These terms, of course, were initially formulated not with the heat death of the universe in mind, but in order to theorize the limits of efficiency of heat engines, that is, closed mechanical systems. It was only through a long historical course that the concept of entropy was then able to gain a progressive foothold from physical to chemical processes, then biological processes, and eventually (in some way by mathematical analogy, and in the search for another kind of technological efficiency) to informational processes. In falling back on mechanistic misconceptions, Freud's 'gaping discontinuities' in this regard prove to be largely continuous with those of his age: how closed systems of the kind described by Carnot, Clausius and

Helmholtz relate to the programming involved in the open homeostatic systems of organized life remained an open question in 1895, and even in 1920.

It is this complicated origin of the second law of thermodynamics that leads to all the confusions that underlie Freud's borrowing of the energetic model, and it is the complicated origin of information theory that leads to all confusions associated with the 'isomorphism' and 'inseparability' of entropy and information. This proliferation of confusions remains to be disentangled, including in relation to the economic 'detour that suspends the accomplishment or fulfillment of "desire" or "will".'[602] It is *all this* that might have been elucidated, deconstructed and reconstituted, had Derrida not 'arbitrarily left aside' these energetic questions, and had he not *already* wavered in indecision about the questions he himself asked eight years prior to giving his seminar on life: 'What differs? Who differs? What is *différance?*'[603]

The issue is not the undecidability of the term but the indecisiveness of its elaboration, and it stands as the symptom of what, despite everything, amounts to Derrida's own repression of technics. It is not that one cannot understand différance as *Of Grammatology* does, as the history of life: on the contrary, Derrida reiterates this understanding of différance as the history of life as late as 2002.[604] But this gesture cannot, on the one hand, authorize a thought of différance as an 'exteriorization always already begun', while, on the other hand, accepting the *specificity* of exteriorization as a '*third* emergence' that opens onto all the 'others' of *phusis* – or at least, it cannot do so without theorizing the relationship between these alternative formulations. Between these two possibilities, the passage remaining to be thought consists in the différance that exosomatization makes to the history of life qua différance:

> At issue is the specificity of the temporality of life in which life is inscription in the nonliving, spacing, temporalization, differentiation, and deferral by, of, and in the nonliving, in the dead.[605]

There can be no *bio*-deconstruction that would not always already have been a *psycho*-deconstruction and a *techno*-deconstruction, because the *grammatological* question is fundamentally organological, in Stiegler's sense.

It is true that this term, organology, does not appear until the second phase of Stiegler's work, where it will be shown to be irreducibly a pharmacology, for which grammatization will be the key analytical concept and proletarianization the fundamental political one.[606]

Together, these concepts alone make it possible to understand how the steps taken in the unfolding of différance in the nineteenth, twentieth and twenty-first centuries were what enabled the grammatized exploitation of desire and its proletarianizing regression to the drives, which bears crucial responsibility for the advent of our current predicament consisting in a global techno-economic system that is reaching the limits of its functioning while threatening the very biosphere itself.

It is thus only in this second phase of Stiegler's work that it becomes totally clear that what he develops are the concepts for thinking the history of noetic différance as the history of the intertwined character of desire and technology, giving rise to the current dysfunctional system and also to the inability to muster the collective intelligence or will to address the crisis it has produced. It is nevertheless also clear that, *already* in *Technics and Time, 1*, the critique of Derridian différance amounts to the question of the differing-deferring that is the history of life referred to by Schrödinger as the history of 'negentropy', and where the decisive *question* to be addressed to Derrida, Schrödinger and Wiener is what différance (it) makes when this localized systemic struggle against entropy, this pursuit of life by means other than life, plays out no longer just endosomatically but *exosomatically*, and what différance (it) makes when this playing out is no longer just technological but industrial, and then hyper-industrial.

The seeds of everything that will be cultivated and ultimately bear fruit in the most recent, *third* epoch of Stieglerian thought are thus planted in his initial critique of this passage that Derrida might have thought, had not the latter's own readings of Leroi-Gourhan and Laplanche suffered from what seem to be bouts of retentional finitude that prevented him from opening a conjunction between Jacob and Freud in which the future of différance might have begun to play out. Hence Stiegler has argued that différance as the history not just of life but of life-death requires at least a doubling of the concepts of entropy and negentropy with anthropy and neganthropy. It is by reading *and rereading* Derrida that Stiegler, *unlike* Derrida, has supplied the weapons with which we can reinvent the question and the problem that towards the end of Derrida's life was given the more-than-epochal and less-than-epochal name of the Anthropocene – and which amounts to an anthropic, all too anthropic Entropocene.

9 The End of the Metaphysics of Being and the Beginning of the Metacosmics of Entropy

> On the ethical plane the most conspicuous and enigmatic feature of human nature is the extent of Man's ethical gamut. The range of his ethical potentialities between the two poles of diabolism and saintliness is as remarkable a feature of human life as the ethical dimension itself. Both features are peculiar to Man among all the denizens of the biosphere. Now that Man has acquired the power to wreck the biosphere, we cannot be sure that he will not commit this suicidal crime; but we also cannot be sure that he will not redeem the biosphere from the state of nature in which, so far, love and strife have been at issue with each other inconclusively. It is conceivable that, instead of wrecking the biosphere, Man may use his power over the biosphere to replace the state of nature by a state of grace in which love will prevail. This would transfigure life from a pandemonium into a communion of saints.
>
> Arnold Toynbee, *Mankind and Mother Earth*

Introduction: on aethers and souls

What follows is an oblique attempt to say something about what locality means in relation to an account of what Bernard Stiegler has called a neganthropology.[607] It might also be construed as the first visible rising to the surface of some questions and themes that have been brewing for some time but hitherto remained latent. Whether the distillation of those questions and themes leads to a genuine step of thought will probably have to be determined on the basis of future works and decided by future hypothetical readers of those future hypothetical works. Nevertheless, if what follows is offered under the limited auspices of these kinds of qualifications, it is nevertheless an earnest attempt to cultivate some prospects for a speculative venture, with hopes that it will at some point prove to be an investment capable of yielding fruit worth savouring.

The chapter consists of two halves stitched together with rather rough sutures. The first part asks whether what has been called metaphysics could be conceived as the history of a repression of a style of thinking that we can discern by reading Empedocles, a suppression that we would thus claim begins with Aristotle. It then posits a kind of continuation of what failed to get going after this putative initial Empedoclean foray. We will risk a new term, 'metacosmics', for what might then become a kind of reinitiating (including in the sense of rites of initiation) or reinitializing (including in the sense of computing) of thinking after the *factual* history of what has been metaphysics up until now, which is to say, up until the long history of its end.

The second part asks what conceptual room might be opened up in this future history for an encounter between Stiegler's exorganological neganthropology and Peter Sloterdijk's immunological spherology. The original paper that became this chapter arose mainly from a longstanding interest in Stiegler's work in general, and in his efforts aimed at reinscribing philosophical concepts in terms of questions of entropy in particular, but also, in part, from what might loosely be called 'political' complications emerging from his internation project (which is a renewal in other terms of Marcel Mauss's reflections on the fate of the national and international, but can additionally and with a bit more imagination be conceived as a kind of response to Peter Szendy's call for a new 'geopolitics of the sensible'[608]), and in part from ongoing email and WeChat discussions I continue to have with Anne Alombert and Ouyang Man. As per usual, all responsibility for any failures of thinking lies with the author, but, beyond this standard disclaimer, is there anything worth saying, by way of setting the scene for a theatre of the individuation of locality, about this context of friendly discussion?

This four-handed scene (involving myself, Bernard, Anne and Man) is obviously conceivable in terms of what Gilbert Simondon calls a process of collective individuation, specifically in the sense that four perpetually unfinished psychic individuation processes have been aiming, via processes of one or another kind of analysis and synthesis, however vaguely or waywardly or hesitatingly at times, towards some kind of commonality of understanding and reason (despite the fact that they are not all involved in a joint collective project). This diffuse aim, due to its very singularity, could only ever be asymptotic, the consequence of which is that the collective individuation process, too, remains perpetually unfinished – even if all these processes are bound one day to be finished off.

But these processes can also be described in terms of locality, whereby the locality that I constitute, or in other words the simple exorganism that I am, or who I am, interacts with those localities and simple exorganisms who are Bernard, Anne and Man. And through this interaction, these localities aim to produce the coherence of another locality, a slightly large scale of exorganism, and a collective individuation process, one operating across the tertiary retentional supports of global digital networks. At the risk of sounding grandiose, we might describe this locality, distributed between Paris, Shanghai and Melbourne, hence in a geophysical location not much smaller than the limits of the biosphere itself, as a kind of cosmological sphere, characterized by a certain warmth, produced by a certain productive tension, that is, a resonance, and within which Bernard's position might be conceived as in some way paternal, raising his philosophical progeny, or again, as a saint who inspires by his no doubt imperfect but still rationally miraculous exemplarity.

I deploy these admittedly rather ingratiating metaphors not to flatter but to suggest the psycho-techno-anthropological multidimensionality involved in conceiving locality in terms of cosmologies harbouring processes that are less a matter of the harmony of encircling spheres than of inwardly and outwardly spiralling tendencies: there is, after all, no such thing as a truly stable orbit, but only a relationship between gravitational and centrifugal forces; nor, more fundamentally, is there after general relativity any formation of the fabric of spacetime that is not either expanding or contracting (as Alexander Friedmann showed as early as 1922). Even at the level of the physics of space and time, then, there is no such thing as true stability.

Take 'warmth', for example: functionally speaking, the concept of warmth is not physical but biophysical, naming one of the conditions under which the negentropic processes of biological life can flourish safely, comfortably and fruitfully, referring to the threshold limits of tolerability of atmospheric temperature (or water temperature for marine or fluvial life), in the struggle against the freezing cold (a coldness that, indeed and in fact, *lowers* the rate of physical entropy, but also kills the potential for biological life to temporarily thwart the entropic processes against which it struggles). In the case we are describing here, it is not a question of biological or endosomatic life that has evolved in the terrestrial locality we call the biosphere, but of noetic or exosomatic life, where 'warmth' would thus be a metaphorical name for the psychosocial conditions in which exosomatic life can flourish safely, comfortably and fruitfully. It is a question of the atmospheric conditions of transindividuation, that is, the conditions of that medium which fills the apparent void between brains and bodies and gives it its character, a transparent element we might also describe metaphorically in terms of nineteenth-century physics as a kind of *aether*.

This invisible medium through which waves of noetic warmth propagate is, however, inaccessible to any interferometer, the instrument used in the Michelson-Morley experiment. When Ernst Cassirer considers the question of the cosmos in Renaissance philosophy, and wants to describe the transformation introduced into the movement and principle of knowledge by Nicholas of Cusa, for whom measurement was fundamental (which is to say, measuring *instruments*), he argues that even if this still relies on fixed points, these are no longer 'prescribed once and for all' as an 'unbridgeable gap [that] separates the "above" from the "below", the "higher" heavenly world from the "lower" sublunary world'.[609] Rather than this predetermined Aristotelian cosmos, knowledge in the Cusanian world must navigate without fixed central points and pre-given interpenetrating spheres, and instead the 'intellect must learn to move in its own medium, in the free aether of thought'.[610]

This noetic character is further indicated when Cassirer describes the cosmos according Giordano Bruno, which, unlike 'the rigidity of the Aristotelian-Scholastic cosmos', is one in which 'the concept of space merges with that of the aether, and this, in turn with the concept of the world soul'.[611] Like the aether through which nineteenth-century physics speculated that light propagated, no physical experiment will ever confirm that warmth propagates through such a noetic aether. Yet despite this physical non-existence, we are indeed entitled to wonder in what way it remains a question of measurement, and by what instruments it might prove measurable, given that, irrespective of this non-existence, it constitutes a fundamental condition of possibility for the fruitful cultivation of certain kinds of transindividuation processes occurring between psychic individuals aiming towards a commonality, that is, a *philia*.

In other words, this is, undoubtedly, a question of knowing something *after* physics. In regards to this 'after physics', it is worth recollecting that Aristotle begins his *Metaphysics* with a declaration tying desire and knowledge together at the heart of the nature (*physei*) of human beings: 'All men by nature desire to know.'[612] If this is taken to be a statement about metaphysics, which might be taken as 'psychological' in the sense that it concerns the *psyche*, the desiring soul, which is to say a soul that is noetically concerned with its relationship to the future, it nevertheless also counts as epistemological to the extent that Aristotle follows it by making a distinction between animals and humans on precisely this score: the knowledge possessed by animals relies upon sensation and memory, and therefore on a *phantasia* that knows little of experience as such, *empeiria*. And this means, says Aristotle at the beginning of *Metaphysics*, that the human desire to know implies that *anthropoi*, that is, *oi thanatoi*, mortals, live by other means than do the animals, and specifically by the means of *tekhnē* and *logos*.

It is not at all difficult to see how this thought of two kinds of knowing possessed by animated beings – those whose *phantasia* is woven from perception and memory, and those who can rely not just on sensation but on the sensational experience that is *empeiria*, which is also to say on the kind of knowing made possible by measurement and measuring instruments, by *logos* and *tekhnē* – is entirely congruent with the distinction between the sensible and noetic souls described in *De Anima*. In other words, this consideration that opens up the long path of what will be called metaphysics – which according to Heidegger attempts to get the whole of being in view, and which in modern philosophy becomes the question not of the being who desires to know but of the metaphysics of will – this consideration begins with the delimitation of different planes of interaction between different kinds of individuals and their milieu, which we can rename with Stiegler as the negentropic or endosomatic plane and the neganthropic or exosomatic plane.

Aristotle, Nietzsche and Freud read Empedocles

It goes without saying that Aristotle did not himself refer to the negentropic plane, let alone the neganthropic, firstly because Aristotle *also* opens the path of metaphysics by opposing the fixed sphere of heavenly bodies, which is to say the sphere of timeless 'being', to the sublunar world of temporal 'becoming' characteristic of life *down here*. From the outset, these beings of *phantasia* that we are calling negentropic, and the beings of *empeiria* that we ourselves are and that we are calling neganthropic, are both *opposed* to a cosmic fixed sphere characterized precisely by the *absence* of any entropic tendency and therefore any struggle against it, and which is the sphere of those eternal beings that are the immortals.

But rather than stopping at the absurdity of this anachronistic observation (that it never occurred to Aristotle to discuss negentropy or neganthropy), rather than allowing ourselves to relax contentedly at the thought that the ancient world simply lacked the physical concepts with which to apprehend the world about them, and consequently lacked the ability to make metaphors out of these concepts, what happens if we instead follow this line of thinking all the way out to the end? Let us abandon well-trodden pathways into the question 'what is metaphysics?' and instead pose the question: *what conceptual absences prevented anything resembling negentropy from entering the Aristotelian conceptual universe?* One possible waystation through which such an unconventional path might lead is Aristotle's dismissal of Empedocles, and specifically of two aspects of Empedoclean thought, both of which will be discovered two and a half millennia later, independently it seems, by Friedrich Nietzsche and Sigmund Freud.

When in 'Analysis Terminable and Interminable' (1937) Freud discusses the struggle between Love and Strife, he differentiates the 'cosmic phantasy' of Empedocles from what he himself seeks, which would be, on the contrary, 'biological validity', that is, *empeiria* valid across the negentropic biosphere, yet he acknowledges that the account of *philia* and *neikos* 'approximates so closely to the psychoanalytic theory of the drives that we should be tempted to maintain that the two are identical', that is, that these 'two fundamental principles', love and strife, amount to what Freud himself calls the drives of life and destruction, love and strife together producing a 'process of the universe' conceived as a 'continuous, never-ceasing alternation of periods, in which the one or the other [...] gain the upper hand'.[613]

It is thus a question of the way in which the Empedoclean cosmos is – like every mythological view of the world according to Freud, as he said several decades earlier – '*nothing but psychology projected into the external world*', an 'endopsychic projection', thus opening the analytic prospect that it could 'be changed back once more by science into the *psychology of the unconscious*', and through which it would become possible 'to transform *metaphysics* into *metapsychology*'.[614] At the same time, as Sarah Kofman points out, Freud accepts the idea that there is something about the drives that involves an irreducible relationship to mythology, an *art* of mythology, but which, he argues in 'Why War?', can probably be said about every science, even Einstein's physics.[615] There is thus a double gesture involved in Freud's relationship to Empedocles: the claim to turn mythological metaphysics into scientific metapsychology, and the claim that science itself contains an irreducible mythological element whose conceptual openness, elusiveness and indefiniteness are all essential to the promulgation of a new science.

Nietzsche, too, draws attention to this struggle between competing drives that, as Kofman says, are not opposites but rather rivals – from which she concludes that 'Empedocles' model is a political one'.[616] In his lectures on the 'pre-Platonic' philosophers, Nietzsche focuses on these 'drives [that] struggle with each other' and on the way in which this *duplicity* somehow arises from a '*oneness of all living things*' in which what 'renders them asunder' somehow can also be that which 'presses them toward mixture and unification', the result of 'desire and aversion' as the 'ultimate phenomena of life'.[617] For Freud, for whom the life drive can sometimes seem to subsume the death drive, taking advantage of the latter so that it might be bent towards its own ends, but where at other times it is the death drive that seems to dominate, with all of life ultimately amounting to an entropic journey back to an inorganic state, this Empedoclean conflict is irreducible.[618]

What both Nietzsche and Freud thus make clear is that what they see in Empedocles's doctrine of the struggle between *philia* and *neikos* is a genuine theory of tendency and counter-tendency, characterizing the universe insofar as it is the domain of life, in which the counter-tendency somehow emerges from out of the tendency and is locked with it in a spiralling transductive embrace. In *Metaphysics*, however, Aristotle sees in this Empedoclean account only a deficiency of analysis, a failure to make a clean cut between one concept and the other, so that, he says, Empedocles 'in many cases [...] makes friendship segregate things, and strife aggregate them'.[619]

For Nietzsche and Freud, this rivalry of tendencies, this play of tendency and counter-tendency that describes the 'ultimate phenomena of life', amounts to a futural and negentropic relationship to the milieu, which is to say, precisely, a question of the relationship between knowledge and the world in that function of reason that is always an art of living (as Whitehead puts it). As Kofman summarizes Empedocles:

> The conditions of possibility of knowledge are, above all, vital: to understand the being of things is to increase one's own vital forces. The art of directing one's thought depends on an art of living. [...] This is why, once again, desire is at the root of a successful exchange between knowing subject and the world.[620]

Freud and Nietzsche thus see the distinction between these two tendencies compositionally. For Empedocles, *philia* produces that admixture in which the elements lose their properties in being united, while *neikos*, 'paradoxically [...] favours the conservation of the elements'. Hence it is the latter that forms the 'basis of knowledge since it alone can tear the parts of the elements from the tissue of their compounds and allow like to rejoin like' – in other words, *analysis*. But with this separating out of elements comes also the risk of error and forgetfulness, for which *philia* is necessary as being the sole possibility of a *synthesis* that recollects a prior unity, 'since only it can bring about a conjunction of elements in the correct proportions'.[621]

In this reading, which we are construing as the necessity for analysis to be both informed and redoubled by synthesis, and which we could also construe as the composition of Dionysian and Apollonian tendencies, Empedocles composes rather than opposes these entropic and negentropic tendencies, but this is then precisely what opens up the compositional relationship of analysis and synthesis at the root of all knowledge.[622] For Aristotle, however, the problem with Empedocles's cosmological account lies in his failure to adequately describe an analytical opposition. No doubt we could refer this Aristotelian reduction of the compositional to the oppositional to the replacement of *alētheia* by *orthōtes*, which for Heidegger was the hallmark of the fall into metaphysics. This would be to suggest that Aristotle dismisses Empedocles as lying conceptually on the wrong side of exactitude (whereas we would wish to argue, *contra* Heidegger and *à la* Stiegler, that this exactitude is the very thing that *opens up* the possibility of an account of the composition of tendencies).

Yet how is it that 'mixture and unification' *can* arise from what pulls things apart, which is to say, how can a tendency towards proliferation, and towards the conservation of order, arise from out of the overwhelming tendency towards disorder characteristic of the physical universe? Again, Nietzsche and Freud, who lived in the age of thermodynamic entropy but prior to the Schrödingerian account of negentropy, both note the extraordinary perspicacity of Empedocles in this regard. For Empedocles's solution to this problem is simply to conceive this counter-tendency as an effect generated by chance over time, or in other words, to interpret this in the light of Darwin and Schrödinger, to conceive the negentropic possibility probabilistically.

As Freud notes, in this way Empedocles really anticipates the theory of natural selection in biological evolution: 'he also included in his theoretical body of knowledge such modern ideas as the gradual evolution of living creatures, the survival of the fittest and a recognition of the part played by chance (*tukhē*) in that evolution'.[623] Kōjin Karatani describes this relationship between Empedocles's cosmological conception of contending tendencies and his foreshadowing of negentropic evolution in similar terms:

> Love and strife here are not to be understood as psychological categories; they are rather physical forces like gravitation and repulsion. Empedocles utilized these principles of combination and separation to conceive a kind of evolution of the creatures. [This] did not involve a teleology, but rather was an evolution by natural selection.[624]

What Karatani describes thus seems quite distant indeed from any 'psychology projected into the external world', and still less does he understand Empedocles as describing a rivalry of drives that would really amount to a 'political model'. Nevertheless, Karatani agrees that the cosmological account given by Empedocles contains the fundamental elements of the theory of biological evolution.

In sum, Freud finds in Empedocles the same two ideas he learns from Helmholtz (via Brücke): natural selection (that is, Darwin's theory of the basis of endosomatic organogenesis) and entropy (or more specifically, for Freud, Helmholtz's distinction between free and bound energy, which will be translated into his account of the life and death drives).[625] Much of what Freud refers to as metapsychology can be interpreted as the outcome of an attempt to conceive the fundamental significance of these two ideas for psychic and collective life in a world that was yet to acquire the concept of negentropy as Schrödinger conceived it.

Nietzsche is even clearer that this is a matter of the possibility of order arising from disorder without design, or, in other words, Nietzsche sees that for Empedocles, purposiveness is not the cause but the cumulative effect of chance over time. A mere decade after the publication of *The Origin of Species*, Nietzsche, himself only twenty-five years old, describes Empedocles as 'the *tragic* philosopher',[626] and writes of him as providing these fundamental tenets of what he calls 'materialist systems':

> His main difficulty, however, is to allow the *ordered world* nonetheless to arise from these opposing forces without any purpose, without any mind, and here he is satisfied by the grandiose idea that among countless deformations and limits to life, some purposive and life-enabling forms arise. Here the purposiveness of those that continue to exist is reduced to the continued existence of those who act according to purposes. Materialist systems have never again surrendered these notions. We have here a special connection to Darwinian theory.[627]

With his account of the rise of separate and detached body parts, which are subsequently joined on the basis of likeness, and only later through the combination of dissimilar organs, Empedocles can be anachronistically interpreted as describing the evolution that runs from unicellular to multicellular organisms, which are then increasingly characterized by the functional unity of diverse organs. In *Physics*, however, Aristotle critically evaluates this place of chance and natural selection in Empedocles, which Aristotle describes as the notion that it is merely a 'coincident result' that we find ourselves with 'the front teeth sharp, fitted for tearing, the molars broad and useful for grinding down the food'.[628] His conclusion is that it is impossible that such a differentiation and proliferation of functional organs could be the outcome of chance or coincidence: such phenomena, he states, are evidently 'for the sake of something', and must therefore be taken as proof that 'action for an end is present in things which come to be and are by nature'.[629]

With this dual Aristotelian dismissal of Empedocles, and specifically of

- the notion of a compositional and transductive relationship of tendency and counter-tendency lying at the origin of the phenomenon of life,
- the notion that this negentropic tendency, giving rise to biological order (organic organisms), can be explained probabilistically (or improbabilistically) rather than in terms of pre-existing final causes,

the path towards a metaphysics of will founded on an oppositional logic was set.

Were things otherwise, had Aristotle not rejected Empedocles and the notion of counter-tendency, had he not rejected the notion that chance and selection could give rise to purposiveness rather than the other way around, what *else* might he have been drawn to conclude about the distinction and relationship between endosomatic beings limited to sensation, memory and *phantasia*, and exosomatic beings open to *tekhnē*, *logos* and *empeiria*? Putting such counterfactual and slightly absurd questions to one side, *the 'end of metaphysics' might as well amount, we are proposing, to the end of the Aristotelian forgetting of Empedocles*, an end that would be philosophically initiated by Nietzsche and Freud but prepared by Clausius, Boltzmann, Helmholtz and Darwin, in ways that neither Nietzsche nor Freud could fully deal with, even though we might well describe their thinking as never fully successful attempts to think in precisely this direction.

From metaphysics to metacosmics

Such resources already equip us with means sufficient to contest Heidegger's account of the end of metaphysics as well as his account of Nietzsche's place in that end. We may well see the history of metaphysics in terms of the fate of that 'desire to know' with which Aristotle opens *Metaphysics*, and which eventually becomes, in Hegel, 'the unity of knowing and willing', and finally becomes, in Nietzsche (according to Heidegger), the 'absolute subjectivity of the body; that is, of drives and affects; that is to say, of will to power'.[630] For Heidegger's Nietzsche, then, the final metaphysical reversal consists in folding the rationality of the *animal rationale* into these drives and affects, which Heidegger then presumes to be reducible to the level of *animalitas*.

If we allow ourselves to credit the notion of bringing to an end the Aristotelian forgetting of Empedocles, however, then what Heidegger himself continues to forget is not *only* that these drives and affects are not at all 'animal', neither in Nietzsche nor in Freud, since they are instead what opens onto the very possibility of the desire to know as *logos* and *tekhnē*, but also that all of these, instinct, drive, desire, arise from those highly improbable, if not indeed singular (happening once ever) processes that inaugurate, in turn, negentropy and neganthropy. With this thought, we can take Heidegger's own conclusion regarding the end of metaphysics as itself raw metaphysical material in want of complete reinterpretation:

> The end of metaphysics that is to be thought here is but the beginning of metaphysics' 'resurrection' in altered forms; these forms leave to the proper, exhausted history of fundamental metaphysical positions the purely economic role of providing raw materials with which – once they are correspondingly transformed – the world of 'knowledge' is built 'anew'.[631]

What does 'raw materials' mean here? The raw materials at stake here are not akin to those simple atomic elements such as copper or iron, to be dug up, smelted and shaped into new inorganic but organized forms, as was formerly done by an artisan and is now accomplished industrially. Rather, these materials are more like those remnants of ancient life, whose highly complex (highly organized) organic molecular constituents over aeons gradually become the still highly complex hydrocarbons of oil and coal, the complexity of which makes possible their combustibility, that is, their possibility of releasing reserves of potential energy. Or, even more so, like those less ancient organic remnants that have been turned from biomass into necromass, at the microcosmic scale forming the humus, and at the macrocosmic scale the pedosphere, which is to say, the set of highly complex components deriving from the diversity of past endosomatic organisms and forming an essential precondition for the continued existence of the biosphere. In other words, Heidegger's account of the fate of the history of metaphysics should be construed in terms of its constituting what Stiegler calls the *noetic necromass*.[632]

The interpretation of the end of metaphysics becomes a question, then, of *desiring to know* what is being left behind to form this noetic necromass, and what is being resurrected from out of this complex humus that is at the same time the transindividual aether that forms the cosmic 'element', where this 'knowing' must itself pass through the question of a future in which, indeed, the world of knowledge must be built 'anew'. This raw material does not consist just in a set of hypotheses, arguments and theorems to be pieced together in new ways like prefabricated building blocks. For the Heidegger of 1942, it is a matter of seeing that the fate of metaphysics lies in 'modern machine technology', and that the question of what comes after that fate (in a lecture course devoted to the complex entanglement of 'locality and journeying') is that of the possibility of a new path:

> For our thinking remains everywhere metaphysical, [...] because metaphysics first begins to achieve its supreme and utter triumph in our century as modern machine technology. It is a fundamental error to believe that because machines themselves are made out of metal and material, the machine era is 'materialistic'. Modern machine technology is 'spirit', and as such is a decision concerning the actuality of everything actual. [...] It is just as childish to wish for a return to previous states of the world as it is to think that human beings could overcome metaphysics by denying it. All that remains is to unconditionally actualize this spirit so that we simultaneously come to know the essence of its truth. [...] Yet in truth, this 'all that remains' is not the last escape route. Rather, it is the first historical path into the commencements of Western historicality, a path that has not at all been ventured into.[633]

This triumph of metaphysics as the spirit of modern machine technology described by Heidegger in 1942 is what *we* are describing as the fate of metaphysics at the end of the long history of the Aristotelian repression of the Empedoclean account of tendency and counter-tendency.

In 1964, Heidegger will describe this in terms of the process by which philosophy 'turns into the empirical science of man', and explain how the empirical sciences of man are in turn bound to succumb to the dictates of cybernetics, by which 'scientific truth is equated with the efficiency' of the effects of its application, so that '"Theory" means now: supposition of the categories which are allowed only a cybernetical function...'.[634] The cybernetic pre-allocation of the categories of thought threatens, Heidegger is clearly stating, to lead to the elimination of thinking itself, and this at a time when we have still barely begun to think. How close is Heidegger here to Stiegler's position, for instance when the latter writes:

> Digital technology [...] is based on the computer, which, more than anything, is an artificial organ of *automated*

categorization, that is, it automatically produces digital tertiary retentions on the basis of other digital tertiary retentions. The automation of categorization makes it possible for *operations of analysis and understanding to be delegated to digital systems*.

Interpretation cannot be delegated to an analytical system of tertiary retentions: on the contrary, it always consists in *deciding between possibilities opened up by tertiary retentions*, but [which] *these tertiary retentions are not themselves capable of choosing between*, however automated they may be – for here, *to choose means, precisely, to disautomatize*.[635]

But Heidegger continues: '...which are allowed only a cybernetical function, *but denied any ontological meaning*'.[636] With this, as with everything he writes, Heidegger shows that he can only partly undo the Aristotelian repression: not because this 'cybernetical function' *has* an ontological meaning but because Heidegger never exposes his notion of being to the tragic notion of tendency and counter-tendency unearthed in the wake of the second law of thermodynamics by Nietzsche and Freud.

This is not to say that Heideggerian concepts are not susceptible to being understood compositionally – quite the opposite, given that for Heidegger existence precedes essence and being is always and inevitably a question of singular forms of being-in-becoming. Heidegger's is indeed a processual form of thinking, and this is why, for example, he rejects objections based on the argument of 'circular reasoning':[637] there is no static starting point at which to begin drawing the circle of thought, and one has always already entered the circuit that one is trying to penetrate, the process of thinking thus constituting a spiral.[638]

What Heidegger cannot see, however, is that the *Da* of Dasein, and the fundamental *locality* of all knowledge and truth, arise from the fact that Dasein, the noetic soul, is engaged in a counter-entropic struggle not just through biological evolution or metaphysical history but through what Alfred Lotka calls 'exosomatic evolution',[639] operating according to criteria that are always thermodynamically local and informationally idiomatic. To interpret this fate of knowledge, truth and philosophy under cybernetics beyond metaphysics, we maintain, is to interpret the meaning of this transformation of 'language into an exchange of news', of the arts into an industry of 'regulated-regulating instruments of information', and of the 'ontologies of the various regions of beings (nature, history, law, art)' into the 'operational and model character of representational-calculative thinking'[640] – it is to interpret the meaning of all of this in terms of the irreducibly local struggle against both thermodynamic and informational entropy (where the latter, as a circuit of knowledge and memory through the necessity of exosomatic hypomnesic organs, is what opens that error and forgetting identified by Empedocles with *neikos*).

If this is indeed a question premised on the necessity of knowing and desiring the future of knowledge itself, which means *building* that future – where this 'building', however, is not a matter of constructing it from building blocks but rather concerns a complete reinvention (a 'transformation in our ways of thinking and experiencing, one that concerns being in its entirety'[641]) – then we can contend that it must also pass through the formulation of that challenge that is discernible in the statement with which Freud concluded his treatment of Empedocles: 'no one can foresee in what guise the nucleus of truth contained in the theory of Empedocles will present itself to later understanding'.[642] Likewise, François Jacob will end *The Logic of Life* by noting that the scientific understanding of endosomatic and exosomatic systems and processes might 'today' (in 1970) be seen in terms of the cybernetical functions of 'messages, codes and information', but he immediately adds that tomorrow's analysis may well 'reconstitute them in a new space'.[643]

Such challenges and professions amount to versions of the Simondonian epistemological dictum that individuation ultimately remains unknowable because the only way of pursuing this knowledge (of individuation) is by individuating. The future guise of the Empedoclean 'cosmic phantasy', after the end of metaphysics, corresponds to a resurrection that leaves the physics of metaphysics behind in an act of anamnesic reinitiation that we are proposing to call the beginning of *metacosmics*, which would be less an anti-physics than an *a*-physics. This would be to recall Bataille's reference to atheology, which he defines, for instance, as 'the science of the death or destruction of God'.[644]

Nevertheless, it is not just a question of death or destruction, or of leaving behind the *physics* of metaphysics, but of no longer dreaming that the oppositions on which it has always been founded could be disengaged from one another, such as the opposition of the sensuous and the nonsensuous, which for Heidegger constitutes 'the fundamental configuration of what has long since been called metaphysics'. Hölderlin's work, for example, exceeds metaphysics, for Heidegger, because the rivers of the Ister hymn cannot be reduced to 'symbolic images', where something sensuous (the work) exists for the sake of something nonsensuous or suprasensuous.[645] The enigma of the place occupied by the rivers in Hölderlin's poetry as delineated by Heidegger, and how they (and the poets) *are* locality and journeying, approaches towards the question of metacosmics as we are raising it here. Yet Heidegger himself cannot conceive how this question of locality and journeying, however far beyond physics it may venture, must *also* never *forget* physics, even if it can never be reduced to it, and more specifically it must always retain, and never fully disengage from, the physics of the second law of thermodynamics and the always improbable possibility of localized counter-entropy.

Such a metacosmics would delimit the conditions under which it would be possible to inaugurate what I have in a previous chapter called a 'theory of general entropy', whose generality would imply the a-systematicity of Bataille's general economy more than Einstein's general relativity. Such a theory of general entropy would also be, by definition, a general theory of negentropy, that is, of life and evolution, but also, beyond Schrödinger, of exosomatic life and *its* (technological) evolution. The *generality* of such theory would consist above all in its not being able to be kept within the bounds of a physical theory: it is a question not just of the thermodynamic entropy characteristic of the universe and revealed by the consideration of the inefficiency of heat engines (through being generalized to all closed systems), but also of a 'cosmic' entropy that is opened up at least from the onset of that localization not of space but of *places* that gets going with the conquest of fire, which becomes the hearth and ends with the final stages of the so-called Anthropocene.[646]

If the artefact of technics is always a *pharmakon*, both poison and cure, it is first of all because the circuit between the living and the dead (the dead matter of which it is composed) remains subject to the probabilistic tendencies of the second law while being itself an expression of a neganthropic improbability that is the singular expression of a dynamic. This dynamic itself amounts to an improbable tendency, a tendency to produce diversity in the deferral of its probable erasure, and this occurs not just thermodynamically or biologically but noetically: because such an improbable tendency (for the noetic soul to rise up rather than fall, to move forward rather than regress, against all odds, and only ever intermittently) is fundamentally singular, it is in all likelihood not reducible to mathematical laws.

Or: it may always be possible to apply mathematical approaches to the *past* of such a tendency, in a way that can, with hindsight, successfully (but only ever partially) illuminate the dynamic of which such a tendency forms a part, but it is not possible to apply a mathematical approach capable of describing the future of that tendency, subject as it always is to surprising improbabilities, at least insofar as the possibility of an improbable future persists, however improbably – here lies the whole question of the Anthropocene considered as the twilight of reason and the fulfilment of nihilism. And it is in this way that we must interpret and confront the *shock* of the Anthropocene, as Bonneuil and Fressoz[647] call it, so that we feel the slap in the face to humankind that it implies, feel it as those primary retentions that are always already being interpreted through the selections we make on the basis of our secondary retentions, and which are in that way very far from being the data with which we could calculate our relationship to the entropic future of that nihilistic tendency (however much we must *also* continue to calculate the implications of climate data and so on):

> When one takes a slap, it is the given: sense data. To receive a slap in the face, to suffer it, is to receive sense data in the form of a shock. To learn that one's father has died: this is to receive the given (which becomes not sense data but a data of sensibility, feeling, since the father is effaced, withdrawn from the sensible, and has become, if not 'spiritual' or 'suprasensible', at least *revenantial*: spectral).[648]

This shock resonates, and this resonance of what is given (and not just data), which involves nothing more than recursive waves of mutually-entangled primary, secondary and tertiary retentions, must be *felt*, so that, in affecting us, it can through us affect the motives of reason that make possible procursive surprises. It is for this epistemological reason that, ultimately, such a theory of entropy must be *general* rather than physical – or in other words, it implies what we are calling a metacosmics, for which both physics and metaphysics remain as a shadow from which it cannot ever disengage.

As Barbara Stiegler points out, the twentieth-century preoccupation with the 'advance' and 'delay' of the species in the organism's struggle with its environment, this preoccupation with the 'lag' of the human species compared with the acceleration of the milieu it has itself created, a preoccupation that set the terms of the kinds of economic theories and practices associated with neoliberalism (Lippmann) and ultra-liberalism (Hayek), *also* led the *opponents* of these twentieth-century 'liberalisms' to *abandon* the question of the relationship between biology and politics, ceding the ground to the most reductive versions of these relationships. The result has been what itself amounts to a metaphysical opposition: between the 'naturalism' or 'biologism' of those who all too *easily* link the bio- to the political, and a 'constructivism' of those who unthinkingly *refuse* this connection, leading to oppositional forms of thought, but also to forms of denial that amount to new forms of reactivity and resentment (including and especially, we contend, in the realms of desire and sexuality). Barbara Stiegler's conclusion is that this demands

> that a new philosophical and political conception of the meaning of life and evolution be reconstructed, one that goes beyond the sterile standoff between constructivism and biologism, so that philosophy can play a full role in the arena of the political battles to come, so that the history and meaning of the politics of evolution can be clarified, and so that it can contribute to reclaiming a collective, democratic and enlightened government of life and the living.[649]

Beyond Barbara Stiegler's explicit conclusion, which she draws from a consideration and confrontation of Lippmann's neoliberalism and Dewey's pragmatism, we would argue, with Bernard Stiegler, that these questions of life and evolution, and of exosomatic life and artificial selection, cannot avoid the admittedly difficult conceptual terrain of thermodynamic, biological and informational entropy and negentropy. As Stiegler *père* points out (in a manner not dissimilar to that of Philip Mirowski), the origins of neoliberalism *also* lie in the informational entropy propagated with the rise of computational cognitivism.[650]

The path beyond biologism and constructivism rightly called for by Barbara Stiegler is, we would argue, ultimately required to pass through Bernard Stiegler's effort to think, create and take care of a sur-real cosmology, whose prospects are first opened up around 2013, when he begins to deploy the concepts of anthropy, neganthropy, neganthropology, Entropocene and Neganthropocene. At the same time, it may well be that there are questions of biological negentropy, questions of the retentional forms characteristic of endosomatic life, that have been left open in the work of Bernard Stiegler, as we will suggest below. Hence it is that we propose the name of 'metacosmics' for the theatre in which such a fruitful encounter could be staged and brought to light, that is, to life. It becomes a question, then, of meeting the obligation of justifying the necessity of this new term, metacosmics, not least in the face of the risks and dangers it may also contain of falling *back* into metaphysics: our suggestion is that, if there is such a justification, it lies in the question and the problem of neganthropological locality.

Troubles of belonging

This theatre will undoubtedly involve other characters and others figures, among them Georges Bataille, Pierre Klossowski and Maurice

Godelier, all of whom should be analysed, reread, critiqued and reinterpreted from a metacosmic standpoint that asks about the relationship of life and evolution to a new philosophy and politics of desire, sexuality and kinship, where all of these are themselves understood within the framework of an exorganological neganthropology of locality. This theatre is thus bound to stage a play of several acts, or a series of interconnected chamber pieces, which will have to remain for another occasion. In what follows, it will be just one of these characters, Peter Sloterdijk, who will be put on stage, and even he only in relation to a portion of his complex and multi-dimensional singularity, and in a way that both his supporters and his opponents might feel is lit in a strange way that somewhat distorts his best-known features.

If locality is a question, it is first of all because we see the evidence of the problem of locality all about us: Sloterdijk describes the twentieth century as 'an era of political psychoses at whose core emerges [...] troubles of belonging'.[651] From his spherological viewpoint, he sees such troubles as symptoms of no longer knowing who one is or who others are, since such forms of knowledge arise only 'where a sufficient number of good primary spheres blossom', or, to put it another way, where there are what Donald Winnicott calls transitional spaces whose rich noetic necromasses and resonant noetic aethers allow what Stiegler calls processes of transindividuation to flourish neganthropically, that is, to enchant worlds. The destruction of this kind of knowledge of who one is and who others are, which is to say (in Stiegler's terms) its proletarianization, leads Sloterdijk to conceive modern nations as 'asylums', spaces of protection for the uprooted.

Today, however, 'the uprooted' refers, says Sloterdijk, not just to the asylum *seeker* but to the local and the indigenous: we are all in want of asylum inasmuch as we are in want of being a *we*, for lack of the knowledge of *how* to form any such *we*, that is, any locality, in a twentieth and now twenty-first century in which individuals are, as Sloterdijk puts it, 'driven to undertake reformattings of the world [...] without first developing the psychic means to enable them to get acclimatized and familiarized with their new conditions of life'.[652] In such a situation, according to Sloterdijk, 'national asylums' possess only the limited function of entertaining 'the necessary illusion of anchorage, of territorial immunity, of solidary integration, and wherever this asylum function does not operate, violence erupts'.[653]

What does it mean to say that we are *driven* to undertake 'reformattings' without being capable of 'acclimatizing' to 'new conditions'? What Sloterdijk seems to be describing here are the consequences of the acceleration of changes occurring within technical systems, where these changes constitute shocks that leave former ways of living with these conditions no longer workable, which is to say that the knowledge of how to live within these former conditions is exposed as no longer able to function *as* knowledge. New forms of knowledge are therefore required – or must be invented – but the formation of such new knowledge is itself prevented by the perpetual transformation occurring precisely because of this acceleration. The turmoil of this adaptive rather than adoptive situation is what Sloterdijk calls reformattings without acclimatization, leaving those thereby 'uprooted' stranded in, at best, asylums built of spheres that fail to blossom.

What is gained, if anything, by referring to 'acclimatization' and 'familiarization' in this context, with its seeming reference to the 'atmosphere' of an epoch or a location? To acclimatize is to undergo or undertake a process of adjustment in relation to one's climatic surroundings, to 'get used to' one's conditions so as to be able to function well within them. More specifically, it is a question of the 'elemental' conditions of that existence, the way in which it is necessary to have an organized relationship to the time and space of collective life, for example, which Stiegler refers to as calendarity and cardinality:

> Adoption is that which is presupposed by the constitution of a *we* in general. A *we* is always constituted by calendarity and cardinality. For us to be able to say *we*, we must share the same calendar system and the same cardinal system. If we cannot refer to the same calendar, that is, if we do not share common time, and if we do not have a common representation of the spatial world in which we share systems of orientation – for example, if we cannot read street names, maps, or road signs – we amount to strangers. We have no sense of familiarity with a *we* other than on condition of such a sharing. Today, however, calendarity and cardinality are submitted to the control of global cultural industries.[654]

The organization of time and space this implies is not just a question of printed maps or printed calendars, of course: it is a matter of *all* the manifold ways in which the division and organization of time and space become collective phenomena, that is, *shared* memories and understandings. What is it that is shared in this way, and how are memories shared collectively? The answer is obvious: through tertiary retentions that form the common fabric by which a collective individuation process weaves a relationship running from past to future. It is through such tertiary retentional calendarities and cardinalities that time and space gain the noetic possibility of coalescing into an epoch and a locality – amounting to the dream and the promise of a collective future. And if those cardinalities and calendarities are not just a matter of literal maps and calendars, it is because they start with the shared geography itself, including in the ways it is negentropized biologically and neganthropized psychosocially. If elements of geography *can* function as a tertiary retentional foundation for the adoption of a way of life for a *we*, it is because they have *become* shared aspects of common *significance* through the weave of transgenerational time that turns spaces into places, that is, neganthropic localities. It is this ability for a geographical territory to function, 'tertiary retentionally', as a locality that is short-circuited by this submission to the 'delocalized' culture industries.

What Sloterdijk and Stiegler *both* describe, then, is a 'reformatting' that overlays a territory without enabling the persistence of any localization, with the consequence that the process of adoption that makes possible 'belonging' is disrupted – troubled by the impossibility of familiarization. Coming back to the question of 'acclimatization', then, and to the atmospherics it implies, if this is a question of *resonating* with a locality and an epoch, then the waves of this resonance are composed of the elemental sea of tertiary retention within which local-epochal collective life is always embedded and suffused. If the language of wave harmonics might seem to invoke a kind of mysticism, it is worth remembering that the atmospheric waves that waft in the form of a warm gentle breeze are themselves obviously composed of countless atoms and molecules, and this warmth is but an effect of countless collisions between these discrete elements. In other words, what makes possible the resonating warmth or sweetness of a locality or an epoch, what makes possible the knowledge of how to live within the conditions of life operating in an anthropized territory, are the forms of grammatization that grant the possibility for *anything and everything* within a territory to function *as* a locality. And this is what also grants the possibility of a dysfunctioning of locality – the proletarianization of our relationship to the time and space of our existence.

What such a diagnosis suggests is that the problem is not the territory and its deterritorialization resulting from anthropization, that is, technicization: deterritorialization is always in effect and underway, because all localization occurs in a relationship between smaller and larger scales of locality, microcosms and macrocosms. Troubles of belonging arise not simply from this perpetual process of deterritorialization, but from the inability to form new localizations when these reformattings can no longer be accompanied by forms of acclimatization and familiarization, and where these processes must always be conceived in terms of the resonances made possible by the grammatization of hypomnesic tertiary retentions. In other words, it is not a question of space 'itself' or time 'itself', but of the chances or otherwise for a redoubling of space via the knowledge through which it has had and continues to have the possibility of becoming a place, and through the redoubling of time via the knowledge through which it has had and continues to have the possibility of possibility of becoming an epoch. But these questions of local and epochal acclimatization and its troubled future cannot be asked without the critique of Husserlian phenomenology that introduces the question of tertiary retention, and without the analytical concept of the grammatization of tertiary retention, through which alone it becomes possible to conceive a theory and politics of proletarianization and deproletarianization.

The quotation from Stiegler about calendarity and cardinality was from a short book that he dedicated to those who voted for the French National Front. It was a way of indicating that troubles of belonging – or forms of suffering – lie behind these symptomatic reactions, and that the fundamental issues raised by such troubles and such suffering should not be matters abandoned to the ideologues of the far right. This is how we should also choose to read and interpret Sloterdijk on these same matters, and he himself seems to want to encourage such a conclusion:

> Even a left-wing cultural politics must take account of it, by assisting local impulses, or spherical needs, to find non-reactionary solutions. If it fails to fulfil this social and ecological mission, explosions will never fail to materialize.[655]

Almost always, such troubles are conceived in terms of a problematics of identity and difference or same and other. But these *bipolar* ways of conceiving such disturbances and disruptions almost always prove to be founded on anything but a transductive or compositional understanding: they are always inherently metaphysical, if not derivative of the pathological opposition between biologism and constructivism diagnosed by Barbara Stiegler, and as such in no way metacosmic. Consequently, these bipolar forms of conceiving such troubles almost always end up designating enemies and scapegoats.

We should instead conceive such troubles of belonging, troubles brought by the proletarianization of the knowledge of the *I* and the *we*, neither simply as symptoms of a deficiency of identity nor of a deficiency of difference. Sloterdijk might be thought to indicate this necessity when he suggests that every attempt of human beings to live together is 'made of continuities and discontinuities'. This would be in contrast, he argues, to 'the attempt to invert [this formula] and prop thought up essentially on discontinuities, as certain types of thought that stem from philosophies of difference suggest'.[656]

Leaving aside the question of whether this amounts to an effective riposte to so-called 'philosophies of difference' (the dismissive tone alone suggests that it does not rise to the level of a critique), we can at least credit Sloterdijk with acknowledging the tendency towards an endless unwinnable war, perpetually 'choosing diversity over normativity' but in the same stroke wanting to 'choose unity over division', and on and on, as if the struggle between tendencies could ever be reduced to such 'choices'. It may be a war waged on the terrain of culture, but its unwinnability stems from never being able to perceive the character or causes of the cultural aether itself, an aether amounting to a rich but now depleted noetic atmosphere emanating from the rich but now depleted soil of the noetic necromass. It is, in short, a war for access to scarce resources, conducted in a desert but without recognizing that this scarcity is primarily the result of a systemic destruction of the knowledge of how to fashion tools (and in the first place, tools of grammatization) capable of excavating what we need in order to subsist – and to exist.

It certainly cannot be a matter of concluding that so-called 'philosophies of difference' are outmoded, and can therefore be abandoned: différance, repetition, inscription – all of these amount to a fundamental step of thought from which there is no turning back. It is crucial, however, to also recognize that the deconstruction of the logic of identity and opposition must not mean the elimination of distinctions. What remains to be found, or re-found, or re-founded, are the terms with which to transform the relationships between identity and difference, or same and other, into relationships that are not just polar but transductive, or to find or re-find or re-found the terms with which to describe the finitude and openness of localities in terms of the *composition* of tendencies. Such terms will lead to a philosophy neither of identity nor of difference, but of tension and resonance, and of the perpetual possibility of their being lost.

There is more than one place to look in order to seek such a form of thinking. Anne Alombert, for example, has recently shown in a lecture given at Sussex that tension between individual and milieu is the very condition of the development of knowledge, and that the loss of knowledge induced by algorithmic performativity amounts to the collapse of that tension:

> Indeed, the totally automated, self-regulated, and adaptive infrastructures which can be applied everywhere and are supposed to eliminate any kind of tension between individuals and their environments in fact prevent these individuals from encountering any specific tensions or from overcoming

them through the invention of new local, collective and singular knowledge. As Canguilhem has shown, it is because tensions appear in their relation to their milieu that human living beings develop knowledge – knowing how to do, how to live and how to theorize – all of which are ways of resolving the problems encountered in the relationship with their milieu (technical shocks or social tensions).[657]

Here, it would be necessary to enter further into the relationship between these (technical) shocks and (social) tensions. As Alombert argues, high-speed algorithmic performativity eliminates the *tension* between organism and milieu that alone produces the knowledge that, as she puts it, enables *resolution* of the problems between the individual and its environment. It would then be a matter of articulating this thought with Gilbert Simondon's attempt to reconceptualize information in a non-quantitative fashion, which, as Yuk Hui has shown, is based on conceiving information as a tension, within a cybernetic system, between a signal and a receiver, and where the production of significance amounts to the *resolution* of this tension.[658] It is a question of how such a thought can also be brought together with Simondon's notions of associated milieu and internal resonance or Giuseppe Longo and Maël Montévil's notion of bio-resonance in the extended critical transitions of biological phase space, strongly correlating the parts and the whole of anti-entropic systems.[659] The basis of such articulations could only be that the significance to which the resolution of informational tension amounts equates to knowledge as a function of the relationship between organism and milieu (and then a matter of investigating to what extent this articulated account is or is not mathematizable, that is, how it relates to the question of the limits of calculability).

But what we must then also say is that this relationship between organism and milieu is itself a relationship between two scales of cosmic sphere. What does it mean to refer to different 'scales of cosmic sphere'? Stiegler has in recent years been engaged in addressing this question, and he does so, in part, precisely by articulating Canguilhem's concern with the technical form of life (as the noetic tension between the individual and the milieu) with Simondon's concern with rethinking information and its theory, in addition to retaking Derrida's notion of différance as distinguishable into two forms of the struggle against entropy (negentropic and neganthropic), on this basis reinterpreting the work of Whitehead (on the function of reason), Lotka (on exosomatization) and Winnicott (on transitional space and the transitional object) to outline a 'hyper-materialist epistemology' in which knowledge and the *desire* to know are construed as functions and faculties of a *sur-real cosmology*.[660] In such a cosmology, we could say, the tension and resonance holding parts and whole within a metastable cohesion arise from the aesthetic or *cosmetic* sphere, conceived in a general sense as the socialization of desire.[661] This must always be founded on the relationship between retentional forms, from the genetic to the nervous to the grammatized forms of tertiary retention, but the articulation of these fundamental retentional forms requires profound analysis and interpretation (to which we will return elsewhere, but where we can immediately state that the cosmetics of such a cosmos are always noetic artifices, in all senses of the word, and where this would also necessarily involve questions of sexual difference).

To what extent can spherology be conceived as a pharmacology?

Let us now give a few indications about how and why Sloterdijk's spherological project might *also* be roped in to the metacosmic project being proposed here. For this preliminary foray, scouting this foreign but not completely unfriendly territory (or perhaps it is better to say: the territory of our best frenemy), some precautions with respect to Sloterdijk may prove prudent, as might some modifications – if not a thoroughgoing critique. Sloterdijk does not shy away from a rather wild form of 'exaggerated' thinking that can be both a virtue and a vice, making it a delicate matter to pick out those kernels with the potential to cross-fertilize with Stiegler's neganthropology and sur-real cosmology.

A fundamental starting point for comparing their work would be to acknowledge the significant overlap between Stiegler and Sloterdijk in terms of their conception of the complicated origin of the kinds of beings that we ourselves are, despite Sloterdijk's apparent distate for philosophies of difference. For his part, Stiegler's notion of an originary default at the onset of technical life (or hominization, but which it is better to call exosomatization) involves a fault that would be anything but a lack because it is the opening of the excessive character of noetic souls that would also be *exclamatory* souls:

> This becoming-symbolic as *logos*, which only is in the course of its being ex-pressed, is what I call an *ex-clamation*: the *noetic* experience of the sensible is *exclamatory*. It exclaims itself before the sensible insofar as it is *sensational*, that is, experience of a *singularity* that is *incommensurable*, and *always in excess*. The exclamatory soul, that

is, sensational and not only sensitive, *enlarges* its sense by exclaiming it symbolically.[662]

And from Sloterdijk's side, he undertakes a critique of Arnold Gehlen's notion that human existence evolves from the outset as a neotenic, helpless form of *Homo pauper*. For Gehlen, human being is a 'deficient being', as Sloterdijk describes:

> This phrase is not only meant to refer to the biological 'negative endowments' of *homo sapiens*, with all its maladjustments, non-specializations, undeveloped traits and so-called 'primitivisms'; it also recalls the increased burden that has, according to Gehlen, weighed down this excessively unprotected, environmentally disconnected, instinct-deprived, organically destitute animal, abandoned by all innate inner guidance, from the start.[663]

As Sloterdijk points out, however, if this is 'meant to be the starting point for a grand narrative of primordial deficiency and its immediate compensation through cultural abilities', the problem is that it 'is impossible to derive such a dramatic dowry of deprivations from a natural history of humanity's precursors'.[664] In other words, given that natural selection functions to eliminate monstrosities and conserve mutations that are beneficial to the relationship between organism and milieu, it appears impossible to reconcile the purported rise of such 'de-specialized and juvenilized' beings with the theory of biological evolution:

> If biologically and culturally motivated development led to the results that are evident in early humans, then their evolutionarily preferred qualities must not be interpreted as deprivations; on the contrary, they would predominantly possess qualifying or, in Darwin's terms, fitness-increasing virtues.[665]

More pointedly, it makes no sense to propose an evolutionary sequence in which endosomatic deficiency *precedes* its exosomatic supplementation, in which the 'primal scene of anthropogenesis' would occur as 'the appearance of a creature unfit for life' so that it 'immediately had to withdraw into the protective shell of a prosthetic cultural armor in order to compensate for its own biological impossibility'.[666] Against the fiction of a 'deficient being', Sloterdijk thus postulates that this 'developmental trait can only be grasped as a self-reinforcing incubator effect' that turns our species into 'beneficiaries of a pampering, cerebralizing and infantilizing tendency' that unfolds 'without any long-term or species-wide reduction of evolutionary chances for the neotenically daring living being':

> The success story of the 'symbolic species' could not have turned out as we see today in retrospect if its basic character had not led to a productive interconnection of somatic refinements and psychoneuro-immunological and technical reinforcements.[667]

Rather than the fiction of a deficient being who compensates for its poverty through exosomatic compensations, then, anthropogenesis is the story of a 'luxury being' whose capacity for exosomatization grants potentials for defunctionalized openness:

> *Homo sapiens* is a basally pampered, polymorphically luxuriating, multiply improvable intermediate being whose formation resulted from the combined action of genetic and symbolic-technical forces.[668]

In other words, both Sloterdijk and Stiegler offer accounts of the origin of the distinction of the noetic soul as a being whose seeming 'lack of qualities' both conceals and arises conjointly with an *excess* made possible by and making possible another kind of evolution beyond the biological: that of exosomatic beings who are as such irreducibly open, improbable, excessive and symbolic.

In *Neither Sun Nor Death*, Sloterdijk describes the distinction between these two kinds of evolution – or two kinds of différance – in terms of a difference between two kinds of 'special machines': firstly, 'autoplastic or autopoetic' 'living machines', and then that second evolutionary process through which

> man became more than a living machine, but also a sort of machine of the spirit, insofar as he has formed the possibility, in thought, of thinking and of letting the world emerge as world.[669]

It is perhaps unclear, here, to what extent Sloterdijk is using the term 'machine' in a metaphorical sense, as so often happens in the history of philosophy, and to what extent he could instead be construed as attempting to describe the exosomatic existence of simple exorganisms as an inextricable relationship between endosomatic and exosomatic organs. If we take it that Sloterdijk is describing a double emergence corresponding to the advent of endosomatization and then exosomatization, then this phrase, 'machine of the spirit', might be understood as indicating the impossibility of reducing the relationship of the endo- and the exo- in exosomatic life to a mere addition of biological and physical components. This 'spirit' would thus refer to the excessiveness of the noetic and exclamatory soul, and this 'coming-into-the-world' (emphasizing 'beginnings more than ends') that is also the Heideggerian emergence of the world-as-world (and ending with 'modern machine technology *as* spirit') would then also correspond to the negentropogenesis and neganthropogenesis that each individual must traverse as a kind of double birth.

Sloterdijk describes this double birth in the following terms:

> Because humans must not only be liberated from a mother, they also find themselves confronted with the challenge of entering into the 'house of Being'. Coming-into-the-world is the philosophical formula for a biological event charged with an ontological character.[670]

Clearly there is something quasi-Heideggerian and something quasi-Winnicottian going on in this account: the entrance into world-as-world corresponds to a process of substitution for the first sphere, that is, the maternal sphere. If Sloterdijk holds to ontological rather than organological terminology, or in other words if he tends to not *quite* see this double sense of coming-into-the-world as the doubling of the endosomatic by the exosomatic, nevertheless Sloterdijk does also stress Heidegger's understanding that 'the question of Being emerges through questions of power and of technology'.[671] He emphasizes the continuity of his thinking with Heidegger's non-physical conception of space, which he says 'broke the habit that consists in interpreting being-in from the angle of everyday physics, and showed that human being-in-something [...] must be interpreted as a standing-outside, an ecstatic positionality, or a being-held-on-the-outside'.[672]

This being-in in the form of an ecstatic positionality is also expressed as a kind of spatial différance (though he does not use this term from the 'philosophy of difference') that opens up the possibility of a locality that is not just a space:

> From the outset, what it [the sphere] thus expresses is the idea that all inhabiting implies a milieu of transference – or again, to employ Deleuze and Guattari's jargon, a deterritorialization within a subsequent reterritorialization. One lives to the extent that one projects an elsewhere into a here. There is no place without a here-there difference.[673]

This Heideggerian-seeming différance of here and there, phrased in Deleuzian terms and opening up the possibility of a place and the whole proto-pharmacology of locality and journeying that occupies Heidegger in 1942, is then extended out to a Winnicottian-seeming liberation from and by the mother (thus opening up a 'milieu of transference'), but where, as in Stiegler's extension of the transitional object and transitional space beyond the confines of the good-enough mother, Sloterdijk turns this into a socio-technological pharmacology:

> My theory of space formation in modernity is backed by the observation that, in the process of civilization, interiority gets replaced by exteriority. Otherwise said, it belongs to the essence of socio-technology to play with maternal capacities in non-maternal media. Modernity consists in finding technological substitutes for maternity, in every sense of the word. [...] Mothers, the bio-patrons, get replaced by artificial patronage systems.[674]

It would no doubt be possible to interpret this last statement – concerning the shift from that primary maternal sphere common to all placental mammals to that secondary exosomatic sphere characteristic of luxury beings alone – metaphysically or non-pharmacologically, to the extent that it seems open to the possibility of being understood as constructing an *opposition* between bio-maternity and artificial patronage in non-maternal media.

In correspondence after the lecture that became this chapter was originally delivered, Anne Alombert raised the question of the pharmacological character of Sloterdijk's project in general, by wondering if his account of 'spherization' is equally an account of 'de-spherization'. One way of approaching this question could be to ask what Sloterdijk means when he describes 'all inhabiting' as implying 'a deterritorialization within a subsequent reterritorialization'. It would also be possible to refer again to his critique of Gehlen. After quoting the latter ('In the light of this reflection, world-openness is fundamentally a *strain*'), Sloterdijk writes:

> This means – even if the author does not state it openly – that the main characteristic of the way *homo sapiens* experiences the world and acts within it lies in a problematic overabundance of sensory impressions as well as possibilities of experience and action, and by no means in a prior poverty and deprivation. Its underspecialized, multiply adaptable or 'open' nature results firstly in an overly impressionable receptiveness, and secondly in an extremely broad spectrum of action options – which deviate from the trivial middle value and extend to the improbabilities of art, asceticism, orgies and crime.[675]

Sloterdijk thus invites us to understand that the luxury beings that we are find ourselves exposed to the full range of pharmacological improbabilities, as well as to the pharmacological character of the trivial and the average (the probable), because, or so it seems, we are characterized by the 'detachability' of drives that can be reattached to those improbably singular aims that are the infinite objects of desire of every kind.

On this basis, we might well reinterpret the replacement of the maternal 'bio-patron' with 'artificial patronage systems' in a non-metaphysical way, as Sloterdijk's description of the changing relationship to the external milieu that occurs when genetic forces are increasingly replaced by symbolic-technical forces, leading in 'modernity' to a formation of space that is no longer just technical but techno-logical, industrial, not to mention bio-technological and bio-industrial – at every level of 'reproduction'. It is thus tempting and conceivable to conclude that Sloterdijk's general account of reproduction implies a form of thinking that *exceeds* metaphysics while also responding to the imperative to overcome the division between the scientific and the philosophical in the direction of knowledge built 'anew':

> It is always necessary to question anew the phenomenon of how it is that life organizes its continuity. With which advanced fortifications, with which war-machines [...]? How do living systems manage to reproduce themselves? How do they make themselves a future? In this, philosophy converges with systemic concerns, and it does so, in the first place, under metabiological auspices.[676]

For Sloterdijk, such auspices mean that the

> anthropotechnical theory of space in contradistinction to that of physics resides in the fact that I define the container as autogenous, that is, as a surreal form of space, wherein several selves together constitute something that I call a sphere. This, precisely, is the space of psychic resonance.[677]

That these metabiological auspices imply an anthropotechnical account of the pharmacological character of noesis, and that, in the Anthropocene, this also has fundamental implications for a pharmacology of locality at the scale of the biosphere, seems obvious from the following passage:

> I start from a strong ontological thesis: intelligence exists. This leads to a strong ethical thesis: there is a positive correlation between intelligence and the will to self-preservation.

Since Adorno, we have known that this correlation can be questioned—that was the most promising idea of older Critical Theory. It started from the observation that intelligence can go in the wrong direction and confuse self-destruction with self-preservation. [...] What is on the agenda now is an affirmative theory of global co-immunity. It is the foundation of, and orientation for, the many and varied practices of shared survival.[678]

On the question of immunity as metaphor

Sloterdijk's conception of spherological space, then, involves what he calls a 'constitutive surrealism', an 'original spatialization' that is also a 'perpetual space-delusion' arising from the fact that human existence is a co-existence.[679] In other words, here-there différance structures the noetic production of knowledge and reason as functions of neganthropic life, which always occupies spheres that are themselves always delusional, that is, noetic dreams of one or another world-as-world, worlds whose fabric is conditioned by the mediating tension and resonance of an aesthetic atmospherics. It is for this reason that Sloterdijk refers to immunity, as can be seen in his attitude to the history of metaphysics:

> I read classical metaphysics as a library of effective propositions about the globality of the world, where world is construed as an immune system. Ontology is therefore the first immunology.[680]

> classical philosophy's premises were the premises of a theory of the space of shelter, and therefore of a cosmological and theological spherology, or even better of a sphero-immunology.[681]

Ought we not be suspicious and reticent, however, about the use of this 'metaphor' of immunity? Does not its 'biologism' tend to encourage the notion that 'we' must defend ourselves against invasion from foreign elements, with all of the unpalatable political suggestions this may seem to encourage or legitimize? Although both Derrida and Sloterdijk indulge in the language of immunity, auto-immunity, co-immunity and so on, isn't this just to make the mistake of allowing into play a metaphor that suggests a false equivalence between very different regimes of individuation? Is it not fundamentally *dangerous* to import such a 'biologistic' metaphor into fields for which this can only be a foreign element?

It is worth remembering, however, that this paradigm is not *firstly* biomedical at all. Immunity begins as a political or legal or indeed economic concept, referring to an exemption from an obligation or a requirement or a law that is generally applicable to everyone who does not possess such immunity. We insist on the economic aspect not just because immunity starts as an exemption from a tax or tribute, but more generally because this implies a suspension of the exchange relationship that *materializes* ob-ligation from a very general anthropological standpoint, as Roberto Esposito points out:

> This is where its anti-social, or more precisely, anti-communal character comes to the fore: *immunitas* is not just a dispensation from an office or an exemption from a tribute, it is something that interrupts the social circuit of reciprocal gift-giving, which is what the earliest and most binding meaning of the term *communitas* referred to. If the members of the community are bound by the obligation to give back the *munus* that defines them as such, whoever is immune, by releasing him- or herself from the obligation, places himself or herself outside the community.[682]

It is by extension of this politico-economic immunitary paradigm that the biomedical paradigm is established, by which immunity refers to 'a protective response in the face of a risk', or more precisely, in the face of a 'rupture of a previous equilibrium and the consequent need for its reconstitution', and more precisely still, where that threat comes from 'trespassing or violating borders', located 'always on the border between the inside and the outside, between the self and other, the individual and common'.[683] This biomedical immunitary paradigm is not just a translation of the politico-economic paradigm, however – it is a transformation whose roots lie in the discovery of the possibility of acquiring immunity, and of doing so artificially, that is, technologically:

> But what makes it significant for the purposes of our reconstruction is the turn it takes within its own field between the eighteenth and nineteenth centuries, first with the discovery of a measles vaccine by Jenner, and then with the experiments by Pasteur and Koch, the birth of medical bacteriology proper. The passage that most interests us is the one leading from natural to acquired immunity – in other words, from an essentially passive condition to one that is actively induced.[684]

This technological, 'active' immunity is produced by the first genuinely endosomatic turn of exosomatization (internalizing exosomatic elements). It is also a step in the history of technics: not just a question of organized inorganic matter but of re-organized organic matter (biotechnology). It is *through* this turn and this step that it amounts to a transformation of the earlier paradigm of immunity, because it contains a new idea, absent from the political and economic conception:

> The basic idea that came into play at a certain point was that an attenuated form of infection could protect against a more virulent form of the same type.[685]

In other words, immune protection does not involve 'a strategy of frontal opposition', nor one that operates by 'keeping [ills] at a distance', but instead a strategy of 'exclusion by inclusion'. As Esposito states:

> The body defeats a poison not by expelling it outside the organism, but by making it somehow part of the body. Its salvation thus depends on a wound that cannot heal, because the wound is created by life itself. [...] It must incorporate a fragment of the nothingness that it seeks to prevent, simply by deferring it. [...] In so doing, it retains its objective in the horizon of meaning of its opposite: it can prolong life, but only by continuously giving it a taste of death.[686]

Can we not see, in this economico-political concept extended *to* the biomedical and biotechnological field, a *pharmacology* of immunity, in which the body must adopt its own wound and where only what is poisonous contains that which makes possible the *protection* of the organism? If so, was it not through this internalization of biotechnological exosomatization that this general pharmacological characteristic was exposed, just as it was through the development of those exosomatic organs that are heat engines that the general entropic tendency was exposed? Moreover, in this necessary incorporation of the fragment of the poisonous foreign, is it not, as a differentiating deferral, precisely a of the play of tendency and counter-tendency in the struggle against entropy:

> The first thing to point out is that the immunitary paradigm does not present itself in terms of action, but rather in terms of *reaction* – rather than a force, it is a repercussion, a counterforce, which hinders another force from coming into being.[687]

Hence if we can say, for example, that the *pharmakos* is a reaction to the shock produced by the *pharmakon*, then are we not entitled to see this pathological shock reaction as precisely constituting a kind of auto-immune response? The question is: under what conditions are we justified in making this kind of analysis? And the answer will be, *beyond* just the question of tendency and counter-tendency: provided that we do not repress or deny the fact that the basis of this reaction lies in *arrangements of retentions and protentions*.

Immune systems are retentional systems, and more than that, interpretive systems

If the pharmacological character of the *pharmakon* ultimately stems from the anthropic and neganthropic *extension* (by other means) of the negentropic struggle against entropy, in the sense that it concerns the struggle against the elimination of improbabilities and the reduction of the improbable to the probable and the average, where these struggles involve not just life but the articulation of the living with the non-living, and if this question of probabilities and the improbable is always a matter of the conservation of the past that opens up the possibility of improbable and incalculable futures, then we are saying that, ultimately, the pharmacological character of the *pharmakon* is *always* a question of organized, retentional systems that open up protentional possibilities, possibilities of the transformation and diversification of order – new noetic dreams. From this, it follows that conceiving immunity beyond the danger of biological metaphoricity is a matter of reconceiving it in terms of retentionality. It is a matter of writing it as the *immuno-logical* with a hyphen, just as Stiegler refers to the *techno-logical* as the composition of *tekhnē* and *logos* that opens up the possibility of what Heidegger in 1942 calls the spirit of modern machine technology.

The possibility of such an *immuno-logical* account can be opened up by reflecting on the 'informational' mechanism of the biological immune function. Jean Claude Ameisen's account of the 'sculpture of the living',[688] which Francesco Vitale enlists in the service of elaborating a Derridian 'biodeconstruction',[689] makes clear that we have good reason to conclude that the immune system is nothing but a retentional system *separate* from the memory of the nervous system, an endosomatic system devoted to endosomatic memory (whereas the nervous system of human beings is an exosomatized system inseparable from exosomatic memory). The immune system develops its *own* set of secondary retentions, its own accumulation of retained traces of past history, precisely by cutting off molecular strands of invading organisms, keeping them as a private epidemiological archive, and using these supports protentionally to determine *how to react or not react* in future encounters. It is only *through* this retention of *preceding but necessary* exposures to immunological risk that the immune system can function. In other words, the immune system is nothing more than a somatic system regulating the here-there difference between the endo- and the exo-, prone to auto-immune disorderliness due precisely to retentional and protentional errors and mishaps in the struggle to maintain improbable negentropy.

Why, after all, did the immune system evolve in vertebrates? What the sensorimotor apparatus gives to the endosmatic organism is a set of abilities with which to navigate its exterior milieu and its inconstancies (as Canguilhem described them), endosomatic mechanisms allowing the organism to conquer space and time (which is to say, speed). The rate at which the inconstancies of its milieu *are* inconstant, however, the rate at which the exterior milieu changes, is generally far slower than the life of a single organism inhabiting that milieu. And the reason is clear: ecosystems change, more or less, at the rate of genetic drift orgeological change.

Yet there are inconstancies that can vary at a rapid enough rate that they transform the conditions of life for organisms and species in an exponentially threatening way: this is what occurs with the advent of a new viral or bacterial pandemic. The Covid-19 pandemic can almost literally be described as a situation in which one little viral fellow jumped into a human being, finding a species-home so conducive to its lifestyle that within a few months its children, grandchildren and great-grandchildren had spread throughout the biosphere, producing billions of 'offspring' at a generational rate that vastly exceeds the genetic adaptive capacities of its hosts (and in this case, where the speed of geographical movement is obviously a product of the exosomatic character of those twenty-first-century hosts). In other words, there is a vast difference in speed between the rate of viral transmission and the pace of human genetic drift: it is precisely because of such disparities that the *immune* rather than genetic retentional system can prove to be the difference between survival and extinction in the face of such rapidly changing inconstancies.

In the case of this endosomatic but non-nervous system, the operation of the retentional and protentional process may not be *sensible* (*to* the nervous system), but it is indeed a retentional system possessed by the organism and through which it struggles to maintain its biological negentropy. This is why a vaccine is nothing other than an exosomatic-endosomatic biotechnological tool that takes advantage of the retentional basis of immune functioning, not *just* to boost the immunity of the individual, but to try to respond to the inconstancies of the milieu in such a way that it protects an entire population, which is to say that a vaccine is a form of the transindividuation of immunological knowledge.

The separateness of the two endosomatic retentional systems is also expressed physiologically as the so-called 'blood-brain barrier', and this, too, needs to be understood if we are to think the prospects of an encounter between exorganology or neganthropology and immunology or spherology. In fact, it is not just the brain and nervous system that are *protected* from the immune system: other organs and parts of the body receive this *'immune privilege'*, as it is called, where the immune system is partially or wholly excluded from normal functioning. The uterus, for example, must become a site of immune privilege prior to conception, because of the risk that the fertilized egg will be judged by the immune system as foreign to the body and therefore eliminated.

The immune system is thus wholly or partially 'switched off' or excluded from areas of the body that are vital to survival and reproduction, where the risk of autoimmunity or unwanted immune effects needs to be minimized. But what is the root cause of this risk that requires immune privilege? Does the possibility of such anaphylactic effects not precisely derive from the fact that the immune system is *not only a retentional system, but an interpretive system*, that is, from the fact that it is a *sensitive instrument*, always susceptible to the risk of *misinterpretation, misidentification* of an element as being poisonous or otherwise?

It is, of course, not interpretive in the *same way* that, for example, written language is always a question of interpretation, including as written law that must be interpreted in order to open the possibility of reasoned judgment. At the same time, however, it is exactly a question of an endosomatic system that must encounter a situation, compare that situation with its accumulated retentional history, and on that basis cross the threshold into action, and where this is *always* a process that can go poorly or well for the organism, that is, entropically or negentropically, given that interpretation is *difficult* and the organ of interpretation *delicate*: *recognition* can always and easily fail. This is precisely why Canguilhem can say that immunity and anaphylaxis are two *normal* responses that only differ in their being either physiological or pathological *in their consequences*.[690]

Towards a neganthropological immunology

What would such a thought imply for a social psychology appropriate to any neganthropological approach? First, it implies that any account of the pharmaco-*logy* of immunity and auto-immunity in exosomatization cannot avoid the question of the *logos* and more specifically of the 'history' of tertiary retention. Second, it implies that, for this reason, it cannot avoid the question of *grammatization*, which is also to say, of proletarianization. But the latter should then be construed as the tertiary retentional auto-immune tendency that destroys knowledge and leads to the regression of the sensational soul as it succumbs to the sensationa*list* tendencies that engender the panic behaviour of crowds lying behind so many contemporary troubles of belonging.[691]

Hence it should not be a surprise that it was in the context of a discussion of the way in which 'analogical and digital mnemo-technical grammatization' produces the figure of the consumer and the proletarianization of this consumer that Stiegler will write that 'my belief remains that this becoming is self-destructive, or, to put it in the words of Jacques Derrida, auto-immune',[692] to which he attaches a note explaining that capitalism is a process of adoption operating via the continuation of the process of grammatization and 'exposed to the entire question of the auto-immunitary reaction'[693] explored by Derrida. Might it be possible, then, that what is missing from *Sloterdijk's* immunological spherology is a systematic account of grammatization, and that such an absence leads to an inadequate consideration of the *auto*-immunitary characteristics of contemporary spherization and despherization?

As for a 'systematic account', no doubt this is indeed missing, but, somewhat surprisingly, something like grammatization is indeed discernible in his text (even if only between the lines, in the sense that no major theses are drawn from it), and specifically in the way Sloterdijk treats psychoanalysis, which is to say the social psychology of desire. Having noted that 'linear mentality [...] is a consequence of the letterpress [that] follows from the one-sidedness engendered by alphabetization',[694] having noted that with the invention of the phonetic alphabet, 'the operative handling and observation of being takes a massive leap forward'[695] because the 'Greek alphabet is the first triumph of analysis', having noted that 'with analytic success an interest for synthesis also comes to the fore, that is to say, the possibility [...] to write new things', he concludes that analysis *'qua* process of elementarization is the preschool of synthesis'.[696]

What Sloterdijk means by elementarization is more or less what Stiegler, reading Sylvain Auroux, means by discretization: turning a temporal flow into discrete spatial elements that can be analysed and reproduced. While Sloterdijk doesn't at all seem to see how this question of elementarization is *also* that of the grammatization of *gesture* that lies behind the industrial revolution (which is Stiegler's stroke of genius, even if it comes from rereadings of Auroux, Leroi-Gourhan, Simondon and the *Grundrisse*), which is to say behind what Sloterdijk calls modernity and what has more recently come to be called the Anthropocene, he does acknowledge that the nineteenth century was 'shot through' with analysis 'at the level of empiricism', based on 'the elementarization of the various domains of being'.[697]

What is odd is that this whole account is merely a prelude to his assessment of psychoanalysis qua analysis:

> But behind the pathos of professions of faith in the primacy of analysis what is dissimulated is an avowal of theoretical perplexity, because what psychoanalysis thereby admits, at bottom, is that its discipline has not accomplished any convincing elementarization.[698]

Now, we may well have a sense of what he means, if he is suggesting that, despite *The Interpretation of Dreams* and its claim to have discovered the royal road to the unconscious, Freud could never really 'discretize' the continuum of dreaming and the fluxes and flows of the unconscious mind, in lieu of which psychoanalysis all too easily succumbs to a kind of esoteric priestliness. But if this is the case, we first have to ask: is Sloterdijk making the error of imagining that, in the systems and structures of desire, the elementary is necessarily *simple*, or is he ascribing this conceptual error to psychoanalysis itself?

In any case, it is surely impossible, in this respect, to avoid the significance of Freud's nephew, Edward Bernays, or more particularly of all those who followed in his wake in the technosciences and neurosciences and other associated pseudo-sciences of marketing – eventually including neuroeconomics and neuromarketing. Surely Bernays and his heirs have been engaged in nothing other than an elementarization of dreams and desires, in order to produce a wholly unholy (wholly calculable, and hence unpriestly) 'psycho'-'analysis', the better to synthesize artificial dreams, an elementarization now carried out algorithmically on 'big data'. Is this not precisely a question of the auto-immuno-logical production of what Sloterdijk calls 'exoneuroses',[699] generated through those non-maternal patronage systems that are socio-technologies (now mostly via 'social media' that are in fact anti-social)?

It is a question, here, of producing the outlines of a metapsychology of exosomatization for any possible neganthropology. In addition to the seeming deficiency of Sloterdijk's account of the fate of what Stiegler calls grammatization, we can also wonder about the adequacy of his account of the maternal relationship as the 'first sphere'. That this leads Sloterdijk to a several-hundred-page account of intra-uterine existence gives the reader a true sense of the risks entailed by his celebration of a 'philosophy of exaggeration'.

Yet this, too, is potentially ameliorable, for instance by referring to the first chapter of *Life and Death in Psychoanalysis*, where Jean Laplanche carefully traces the relationship between instinct and drive in Freud, and does so by drawing out its four constituent and elemental dimensions:

- 'impetus', *Drang*, the pressure or the 'motor factor in the drive', where to 'define a drive by its impetus [...] is, from an epistemological point of view, almost a tautology';
- 'aim', *Ziel*, the 'act to which the drive is driven', and where 'the only "final" aim is always satisfaction, defined [as] the appeasing of a certain tension caused precisely by the *Drang*';
- 'object', *Objekt*, the 'thing in regard to which or through which the drive is able to achieve its aim', and which may or may not be a person or a *part* of a person, such *partial* objects 'being, in fact or in fantasy, *detached* or *detachable*', but which may also be a *function*;
- 'source', *Quelle*, an 'unknown but theoretically knowable somatic process, a kind of biological *x*, whose psychical translation would in fact be the drive' or 'represented in mental life by a drive', or *delegated* to a drive.[700]

(It would seem eminently possible to connect these four dimensions to the four causes in Aristotle, although Laplanche himself does not do so.)

Laplanche's whole account here merits careful consideration, not just as a way of supplementing Sloterdijk's account of the maternal sphere, but because of the clarification he offers of the relationship between instinct, drive and desire, and the *mechanisms* involved in their compositional distinction.[701] Laplanche also suggests a kind of analogy between (1) instinct and wanting milk (an object whose function is nutrition), (2) drive and sucking the nipple, and (3) desire and sucking the thumb (or, *supplementing* these elements, sucking the artificial dummy). In other words, more may remain to be said about the role of the maternal in any such socio-technical psychology, which will be *both closer to* and *more distant from* biology than any existing psychology (or, for that matter, any existing anthropology).

In short, where all of this leads Laplanche is to the notion that the partial object (the breast) may be lost at the moment when the total object ('the mother as person') emerges, that this finding of an object as its *re*-finding (as Freud says) involves, when it concerns the drive of sexuality, not the rediscovery of the lost object but its 'substitute by displacement' (its différance), by which 'the aim has become the scenario of a fantasy' and thus that sexuality 'in its entirety' amounts to 'the slight deviation, the *clinamen* from the function'.[702] All of *this*, too, is a question of escaping the hermeneutic circle by entering into a cosmic or noetic spiral, and, *as such*, all of this, *too*, is a recapitulation, differently, of the question of *Meno*.

As Laplanche well understands, with the question of deviation, the notion of *perversion* is automatically brought into play, and hence one is immediately confronted by the paradox involved in defining sexuality as a functional deviation. We will quote his conclusions at length, even if we cannot here give them the analysis and interpretation they deserve:

> The movement we sketched above, a movement of exposition which is simultaneously the movement of a system of thought and, in the last analysis, the movement of the thing itself, is that the *exception* – i.e., the perversion – ends up by *taking the rule along with it*. The exception, which should presuppose the existence of a definite instinct, a pre-existent sexual function, with its well-defined norms of accomplishment; that exception ends up by undermining and destroying the very notion of a biological norm. [...] What is perverted is still the instinct, but it is as a vital function that it is perverted *by* sexuality. [...] The drive properly speaking, in the only sense faithful to Freud's discovery, *is* sexuality. Now sexuality, in its entirety, in the human infant, lies in *a movement which deflects the instinct, metaphorizes its aim, displaces and internalizes its object, and concentrates its source on what is ultimately a minimal zone, the erotogenic zone*. [...] This zone of exchange is also a zone of care, namely, the particular and attentive care provided by the mother [...]: these zones *focalize parental fantasies*, so that we may say, in what is barely a metaphor, that they are the points through which is *introduced into the child that alien internal entity* which is, properly speaking, *the sexual excitation*.[703]

For Laplanche, then, the neotenic character of exorganic life (not its deficiency but its luxury, not its lack but its excess) lies precisely in this co-implicated question of the relationship between drive and function, a complication that amounts to a default of origin:

> on the one hand, the proposed genesis implies in fact that what comes first – say, the vital order – contains what might be called a fundamental imperfection in the human being: a dehiscence. What is 'perverted' by sexuality is indeed the function, but a function which is somehow feeble or premature. [...] On the other hand, to that very extent, it is the *later* which is perhaps more important, and alone allows us to understand and to interpret what we persist in calling *the prior*.[704]

Laplanche is well on the way, here, to offering fundamental elements of a neganthropological metapsychology, which continues his work with Jean-Bertrand Pontalis on 'fantasy and the origins of sexuality',[705] and which a later chapter of *Life and Death in Psychoanalysis* conjoins to questions of the relationship between the life and death drives and negentropy and entropy, respectively.

But leaving this *movement* of Laplanche to one side, one might say, more programmatically, that Sloterdijk is arguing that what Freud called metapsychology must be supplemented and deepened with a metabiology that would also be a metacosmology. To this we should also add, *conversely*, that what Vitale calls biodeconstruction must be supplemented with a psychodeconstruction that would also be a cosmodeconstruction: our argument is that this is the terrain on which a general theory of entropy, a neganthropology, an exorganology and a metacosmics must be played out.

If we are willing to indulge the possibility of believing in the movement of such a metacosmic and exorganic neganthropology, that is, a movement of thought that would inextricably also be a movement of 'the thing itself', this in no way involves delineating a 'domain of being' but rather concerns the invention of a highly improbable future. We might conceive this future in terms of what the thinker whom Nietzsche in 1861 described as 'my favourite poet',[706] that is, Friedrich Hölderlin – Nietzsche observing in the same letter that Hölderlin 'hated in Germans the mere specialist, the philistine',[707] a hatred of philistinism that we can see clearly expressed in the *Trauerspiel* concerning the suicide of Empedocles at Mount Etna – has Empedocles say in the first version of this play (later filmed by Jean-Marie Straub and Danièle Huillet in their unique cinematic style, the extreme austerity of which draws attention firstly to the locality of words, secondly to their idiomatic concreteness, and thirdly to their uncanny strangeness). In his *Der Tod des Empedokles*, the eponymous philosopher, almost a mythological and fictional character projected from out of the Greek noetic necromass and filtered through Hölderlin's singular German imagination, expresses the hope that a path can be opened up, a resurrection producing new, highly improbable states of a cosmos in which 'the green of earth will glisten once again'.[708]

It is a matter of hearing in this hope for a glistening green the possibility of finding a zone of care and a way of caring not just for our biospheric negentropic fate, but also for our psychospheric and noospheric neganthropic fate, and a renewed capacity for receiving a sensational 'glistening' that will open new exclamatory paths. Without a path towards such a multidimensional cosmic and cosmetic resurrection, the cellular suicide that Ameisen sees as opening new voids in the sculpture of the living via the genetic milieu, and the anaphylactic endosomatic suicide that can occur when the retentional systems of the immune system overreact, and the psychic auto-immunity that can lead the thinker to abandon his own noetic garden and instead contemplate the void of the volcano, and the civilizational suicide that Toynbee sees as inherent to what Valéry already saw as the mortal character of civilizations, will find a whole new counterpart in the technospheric suicide brought about by the pharmacological character of locality, now operated by automated tertiary retentional systems distributed at the macrocosmic level of the biosphere, destroying not just knowledge but also the desire to know, and leading, ultimately and irreversibly, to a terrestrial Pandaemonium.

Afterword: On Positive Pharmacology

Bernard Stiegler

Grammatology, retention and the play of traces

Jacques Derrida investigated the possibility of grammatology 'as a positive science'[709] – but he did so by positing from the outset that such a possibility would be self-annihilating to the extent (and the excess) that this grammato-logy would shatter its own *logos*: it would be forced to 'solicit logocentrism' while at the same time 'deconstructing' it. We should therefore refer to *graphematics* or *grammatography* – and abandon the possibility that these could present themselves 'as sciences'.

The scientific positivity of a 'positive grammato*logy*', positive *in this sense*, necessarily passes through the question of the *essence* of writing, and therefore of its *being*: it should interrogate the *origin* of writing. Writing, however, if we understand it on the basis of the question of the trace, that is, as archi-trace or archi-writing, is precisely what constitutes the ordeal of a *default* of origin:

> Where does writing begin? When does writing begin? Where and when does the trace, writing in general, common root of speech and writing, narrow itself down to 'writing' in the colloquial sense? [...] A question of origin. But a meditation upon the trace should undoubtedly teach us that there is no origin, that is to say simple origin; that the questions of origin carry with them a metaphysics of presence.[710]

This question of trace and archi-trace builds on those of retention and protention, which emerged in the Derridian corpus in 1962[711] with the 'Introduction' to *The Origin of Geometry*,[712] and which, in 1967 (also the year in which *Of Grammatology* was published), formed the crucial analysis in *Speech and Phenomena*.[713]

In *Speech and Phenomena*, Derrida sets out to show that primary retention and the privilege accorded to it by Husserl in *On the Phenomenology of the Consciousness of Internal Time* falls within a 'metaphysics of presence'. Beyond the difference between the two kinds of retentions identified by Husserl and qualified as primary and secondary, we must pose the question of the trace that *exceeds* all presence, that is, all opposition between presence and absence

– which is also to say, the opposition that Husserl erects in principle between primary retention and secondary retention.

Of Grammatology takes up this problematic of retention deconstructed on the basis of the concept of the trace, and as the deconstruction of this 'metaphysics of presence', that is, the privileging of the present, and of which the privilege of primary retention over secondary retention would be the index – deconstruction passing on this occasion through Heidegger and the question of being, as well as through Saussure, Leroi-Gourhan, Lévi-Strauss and Rousseau. The absent presence, and the absence forming or giving presence, is the trace.

Nevertheless, 'that there is no origin, that is to say simple origin':[714] should this not lead us to question the question of the archi-trace, or even of *the* trace itself? If there will never have been a simple origin, then, rather than referring to *the* trace or *the* archi-trace, is it not a matter of investigating and problematizing, *even older than 'the trace'*, that *complex of traces* which would from the outset constitute that which would, through a retrospective illusion, initially present itself as 'the' trace?

From the trace to traces: being, becoming, différance and process

To submit the question of the trace to that of traces, and as the *primordial multiplicity of traces* – by positing that there is no simple origin, and that in the primordial complex of traces that the *default* of origin *unceasingly becomes* (rather than being it, it being a question not of the *being of the trace*, this copula being erased, but of the *becoming of traces*), *the* trace *must* 'always already' have become *an indefinite plural* – we must return to the question of the relationship between primary and secondary retention as defined by Husserl, and to Derrida's commentary on this question in *Speech and Phenomena*:

> As soon as we admit [with primary retention] this continuity of the now and the not-now, perception and nonperception, in the zone of primordiality common to primordial impression and primordial retention, we admit the other into the self-identify of the *Augenblick* [...]. The difference between retention and reproduction, between primary and secondary memory, is not the radical difference Husserl wanted between perception and nonperception; it is rather a difference between two modifications of nonperception.[715]

I have already commented on this commentary as follows:

These considerations are perfectly legitimate, and I have taken them up in my own work, but with several specifications that I consider indispensable: the *difference* between primary and secondary retention is not a *radical* difference insofar as primary retention is unceasingly composed *with* secondary retention, that is to say, insofar as perception is always projected *by, upon,* and *in* imagination – contrary to what Husserl thinks, and Brentano as well. But it is no less the case that the *difference* remains and *constitutes* a distinction that is not an *op-position*, but precisely what I have called a *com-position*. Now this constitutive character of composition – that is, *the woof of time* – constructed by the difference between primary and secondary is a distinctive philosophical discovery on Husserl's part. At the end of his career, he supplements it with the discovery of retentional finitude and its primordial technicity in geometry. Neither of these advances were, in the end, fully acknowledged or explored in Derrida's thought. *Différance* passes through this difference, but the latter in turn presupposes the differentiation (and thus the identification) of what I have called tertiary retention – the name for everything at stake in *The Origin of Geometry*.[716]

That there is no *radical* difference between primary retention and secondary retention does not mean *that there is no* difference between them. But nor this does mean that *the* difference that there is *in fact(s)* [*en effet(s)*] between them could be turned into the question of *the* trace, such that it would itself be indifferent to this difference (because it stands on another plane) and could therefore *give* or *make* this difference – and as différance – *before* the appearance of these retentional forms themselves.

For in order for there to be what Derrida calls the trace, which he also understands not just as *the* difference (and this is why we speak of the 'philosophy of difference'), but as différance, we need *terms* that are *transductively constituting* as well as *transductively constituted* by this difference that différance gives: we need a process. Such a process obviously does not precede its terms, but nor do the terms precede the process.

Such a question of process is that of *individuation* qua *process* of individuation that cannot be thought on the basis of the origin that *the* individual would be, but which individuates this individual such that, structurally in want of itself [*en défaut de lui-même*] (unfinished [*inachevé*]), it is always becoming and co-individuating with other individuals within a process that, incapable of being thought within the framework of substantialism or the hylomorphic schema, opens up the question of the preindividual as the phase in which the individual individuates itself by shifting phase [*se déphasant*], where phasing and dephasing constitute the process itself.

The default of différance – between the One and the Many

Différance is what Simondon tried to think as the process of individuation – where *the* difference, that is, *the* trace, 'commences' in différance through individuating (dephasing) differences, that is, through traces in which the preindividual shifts phase as this différance: it is what does not commence (on its own); it is *that which is not the commencement.* It is what not only has no simple origin, but, ultimately and *literally,* has no origin at all: it is the default of origin that is necessary, and that is necessary *in diverse ways.* And here lies the whole question – in this *diversity* of which the metaphysical obsession will be to subsume it under the One of the concept, and of which the concept of the trace or the archi-trace (as *the* trace or as *the* archi-trace) still seems to be a ghost.

This multiplicity that arises in the default of origin, and as this very default (as the default of the One), that is, as the individuation of the preindividual fund or background [*fonds préindividuel*] of which one cannot say that it 'is' this default, but that it *makes* this default, where defaults 'swarm', as Deleuze and Guattari would have said, is the process through which an arrangement is effected between primary, secondary *and tertiary* retentions, that is, *as the emergence of a complex of traces articulating the living and the non-living.*

Yet by downplaying the difference between primary and secondary retention as Husserl conceives it – and despite his interpretation of *The Origin of Geometry* and of the place that technics occupies in it as that which gives access to idealities through polishing, surveying and writing, that is, as a *praxical* space remedying the retentional finitude of the protogeometer – Derrida avoids investigating and describing what we should understand as tertiary retention. It is here that the whole problem of this 'grammatology as positive science' lies, a grammatology that is, however, constituted from beginning to end as the question of the relationship between protention(s) and retention(s), as *Of Grammatology* indicates on many occasions, for example in Derrida's commentary on Leroi-Gourhan, where the trace becomes the *grammē* of which différance is the history.

In *Gesture and Speech,* Leroi-Gourhan describes the unity of man, Derrida writes,

> as a stage or an articulation in the history of life – of what I have called differance – as the history of the *grammè*. [...] [T]he notion of *program* is invoked. It must of course be understood in the cybernetic sense, but cybernetics is itself intelligible only in terms of a history of the possibilities of the trace as the unity of a double movement of protention and retention.[717]

As can be seen perfectly clearly here, différance is life – as the history of the *grammē*. This is also to refer to what with Simondon we would call the *process of vital individuation* – such that it can lead to a process of *psychic and collective* individuation.[718] The history of the possibilities of the trace within *différance as the 'history of life'*: it is this that constitutes the 'unity of a double movement of protention and retention'.

Intentional consciousness and tertiary retention

In life, however, an articulation of the living and the non-living makes it possible that in this 'double movement of protention and retention', that is, in this différance that is life, there appears 'the *grammē* as such', which 'intentional consciousness' makes appear, *or indeed* that makes 'intentional consciousness' appear, from which it emerges – unless this 'emergence', which 'undoubtedly makes possible the emergence of the systems of writing in the narrow sense',[719] is, like the invention of man, a transductive relation such that, just as man is the inventor of technics only because he is invented by it, so too intentional consciousness is conscious of the *grammē* as such only because the *grammē* as such makes intentional consciousness possible – and does so through what I call a process of grammatization, of which Sylvain Auroux proposed a 'positive science', so to speak (with limits that I have tried to analyse on various occasions), and where the discretization that conditions this 'as such' is accomplished not consciously, but technically.

One wonders how we are to understand this rather surprising statement in which Derrida, who does not reason in these Simondonian terms, suggests that writing systems in the narrow sense would be made possible by the emergence of intentional consciousness – when we would be tempted to think, if we were completely faithful to the logic of the supplement as well as to its historicity or its prehistoricity, that the formation of intentional consciousness is the psychic side (as a stage of its individuation) of the technical formation of those tertiary retentions that are the systems of writing in the narrow sense.

Be that as it may, more generally, does not the thought of différance rush here *prematurely* towards 'systems of writing in the narrow sense', if it is true that there is tertiary retention long before this writing in the narrow sense, and if it is true that this proto-tertiary retention is already an articulation of the living and the non-living that induces a retentional/protentional process (a différance) thoroughly overdetermined *and undetermined* by this default of origin?

This default of origin is a new modality of the individuation of the preindividual fund *that is hollowed out in life* (like the 'collapsed zones' of genetic coding[720]) as what Derrida himself will call life/death. And this is so precisely through tertiary retention and through what will become the technical system that individuates itself by shifting phase, and, in this way, by individuating *what only thus becomes* psychic and collective individuation – a meta-individuation of the preindividual fund from out of which tertiary, that is, *accidental*, retentions will arise.

This meta-individuation would amount to a *bifurcation in the retentional and protentional conditions of individuation*, such that, intrinsically différant, psychic individuation and collective individuation are in transductive relation with technical individuation, that is, across the *proliferating multiplicity of transductive relations that are woven by the play of these tertiary retentions* that are technical traces with primary and secondary retentions, *forming a new protentional regime that is desire – by which becoming [devenir] is trans-formed into future [avenir], that is, into temporality (the condition of what Husserl calls intentionality)*.

Desire and protention

This proliferation is that of desire qua idealization, the latter constituting a new protentional regime – and it is only on this ground that a mathematical-philosophical ideality can be constituted, on the basis of which, by passing through this specific form of tertiary retention that is writing in the narrow sense, the thought of the *grammē* as such will become possible. But this new protentional regime is not just that of consciousness: it is also that of the unconscious.

(We should ask ourselves here to what extent Derrida is able to take hold of the concepts of retention and protention, formulated by Husserl in order to think consciousness, and extend them to différance as the history of life without, however, thematizing the immense phenomenological problem opened up by this extension, and despite the fact that Derrida always ultimately places himself under the authority of phenomenology so as to defend, for example, the Saussurian position that requires distinguishing the appearing sound and the appearing of the sound,[721] etc.).

Here, the question of tertiary retention must be understood in relation to the question of the transitional object – that is, by having recourse to Winnicott. But if tertiary retention emerges from a différance that, qua process of vital individuation, is composed of retentions and protentions that are in a way pre-intentional, then we must also turn to Bowlby,[722] whose work and material is close to that of Winnicott, and who raises the question of the relationship between the instincts and the drives, that is, between elementary protentional forms. We must do so, if we want to take seriously (and it is imperative that we do so) the Derridian propositions regarding pre-intentional différance, and if we want to take seriously, not the passage from archi-writing or the archi-trace to writing (and the trace) in the narrow sense, but the question of the relationships between the living and the *organized* non-living, organized as technical *organs* – which is the question of general organology.

If tertiary retention is not qualified in such a way, that is, as *governing and overdetermining by indetermining the compositions* of primary and secondary retentions, it becomes very difficult not to drown in the aporias of *the* trace, for example, by wondering where and when *the* trace begins, which is also called, here, (*the*) writing.

Traces of the default: Derrida's future passes through Simondon

While it is obvious – and I have tried to show this on many occasions – that primary retention is ceaselessly composing with secondary retention, and that in this sense their difference is not radical because they form a *system* of traces (which are always arranged by retentional systems[723] and through which attentional forms are metastabilized[724]), but where we must also analyse the way in which tertiary retentions condition and 'factorize' the play of primary and secondary retentions, it is just as obvious that a primary retention is not a secondary retention, which is obviously not a tertiary retention, even though no one of them occurs without the others.

This *play* of *three types of traces* not only begins well before writing 'in the ordinary sense', but also before the traces that Derrida observes via Leroi-Gourhan: those rupestral inscriptions or carved bones found on the excavation sites of the Upper Palaeolithic.[725] The play of these three types of retentions begins long before even that, with the very first flint tools – this at least is what I have tried to show in *Technics and Time, 1*.

This having been said, what of the question of *scientificity* in these matters, and of 'grammatology as a positive science'? To understand this problem other than in a purely speculative and logical way, that is, steeped in this *logos* of which it would be a matter of overcoming the metaphysics of presence, is to approach it as a *practical* question of the default of origin as that which *is necessary* (in modern French we would say *'il faut ce défaut'*, and in old French *'ce défaut faut'*, from the verb *'falloir'*). This default is necessary, but even though it is necessary, this necessity is itself always flawed: always faulty, faltering, that is, *forgotten, repressed* – not as a lack or as something missing, but such that it is always *to come* [*à venir*], and *in this way protentional*.[726] Such is the structure of desire, that is, of 'intentional' différance, changeable by the *grammē* as such, which is also to say by what Heidegger would have called the *question*,[727] and as the structure of what Derrida called exappropriation.

'The' trace that *Of Grammatology* tracks down, in tracking down the 'metaphysics of presence', and as archi-trace (which would later lead Derrida to refer to the 'quasi-transcendental'), dates from *before* tertiary retention: it would thus concern *life as such*, long before technicized life that articulates itself with the non-living while organizing it (as, precisely, an artificial organ), as the genetic program and so on. As *grammē*, it amounts to memory in all its forms, and first of all as biological memory. But it is also the 'magnetic storage facility' [*magnétothèque*] to which Leroi-Gourhan refers[728] – and who discusses the advent of the global mnemotechnological system – and the cybernetics that was then being imposed, in an age that was also that of structuralism, molecular biology and so on.

Furthermore, the question of the originary default of origin, of which the technicization of life is the direct inscription of this *life* becoming *life/death*, and which comes to oppose the possibility of grammatology as positive science, is not just the question of 'the' trace: it is that of a play between traces such that *in* this play, they *give this play* [*jeu*], and more precisely games [*jeux*], and *stakes* [*enjeux*] that are each time *unprecedented and unheard of* and that open up as the *protentions* of all these plays and games – as games of love and chance that fall within what is not just a 'logic of the supplement', but a 'quasi-causal logic'.

That these questions can be posed to and as a grammatology, which is a deconstruction, stems from a *genealogy* and a *retrospective of traces* that must abandon the question of a *one* (*the* trace) that would not be always already many, and that must in this way shift from the question of the *individual* to that of *individuation*: the future of Derrida passes through the work of Simondon (which does not contain it). Such is the future of what will have been opened up under the name and as the enterprise of *deconstruction*. At the default of origin of deconstruction, there will have always been a multiple.

Organology of transductive relations linking traces

The play of traces that continues to unfold until it reaches the point of being capable of considering the '*grammē* as such' results from an arrangement between *three organological levels*:

- the level of the psychosomatic organs of the psychic individual;
- the level of the technical and artificial organs of the technical individual (forming a technical system);
- the level of the social organs that are institutions and organizations of all kinds, constituting the social systems through which collective individuation is concretized.

As a *method of investigating the transductive relations* between the processes of psychic individuation, the processes of technical individuation and the processes of collective individuation, general organology undertakes the genealogy of the relations between primary, secondary and tertiary retentions. Amounting in this way to a 'history of the supplement', it develops the concept of 'grammatization',[729] a process that concerns gesture and the body as much as it does *logos*, and which, as the history of writing understood in this sense, is the condition of an intelligible understanding of industrial development. In addition, it studies the unfolding of transductive relations and their effects as a process of transindividuation forming circuits of all kinds, and at all three organological levels, which is also to say *between* these three levels.

Over the course of this process of transindividuation that is différance, *psychic* secondary retentions are always becoming *collective* secondary retentions (forming the transindividual, that is, meaning [*signification*]), while at the same time:

- *collective secondary protentions* are also being formed;
- tertiary retentions as *pharmaka* make it possible to control (which does not mean to master) the production of these psychic and collective secondary retentions through *retentional systems* and *criteriologies* (formed by long circuits of transindividuation[730]), which are constituted by social organizations;

- these retentional systems and criteriologies, which belong to the third level of general organology (the level of the social body concretizing collective individuation through the social systems), tend today to be absorbed by the technological level of the planetarized technical system, becoming thoroughly mnemotechnical and thus constituting a process of generalized proletarianization;
- the psychic individual henceforth finds itself disindividuated, deprived of the possibility of participating in collective individuation (being proletarianized).

Pharmacology as positive knowledge

The grammatological question that Derrida formulates in 1967, five years after the question of writing appeared in the phenomenology of geometrical knowledge belatedly formulated by Husserl, leads in 1972 to a *pharmacological* question: writing – on which at the end of his work Husserl confers a constitutive status, thus forming what Jean Hyppolite will famously call a 'transcendental field without a subject'[731] (which obviously does not mean that there is no *I* in this field, as 'mediocre thinkers'[732] will have believed, but that *if there is* anything transcendental, it *exceeds* the subject, and does so as its default) – thus becomes a *pharmakon*, which may be a remedy for 'retentional finitude' but is also what, through the retentional extension in which it consists as tertiary retention, makes possible *short-circuits* of the anamnesic retentional activity in which thinking *consists*.

If in 1967 grammatology could pose the question of its possible and impossible scientificity, in 1972 this ambiguous game turns out to be that of a *pharmacy*, if not a pharmacology – of which grammatology is an initial formulation and a field *that exceeds that which was germinated there* and does so precisely as the question of the *pharmakon*.

What we must confront today, beyond grammatology as a positive science, is not just the question but the problem of pharmacology as a *positive knowledge whose positivity is not that of a science but of a practice* – let us say of a *praxis*, and more precisely of *techniques of the self and others* that together form the *question of care*, and of those systems of care that, via retentional systems, form social systems. Yet these social systems are the very thing that the *pharmakon*, having become *industrially techno-logical*, tends to dissolve into prostheses themselves arranged through services promoted by global marketing and aimed at eliminating diachronicities, that is, singularities capable of forming objects of desire irreducible to the generalized computation from which all of this stems, and where all of this occurs under the hegemonic control of a financialized economic system that therefore no longer invests, preferring careless and self-destructive speculation.

In other words, positive pharmacology is not a positive science. On the other hand, it necessarily calls for a general organology that is itself not a positive science, but a paradigm investigating the positive sciences by starting from the question of the *organon* that is common to them not *as logos* but as *tekhnē* – and which is inevitably and invariably transmuted into a *pharmakon* by the revelation of its toxicities, which are never sufficiently foreseen.

Positive pharmacology and political economy

In 'Plato's Pharmacy', the question of grammatology becomes the question of pharmacology. But Derrida himself never understood this as such, nor therefore did he do so from the standpoint of a positive pharmacology, that is, the question of the *investments* made possible by the *pharmakon* (and still less from the standpoint of a 'positive science'). If one *could* and *should* refer to positive *pharmacology*, however, it is therefore precisely *not* as a science, but as a *positive* (and knowledgeable [*savante*]) *technicity* of this technics that is always and firstly a *pharmakon*, inasmuch as, from the outset and irreducibly, it divides itself into a pair of opposites.

A positive technicity is a form of knowledge that is not a science, but which, taking care of what presents itself as a chance and a virtue (a power, a force, an excellence) only in being *accompanied by its opposite* (an expedient, a dependency, a poison), does not try to reduce its duplicity, but on the contrary knows that *this condition of impossibility is the condition of a contingent positivity*, one that is accidental, risky, *tukhē* becoming *kairos*, that is, a *possibility arising from out of impossibility*, and as the *necessity of a fault* (or what Blanchot called the improbable).

It is a question of knowing how to turn this necessity into a virtue – which would involve knowing-how-to-make-a-virtue-of-a-necessity-of-those-needy-ones who are the neotenics (that is, pharmacological beings) becoming noetics.

This amounts to the program of a political economy that could only be a *praxis*. Such a *praxis*, however, needs a theory. This *praxis* is named positive pharmacology, the theory of which is named general organology.

In recent years, I have often tried to think this with Deleuze and his concept of quasi-causality – which remains in and returns from

Hades, making (the) différance with Lyotard and Derrida, ghosts of anamneses to come. *If there are any.*

Translated by Daniel Ross.

Notes

1   Vladimir I. Vernadsky, *The Biosphere*, trans. David B. Langmuir (New York: Copernicus, 1998), p. 118.

2   Jakob von Uexküll, *A Foray into the World of Animals and Humans, with, A Theory of Meaning*, trans. Joseph D. O'Neil (Minneapolis and London: University of Minnesota Press, 2010).

3   Alfred J. Lotka, 'The Law of Evolution as a Maximal Principle', *Human Biology* 17:3 (1945), pp. 167–94.

4   Lotka, 'The Law of Evolution as a Maximal Principle', p. 179.

5   Jacques Grinevald, 'Introduction: The Invisibility of the Vernadskian Revolution', in Vernadsky, *The Biosphere*, p. 25.

6   Lotka, 'The Law of Evolution as a Maximal Principle', pp. 192–93.

7   Arnold Toynbee, *Mankind and Mother Earth* (Oxford: Oxford University Press, 1976), p. 17.

8   Ibid., p. 575.

9   Friedrich Engels, *Dialectics of Nature*, trans. Clemens Dutt (London: Lawrence & Wishart, 1940), p. 17.

10 Toynbee, *Mankind and Mother Earth*, p. 17.

11 Ibid.

12 Ibid.

13 Ibid., p. 596.

14 Georges Canguilhem, *The Normal and the Pathological*, trans. Carolyn R. Fawcett, with Robert S. Cohen (New York: Zone Books, 1991), p. 205.

15 Ibid., p. 200, my italics.

16 Ludwig Boltzmann, 'The Second Law of Thermodynamics (1886)', *Theoretical Physics and Philosophical Problems*, edited by Brian McGuinness, trans. Paul Foulkes (Dordrecht and Boston: Reidel, 1974), p. 24.

17 Erwin Schrödinger, *What is Life?* in *What is Life?, with Mind and Matter and Autobiographical Sketches* (Cambridge: Cambridge University Press, 1992), p. 73.

18 Boltzmann, 'On a Thesis of Schopenhauer's (1905)', *Theoretical Physics and Philosophical Problems*, p. 196.

19 Ibid.

20 Alfred North Whitehead, *The Function of Reason* (Princeton: Princeton University Press, 1929), p. 2.

21 Boltzmann, 'On a Thesis of Schopenhauer's (1905)', p. 197.

22 Boltzmann, 'On Statistical Mechanics (1904)', *Theoretical Physics and Philosophical Problems*, p. 166.

23 Ibid., pp. 166–67.

24 Boltzmann, 'On a Thesis of Schopenhauer's (1905)', p. 196.

25 Ibid., p. 197.

26 Carlo Cercignani, *Ludwig Boltzmann: The Man Who Trusted Atoms* (Oxford: Oxford University Press, 1998), p. 43.

27 And Musil did not hesitate to interpret this Kakania in terms of the question of entropic becoming, and in dialogue with Nietzsche and his concept of nihilism, as shown in Bernard Stiegler, *Qu'appelle-t-on panser? 1. L'immense régression* (Paris: Les Liens qui Libèrent, 2018).

28 Simondon, *L'individuation à la lumière des notions de forme et d'information* (Grenoble: Jérôme Millon, 2013), p. 216. For the following discussion of Simondon, the author would like to sincerely thank Anne Alombert, for drawing attention to these parts of Simondon's work, for her ongoing discussions concerning these questions, and for her thesis on Derrida and Simondon that greatly adds to the sum of our knowledge of these two thinkers by, for the first time, bringing them together in a mutually illuminating manner, thereby increasing the life of their second birth.

29 Ibid., p. 245.

30 Ibid., p. 216.

31 Ibid., p. 217.

32 See Marcel Detienne and Jean-Pierre Vernant, *Cunning Intelligence in Greek Culture and Society*, trans. Janet Lloyd (Chicago and London: University of Chicago Press, 1991).

33 Karl Marx and Friedrich Engels, *The German Ideology: Students Edition*, trans. Clemens Dutt and C. P. Magill (London: Lawrence & Wishart, 1974), p. 42.

34 Friedrich Engels, *Dialectics of Nature*, trans. Clemens Dutt (London: Lawrence & Wishart, 1940), p. 17.

35 Cf., Bernard Stiegler, *Technics and Time, 1: The Fault of Epimetheus*, trans. Richard Beardsworth and George Collins (Stanford: Stanford University Press, 1998), p. 88.

36 Stiegler, *Technics and Time, 1*, p. 177.

37 Georges Bataille, *Lascaux: Or the Birth of Art*, trans. Austryn Wainhouse (Geneva: Skira, 1955), p. 9.

38 See also Bernard Stiegler, 'Elements for a General Organology', trans. Daniel Ross, *Derrida Today* 13 (2020), p. 80.

39 Jacques Derrida, *Of Grammatology*, trans. Gayatri Chakravorty Spivak, corrected edition (Baltimore and London: Johns Hopkins University Press, 1998), p. 84.

40 Stiegler, 'Elements for a General Organology', p. 78.

41 Ibid., p. 88.

42 I argued that Stiegler's work can be divided into three periods in the introduction to Bernard Stiegler, *The Neganthropocene*, trans. and ed. Daniel Ross (London: Open Humanities Press, 2018).

43 Sylvain Auroux, *La révolution technologique de la grammatisation: Introduction à l'histoire des sciences du langage* (Liège: Mardaga, 1994).

44 It should be pointed out that it was Simondon who conceived this transition as the shift from a situation in which the human being, as the tool-bearer, is the 'technical individual' at the heart of the process, to a situation in which the machine becomes the technical individual.

45 Edmund Husserl, *On the Phenomenology of the Consciousness of Internal Time (1893–1917)*, trans. John Barnett Brough (Dordrecht: Kluwer Academic Publishers, 1991) p. 32.

46 Jacques Derrida, *Speech and Phenomena*, trans. David B. Allison (Evanston: Northwestern University Press, 1973), p. 65.

47 In Bernard Stiegler, *Taking Care of Youth and the Generations*, trans. Stephen Barker (Stanford: Stanford University Press, 2010).

48 Naomi Klein, 'Screen New Deal: Under Cover of Mass Death, Andrew Cuomo Calls in the Billionaires to Build a High-Tech Dystopia', *The Intercept* (9 May 2020), available at: <https://theintercept.com/2020/05/08/andrew-cuomo-eric-schmidt-coronavirus-tech-shock-doctrine/>.

49 Bernard Stiegler, *Technics and Time, 3*, p. 74.

50 Stiegler, *The Neganthropocene*, ch. 1.

51 Erwin Schrödinger, *What is Life?*, in *What is Life?, with Mind and Matter and Autobiographical Sketches* (Cambridge: Cambridge University Press, 1992).

52 Alfred J. Lotka, 'The Law of Evolution as a Maximal Principle', *Human Biology* 17 (1945), pp. 167–94.

53 On this distinction between existence and consistence, see Bernard Stiegler, *The Decadence of Industrial Democracies: Disbelief and Discredit, Volume 1*, trans. Daniel Ross and Suzanne Arnold (Cambridge: Polity Press, 2011), pp. 89–93. Suffice it to say here that among those things that do not exist yet consist are God, the geometrical point, the triangle, the number three, justice, the English language – in short, everything that falls under the term, 'the ideas'.

54 Claude Lévi-Strauss, *Tristes Tropiques*, trans. John Weightman and Doreen Weightman (Harmondsworth, Middlesex: Penguin, 1976), p. 543.

55 Stiegler, *Technics and Time, 1*, p. x.

56 Bernard Stiegler, *Acting Out*, trans. David Barison, Daniel Ross and Patrick Crogan (Stanford: Stanford University Press, 2009), p. 32.

57 Bernard Stiegler, *The Age of Disruption: Technology and Madness in Computational Capitalism*, trans. Daniel Ross (Cambridge: Polity Press, 2019), pp. 205–6.

58 Ibid., p. 219.

59 Bernard Stiegler, *Qu-appelle-t-on panser? 1. L'immense régression* (Paris: Les Liens qui Libèrent, 2018), p. 56.

60 Ibid., pp. 329–30.

61 Bernard Stiegler, *Qu-appelle-t-on panser? 2. La leçon de Greta Thunberg* (Paris: Les Liens qui Libèrent, 2020), pp. 44–45.

62 Bernard Stiegler, 'Démesure, promesses, compromis', *Mediapart*, part 1/3 (5 September 2020), available at: <https://blogs.mediapart.fr/edition/les-invites-de-mediapart/article/050920/demesure-promesses-compromis-13-par-bernard-stiegler>

63 Ibid.

64 Stiegler, *Acting Out*, p. 3.

65 Stiegler, 'Démesure, promesses, compromis', *Mediapart*, part 2/3 (7 September 2020), available at: <https://blogs.mediapart.fr/edition/les-invites-de-mediapart/article/070920/demesure-promesses-compromis-23-par-bernard-stiegler>.

66 Stiegler, *Acting Out*, p. 82, translation modified.

67 According to a 2016 Nielsen audience report, Americans spend more than *ten and a half hours per day* consuming media on various devices: <http://www.nielsen.com/content/dam/corporate/us/en/reports-downloads/2016-reports/total-audience-report-q1-2016.pdf>.

68 Georges Canguilhem, 'The Decline of the Idea of Progress', trans. David Macey, *Economy and Society* 27 (1998), p. 323.

69 Theodor W. Adorno and Max Horkheimer, *Dialectic of Enlightenment: Philosophical Fragments*, trans. Edmund Jephcott (Stanford: Stanford University Press, 2002), p. xiv.

70 On the hubris of the Straussians, see Daniel Ross, *Violent Democracy* (Cambridge: Cambridge University Press, 2004), ch. 1.

71 Peter Thiel, 'The Straussian Moment', in Robert Hamerton-Kelly (ed.), *Politics and Apocalypse* (East Lansing: Michigan State University Press, 2007), p. 209.

72 Ibid., p. 212.

73 Ibid., pp. 214–15.

74 Peter Thiel, quoted in Quentin Hardy, 'René Girard, French Theorist of the Social Sciences, Dies at 91', *New York Times* (10 November 2015), available at: <https://www.nytimes.com/2015/11/11/arts/international/rene-girard-french-theorist-of-the-social-sciences-dies-at-91.html>. See also Geoff Shullenberger, 'The Scapegoating Machine', *The New Inquiry* (30 November 2016), available at: <https://thenewinquiry.com/essays/the-scapegoating-machine/>.

75 René Girard, 'The Evangelical Subversion of Myth', in Hamerton-Kelly (ed.), *Politics and Apocalypse*, p. 39.

76 Maurice Godelier, *The Metamorphoses of Kinship*, trans. Nora Scott (London and New York: Verso, 2011), p. 552.

77 Claude Lévi-Strauss, 'The Future of Kinship Studies', *Proceedings of the Royal Anthropological Institute of Great Britain and Ireland* 1 (1965), p. 16. Note, however, that Lévi-Strauss himself, as per his general aversion to diachronic questions, introduces this categorization 'without loading these terms with historical content'. See also Godelier, *The Metamorphoses of Kinship*, pp. 421–22.

78 René Girard, *Violence and the Sacred*, trans. Patrick Gregory (Baltimore and London: Johns Hopkins University Press, 1977), p. 296.

79 Theodore Kaczynski, *Anti-Tech Revolution: Why and How* (Scottsdale, AZ: Fitch and Madison, 2016), p. 1.

80 Ibid., p. 43.

81 Ibid., p. 153.

82 Immanuel Kant, 'The Contest of Faculties', *Political Writings*, 2nd edition, trans. H. B. Nisbet (Cambridge: Cambridge University Press, 1991), p. 179, a conception according to which it 'seems that the day of judgement is at hand, and the pious zealot already dreams of the rebirth of everything and of a world created anew after the present world has been destroyed by fire'.

83 Ibid., p. 184.

84 Nietzsche, *The Anti-Christ*, §11, in *The Anti-Christ, Ecce Homo, Twilight of the Idols, and Other Writings*, trans. Judith Norman (Cambridge: Cambridge University Press, 2005), p. 10.

85 Canguilhem, 'The Decline of the Idea of Progress', p. 316.

86 Ibid., my italics.

87 Jean-Paul Sartre, *Critique of Dialectical Reason, Volume One*, corrected edition, trans. Alan Sheridan-Smith (London and New York: Verso, 1991), pp. 136–37.

88 Claude Lévi-Strauss, *Tristes Tropiques*, trans. John Weightman and Doreen Weightman (Harmondsworth, Middlesex: Penguin, 1976), p. 543, my italics.

89 Martin Heidegger, 'Insight Into That Which Is: Bremen Lectures 1949', *Bremen and Freiburg Lectures: Insight Into That Which Is and Basic Principles of Thinking*, trans. Andrew J. Mitchell (Bloomington and Indianapolis: Indiana University Press, 2012), p. 40.

90 Erwin Schrödinger, 'What is Life? The Physical Aspect of the Living Cell', *What is Life?, with Mind and Matter and Autobiographical Sketches* (Cambridge: Cambridge University Press, 1992).

91 Oswald Spengler, *The Decline of the West, Volume 1: Form and Actuality*, trans. Charles Francis Atkinson (New York: Alfred A. Knopf, 1947), pp. 421–24. Perhaps the most earnest attempt to incorporate the meaning of the second law of thermodynamics into a metaphysics premised on a cosmic suicidal tendency is shown in the work (and life) of Philipp Mainländer, for whom all things express 'the deepest longing for absolute annihilation'. See Frederick C. Beiser, *Weltschmerz: Pessimism in German Philosophy, 1860–1900* (Oxford: Oxford University Press, 2016), p. 218.

92 Sigmund Freud, *Beyond the Pleasure Principle*, in Volume 18 of Freud, *The Standard Edition of the Complete Psychological Works of Sigmund Freud*, trans. and ed. James Strachey (London: Hogarth, 1953–74), p. 48.

93 Jacques Derrida, *Of Grammatology*, trans. Gayatri Chakravorty Spivak, corrected edition (Baltimore and London: Johns Hopkins University Press 1998), p. 84.

94 Alfred North Whitehead, *The Function of Reason* (Princeton: Princeton University Press, 1929), Introductory Summary (no page number).

95 Ibid., p. 5.

96 See Gerald Moore, 'On the Origin of *Aisthesis* by Means of Artificial Selection; or, The Preservation of Favored Traces in the Struggle for Existence', *Boundary 2* 44 (2017), pp. 191–212.

97 Bernard Stiegler, 'Du temps-carbone au temps-lumière', in Bernard Stiegler, Alain Giffard and Christian Fauré, *Pour en finir avec la mécroissance* (Paris: Flammarion, 2009), pp. 11–43. See also Bernard Stiegler, *For a New Critique of Political Economy*, trans. Daniel Ross (Cambridge: Polity Press, 2010), pp. 23–24; and '*Ars Industrialis*: 2010 Manifesto', in Bernard Stiegler, *The Re-Enchantment of the World: The Value of Spirit against Industrial Populism*, trans. Trevor Arthur (London and New York: Bloomsbury, 2014), p. 25.

98 Bernard Stiegler, *Automatic Society, Volume 1: The Future of Work*, trans. Daniel Ross (Cambridge: Polity Press, 2016), p. 244.

99 Bernard Stiegler, *Technics and Time, 1: The Fault of Epimetheus*, trans. Richard Beardsworth and George Collins (Stanford: Stanford University Press, 1998), pp. 68–69.

100 Ibid., p. 61.

101 Bernard Stiegler, 'The Theater of Individuation: Phase-Shift and Resolution in Simondon and Heidegger', trans. Kristina Lebedeva, in Arne De Boever, Alex Murray, Jon Roffe and Ashley Woodward (eds), *Gilbert Simondon: Being and Technology* (Edinburgh: Edinburgh University Press, 2012), pp. 193–94.

102 Erich Hörl, 'A Thousand Ecologies: The Process of Cyberneticization and General Ecology', trans. James Burton, Jeffrey Kirkwood and Maria Vlotides, in Diedrich Diederichsen and Anselm Franke (eds), *The Whole Earth: California and the Disappearance of the Outside* (Berlin: Sternberg Press, 2013), p. 126, n. 35.

103 Erich Hörl, 'The Technological Condition', trans. Anthony Enns, *Parrhesia* 22 (2015), p. 4, and Hörl, 'Other Beginnings of Participative Sense-Culture: Wild Media, Speculative Ecologies, Transgressions of the Cybernetic Hypothesis', trans. Anne Ganzert and James Burton, in Mathias Denecke, Anne Ganzert, Isabell Otto

and Robert Stock (eds), *ReClaiming Participation: Technology – Mediation – Collectivity* (Bielefeld: Transcript Verlag, 2016), p. 110.

104 Hörl, 'Other Beginnings of Participative Sense-Culture', p. 116.

105 Ibid., p. 95.

106 Hörl, 'The Technological Condition', p. 10.

107 Hörl does not elucidate his critique of Stiegler's purported anthropocentrism in his long introduction to Erich Hörl and James Burton (eds), *General Ecology: The New Ecological Paradigm* (New York: Bloomsbury, 2017), to which Stiegler contributes an important chapter. See also Hörl, 'Prostheses of Desire: On Bernard Stiegler's New Critique of Projection', trans. Arne De Boever, *Parrehsia* 20 (2014), pp. 2–14, for what seems a somewhat more sympathetic treatment of Stiegler's account of desire. A key question to be posed to this critique would concern the repeated conflation of 'default and lack', which thereby seems to both aim at and miss Stiegler's philosophy.

108 Mark B. N. Hansen, 'Bernard Stiegler, Philosopher of Desire?', *Boundary 2* 44 (2017), p. 185.

109 Ibid.

110 Ibid., p. 186.

111 Ibid.

112 Ibid., p. 187.

113 Ibid., p. 189.

114 Ibid., p. 190.

115 Ibid., pp. 188–89.

116 Ibid., p. 189.

117 That being said, Stiegler has himself recently acknowledged that the *question* of a new *regime* of individuation is indeed at stake today: this is not just a matter of rapid advances in artificial intelligence but of the fact that new biotechnologies themselves amount to a 'new age of exosomatization'. Hence he has recently argued that potential developments in neurotechnology raise the question, and the *problem*, of a new *endosomatization*, new interfaces of the relationship between interiorization and exteriorization. See Bernard Stiegler, *The Neganthropocene*, trans. Daniel Ross (London: Open Humanities Press, 2018), chs 4 and 12.

118 Bernard Stiegler, 'The Proletarianization of Sensibility', trans. Arne De Boever, *Boundary 2* 44 (2017), p. 14.

119 Francis Fukuyama, *The End of History and the Last Man* (New York: Macmillan, 1992), p. 336: 'Looking around contemporary America, it does not strike me that we face the problem of an excess of *megalothymia* [Fukuyama's name for the desire to be recognized as superior to one's fellows]. Those earnest young people trooping off to law and business school, who anxiously fill out their résumés in hopes of maintaining the lifestyles to which they believe themselves entitled, seem to be much more in danger of becoming last men, rather than reviving the passions of the first man.'

120 Ibid., p. 328.

121 Ibid., p. 336.

122 Samuel P. Huntington, *The Clash of Civilizations and the Remaking of World Order* (New York: Simon and Schuster, 1996), pp. 31–32.

123 Ibid., p. 20.

124 Huntington argues that global politics has for the first time become 'multipolar and multicivilizational', that modernization is different from Westernization, that the balance of power between civilizations is shifting and destabilizing, that the West's 'universalist pretensions' are bringing it into conflict with other civilizations (Islam and China in particular), and that the 'survival of the West depends on Americans reaffirming their Western identity and Westerners accepting their civilization as unique not universal and uniting to renew and preserve it against challenges from non-Western societies'. Hence for Huntington, avoiding 'a global war of civilizations depends on world leaders accepting and cooperating to maintain the multicivilizational character of global politics' (ibid., pp. 20–21).

125 As stated by the World Bank, emissions rose by 25 per cent in the decade following the signing of the Protocols. See World Bank, *World Development Report 2010: Development and Climate Change* (Washington, D.C.: The World Bank, 2010), p. 233.

126 Antoine Berman, *The Experience of the Foreign: Culture and Translation in Romantic Germany*, trans. Stefan Heyvaert (Albany: State University of New York Press, 1992), p. 176.

127 Matt Taibbi, 'Why Aren't We Talking More About Trump's Nihilism', *Rolling Stone* (1 October 2018), available at: <https://www.rollingstone.com/politics/politics-news/trump-white-house-climate-change-731440/>.

128 The question of how we must understand *Ereignis* is thus a matter of hearing Heidegger otherwise than he has tended to be heard (including by himself), and for obvious reasons. For instance, what would it mean to hear the following statement (of a problem) and question (of a solution) and confession (of having no solution) and suspicion

(about what may *not* be a solution) from 1966 (half a century ago), not as an example of some anti-cosmopolitan 'conservatism' but as an instance of his most *radical* speculation?

> During the past thirty years, it should meanwhile have become clearer that the planetary movement of modern technology is a power whose great role in determining history can hardly be overestimated. A decisive question for me today is how a political system can be assigned to today's technological age at all, and which political system would that be? I have no answer to this question. I am not convinced that it is democracy.

Martin Heidegger, 'Der Spiegel Interview', in Günther Neske and Emil Kettering, *Martin Heidegger and National Socialism: Questions and Answers*, trans. Lisa Harries (New York: Paragon House, 1990), p. 54. I have previously discussed this quotation (which is from the same interview in which Heidegger famously states that, now, 'only a God can save us') in Daniel Ross, 'Democracy, Authority, Narcissism: From Agamben to Stiegler', *Contretemps* 6 (2006), available at: <https://www.academia.edu/12687280/Democracy_Authority_Narcissism_From_Agamben_to_Stiegler_2006_>, esp. pp. 77–78, but it requires further consideration in the contemporary context.

129 'Doubling down' being a reference to the card game blackjack, which indicates the degree to which all this is a matter of gambling, but in this case by betting on the highly improbable, with all the risks that entails. But it also serves as a reminder that playing cards are themselves a technological and civilizational artefact and invention of Chinese origin, possibly from the Tang dynasty and utilizing the woodblock printing technology that is one of the Four Great Inventions, and hence as a reminder that all this raises the question of the porosity of civilizational borders, and the proliferating effects of processes of inter-civilizational transmission, trade and borrowing, crucial examples of which are technologies of addiction such as opium and games of chance.

130 Bernard Stiegler, *Technics and Time, 1: The Fault of Epimetheus*, trans. Richard Beardsworth and George Collins (Stanford: Stanford University Press, 1998), p. ix.

131 Jacques Derrida, *Of Grammatology*, corrected edition, trans. Gayatri Chakravorty Spivak (Baltimore and London: Johns Hopkins University Press, 1998), p. 6.

132 Stiegler, *Technics and Time, 1*, p. 1.

133 Jacques Derrida, 'Violence and Metaphysics: An Essay on the Thought of Emmanuel Levinas', *Writing and Difference*, trans. Alan Bass (London and Henley: Routledge and Kegan Paul, 1978), p. 79.

134 Ibid.

135 Bernard Stiegler, *Philosophising by Accident: Interviews with Élie During*, trans. Benoît Dillet (Edinburgh: Edinburgh University Press, 2017), p. 31.

136 It becomes our accidental necessity in the sense of being the originary fault that we must quasi-causally adopt, and so transform.

137 Bernard Stiegler, *Acting Out*, trans. David Barison, Daniel Ross and Patrick Crogan (Stanford: Stanford University Press, 2009), p. 3.

138 Friedrich Nietzsche, *Twilight of the Idols*, in *The Anti-Christ, Ecce Homo, Twilight of the Idols, and Other Writings*, trans. Judith Norman (Cambridge and New York: Cambridge University Press, 2005), p. 162.

139 Ibid.

140 Ibid., p. 164. But, we might wonder here, could it be that Nietzsche is mistaking Socrates for Plato, for whom alone dialectics becomes a method?

141 Ibid., p. 165.

142 Ibid., p. 166.

143 Ibid.

144 Ibid.

145 Is not the arrival of the first stages of that hellish prospect what is depicted, for example, in the 2018 documentary entitled *People's Republic of Desire*, directed by Hao Wu?

146 Nietzsche, *Twilight of the Idols*, p. 165.

147 Ibid., p. 166.

148 Ibid.

149 Ibid.

150 Laurence Lampert begins his book on Nietzsche by asking 'What is a philosopher?', and he indicates on the first page that Nietzsche's answer to this question was that 'a philosopher naturally generated the highest "art", the highest making, a way of living that could structure the life of a whole people'. While this association of philosophical questioning with the problem of collective existence, and with its *making*, is that to which we, too, are drawing attention, everything depends on what is meant by 'naturally generated', 'structure' and 'whole people', and the degree to which this 'making' of collective life is understood *pharmacologically* (in Stiegler's sense): the question of the generation of resentment, for example, is absent

from Lampert's account. See Laurence Lampert, *What a Philosopher Is: Becoming Nietzsche* (Chicago and London: University of Chicago Press, 2017), p. 1.

151 Nietzsche, *Twilight of the Idols*, p. 228.

152 Friedrich Nietzsche, *Philosophy in the Tragic Age of the Greeks*, trans. Marianne Cowan (Washington D.C.: Regnery Gateway, 1962), p. 33.

153 Alfred North Whitehead, *The Function of Reason* (Princeton: Princeton University Press, 1929), p. 28.

154 Ibid., p. 5.

155 Ibid., 'Introductory Summary', no page number.

156 Ibid., p. 5.

157 Karl Marx and Friedrich Engels, *The German Ideology*, trans. Clemens Dutt and C. P. Magill (London: Lawrence & Wishart, 1974), p. 42.

158 Ibid., pp. 42–43.

159 Jacques Derrida, '"Genesis and Structure" and Phenomenology', *Writing and Difference*, p. 167.

160 Derrida, 'Structure, Sign and Play in the Discourse of the Human Sciences', *Writing and Difference*, p. 291.

161 Claude Lévi-Strauss, quoted in ibid. See Claude Lévi-Strauss, *Introduction to the Work of Marcel Mauss*, trans. Felicity Baker (London: Routledge and Kegan Paul, 1987), p. 59.

162 Anne Alombert, 'Penser dans l'après-coup de la postmodernité', *Implications Philosophiques* (2017), published in two parts, available at: <http://www.implications-philosophiques.org/actualite/une/penser-dans-lapres-coup-de-la-postmodernite-12/> and <http://www.implications-philosophiques.org/actualite/une/penser-dans-lapres-coup-de-la-modernite-22/>.

163 Jacques Derrida, *Positions*, trans. Alan Bass (Chicago: University of Chicago Press, 1981), pp. 57–58.

164 André Leroi-Gourhan, quoted in Stiegler, *Technics and Time, 1*, p. 58.

165 Ibid., p. 59.

166 Derrida, *Of Grammatology*, p. 8.

167 André Leroi-Gourhan, *Gesture and Speech*, trans. Anna Bostock Berger (Cambridge, Massachusetts and London: MIT Press, 1993), p. 413, n. 14.

168 Here we must observe that in the note just referred to, Leroi-Gourhan divides memory into three epochs in another way than we are going to here – first, 'species-related memory', second, 'ethnic' memory that ensures the reproduction of behavioural patterns in human societies, and third, 'artificial' memory that ensures the reproduction of 'mechanical actions'. In other words, the differentiation we are about to make between genetic and nervous memory is in this note assimilated to the single memory that is being called 'species-related', and the memory that we are here referring to in terms of exteriorization (which means that ethnic memory is *already* technical *as well as ethnic* memory) is being distinguished by Leroi-Gourhan from an artificial memory *divorced* from the reproduction of human behavioural patterns. He later refers to this as a tripartite distinction between animal, human and mechanical memory (p. 258). The status of the distinction between the human and the mechanical (where both are *already* the product of exteriorization and therefore technical) is precisely the question we face *today*, in our epoch, as well as being the question that Leroi-Gourhan anticipates in chs 9 and 15.

169 Exactly how long or complex the period was that led from a world of inorganic compounds to the world of DNA remains a mystery, and most likely will always remain something about which it is only possible to speculate, poorly or well. It has been suggested, for example, that an 'RNA world' could have preceded the DNA world, and no doubt there are grounds for this speculation, but its character and duration remain completely unknown. See, for example, Michel Morange, *Life Explained*, trans. Matthew Cobb and Malcolm DeBevoise (New Haven and London: Yale University Press, 2008), pp. 16–18.

170 See Brendan B. Larsen et al., 'Inordinate Fondness Multiplied and Redistributed: The Number of Species on Earth and the New Pie of Life', *Quarterly Review of Biology* 92 (2017), pp. 229–65.

171 Leroi-Gourhan, *Gesture and Speech*, p. 222.

172 That is, beyond non-nervous 'responses' such as plant phototropism, which consists in alterations in gene expression regulated via auxins, a type of plant hormone.

173 See Stiegler, *Philosophising by Accident*, pp. 35–36.

174 Leroi-Gourhan, *Gesture and Speech*, p. 134.

175 Ibid., pp. 141–42.

176 See Bernard Stiegler, *States of Shock: Stupidity and Knowledge in the Twenty-First Century*, trans. Daniel Ross (Cambridge: Polity Press, 2015), §31.

177 Derrida's wife Marguerite wrote her thesis in ethnology under the supervision of André Leroi-Gourhan, and the article by Jacques Derrida that would grow into *Of Grammatology* was first published as a review of several books including *Gesture and Speech*. See Benoît Peeters, *Derrida: A Biography*, trans. Andrew Brown (Cambridge: Polity Press, 2013), pp. 113 and 159.

178 See Christopher Johnson, *System and Writing in the Philosophy of Jacques Derrida* (Cambridge and New York: Cambridge University Press, 1993), p. 216, n. 19, and especially Johnson, 'Derrida: The Machine and the Animal', *Paragraph* 28:3 (2005), pp. 102–20. Johnson reckons with *Technics and Time* in 'The Prehistory of Technology: On the Contribution of Leroi-Gourhan', in Christina Howells and Gerald Moore (eds), *Stiegler and Technics* (Edinburgh: Edinburgh University Press, 2013), but not always convincingly: for example, he argues (pp. 43–44) that Stiegler is too keen to consider evolution in terms of a 'philosophy of *difference*', arguing that this erases Leroi-Gourhan's account of the increase of brain capacity as 'the progressive layering of brain functions', but is it not obvious that what underlies such accretions and layerings is a selection process that leads precisely to genetic differentiation, and does so in the pursuit of the deferral of entropy?

179 Jacques Derrida, 'Différance', *Margins of Philosophy*, trans. Alan Bass (Hemel Hempstead: Harvester Press, 1982), p. 7, translation modified.

180 Jacques Derrida, *Of Grammatology*, p. 5, translation modified.

181 Derrida, 'Différance', p. 15.

182 Jacques Derrida, *Speech and Phenomena, And Other Essays on Husserl's Theory of Signs*, trans. David B. Allison (Evanston: Northwestern University Press, 1973), p. 80.

183 Ibid., p. 81.

184 Ibid., p. 82.

185 Ibid.

186 Derrida, 'Différance', p. 8.

187 Ibid., p. 14.

188 Derrida, *Of Grammatology*, p. 83.

189 Ibid., p. 84.

190 Ibid.

191 Stiegler, *Technics and Time, 1*, p. 138.

192 Leroi-Gourhan, *Gesture and Speech*, p. 224.

193 Francesco Vitale, *Biodeconstruction*, trans. Mauro Senatore (Albany: State University of New York Press, 2018), p. 22, justifies Derrida's linkage of Leroi-Gourhan's 'program' to cybernetics by drawing attention to the fact that Leroi-Gourhan 'compares the function of the nervous system and the brain of the animal to that of the machine'. Indeed, Leroi-Gourhan states that 'the nervous system is not an instinct-producing machine but one that responds to internal and external demands by designing programs' (Leroi-Gourhan, *Gesture and Speech*, p. 221). Yet even if this reference to machines and programs does show that Leroi-Gourhan sees computational technology as the latest step in the adventure of life's conquest of speed, it is much less certain that he is working with an animal/machine analogy in order to show that everything from genetics to electronics falls unproblematically *within* the terms of the cybernetic paradigm.

194 Derrida, *Of Grammatology*, p. 84.

195 Ibid.

196 See Vitale, *Biodeconstruction*, p. 24: 'If the life of the animal depends on interaction with the environment as it is described by Leroi-Gourhan, then it is regulated by the possibility of elaborating iterable traces: before any opposition between humans and animals, the animal in general must be endowed with a structure of retention and protention and, thus, must be capable of memory. In the wake of Leroi-Gourhan, Derrida can say that the intentional consciousness described by phenomenology is only a particular emergence of the general structure of the living programmed to respond to the necessity of survival. Therefore, arche-writing would be already at stake in the animal life, in the necessity of recognizing sources of food, reproductive partners, and dangers.'

197 Derrida, *Of Grammatology*, p. 84, my italics.

198 Ibid., p. 85. And, we might add, where this exorbitant thought is *also* the history and the story of an adventure that will travel all across the orb, turning the biosphere into a technosphere, and, eventually, *beyond* the orb, as this technics journeys into orbit and beyond the solar system, and, most significantly, as it produces an apparatus of memory and communication that is orbitally connected via artificial satellites that become the exospheric means and possibility of the latest phase of this technospheric interconnection commonly known as globalization. But this formulation of the ex-orbitant is one that Stiegler will not pursue *explicitly* until long after the first volume of *Technics and Time*, even if we can say that it is already *implied*, however faintly, by Derrida's suggestion that the history of life is an adventure extending to electronic card indexes and reading machines,

echoing Leroi-Gourhan's own reference to the future possibility of electronic libraries (the first artificial communications satellites being the Echo balloon satellites, first launched in 1960, and then the Telstar satellites, owned by AT&T and launched in 1962 as part of a multi-national agreement between AT&T, Bell, NASA and the British and French general post offices, that is, five years before the publication of *Of Grammatology*).

199 Vitale, *Biodeconstruction*, pp. 21–22.

200 Derrida, *Of Grammatology*, p. 65.

201 Stiegler, *Technics and Time, 1*, p. 139.

202 Derrida, *Of Grammatology*, p. 65.

203 Stiegler, *Technics and Time, 1*, p. 139.

204 Ibid., p. 186.

205 Derrida, 'Différance', p. 17.

206 Stiegler, *Technics and Time, 1*, p. 139.

207 Ibid., p. 140.

208 Martin Heidegger, *Being and Time*, trans. Joan Stambaugh, rev. by Dennis J. Schmidt (Albany: State University of New York Press, 2010), p. 20 (all references to this work will be to the German pagination).

209 Ibid.

210 Ibid., p. 19.

211 Ibid., p. 20.

212 Ibid.

213 Stiegler, *Technics and Time, 1*, p. 140.

214 Ibid., pp. 140–41.

215 Bernard Stiegler, *Qu'appelle-t-on panser? 1. L'immense régression* (Paris: Les Liens qui Libèrent, 2018), p. 107.

216 Stiegler, *Technics and Time, 1*, pp. 262–63.

217 Bernard Stiegler, 'Elements for a General Organology', trans. Daniel Ross, *Derrida Today* 13 (2020), p. 80.

218 Stiegler, *Philosophising by Accident*, p. 35.

219 For this statement to be definitive, we would need to add mention of the critique that Stiegler outlines in *Technics and Time, 1* of

Heidegger's concept of 'world-historiality', but there was not time to do so in the previous lecture.

220 And it will be this same Rudolf Boehm who writes an article on Heidegger's thinking of technology that will become crucial to Stiegler's own 'going back' to Heidegger.

221 John Barnett Brough, 'Translator's Introduction', in Edmund Husserl, *On the Phenomenology of the Consciousness of Internal Time (1893–1917)*, trans. John Barnett Brough (Dordrecht: Kluwer Academic Publishers, 1991), p. xiv.

222 Ibid., p. xvi.

223 Edmund Husserl, quoted in Theodore Kisiel and Thomas Sheehan (eds), *Becoming Heidegger: On the Trail of his Early Occasional Writings, 1910–1927*, 2nd revised edition (Seattle: Noesis Press, 2010), pp. 414–15.

224 Martin Heidegger, quoted in ibid., p. 419.

225 Martin Heidegger, quoted in ibid., p. li, n. 13. The italicization of the word 'system' may here be the most telling part of the statement.

226 Edmund Husserl, 4 May 1933, quoted in ibid., p. 412.

227 Waltraud Herbstrith, *Edith Stein: A Biography*, trans. Bernard Bonowitz (San Francisco: Harper and Row, 1985), p. 186.

228 Edith Stein, 'Martin Heidegger's Existential Philosophy', trans. Mette Lebech, *Maynooth Philosophical Papers* 4 (2007), p. 77.

229 Ibid., p. 79.

230 Stein's bust does not appear in the film *The Ister* (2004), however, because it was not added until 2009.

231 Edith Stein, quoted in John Felstiner, *Paul Celan: Poet, Survivor, Jew* (New Haven and London: Yale University Press, 1995), p. 306, n. 45.

232 Ibid., p. 103.

233 Hans-Georg Gadamer, quoted in ibid., p. 105.

234 Günter Grass, quoted in James K. Lyon, *Paul Celan and Martin Heidegger: An Unresolved Conversation, 1951–1970* (Baltimore: Johns Hopkins University Press, 2006), p. 63.

235 Bernard Stiegler, *Technics and Time, 2: Disorientation*, trans. Stephen Barker (Stanford: Stanford University Press, 2009), pp. 191–92.

236 Ibid., p. 194, translation modified.

237 Ibid., p. 195, translation modified.

238 Ibid., pp. 195–96, translation modified.

239 Ibid., p. 196, translation modified.

240 Ibid., p. 197, translation modified.

241 Stiegler, *Technics and Time, 1*, p. 248.

242 Husserl, *On the Phenomenology of the Consciousness of Internal Time*, p. 24.

243 It is precisely in terms of the gulf between the time of computation and the temporality of phenomenological lived experience that Stiegler will introduce the entire discussion of Husserlian temporality at the beginning of ch. 4 of *Technics and Time, 2*. If there is no sense in which the computer is founded on the experience of temporal *passage*, of what we will see can be called the 'large now' of retention and protention, then is this not a fundamental flaw in all 'cognitivist' approaches to the notion of human experience being somehow 'like' a computer? But at the same time, could it be that what Husserl missed, and could never have grasped, is the way in which, in a becoming-temporal-object of everything, through the massive dissemination of *industrial* temporal objects, it is *in fact* possible to *reduce* that large now of retentionality-protentionality *to* the simultaneity and instantaneity of objectivated time?

244 Husserl, *On the Phenomenology of the Consciousness of Internal Time*, p. 24.

245 Stiegler, *Technics and Time, 2*, p. 199.

246 Husserl, *On the Phenomenology of the Consciousness of Internal Time*, p. 37.

247 See Stiegler, *Technics and Time, 1*, p. 246.

248 Like an imaginary version of the bouncing ball used in karaoke videos so that singers can reproduce the lyrics with 'correct' musical timing, a technique that was in fact pioneered in 1924 with the 'Song Car-Tune' of 'Come Take a Trip on My Airship', that is, three years *prior* to the first 'talkie', *The Jazz Singer*.

249 Husserl, *On the Phenomenology of the Consciousness of Internal Time*, p. 37.

250 Ibid., p. 61.

251 Stiegler, *Technics and Time, 2*, p. 203.

252 Ibid., p. 205.

253 Ibid., p. 204, translation modified.

254 Ibid., p. 213.

255 Stiegler, *Philosophising by Accident*, p. 70, translation modified.

256 Stiegler, *Technics and Time, 2*, p. 224.

257 Derrida, *Speech and Phenomena*, pp. 64–65.

258 Stiegler, *Technics and Time, 2*, p. 218.

259 Derrida, *Speech and Phenomena*, p. 67.

260 Bernard Stiegler, 'Derrida and Technology: Fidelity at the Limits of Deconstruction and the Prosthesis of Faith', trans. Richard Beardsworth, in Tom Cohen (ed.), *Jacques Derrida and the Humanities: A Critical Reader* (Cambridge: Cambridge University Press, 2001), p. 243.

261 Derrida, *Speech and Phenomena*, p. 67.

262 Bernard Stiegler, 'The Magic Skin; or, The Franco-European Accident of Philosophy after Jacques Derrida', *Qui Parle* 18 (2009), p. 105.

263 Ibid.

264 Bernard Stiegler, *Symbolic Misery, Volume 2: The Katastrophē of the Sensible*, trans. Barnaby Norman (Cambridge: Polity Press, 2015), §§48–49.

265 Stiegler, *Technics and Time, 2*, p. 229, translation modified.

266 Ibid., p. 231, translation modified.

267 Husserl, *On the Phenomenology of the Consciousness of Internal Time*, p. 61.

268 Stiegler, *Technics and Time, 2*, p. 217.

269 See ibid., pp. 234–37.

270 Jacques Derrida, *The Problem of Genesis in Husserl's Philosophy*, trans. Marian Hobson (Chicago and London: University of Chicago Press, 2003), p. 167.

271 Jacques Derrida, *Edmund Husserl's Origin of Geometry: An Introduction*, trans. John P. Leavey Jr. (Lincoln and London: University of Nebraska Press, 1989), p. 57.

272 Ibid., p. 61.

273 Ibid., p. 64.

274 Ibid., p. 66.

275 Ibid., p. 88.

276 Stiegler, *Technics and Time, 2*, p. 238.

277 Stiegler, 'Derrida and Technology', p. 241.

278 Husserl, *On the Phenomenology of the Consciousness of Internal Time*, p. 185,

279 Stiegler, *Technics and Time, 2*, p. 242, translation modified.

280 For a brief summary of these concepts and phases, see Ross, 'Introduction', in Stiegler, *The Neganthropocene*.

281 This was originally written as a background paper for the panel of the 2018 Serpentine Galleries 'Work' Marathon entitled 'Acceleration, Disruption, Bifurcation', presented together with Gerald Moore and Shaj Mohan on 22 September 2018. Prior to the panel discussion, an excerpt from the documentary *Lo and Behold: Reveries of the Connected World* (Werner Herzog, 2016) was screened, consisting of the director's interview with Elon Musk, available here: <https://www.youtube.com/watch?v=we6rMEIGp9s&t=13s>.

282 On these synergistic and antagonistic problems, see Daniel Ross, 'Introduction', in Bernard Stiegler, *The Neganthropocene*, trans. Daniel Ross (London: Open Humanities Press, 2018), pp. 9–13.

283 Report by the secretariat of the United Nations Conference on Trade and Development, *Trade and Development Report 2018: Power, Platforms and the Free Trade Delusion* (New York and Geneva: United Nations, 2018), available at: <https://unctad.org/en/PublicationsLibrary/tdr2018_en.pdf>, p. 126.

284 Paavo Järvensivu et al., 'Governance of Economic Transition', invited background document on economic transformation, to chapter, 'Transformation: The Economy', for the *Global Sustainable Development Report 2019*, available at: <https://bios.fi/bios-governance_of_economic_transition.pdf>, p. 6.

285 Alfred North Whitehead, *Religion in the Making: Lowell Lectures, 1926* (Cambridge: Cambridge University Press, 1927), p. 10.

286 Ibid., pp. 10–11.

287 Ibid., p. 11.

288 Ibid., p. 16.

289 Akira Kurosawa, 'Kurosawa on Kurosawa: Part Two', *Sight and Sound* 33 (October 1964), pp. 200–1.

290 Quoted in Michael Hoffman, 'Forgotten atrocity of the atomic age', *Japan Times* (28 August 2011), available at: <https://www.japantimes.co.jp/culture/2011/08/28/culture/forgotten-atrocity-of-the-atomic-age/#.W57kTy17HjA>.

291 This is a slight exaggeration: while my father, David Ross, would later become a psychologist, at the time of the Second World War he was an accountant working at a government accounting office, where he would receive invoices headed 'Manhattan Project' involving gigantic sums far exceeding those for any other accounts. At the time, none of his fellow workers had any idea of what this project could be, but it was obviously some very big, very secret undertaking to do with the war effort. With the attacks on Hiroshima and Nagasaki, it was suddenly clear on the invention of what device these vast sums had been spent.

292 Kurosawa, quoted in 'Kurosawa on Kurosawa', p. 201.

293 Ibid.

294 See Bernard Stiegler, *Acting Out*, trans. David Barison, Daniel Ross and Patrick Crogan (Stanford: Stanford University Press, 2009), p. 2.

295 Elon Musk, on *The Joe Rogan Experience* podcast (7 September 2018), available at: <http://podcasts.joerogan.net/podcasts/elon-musk>.

296 Will Steffen et al., 'Trajectories of the Earth System in the Anthropocene', *Proceedings of the National Academy of Sciences of the United States of America* 115:33 (14 August 2018), available at: <https://doi.org/10.1073/pnas.1810141115>.

297 This idea is thematized in Alexander Payne's 2017 movie, *Downsizing*, through the final plan of the Norwegians (a kind of less 'American' variation on Musk's Mars strategy).

298 Barack Obama (7 September 2018), transcript available at: <https://www.vox.com/policy-and-politics/2018/9/7/17832024/obama-speech-trump-illinois-transcript>.

299 Musk, *The Joe Rogan Experience*.

300 Ibid.

301 On Neuralink, see Tim Urban, 'Neuralink and the Brain's Magical Future', *Wait But Why* (20 April 2017), available at: <https://waitbutwhy.com/2017/04/neuralink.html>.

302 See Stiegler, *The Neganthropocene*, ch. 4.

303 Musk, *The Joe Rogan Experience*.

304 Thomas Lewis, Fari Amini and Richard Lannon, *A General Theory of Love* (New York: Random House, 2000).

305 Ibid., pp. 63–64.

306 Ibid., p. 68.

307 Ibid., p. 70.

308 Ibid., p. 84.

309 Ibid., p. 85.

310 Ibid., p. 169.

311 Ibid., p. 177.

312 Ibid., p. 178.

313 Ibid., p. 183.

314 Ibid., p. 191.

315 Ibid., p. 192.

316 Ibid., p. 196.

317 Ibid., pp. 198–99. The quotation at the end is from Maria Semineiro, 'The Web Got You Down? Report Links Internet Use to Depression, Loneliness', *ZDNet* (31 August 1998), available at: <https://www.zdnet.com/article/the-web-got-you-down-report-links-internet-use-to-depression-loneliness/>.

318 Charles Eric Maine, *The Man Who Couldn't Sleep* (Philadelphia and New York: J. B. Lippincott, 1956), published in England under the title, *Escapement*.

319 Ibid., pp. 114–19.

320 Ibid., p. 117.

321 Nick Bostrom, 'Are You Living in a Computer Simulation?', *Philosophical Quarterly* 53 (2003), pp. 243–55.

322 Maine, *The Man Who Couldn't Sleep*, p. 181.

323 Ibid., p. 122.

324 But Musk notes in conversation with Joe Rogan that (non-democratic) China seems very different in this regard, with many important leaders also having high-level degrees in scientific fields. Of course, this does not mean that China will actually decarbonize its production, let alone deproletarianize its consumers. The point, however, is that the former may well be impossible without the latter.

325 Järvensivu et al., 'Governance of Economic Transition', p. 1.

326 Similar arguments with respect to the implications of EROI shift and Chinese economic growth (with obvious implications for the global economy) are presented in Jingxuan Feng et al., 'Modeling the point of use EROI and its implications for economic growth in China', *Energy* 144 (1 February 2018), pp. 232–42.

327 Nicholas Georgescu-Roegen, *The Entropy Law and the Economic Process* (Cambridge, Massachusetts and London: Harvard University Press, 1971), p. 280.

328 Järvensivu, 'Governance of Economic Transition', p. 5, my italics.

329 Ibid.

330 Theodore Kaczynski, *Anti-Tech Revolution: Why and How* (Scottsdale: Fitch and Madison, 2016). And see ch. 1.

331 Järvensivu, 'Governance of Economic Transition', p. 6.

332 Niccolò Machiavelli, *The Prince*, in Peter Bondanella and Mark Musa (eds and trans.), *The Portable Machiavelli* (New York and London: Penguin, 1979), p. 150.

333 See Colin Crouch, 'Privatised Keynesianism: An Unacknowledged Policy Regime', *British Journal of Politics and International Relations* 11 (2009), pp. 382–99, and Crouch, *The Strange Non-Death of Neoliberalism* (Cambridge: Polity Press, 2011), esp. ch. 5.

334 Secretariat of the United Nations Conference on Trade and Development, *Trade and Development Report 2018: Power, Platforms and the Free Trade Delusion* (New York and Geneva: United Nations, 2018), available at: <https://unctad.org/en/PublicationsLibrary/tdr2018_en.pdf>, p. 40.

335 See Daniel Ross, 'Traumas of the Image', *theory@buffalo* 10 (2005), pp. 81–102, and Ross, 'Politics, Terror, and Traumatypical Imagery', in Matthew Sharpe, Murray Noonan and Jason Freddi (eds), *Trauma, Historicity, Philosophy* (Newcastle: Cambridge Scholars Press, 2007).

336 Secretariat of the United Nations Conference on Trade and Development, *Trade and Development Report 2018*, p. 41.

337 Ibid.

338 Ibid., p. 60

339 Ibid.

340 See ibid., p. 73: 'As discussed in *TDR 2017*, the stock of robots remains concentrated in a few developed countries, and in relatively high-wage sectors, despite its recent rapid increase in some developing countries, especially China. The *Report* suggested that, for now at least, robot-based automation per se does not invalidate the traditional role of industrialization as a development strategy for lower-income countries moving into manufacturing activities.'

341 See ibid., p. 94: 'Moving towards a digital economy holds both more and less potential for income and employment creation in developing

countries than often thought. This is because many existing studies overestimate the potential adverse employment and income effects of some digital technologies, such as robots, as argued in *TDR 2017*. At the same time, there is an equally exaggerated tendency, bordering on digital utopianism, that attributes boundless opportunities for developing countries, through further rounds of liberalization, to leapfrog in to high value added and job-creating activities in all segments of the manufacturing process as well as services.'

342 See ch. 1.

343 See Gerald Moore, 'The Pharmacology of Addiction', *Parrhesia* 29 (2018), pp. 190–211.

344 As the *Trade and Development Report 2018* concludes (p. 95): 'But data, unless processed, may be of little value. Big-data analytics using algorithms have revolutionized production as well as distribution services. The limited ability of the developing world to transform data into economically meaningful knowledge has fuelled the growth of highly profitable digital platforms, which through "network effects" have been able to glean more data and use it to facilitate entry into new markets and new business lines. The rising rents of these super-platforms and their ability to kill competition from national platforms remains unchecked because of a lack of regulatory policies.'

345 Robert Smithson, 'Entropy Made Visible', *Robert Smithson: The Collected Writings*, ed. Jack Flam (Berkeley, Los Angeles and London: University of California Press, 1996), p. 309.

346 Smithson, 'Entropy and the New Monuments', *Robert Smithson: The Collected Writings*, pp. 17–18.

347 Smithson, 'Entropy Made Visible', p. 303: With this last statement, the possibility arises of reading Smithson's account of entropy as a kind of general economy in Georges Bataille's sense of the necessity of expenditure. The necessity of doing so exceeds the scope of this chapter.

348 Percy Bridgman, *The Nature of Thermodynamics*, quoted in Smithson, 'Entropy and the New Monuments', p. 20.

349 Smithson, 'Entropy and the New Monuments', p. 19.

350 Ibid.

351 Crouch, *The Strange Non-Death of Neoliberalism*, p. 179.

352 Smithson, 'Entropy and the New Monuments', p. 18.

353 Smithson, 'Entropy Made Visible', pp. 303–4: 'There's this need to try to transcend one's condition. I'm not a transcendentalist, so I just

see things going towards a … well it's very hard to predict anything; anyway all predictions tend to be wrong. I mean even planning. I mean planning and chance almost seem to be the same thing.'

354 Giuseppe Longo has drawn attention to the utmost positivity and necessity of randomness and accidentality in biological evolution, and to the way in which the failure to understand this leads to the sterile entropy of the crystallized digital palaces of contemporary capitalism. See Giuseppe Longo, 'Complexity, Information and Diversity in Science and in Democracy', trans. M. R. Doyle and S. Savic, *Glass Bead*, available at: <https://www.glass-bead.org/research-platform/complexity-information-diversity-science-democracy/>.

355 Bernard Stiegler, 'The Proletarianization of Sensibility', trans. Arne De Boever, *Boundary 2* 44 (2017), p. 10.

356 Alfred North Whitehead, *The Function of Reason* (Princeton: Princeton University Press, 1929), p. 5.

357 IPCC, 'Global Warming of 1.5°C: An IPCC special report on the impacts of global warming of 1.5°C above pre-industrial levels and related global greenhouse gas emission pathways, in the context of strengthening the global response to the threat of climate change, sustainable development, and efforts to eradicate poverty: summary for policymakers' (6 October 2018), available at: <http://report.ipcc.ch/sr15/pdf/sr15_spm_final.pdf>.

358 Gerry Shih, 'Xi tells the world China will boost imports while swiping at Trump's "law of the jungle"', *Washington Post* (5 November 2018), available at: <https://www.washingtonpost.com/world/asia_pacific/xi-tells-the-world-china-will-boost-imports-while-swiping-at-trumpslaw-of-the-jungle/2018/11/05/c9b61f9c-e0bc-11e8-a1c9-6afe99dddd92_story.html>.

359 It goes without saying that much hangs on the degree of that commitment. See for example the following article, which implies that China's current mitigation strategies would, if taken as a global benchmark, produce catastrophic warming of 5.1°C by 2100: Yann Robiou du Pont and Malte Meinshausen, 'Warming Assessment of the Bottom-Up Paris Agreement Emissions Pledges', *Nature Communications* 9 (16 November 2018), available at: <https://www.nature.com/articles/s41467-018-07223-9>.

360 Bernard Stiegler, *Qu'appelle-t-on panser? 1. L'immense régression* (Paris: Les Liens qui Libèrent, 2018).

361 Many of the extremely worrying trends in contemporary global politics, for example, can clearly be viewed as in large part symptoms of decisions taken and not taken with respect to the manner in which this transformation has proceeded.

362 It should be noted that the division between carbon technologies and silicon technologies we will elaborate in these pages is essentially a slightly simplified and modified reinterpretation of Bernard Stiegler's distinction between carbon-time and light-time.

363 Alfred North Whitehead, *Science and the Modern World* (New York: Macmillan, 1925), p. 41.

364 Stiegler's general organology is an account of the processes involved with beings (such as ourselves) whose somatic and psychic (bodily and mental) organs are inadequate for life unless they are supplemented with artificial and prosthetic (technical) organs such as tools (but where the ensemble of such technical organs forms a technical system). Because these technical organs are in no way 'natural', however, they require knowledge and care in order to prevent their productive effects from becoming destructive, and this knowledge and care is contained in social organizations. General organology thus posits three inextricably-tied organological levels dynamically unfolding together over the course of proto-human and human history: the individual, the collective and the technical.

365 For Heidegger, swimming was the example through which he raised the epistemological question of how we can *know* our element (which for Heidegger is the element of thinking, given that we are, in Aristotelian and Stieglerian terms, *noetic* beings), and the more-than-epistemological question of how we can *respond* to what we know of our element. See Martin Heidegger, *What is Called Thinking?*, trans. J. Glenn Gray (New York: Harper & Row, 1968), p. 21: 'We shall never learn what "is called" swimming, for example, or what it "calls for", by reading a treatise on swimming. Only the leap into the river tells us what is called swimming. The question "What is called thinking?" can never be answered by proposing a definition of the concept *thinking*, and then diligently explaining what is contained in that definition.'

366 Aristotle, *On the Soul*, 418b–419a. 'The transparent' is the usual translation of *diaphanēs*, alluded to by Joyce, who refers to the 'ineluctable modality of the visible' in order to evoke the 'limits of the diaphane' and Aristotle's being 'aware of them bodies before of them coloured'. James Joyce, *Ulysses. Annotated Student Edition* (London: Penguin, 1992), p. 45.

367 Aristotle, *On the Soul*, 423a33–34. See Bernard Stiegler, *Acting Out*, trans. David Barison, Daniel Ross and Patrick Crogan (Stanford: Stanford University Press, 2009), pp. 13–14.

368 Bernard Stiegler, *The Age of Disruption: Technology and Madness in Computational Capitalism*, trans. Daniel Ross (Cambridge: Polity Press, 2019), p. 13.

369 Sigmund Freud, *Beyond the Pleasure Principle*, in Volume 18 of James Strachey (ed. and trans.), *The Standard Edition of the Complete Psychological Works of Sigmund Freud* (London: Hogarth, 1953–74), pp. 48–49.

370 Norbert Wiener, *Cybernetics, or Control and Communication in the Animal and the Machine*, second edition (Cambridge, Massachusetts: MIT Press, 1961), p. 38.

371 Ibid., p. 39.

372 Ibid., pp. 38–39. With this, it is important to note that automation does not begin with computers, and that Wiener himself describes a genealogy of automation, and more particularly of the automaton as 'a working simulacrum of a living organism', that itself follows the delineation of technical systems he describes across the last three centuries: 'In the time of Newton, the automaton becomes the clockwork music box, with the little effigies pirouetting stiffly on top. In the nineteenth century, the automaton is a glorified heat engine, burning some combustible fuel instead of the glycogen of the human muscles. Finally, the present automaton opens doors by means of photocells, or points guns to the place at which a radar beam picks up an airplane, or computes the solution of a differential equation' (pp. 39–40).

373 See the Wikipedia list available here: <https://en.wikipedia.org/wiki/List_of_largest_companies_by_revenue>. As of January 2020, seven out of the top ten are energy companies, along with two automobile manufacturers, and rounded out (at number one) by Walmart.

374 See the Wikipedia list available here: <https://en.wikipedia.org/wiki/List_of_public_corporations_by_market_capitalization>. As of January 2020, seven out of the top ten are internet or computing companies (Microsoft, Apple, Amazon, Alphabet, Facebook, Alibaba, Tencent).

375 Karl Marx, *A Contribution to the Critique of Political Economy*, trans. S. W. Ryanzanskaya (Moscow: Progress Publishers, 1970), p. 197.

376 Gunpowder was invented or discovered during the Tang Dynasty in China, giving rise to the long history of fire weapons and guns, which were firstly technologies of external war but also of internal social control.

377 Daily atmospheric CO_2 concentration totals recorded at Mauna Loa Observatory, along with all-time highs, are available here: <https://www.co2.earth/daily-co2>.

378 On 11 November 2018, that is, the tenth anniversary of Alibaba's promotion of so-called 'Singles Day' as a kind of consumerist festival, their Tmall shopping platform recorded sales totalling ten

billion yuan (US$1.44 billion) *in the first two minutes and five seconds of the day's trading*. This possibility, involving the processing of *hundreds of thousands of transactions per second*, exposes the true meaning of automation in the current macroeconomic model (even if, in this particular case, many of these transactions may have been 'preordered'). See He Wei, 'Singles Day Achieves New Record', *China Daily* (12 November 2018), available at: <http://www.chinadaily.com.cn/a/201811/12/WS5be881a3a310eff303287e8d.html>. It has also been suggested that these annual 'records' are in fact engineered, evidence for which would be the smoothness of the curve showing year-to-year growth.

379 Once again, carbon technologies and memory technologies are inextricably entangled together throughout their history. To give a seemingly minor example, if writing is a memory technology, the paper on which one writes is a carbon technology (and one producing a significant environmental impact). Or more obliquely: the very possibility of carbon technologies lies in the fact that fossilized organic material still retains traces of the molecular complexity of the organisms of which it is composed – this molecular complexity in the form of hydrocarbons is the source of the potential energy that is liberated in combustion (thereby reducing these hydrocarbons to much *less* complex molecules). Such complexity ultimately derives from the organizational characteristics of organic material, characteristics that are constructed and maintained on the basis of the genetic molecule, which is itself a kind of biological memory. And, on the other hand, every fabricative technology has an *accidental* retentional capacity (a prehistoric flint tool *records* the gestures of the hand that made it): what we are here calling retentional technologies are those in which this memorial function is deliberate rather than accidental.

380 See Bernard Stiegler, *Automatic Society, Volume 1: The Future of Work*, trans. Daniel Ross (Cambridge: Polity Press, 2016).

381 Karl Marx and Friedrich Engels, *The German Ideology: Students Edition*, trans. William Lough, Clemens Dutt and Charles Philip Magill (London: Lawrence and Wishart, 1974), p. 54.

382 Herbert Marcuse, *An Essay on Liberation* (Boston: Beacon Press, 2000), p. 20.

383 Ibid., p. 21. And we should note that in *our* terms, this sensitivity and consciousness are *both* aspects of the *noetic* being, whose *way* of being sensitive is always inscribed in a becoming-symbolic.

384 Ibid., p. 22.

385 The notion of the 'cinesphere' is borrowed from a work of science fiction: Charles Eric Maine, *The Man Who Couldn't Sleep* (Philadelphia and New York: J. B. Lippincott, 1956), published in England under

the horological title, *Escapement*. Here we use it in a way that sees the conjunction of the process of globalization with the process of what, using Husserlian terms, Stiegler calls the 'becoming-temporal-object of everything "that happens", through the operation of media and, beyond them, through the omnipotence of the new programmatology producing space-light-time's weave of rhythms'. Bernard Stiegler, *Technics and Time, 2: Disorientation*, trans. Stephen Barker (Stanford: Stanford University Press, 2009), p. 188.

386 In 'Toutes les Histoires' (1988), the first episode of *Histoire(s) du Cinéma* (directed by Jean-Luc Godard, 1988–98). Note that the first of these statements also appears in Godard's *Contempt* (1963), attributed to André Bazin, but it actually comes from a 1959 article by Michel Mourlet in *Cahiers du cinéma*. See also Bernard Stiegler, *The Neganthropocene*, trans. Daniel Ross (London: Open Humanities Press, 2018), pp. 163–64, and Daniel Ross, 'Moving Images of the Anthropocene: Rethinking Cinema Beyond Anthropology', *Screening the Past* 44 (2019), available at: <http://www.screeningthepast.com/2019/03/moving-images-of-the-anthropocene-rethinking-cinema-beyond-anthropology/>.

387 In fact, the speed at which information circulates in the silicon memory of a computer is 200,000 km per second (two thirds of the speed of light), which is more than 500,000 times quicker than a plane flying at Mach 1 (that is, 0.34 km per second, or 20 km per minute).

388 Note that this distinction between a *hyper*-capitalism of consumption and an *ultra*-capitalism of algorithmic platforms deviates from Stiegler's own terminology. The sense of 'ultra' here is that of 'the furthest possible', 'the ultimate'.

389 See for example Bernard Stiegler, 'Telecracy Against Democracy', trans. Chris Turner, *Cultural Politics* 6 (2010), pp. 171–80.

390 Marcuse, *An Essay on Liberation*, pp. 21. For a critique of Marcuse on these questions, see Bernard Stiegler, *The Lost Spirit of Capitalism: Disbelief and Discredit, Volume 3*, trans. Daniel Ross (Cambridge: Cambridge University Press, 2014), part 2, 'The Automatization of the Super-Ego and the Passage of Desire as Original Diversion of Libidinal Energy'.

391 Percy Bridgman, *The Nature of Thermodynamics*, quoted in Robert Smithson, 'Entropy and the New Monuments', *Robert Smithson: The Collected Writings* (Berkeley: University of California Press, 1996), p. 20.

392 Smithson, 'Entropy Made Visible', *Robert Smithson: The Collected Writings*, p. 303.

393 Smithson, 'Entropy and the New Monuments', p. 17.

394 Philip Mirowski, 'Philosophizing With a Hammer: Reply to Binmore, Davis and Klaes', *Journal of Economic Methodology* 11 (2004), p. 500. And see Philip Mirowski, *More Heat Than Light. Economics as Social Physics: Physics as Nature's Economics* (Cambridge: Cambridge University Press, 1989).

395 Philip Mirowski, *Machine Dreams: Economics Becomes a Cyborg Science* (Cambridge and New York: Cambridge University Press, 2002).

396 Philip Mirowski and Edward Nik-Khah, *The Knowledge We Have Lost in Information: The History of Information in Modern Economics* (New York: Oxford University Press, 2017).

397 Information theory has always been premised on a de-substantialized, de-materialized and de-functionalized conception of information. But in addition to its irreducible materiality (which forms, furthermore, the retentional basis of all counter-entropy), information must be reconceptualized in terms of its tensional and protentional dimensions (in Simondon's sense of tension, and in and beyond Husserl's sense of protention). It is on the basis of this pro-tending outwards to the new and unexpected that a renewed concept of information within a theory of general entropy will be able to think the possibility of *bifurcation* to which we refer below.

398 See the graph available at: <https://www.abc.net.au/news/2019-03-26/carbon-emissions-over-time-1/10942172>.

399 See the charts concerning annual CO_2 emissions by world region available at <https://ourworldindata.org/grapher/annual-co-emissions-by-region>.

400 See the charts concerning global CO_2 emissions by fuel type available at <https://ourworldindata.org/grapher/co2-by-source>.

401 Leo Strauss, *Natural Right and History* (Chicago and London: University of Chicago Press, 1953), p. 4.

402 See p. 50.

403 Theodore Kaczynski, *Anti-Tech Revolution: Why and How* (Scottsdale: Fitch and Madison, 2016).

404 Peter Thiel, 'The Optimistic Thought Experiment', *Policy Review* (February and March 2008), available at: <https://www.hoover.org/research/optimistic-thought-experiment>.

405 Peter Thiel, 'The Education of a Libertarian', *Cato Unbound* (13 April 2009), available at: <https://www.cato-unbound.org/2009/04/13/peter-thiel/education-libertarian>.

406 Jean-Luc Nancy, *The Sense of the World*, trans. Jeffrey S. Librett (Minneapolis and London: University of Minnesota Press, 1997), p. 101.

407 See Frank Pasquale, 'From Territorial to Functional Sovereignty: The Case of Amazon', *OpenDemocracy* (5 January 2018), available at: <https://www.opendemocracy.net/en/digitaliberties/from-territorial-to-functional-sovereignty-case-of-amazon/>.

408 Note that here we will quote from the longer version published as 'Complément à *La nation*' in Marcel Mauss, *La nation, ou le sens du social*, corrected edition (Paris: Presses Universitaires de France, 2018).

409 Bernard Stiegler, 'The Internation and Internationalism', trans. Daniel Ross, *Alienocene* stratum 6 (2019), pp. 9–10., available at: <https://alienocene.files.wordpress.com/2019/12/bs-internation.pdf>.

410 Jean Terrier, *Visions of the Social: Society as a Political Project in France, 1750–1950* (Leiden and Boston: Brill, 2011), pp. 149–50. In the following account of Mauss's conception of the nation and internation, we will rely in part on Terrier's work.

411 Mauss, 'Complément à *La nation*', p. 388.

412 Marcel Mauss, 'La nation', p. 584, quoted in Terrier, *Visions of the Social*, p. 153.

413 Terrier, *Visions of the Social*, p. 154.

414 Ibid.

415 Ibid.

416 Ibid., pp. 155–56.

417 Mauss, quoted in ibid., pp. 167–68.

418 Terrier, *Visions of the Social*, p. 168.

419 Mauss, quoted in ibid.

420 Terrier, *Visions of the Social*, p. 168.

421 Mauss, 'Complément à *La nation*', p. 396 (note that this corrected text differs somewhat from the 1920 version, which makes clearer the distinction between the internation and any nationalism).

422 Arnold Toynbee, *Mankind and Mother Earth* (Oxford: Oxford University Press, 1976), p. 587.

423 Ibid., p. 593.

424 Ibid.

425 Alain Supiot, 'The Territorial Inscription of Laws', trans. Saskia Brown, in Graf-Peter Calliess, Andreas Fischer-Lescano, Dan Wielsch, and Peer Zumbanssen (eds), *Soziologische Jurisprudenz: Festschrift für Gunther Teubner zum 65. Geburtstag am 30. April 2009* (Berlin: Walter de Gruyter, 2009).

426 Ibid., pp. 380–81.

427 Ibid., p. 389.

428 Ibid., pp. 390–91.

429 Ibid., p. 392.

430 Ibid., p. 383.

431 On the question of law and tertiary retention, in relation to ancient Greece and in relation to the question of the relationship between Socrates and Plato, see the 2017 lectures in Bernard Stiegler, *Nanjing Lectures 2016–2019*, trans. Daniel Ross (London: Open Humanities Press, 2020), esp. pp. 109–37.

432 Walter Benjamin, 'Critique of Violence', trans. Edmund Jephcott, *Selected Writing, Volume 1: 1913–1926* (Cambridge, Massachusetts and London: Harvard University Press, 1996), p. 243.

433 Rudolf Boehm, 'Pensée et technique. Notes préliminaires pour une question touchant la problématique heideggérienne' *Revue Internationale de Philosophie* 14 (1960), p. 204.

434 Martin Heidegger, *An Introduction to Metaphysics*, trans. Gregory Fried and Richard Polt (New Haven and London: Yale University Press, 2000), p. 168.

435 Ibid., pp. 162–63.

436 Benjamin, 'Critique of Violence', p. 244.

437 Bernard Stiegler, 'Après les élections européennes, et en vue de préparer le séminaire des 2 et 3 juillet 2019. Considérations sur la question de la localité' (June 2019), unpublished.

438 Martin Heidegger, *Hölderlin's Hymn 'The Ister'*, trans. William McNeill and Julia Davis (Bloomington and Indianapolis: Indiana University Press, 1996), p. 33.

439 See Bernard Stiegler, interviewed by Anaïs Nony, 'On Automatic Society', *Third Rail Quarterly* 5 (2015), available at: <http://thirdrailquarterly.org/wp-content/uploads/05_Stiegler_TTR5.pdf>, p. 16: 'The question is a relation between automaticity and disautomatization. You ask me, what about the self? *Auto* is the common root of two words which are opposite in the philosophical tradition: *automata* and *autonomy*. To be autonomous in ancient Greek philosophy

– although it is also still the case with Kant and even later, for example for the Frankfurt School – to be autonomous is the opposite of being in automatic behavior. And I disagree with that. I believe that this point of view, which is a very classical, metaphysical point of view, is completely wrong, because in reality, to become really autonomous you must integrate a lot of automatisms. For example, if you want to become an autonomous pianist you must transform your body into such a thing like the piano. [...] So the question of automatic society is how to deal with new automatisms, not with automatism in general, because every society deals with a set of automatisms.'

440 Mauro Senatore, 'Drive to Drive: The Deconstruction of the Freudian *Trieb*', *Derrida Today* 12 (2019), pp. 59–79.

441 Jacques Derrida, *Rogues: Two Essays on Reason*, trans. Pascale-Anne Brault and Michael Naas (Stanford: Stanford University Press, 2005), pp. 10–11.

442 Ibid., pp. 100–101.

443 Ibid., p. 88.

444 Ibid., pp. 102–4.

445 Jacques Derrida, *The Beast and the Sovereign, Volume 1*, trans. Geoffrey Bennington (Chicago and London: University of Chicago Press, 2009), p. 290.

446 This is the basis of Heidegger's claim that Hölderlin's poetry exceeds any metaphysics of art based on the opposition of the sensuous and the non-sensuous. See, for example, Heidegger, *Hölderlin's Hymn 'The Ister'*, p. 166:

> At the beginning of these 'remarks' we rejected the obvious view that the rivers are 'poeticized' 'symbols', 'images' or 'signs' that offer a symbolic image of something else. We can now recognize the reason for our rejecting this. The rivers cannot be 'poeticized images' or 'signs of' something else because they in themselves are 'the signs', 'signs' that are no longer 'signs' of something else, nor symbols of something else, but are themselves this supposed 'something else'. The poets, as poets, are these rivers, and these rivers are the poets. 'Poetically' they ground the dwelling of human beings upon this earth. [...] The essence of the rivers does not depict or present the 'meaningful sense' of the essence of the poet. In their essence, the rivers are the signs, as showing and making arable. These signs that show are the poets. The poets are these rivers.

If the poets are signs that show in the sense of being rivers that make arable the locality, then, we might as well say, they are, in this making-arable, nothing but the violence-as-*tekhnē* that opens the possibility of new neganthropic or anti-anthropic bifurcations.

447 See, for example, ibid., p. 9:

> For all essential poetry also poetizes 'anew' the essence of poetizing itself. [...] The 'Now come' appears to speak from a present into the future. And yet, in the first instance, it speaks into what has already happened. 'Now' – this tells us: something has already been decided. And precisely the appropriation that has already 'occurred' [*sich 'ereignet'*] alone sustains all relation to whatever is coming. The 'Now' names an appropriative event [*Ereignis*].

The *polis* is thus poetic *and not political* in the *sense* that its sovereign possibility arises from the poetic as the 'question-worthy' site of locality and journeying (see ibid., pp. 80–83).

448 Jacques Derrida, 'Heidegger's Silence: Excerpts from a Talk Given on 5 February 1988', trans. Joachim Neugroschel, in Günther Neske and Emil Kettering (eds), *Martin Heidegger and National Socialism: Questions and Answers* (New York: Paragon House, 1990), pp. 147–48: 'If [Heidegger] had been tempted to make a statement, let us say a statement made as an immediate moral reaction or a manifestation of his horror or his nonforgiving and thus a statement that would not stem from his work of thinking, at the peak of all that he had already thought, I believe we would then be more likely to feel dismissed from the duty of doing the work we must do today. [...] Without Heidegger's terrible silence, we would not be conscious of the commandment that addresses itself to our sense of responsibility and tells us of the necessity to read Heidegger the way he did not read himself.' And what we are arguing here is also that this duty applies to our reading of Derrida himself, albeit in very different ways.

449 Derrida, *The Beast and the Sovereign, Volume 1*, pp. 290–91.

450 Georges Canguilhem, *The Normal and the Pathological*, trans. Carolyn R. Fawcett, with Robert S. Cohen (New York: Zone Books, 1991), p. 205.

451 Ibid., p. 206.

452 Ibid.

453 Ibid.

454 Ibid., pp. 206–7, my italics.

455 Ibid., p. 207.

456 Cf., Stiegler, 'On Automatic Society', p. 16: 'But what is automaticity in general? Life is automatic. A biological cell, for example, is a sequence of instructions and this sequence of instructions is

automatic. The reproduction of life is automatic. When you have something that is not automatic, it is a mutation, which produces a monster. So automatic repetition is really the basis of life.'

457 Barbara Stiegler, *'Il faut s'adapter': Sur un nouvel impératif politique* (Paris: Gallimard, 2019), pp. 14–15.

458 But it should be noted that for Barbara Stiegler, Lippmann and Hayek are the iconic figures by which the *different* paths of *neo*-liberalism and *ultra*-liberalism can be differentiated; see ibid., p. 311, n. 5.

459 Ibid., p. 284.

460 See Bernard Stiegler, *For a New Critique of Political Economy*, trans. Daniel Ross (Cambridge: Polity Press, 2010), Stiegler, *Automatic Society, Volume 1: The Future of Work*, trans. Daniel Ross (Cambridge: Polity Press, 2016), Stiegler, *The Neganthropocene*, trans. Daniel Ross (London: Open Humanities Press, 2018), p. 36.

461 Karl Polanyi, *The Great Transformation: The Political and Economic Origins of Our Time* (Boston: Beacon Press, 2001), p. 74.

462 Jean Terrier, *Visions of the Social: Society as a Political Project in France, 1750–1950* (Leiden and Boston: Brill, 2011), p. 155.

463 Bernard Stiegler, *The Nanjing Lectures 2016–2019*, trans. Daniel Ross (London: Open Humanities Press, 2020), pp. 309–10.

464 Ibid., p. 310.

465 Bernard Stiegler, 'The New Conflict of the Faculties and Functions: Quasi-Causality and Serendipity in the Anthropocene', trans. Daniel Ross, *Qui Parle* 26 (2017), p. 83.

466 Ibid.

467 Michel Bauwens, 'Introduction', *P2P Accounting for Planetary Survival* (27 June 2019), available at: <http://commonstransition.org/p2p-accounting-for-planetary-survival/>.

468 Colin Crouch, 'Privatised Keynesianism: An Unacknowledged Policy Regime', *British Journal of Politics and International Relations* 11 (2009), p. 383.

469 Gareth Dale, 'Karl Polanyi vs Friedrich von Hayek: The Socialist Calculation Debate and Beyond', in Robert Leeson (ed.), *Hayek: A Collaborative Biography. Part XIV: Liberalism in the Classical Tradition: Orwell, Popper, Humboldt and Polanyi* (Cham: Palgrave Macmillan, 2018), p. 291.

470 Polanyi, *The Great Transformation*, pp. 42–43.

471 Ibid., p. 59.

472 Ibid., p. 61.

473 Ibid., p. 65.

474 Ibid., p. 60.

475 Ibid., p. 75.

476 Ibid., p. 72.

477 Ibid., p. 78.

478 Ibid., pp. 75–76.

479 Friedrich A. Hayek, 'The Use of Knowledge in Society', *Individualism and Economic Order* (Chicago and London: University of Chicago Press, 1948), p. 80, my italics.

480 Dale, 'Karl Polanyi vs Friedrich von Hayek: The Socialist Calculation Debate and Beyond', p. 287.

481 Philip Mirowski and Edward Nik-Khah, *The Knowledge We Have Lost in Information: The History of Information in Modern Economics* (New York: Oxford University Press, 2017), ch. 6.

482 Friedrich A. Hayek, *Law, Legislation and Liberty: A New Statement of the Liberal Principles of Justice and Political Economy*, one-volume edition (London: Routledge, 1982), p. 36.

483 Ibid., p. 37.

484 Ibid.

485 Ibid., p. 38.

486 Ibid., p. 39.

487 Ibid., p. 44.

488 Ibid., p. 47.

489 Ibid., p. 49.

490 Georges Canguilhem, *Knowledge of Life*, trans. Stefanos Geroulanos and Daniela Ginsburg (New York: Fordham University Press, 2008), p. 88.

491 Ibid., pp. 36–37.

492 Martin Heidegger, 'The End of Philosophy and the Task of Thinking', *On Time and Being*, trans. Joan Stambaugh (New York: Harper & Row, 1972), pp. 58–59.

493 Edgar Morin, *Method: Towards a Study of Humankind, Volume 1: The Nature of Nature*, trans. J. L. Roland Bélanger (New York: Peter Lang, 1992), pp. 257ff.

494 Ibid., p. 259.

495 Hayek, *Law, Legislation and Liberty*, p. 42.

496 Ibid., pp. 39–40.

497 Ibid., p. 42.

498 Ibid., p. 51.

499 Ibid., p. 54.

500 Norbert Wiener, *The Human Use of Human Beings: Cybernetics and Society* (London: Free Association Books, 1989), p. 52.

501 Philip Mirowski, 'Philosophizing With a Hammer: Reply to Binmore, Davis and Klaes', *Journal of Economic Methodology* 11 (2004), p. 500.

502 Philip Mirowski, *Machine Dreams: Economics Becomes a Cyborg Science* (Cambridge and New York: Cambridge University Press, 2002), p. 7.

503 Mary Douglas, *How Institutions Think*, quoted in Philip Mirowski, *More Heat Than Light. Economics as Social Physics: Physics as Nature's Economics* (Cambridge: Cambridge University Press, 1989), p. 397.

504 Stiegler, 'The New Conflict of the Faculties and Functions', p. 94.

505 Ibid., 96.

506 Mirowski, 'Philosophizing With a Hammer', p. 502.

507 Mirowski, *Machine Dreams*, p. 13.

508 Ibid.

509 Ibid., p. 15.

510 Ibid., p. 16.

511 Ibid.

512 Ibid., p. 17.

513 Mirowski and Nik-Khah, *The Knowledge We Have Lost in Information*, pp. 54–55.

514 Ibid., p. 56.

515 Ibid., p. 58.

516 Ibid., p. 144.

517 Ibid., pp. 145–46.

518 Ibid., p. 146.

519 See Colin Crouch, *The Strange Non-Death of Neoliberalism* (Cambridge: Polity Press, 2011), ch. 5.

520 Mirowski and Nik-Khah, *The Knowledge We Have Lost in Information*, p. 146.

521 Ibid., ch. 15.

522 Ibid., p. 238.

523 Ibid., p. 240.

524 Ibid., p. 239.

525 Mirowski, 'Philosophizing With a Hammer', p. 506.

526 Ibid.

527 Philip Mirowski, *Never Let a Serious Crisis Go to Waste: How Neoliberalism Survived the Financial Meltdown* (London and New York: Verso, 2013), p. 75.

528 Friedrich A. Hayek, *The Constitution of Liberty: The Definitive Edition* (Chicago and London: University of Chicago Press, 2011), p. 128, my italics.

529 See chapters 7 and 8.

530 Wolfgang Streeck, *How Will Capitalism End? Essays on a Failing System* (London and New York: Verso, 2016), p. 36.

531 Ibid., p. 37.

532 Ibid., p. 39.

533 Ibid., p. 40.

534 Ibid., p. 41.

535 See Bernard Stiegler, 'Noodiversity, Technodiversity: Elements of a New Economic Foundation Based on a New Foundation for Theoretical Computer Science', trans. Daniel Ross, *Angelaki* 25:4 (2020), pp. 67–80.

536 See Georges Dumézil, *Mitra-Varuna: An Essay on Two Indo-European Representations of Sovereignty*, trans. Derek Coltman (New York: Zone Books, 1988).

537 Jacques Derrida, *Learning to Live Finally: The Last Interview*, trans. Pascale-Anne Brault and Michael Naas (Basingstoke, Hampshire and New York: Palgrave Macmillan, 2007), p. 34.

538 Bernard Stiegler, *Technics and Time, 1: The Fault of Epimetheus*, trans. Richard Beardsworth and George Collins (Stanford: Stanford University Press, 1998), p. 139.

539 Jacques Derrida, 'Différance', *Margins of Philosophy*, trans. Alan Bass (Hemel Hempstead: Harvester Press, 1982), p. 7, translation modified.

540 Jacques Derrida, *Of Grammatology*, corrected edition, trans. Gayatri Chakravorty Spivak (Baltimore and London: Johns Hopkins University Press, 1998), p. 5.

541 Ibid., p. 84.

542 But see Daniel Ross, 'Pharmacology and Critique After Deconstruction', in Gerald Moore and Christine Howells (eds), *Stiegler and Technics* (Edinburgh: Edinburgh University Press, 2013), and Daniel Ross, 'Introduction', in Bernard Stiegler, *The Neganthropocene*, trans. Daniel Ross (London: Open Humanities Press, 2018).

543 Derrida, *Of Grammatology*, p. 84.

544 Ibid.

545 Ibid.

546 Francesco Vitale, *Biodeconstruction*, trans. Mauro Senatore (Albany: State University of New York Press, 2018), pp. 21–22.

547 Derrida, *Of Grammatology*, p. 84.

548 André Leroi-Gourhan, *Gesture and Speech*, trans. Anna Bostock Berger (Cambridge, Massachusetts and London: MIT Press, 1993), pp. 222–24.

549 Ibid., p. 19.

550 Ibid., p. 413, n. 14, translation modified.

551 Ibid., p. 228.

552 Ibid., p. 257.

553 Ibid.

554 Bernard Stiegler, 'Elements for a General Organology', trans. Daniel Ross, *Derrida Today* 13 (2020), p. 88.

555 Stiegler, *Technics and Time, 1*, p. 177.

556 Jacques Derrida, *Positions*, trans. Alan Bass (Chicago: University of Chicago Press, 1981), pp. 57–58.

557 See Stiegler, *Technics and Time, 1*, pp. 134–40.

558 Derrida, *Of Grammatology*, p. 65.

559 Derrida, 'Différance', p. 17.

560 See, for example, Geoffrey Bennington, *Interrupting Derrida* (London and New York: Routledge, 2000), p. 171, Tracy Colony, 'Epimetheus Bound: Stiegler on Derrida, Life, and the Technological Condition', *Research in Phenomenology* 41 (2011), p. 86.

561 Bernard Stiegler, 'Elements for a General Organology', p. 80.

562 Jacques Derrida, *Life Death*, trans. Pascale-Anne Brault and Michael Naas (Chicago and London: University of Chicago, 2020), p. 1.

563 See ibid., pp. 3–4, where he indicates that deconstructing a logic of oppositions is not a matter of erecting *another* logic, explaining on p. 6 that he wishes neither to identify nor oppose the concepts of life and death and that the question is not that of another logic but 'another topos, if you will'. On pp. 105–6, however, he restates this question as being a matter neither of the 'is' nor of the 'and', neither of identity nor of opposition, but, precisely, of another logic, that of différance. This would seem to conform to the 'new logic' referred to in *Positions* (1972), but leaves unanswered the question of what is at stake between a 'logic' and a 'topos'.

564 François Jacob, *The Logic of Life: A History of Heredity*, trans. Betty E. Spillmann (New York: Pantheon, 1982), p. 1.

565 Ibid.

566 Ibid., p. 2.

567 Ibid.

568 Ibid., translation modified. We prefer to translate *projet* as project rather than design: the latter makes general sense but obscures the philosophical import we would like to read in to Jacob's use of these terms, which so clearly echo the notions of retention and protention in Husserl, along with their Heideggerian connotations.

569 Derrida, *Life Death*, p. 13.

570 Ibid., p. 14, translation modified.

571 Jacob, *The Logic of Life*, pp. 2–3.

572 Derrida, *Life Death*, p. 17.

573 Ibid., pp. 19–20.

574 Ibid., p. 20.

575 See ibid., p. 23.

576 Cf., Bernard Stiegler, 'The Discrete Image', in Jacques Derrida and Bernard Stiegler, *Echographies of Television: Filmed Interviews*, trans. Jennifer Bajorek (Cambridge: Polity Press, 2002), p. 162.

577 Derrida, *Life Death*, pp. 105–6.

578 Edgar Morin, *Method: Towards a Study of Humankind, Volume 1: The Nature of Nature*, trans. J. L. Roland Bélanger (New York: Peter Lang, 1992), p. 300.

579 Jacob, *The Logic of Life*, p. 253.

580 Derrida, *Life Death*, pp. 118–19.

581 Ibid., p. 3.

582 Ibid., pp. 122–23.

583 Ibid., p. 124.

584 Ibid.

585 Ibid., pp. 125–26.

586 Ibid., p. 126.

587 See Nicholas Georgescu-Roegen, *The Entropy Law and the Economic Process* (Cambridge, Massachusetts and London: Harvard University Press, 1971), p. 11, where he describes the 'way in which Alfred J. Lotka, a physical biologist, explained why the economic process is a continuation of the biological one. In the last process – Lotka pointed out – man, like any other living creature, uses only his *endosomatic* instruments, i.e., the instruments that are part of each individual organism by birth. In the economic process man uses also *exosomatic* instruments – knives, hammers, boats, engines, etc., which he produces himself.' This new process is pharmacological in the sense that it may either go poorly or well, since each new instrument has the irreducible potential to disrupt the functioning of the technical system and the knowledge required to manage those instruments and that functioning, and hence this process requires processes of adoption rather than adaptation. This is at least implied when he continues, describing how this need for adoption can always lead to internal or external problems for the social systems that alone can generate such processes: 'Lotka's framework will help us understand why only the human species is subject to an irreducible social conflict.'

588 See the section 'From Anthropology to Organology' in Daniel Ross, 'Moving Images of the Anthropocene: Rethinking Cinema Beyond Anthropology', *Screening the Past* 44 (2019), no page numbers, available at: <http://www.screeningthepast.com/2019/03/moving-images-of-the-anthropocene-rethinking-cinema-beyond-anthropology/>.

589 Jacob, *The Logic of Life*, p. 324: 'Ultimately all organizations, all systems, all hierarchies owe their very possibility of existence to the properties of the atoms described by Clerk Maxwell's electromagnetic laws. There are perhaps other possible coherences in descriptions. But science is enclosed in its own explanatory system, and cannot escape from it. Today the world is messages, codes and information. Tomorrow what analysis will break down our objects to reconstitute them in a new space? What new Russian doll will emerge?'

590 On the three phases of Stiegler's work, see Ross, 'Introduction', in Stiegler, *The Neganthropocene*.

591 Stiegler, *Technics and Time, 1*, p. x.

592 Derrida, *Life Death*, p. 232. In Jacques Derrida, *The Post Card: From Socrates to Freud and Beyond*, trans. Alan Bass (Chicago and London: University of Chicago Press, 1987), this will be slightly modified by Derrida, to read: 'Let us arbitrarily leave aside all the problems posed by the borrowing of this energetic "model"'.

593 Derrida, *The Post Card*, p. 280, n. 15.

594 Sigmund Freud, *Beyond the Pleasure Principle*, in Volume 18 of James Strachey (ed. and trans.), *The Standard Edition of the Complete Psychological Works of Sigmund Freud* (London: Hogarth Press, 1953–74), p. 9.

595 Freud, *Project for a Scientific Psychology*, in Volume 1 of Strachey, *Standard Edition*, p. 297.

596 Jean Laplanche, *Life and Death in Psychoanalysis*, trans. Jeffrey Mehlman (Baltimore and London: Johns Hopkins University Press, 1976), p. 117.

597 Ibid., p. 119.

598 Ibid., p. 120.

599 Ibid., p. 121.

600 Ibid.

601 One might say that, for Freud, Ernst Brücke represents the point of intersection of the encounter between Helmholtz and Darwin. It was also through Brücke that Freud met Josef Breuer. See Peter Gay, *Freud: A Life for Our Time* (London: Macmillan, 1989), pp. 32–35.

602 Derrida, 'Différance', p. 8.

603 Ibid., p. 14.

604 See Jacques Derrida, *Trace et archive, image et art* (Paris: INA Éditions, 2014), p. 59.

605 Stiegler, *Technics and Time, 1*, pp. 139–40.

606 Grammatization is the process of the spatialization of time made possible by hypomnesic artefacts that allow temporal flows to be made discrete, analysable and reproducible; proletarianization refers to the fact that processes of grammatization may not just lead to an accumulation of knowledge but to its loss, precisely because they open a circuit not just with the living, but with what is dead.

607 This chapter was originally written for an STS conference at Nanjing University at which Bernard Stiegler was in attendance and one of the keynote speakers.

608 Peter Szendy, *Kant in the Land of the Extraterrestrials: Cosmopolitical Philosofictions*, trans. Will Bishop (New York: Fordham University Press, 2013), p. 79.

609 Ernst Cassirer, *The Individual and the Cosmos in Renaissance Philosophy*, trans. Mario Domandi (Mineola: Dover, 2000), pp. 177–78.

610 Ibid., p. 178.

611 Ibid., p. 187.

612 Aristotle, *Metaphysics*, 980a22.

613 Sigmund Freud, 'Analysis Terminable and Interminable', in Volume 23 of James Strachey (ed. and trans.), *The Standard Edition of the Complete Psychological Works of Sigmund Freud* (London: Hogarth Press, 1953–74), pp. 245–46.

614 Sigmund Freud, *The Psychopathology of Everyday Life*, in Volume 6 of Strachey, *The Standard Edition of the Complete Psychological Works of Sigmund Freud*, pp. 258–59.

615 Sarah Kofman, *Freud and Fiction*, trans. Sarah Wykes (Cambridge: Polity Press, 1991), p. 33.

616 Ibid., p. 47.

617 Friedrich Nietzsche, *The Pre-Platonic Philosophers*, trans. Greg Whitlock (Urbana and Chicago: University of Illinois Press, 2001), pp. 115–16.

618 Kofman, *Freud and Fiction*, p. 43.

619 Aristotle, *Metaphysics*, 985a24–25.

620 Kofman, *Freud and Fiction*, p. 46.

621 Ibid.

622 To decide the degree to which it would be possible to ascribe such a compositional relationship to Aristotle himself, it would be necessary to pass through a scrupulous reading of Heidegger's lecture courses of 1924–25 on *Plato's Sophist*.

623 Freud, 'Analysis Terminable and Interminable', p. 245.

624 Kōjin Karatani, *Isonomia and the Origins of Philosophy*, trans. Joseph A. Murphy (Durham and London: Duke University Press, 2017), pp. 97–98.

625 On the first, see Peter Gay, *Freud: A Life for Our Times* (London: Macmillan, 1989), pp. 34–35; on the second, see Jean Laplanche, *Life and Death in Psychoanalysis*, trans. Jeffrey Melhman (Baltimore and London: Johns Hopkins University Press, 1976), pp. 118–19.

626 Nietzsche, *The Pre-Platonic Philosophers*, p. 113.

627 Ibid., p. 116.

628 Aristotle, *Physics*, 198b25–28.

629 Ibid., 199a5–8.

630 Martin Heidegger, *Nietzsche, Volume IV: Nihilism*, trans. Frank A Capuzzi (New York: Harper & Row, 1982), p. 147.

631 Ibid., p. 148.

632 Bernard Stiegler, *Qu'appelle-t-on panser? 1. L'immense régression* (Paris: Les Liens qui Libèrent, 2018), p. 107.

633 Martin Heidegger, *Hölderlin's Hymn 'The Ister'*, trans. William McNeill and Julia Davis (Bloomington and Indianapolis: Indiana University Press, 1996), pp. 53–54. We must also add that this lecture course is *also* devoted to *rejecting* a 'spiritual' notion of art, which would be, precisely, to hold to a metaphysical conception. For this reason, Heidegger's reference to 'spirit' here becomes a question, and that question becomes our problem.

634 Martin Heidegger, *On Time and Being*, trans. Joan Stambaugh (New York: Harper & Row, 1972), pp. 57–58.

635 Bernard Stiegler, 'For a Neganthropology of Automatic Society', trans. Daniel Ross, in Thomas Pringle, Gertrud Koch and Bernard Stiegler, *Machine* (Minneapolis and London: University of Minnesota Press, 2019), pp. 34–35. It is worth pointing out that the translator of this text was not given the opportunity to edit or proofread it prior to publication, and it contains some unfortunate errors that would otherwise have been eliminated.

636 Heidegger, *On Time and Being*, p. 58, my italics.

637 Martin Heidegger, *Being and Time*, trans. Joan Stambaugh, rev. by Dennis J. Schmidt (Albany: State University of New York Press, 2010), p. 7, German pagination.

638 As Stiegler points out, this really amounts to a recapitulation of the question raised in Plato's *Meno*. See Bernard Stiegler, *Nanjing Lectures 2016–2019*, trans. Daniel Ross (London: Open Humanities Press, 2020), p. 148.

639 Alfred J. Lotka, 'The Law of Evolution as a Maximal Principle', *Human Biology* 17:3 (1945), p. 188.

640 Heidegger, *On Time and Being*, pp. 58–59.

641 Heidegger, *Hölderlin's Hymn 'The Ister'*, p. 166.

642 Freud, 'Analysis Terminable and Interminable', p. 247.

643 François Jacob, *The Logic of Life: A History of Heredity*, trans. Betty E. Spillmann (New York: Pantheon, 1982), p. 324.

644 Georges Bataille, *The Unfinished System of Nonknowledge*, trans. Michelle Kendall and Stuart Kendall (Minneapolis and London: University of Minnesota Press, 2001), p. 166.

645 Heidegger, *Hölderlin's Hymn 'The Ister'*, pp. 17–18.

646 See, for example, the incredible paragraphs that Stiegler has written on these questions, after himself asking about the meaning of 'general' in 'general organology', in Stiegler, *Nanjing Lectures 2016–2019*, pp. 43–44.

647 Christophe Bonneuil and Jean-Baptiste Fessoz, *The Shock of the Anthropocene: The Earth, History and Us*, trans. David Fernbach (London: Verso, 2016).

648 Bernard Stiegler, 'The New Conflict of the Faculties and Functions: Quasi-Causality and Serendipity in the Anthropocene', trans. Daniel Ross, *Qui Parle* 26 (2017), p. 89.

649 Barbara Stiegler, *'Il faut s'adapter': Sur un nouvel impératif politique* (Paris: Gallimard, 2019), p. 284.

650 Bernard Stiegler, 'Noodiversity, Technodiversity: Elements of a New Economic Foundation Based on a New Foundation for Theoretical Computer Science', trans. Daniel Ross, *Angelaki* 25:4 (2020), p. 73.

651 Peter Sloterdijk, *Neither Sun Nor Death*, trans. Steve Corcoran (Los Angeles: Semiotext(e), 2011), p. 187.

652 Ibid.

653 Ibid., p. 189.

654 Bernard Stiegler, *Acting Out*, trans. David Barison, Daniel Ross and Patrick Crogan (Stanford: Stanford University Press, 2009), pp. 45–46.

655 Sloterdijk, *Neither Sun Nor Death*, p. 190.

656 Ibid., pp. 200–1.

657 Anne Alombert, 'Technologies, Territories, Power: From "Control Societies" to "Neganthropic Localities"' (2019), unpublished.

658 Yuk Hui, 'Simondon et la question de l'information', *Cahiers Simondon* 6 (2015), pp. 29–46.

659 See Giuseppe Longo and Maël Montévil, *Perspectives on Organisms: Biological Time, Symmetries and Singularities* (Berlin and Heidelberg: Springer, 2014).

660 See Bernard Stiegler, 'The New Conflict of the Faculties and Functions: Quasi-Causality and Serendipity in the Anthropocene', trans. Daniel Ross, *Qui Parle* 26 (2017), pp. 79–99, and Bernard Stiegler, *Nanjing Lectures 2016–2019*, trans. Daniel Ross (London: Open Humanities Press, 2020), '2019 Lectures: Elements of a Hyper-Materialist Epistemology'.

661 See also Daniel Ross and Ouyang Man, 'Towards a Metacosmics of Shame', in Ladson Hinton and Hessel Willemsen (eds), *Shame, Temporality and Social Change: Ominous Transitions* (London and New York: Routledge, 2021), where this is also interpreted in relation to the distinction Winnicott makes between 'regression' and 'withdrawal', regression in this sense having a positive character as that which, in conditions of therapeutic 'holding', opens the possibility for the potential contained in shame to be actualized through a process of individuation. Withdrawal, in this scheme, is due to a loss of the resonant conditions of holding, and consists precisely in withdrawing from this positive potential of regression. At the largest scale, such withdrawal is the withdrawal of the cosmos itself as it gives way to the dominance of an entropic universe, and this is what Nietzsche saw in the nineteenth century (in the industrial revolution) and understood as the 'death of God', which is to say, the rise of nihilism, which should therefore also be interpreted as the loss of the possibility of cosmic holding, a loss that in his view would take two hundred years to reach its culminating point.

662 Bernard Stiegler, *The Decadence of Industrial Democracies: Disbelief and Discredit, Volume 1*, trans. Daniel Ross and Suzanne Arnold (Cambridge: Polity Press, 2011), p. 133.

663 Peter Sloterdijk, *Spheres, Volume 3: Foams. Plural Spherology*, trans. Wieland Hoban (Los Angeles: Semiotext(e), 2016), pp. 654–55.

664 Ibid., p. 656.

665 Ibid.

666 Ibid.

667 Ibid., pp. 656–57.

668 Ibid., pp. 657–58.

669 Sloterdijk, *Neither Sun Nor Death*, pp. 115–16.

670 Ibid., p. 175.

671 Ibid., p. 118.

672 Ibid., p. 176.

673 Ibid., p. 249.

674 Ibid., p. 215.

675 Sloterdijk, *Spheres, Volume 3: Foams*, p. 659.

676 Sloterdijk, *Neither Sun Nor Death*, p. 221.

677 Ibid., p. 222–23.

678 Peter Sloterdijk, *Selected Exaggerations: Conversations and Interviews, 1993–2012*, trans. Karen Margolis (Cambridge: Polity Press, 2016), p. 230.

679 Sloterdijk, *Neither Sun Nor Death*, p. 260.

680 Ibid., p. 181.

681 Ibid., p. 210.

682 Roberto Esposito, *Immunitas: The Projection and Negation of Life*, trans. Zakiya Hanafi (Cambridge: Polity Press, 2011), p. 6.

683 Ibid., pp. 1–2.

684 Ibid., p. 7.

685 Ibid.

686 Ibid., pp. 8–9.

687 Ibid., p. 7.

688 Jean Claude Ameisen, *La sculpture du vivant. Le suicide cellulaire ou la mort créatrice* (Paris: Seuil, 2003).

689 Francesco Vitale, *Biodeconstruction: Jacques Derrida and the Life Sciences*, trans. Mauro Senatore (Albany: State University of New York Press, 2018.

690 On all these questions, see also Ross and Ouyang, 'Towards a Metacosmics of Shame'.

691 Stiegler, *The Decadence of Industrial Democracies*, p. 134.

692 Ibid., p. 150.

693 Ibid., p. 183, n. 22.

694 Sloterdijk, *Neither Sun Nor Death*, p. 266.

695 Ibid., pp. 270–71.

696 Ibid., p. 271.

697 Ibid., pp. 271–72.

698 Ibid., pp. 274–75.

699 Ibid., p. 84.

700 Jean Laplanche, *Life and Death in Psychoanalysis*, pp. 10–13.

701 Another possible source for such a clarification and extension could be Pierre Klossowski, *Living Currency*, trans. Vernon W. Cisney et al. (London: Bloomsbury Academic, 2018), although aspects of his theoretical apparatus remain obscure to this author.

702 Laplanche, *Life and Death in Psychoanalysis*, pp. 19–22.

703 Ibid., pp. 23–24.

704 Ibid., p. 25.

705 Jean Laplanche and Jean-Bertrand Pontalis, 'Fantasy and the Origins of Sexuality', *International Journal of Psychoanalysis* 49 (1968), pp. 1–18.

706 Friedrich Nietzsche, *Selected Letters*, trans. Christopher Middleton (Indianapolis and Cambridge: Hackett, 1996), p. 3.

707 Ibid., p. 4.

708 Friedrich Hölderlin, *The Death of Empedocles: A Mourning-Play*, trans. David Farrell Krell (Albany: State University of New York Press, 2009), p. 91.

709 At the end of Part I of Jacques Derrida, *Of Grammatology*, corrected edition, trans. Gayatri Chakravorty Spivak (Baltimore and London: Johns Hopkins University Press, 1998).

710 Ibid., p. 74.

711 And after a preamble published later as Jacques Derrida, *The Problem of Genesis in Husserl's Philosophy*, trans. Marian Hobson (Chicago and London: University of Chicago Press, 2003), which interprets

The Origin of Geometry in a manner that is almost the opposite of the 1962 'Introduction', of which I proposed an analysis in Bernard Stiegler, *Technics and Time, 2: Disorientation*, trans. Stephen Barker (Stanford: Stanford University Press, 2009), pp. 233–40

712 Jacques Derrida, *Edmund Husserl's Origin of Geometry: An Introduction*, trans. John P. Leavey, Jr. (Lincoln and London: University of Nebraska Press, 1989).

713 Jacques Derrida, *Speech and Phenomena, And Other Essays on Husserl's Theory of Signs*, trans. David B. Allison (Evanston: Northwestern University Press, 1973).

714 Derrida, *Of Grammatology*, p. 74.

715 Derrida, *Speech and Phenomena*, p. 65.

716 Bernard Stiegler, 'The Magic Skin; or, The Franco-European Accident of Philosophy after Jacques Derrida', *Qui Parle* 18 (2009), p. 105.

717 Derrida, *Of Grammatology*, p. 84.

718 On this passage from vital individuation to psychic and collective individuation, I refer to Bernard Stiegler, 'Five Hundred Million Friends: The Pharmacology of Friendship', trans. Daniel Ross, *Umbr(a)* 1 (2012), pp. 59–75, and Stiegler, *States of Shock: Studpidity and Knowledge in the Twenty-First Century*, trans. Daniel Ross (Cambridge: Polity Press, 2015).

719 Derrida, *Of Grammatology*, p. 84.

720 Paul Ricoeur, *Time, and Narrative, Volume 1*, trans. Kathleen McLaughlin and David Pellauer (Chicago and London: University of Chicago Press, 1984), p. 58, translation modified.

721 Derrida, *Of Grammatology*, p. 64.

722 John Bowlby, *Attachment and Loss, Volume 1: Attachment* (London: Pimlico, 1997).

723 On this concept, see Bernard Stiegler, *Technics and Time, 3: Cinematic Time and the Question of Malaise*, trans. Stephen Barker (Stanford: Stanford University Press, 2011), pp. 131 ff.

724 On attentional forms, see Stiegler, *States of Shock*.

725 Derrida, *Of Grammatology*, p. 84.

726 *Translator's note*: I would like to thank Anne Alombert for her assistance in the translation of this paragraph, as did the author himself in an email dated 21 July 2020, in which he wrote: 'Je crois que cette version est au plus près du texte, merci à vous et à Anne. Lorsque

j'avais soutenu ma thèse, Derrida, dans son intervention, avait insisté sur ce verbe falloir en disant qu'il l'avait entendu comme le verbe pleuvoir (il pleut, il faut, etc.).'

727 Here, we would need to go back over Derrida's *Of Spirit: Heidegger and the Question*, of which I proposed a reading in Bernard Stiegler, *What Makes Life Worth Living: On Pharmacology*, trans. Daniel Ross (Cambridge: Polity Press, 2013), pp. 101 ff.

728 André Leroi-Gourhan, *Gesture and Speech*, trans. Anna Bostock Berger (Cambridge, Massachusetts and London: MIT Press, 1993), pp. 261–66 and 404.

729 On grammatization, see, for example, Bernard Stiegler, *Symbolic Misery, Volume 1: The Hyper-Industrial Epoch*, trans. Barnaby Norman (Cambridge: Polity Press, 2014), §30.

730 See Bernard Stiegler, *Taking Care of Youth and the Generations*, trans. Stephen Barker (Stanford: Stanford University Press, 2010), §20.

731 *Translator's note*: On the transcendental field without a subject, see Bernard Stiegler, *Automatic Society, Volume 1: The Future of Work*, trans. Daniel Ross (Cambridge: Polity Press, 2016), pp. 315–14, n. 53.

732 'Les piètres penseurs', to quote the original French title of Dominique Lecourt, *The Mediocracy: French Philosophy since the mid-1970s*, trans. Gregory Elliott (London and New York: Verso, 2001).

References

Adorno, Theodor W., and Max Horkheimer. *Dialectic of Enlightenment: Philosophical Fragments*. Trans. Edmund Jephcott. Stanford: Stanford University Press, 2002.

Alombert, Anne. 'Penser dans l'après-coup de la postmodernité', *Implications Philosophiques* (2017), published in two parts, available at: <http://www.implications-philosophiques.org/actualite/une/penser-dans-lapres-coup-de-la-postmodernite-12/> and <http://www.implications-philosophiques.org/actualite/une/penser-dans-lapres-coup-de-la-modernite-22/>.

Alombert, Anne. 'Technologies, Territories, Power: From "Control Societies" to "Neganthropic Localities"' (2019), unpublished.

Ameisen, Jean Claude. *La sculpture du vivant. Le suicide cellulaire ou la mort créatrice*. Paris: Seuil, 2003.

Auroux, Sylvain. *La révolution technologique de la grammatisation: Introduction à l'histoire des sciences du langage*. Liège: Mardaga, 1994.

Bataille, Georges. *Lascaux: Or the Birth of Art*. Trans. Austryn Wainhouse. Geneva: Skira, 1955.

Bataille, Georges. *The Unfinished System of Nonknowledge*. Trans. Michelle Kendall and Stuart Kendall. Minneapolis and London: University of Minnesota Press, 2001.

Bauwens, Michel. 'Introduction', *P2P Accounting for Planetary Survival* (27 June 2019), available at: <http://commonstransition.org/p2p-accounting-for-planetary-survival/>.

Beiser, Frederick C. *Weltschmerz: Pessimism in German Philosophy, 1860–1900*. Oxford: Oxford University Press, 2016.

Benjamin, Walter. *Selected Writing, Volume 1: 1913–1926*. Edited by Marcus Bullock and Michael W. Jennings. Cambridge, Massachusetts and London: Harvard University Press, 1996.

Bennington, Geoffrey. *Interrupting Derrida*. London and New York: Routledge, 2000.

Berman, Antoine. *The Experience of the Foreign: Culture and Translation in Romantic Germany.* Trans. Stefan Heyvaert. Albany: State University of New York Press, 1992.

Boehm, Rudolf. 'Pensée et technique. Notes préliminaires pour une question touchant la problématique heideggérienne', *Revue Internationale de Philosophie* 14 (1960): 194–220.

Boltzmann, Ludwig. *Theoretical Physics and Philosophical Problems.* Edited by Brian McGuinness. Trans. Paul Foulkes. Dordrecht and Boston: Reidel, 1974.

Bonneuil, Christophe, and Jean-Baptiste Fessoz. *The Shock of the Anthropocene: The Earth, History and Us.* Trans. David Fernbach. London: Verso, 2016.

Bostrom, Nick. 'Are You Living in a Computer Simulation?', *Philosophical Quarterly* 53 (2003): 243–55.

Bowlby, John. *Attachment and Loss, Volume 1: Attachment.* London: Pimlico, 1997.

Canguilhem, Georges. *The Normal and the Pathological.* Trans. Carolyn R. Fawcett, with Robert S. Cohen. New York: Zone Books, 1991.

Canguilhem, Georges. 'The Decline of the Idea of Progress'. Trans. David Macey. *Economy and Society* 27 (1998): 313–29.

Cassirer, Ernst, *The Individual and the Cosmos in Renaissance Philosophy.* Trans. Mario Domandi. Mineola: Dover, 2000.

Cercignani, Carlo. *Ludwig Boltzmann: The Man Who Trusted Atoms.* Oxford: Oxford University Press, 1998.

Colony, Tracy. 'Epimetheus Bound: Stiegler on Derrida, Life, and the Technological Condition', *Research in Phenomenology* 41 (2011): 72–89.

Crouch, Colin. 'Privatised Keynesianism: An Unacknowledged Policy Regime', *British Journal of Politics and International Relations* 11 (2009): 382–99.

Crouch, Colin. *The Strange Non-Death of Neoliberalism.* Cambridge: Polity Press, 2011.

References

Dale, Gareth. 'Karl Polanyi vs Friedrich von Hayek: The Socialist Calculation Debate and Beyond'. In Robert Leeson (ed.), *Hayek: A Collaborative Biography. Part XIV: Liberalism in the Classical Tradition: Orwell, Popper, Humboldt and Polanyi*. Cham: Palgrave Macmillan, 2018.

Derrida, Jacques. *Speech and Phenomena, And Other Essays on Husserl's Theory of Signs*. Trans. David B. Allison. Evanston: Northwestern University Press, 1973.

Derrida, Jacques. *Writing and Difference*. Trans. Alan Bass. London and Henley: Routledge and Kegan Paul, 1978.

Derrida, Jacques. *Positions*. Trans. Alan Bass. Chicago: University of Chicago Press, 1981.

Derrida, Jacques. *Margins of Philosophy*. Trans. Alan Bass. Hemel Hempstead: Harvester Press, 1982.

Derrida, Jacques. *The Post Card: From Socrates to Freud and Beyond*. Trans. Alan Bass. Chicago and London: University of Chicago Press, 1987.

Derrida, Jacques. *Edmund Husserl's Origin of Geometry: An Introduction*. Trans. John P. Leavey Jr. Lincoln and London: University of Nebraska Press, 1989.

Derrida, Jacques. 'Heidegger's Silence: Excerpts from a Talk Given on 5 February 1988'. Trans. Joachim Neugroschel. In Günther Neske and Emil Kettering (eds), *Martin Heidegger and National Socialism: Questions and Answers*. New York: Paragon House, 1990.

Derrida, Jacques. *Of Grammatology*, corrected edition. Trans. Gayatri Chakravorty Spivak. Baltimore and London: Johns Hopkins University Press, 1998.

Derrida, Jacques. *The Problem of Genesis in Husserl's Philosophy*. Trans. Marian Hobson. Chicago and London: University of Chicago Press, 2003.

Derrida, Jacques. *Rogues: Two Essays on Reason*. Trans. Pascale-Anne Brault and Michael Naas. Stanford: Stanford University Press, 2005.

Derrida, Jacques. *Learning to Live Finally: The Last Interview*. Trans. Pascale-Anne Brault and Michael Naas. Basingstoke, Hampshire and New York: Palgrave Macmillan, 2007.

Derrida, Jacques. *The Beast and the Sovereign, Volume 1*. Trans. Geoffrey Bennington. Chicago and London: University of Chicago Press, 2009.

Derrida, Jacques. *Trace et archive, image et art*. Paris: INA Éditions, 2014.

Derrida, Jacques. *Life Death*. Trans. Pascale-Anne Brault and Michel Naas. Chicago and London: University of Chicago Press, 2020.

Detienne, Marcel, and Jean-Pierre Vernant. *Cunning Intelligence in Greek Culture and Society*. Trans. Janet Lloyd. Chicago and London: University of Chicago Press, 1991.

Dumézil, Georges. *Mitra-Varuna: An Essay on Two Indo-European Representations of Sovereignty*. Trans. Derek Coltman. New York: Zone Books, 1988.

Engels, Friedrich. *Dialectics of Nature*. Trans. Clemens Dutt. London: Lawrence & Wishart, 1940.

Esposito, Roberto. *Immunitas: The Projection and Negation of Life/* Trans. Zakiya Hanafi. Cambridge: Polity Press, 2011.

Felstiner, John. *Paul Celan: Poet, Survivor, Jew*. New Haven and London: Yale University Press, 1995.

Feng, Jingxuan, et al. 'Modeling the point of use EROI and its implications for economic growth in China', *Energy* 144 (1 February 2018): 232–42.

Freud, Sigmund. *The Standard Edition of the Complete Psychological Works of Sigmund Freud*, 24 vols. Trans. and ed. James Strachey. London: Hogarth, 1953–74.

Fukuyama, Francis. *The End of History and the Last Man*. New York: Macmillan, 1992.

Gay, Peter. *Freud: A Life for Our Time*. London: Macmillan, 1989.

Georgescu-Roegen, Nicholas. *The Entropy Law and the Economic Process*. Cambridge, Massachusetts and London: Harvard University Press, 1971.

Girard, René. *Violence and the Sacred*. Trans. Patrick Gregory. Baltimore and London: Johns Hopkins University Press, 1977.

Girard, René. 'The Evangelical Subversion of Myth'. In Robert Hamerton-Kelly (ed.), *Politics and Apocalypse*. East Lansing: Michigan State University Press, 2007.

Godelier, Maurice. *The Metamorphoses of Kinship*. Trans. Nora Scott. London and New York: Verso, 2011.

Hansen, Mark B. N. 'Bernard Stiegler, Philosopher of Desire?', *Boundary 2* 44 (2017): 167–90.

Hardy, Quentin. 'René Girard, French Theorist of the Social Sciences, Dies at 91', *New York Times* (10 November 2015), available at: <https://www.nytimes.com/2015/11/11/arts/international/rene-girard-french-theorist-of-the-social-sciences-dies-at-91.html>.

Hayek, Friedrich A. *Individualism and Economic Order*. Chicago and London: University of Chicago Press, 1948.

Hayek, Friedrich A. *Law, Legislation and Liberty: A New Statement of the Liberal Principles of Justice and Political Economy*, one-volume edition. London: Routledge, 1982.

Hayek, Friedrich A. *The Constitution of Liberty: The Definitive Edition*. Chicago and London: University of Chicago Press, 2011.

Heidegger, Martin. *What is Called Thinking?* Trans. J. Glenn Gray. New York: Harper & Row, 1968.

Heidegger, Martin. *On Time and Being*. Trans. Joan Stambaugh. New York: Harper & Row, 1972.

Heidegger, Martin. *Nietzsche, Volume IV: Nihilism*. Trans. Frank A Capuzzi. New York: Harper & Row, 1982.

Heidegger, Martin. *Hölderlin's Hymn 'The Ister'*. Trans. William McNeill and Julia Davis. Bloomington and Indianapolis: Indiana University Press, 1996.

Heidegger, Martin. *An Introduction to Metaphysics*. Trans. Gregory Fried and Richard Polt. New Haven and London: Yale University Press, 2000.

Heidegger, Martin. *Being and Time*. Trans. Joan Stambaugh, revised by Dennis J. Schmidt. Albany: State University of New York Press, 2010.

Heidegger, Martin. *Bremen and Freiburg Lectures: Insight Into That Which Is and Basic Principles of Thinking*. Trans. Andrew J. Mitchell. Bloomington and Indianapolis: Indiana University Press, 2012.

Herbstrith, Waltraud. *Edith Stein: A Biography*. Trans. Bernard Bonowitz. San Francisco: Harper and Row, 1985.

Hoffman, Michael. 'Forgotten atrocity of the atomic age', *Japan Times* (August 28, 2011), available at: <https://www.japantimes.co.jp/culture/2011/08/28/culture/forgotten-atrocity-of-the-atomic-age/#.W57kTy17HjA>.

Hölderlin, Friedrich. *The Death of Empedocles: A Mourning-Play*. Trans. David Farrell Krell. Albany: State University of New York Press, 2009.

Hörl, Erich. 'A Thousand Ecologies: The Process of Cyberneticization and General Ecology'. Trans. James Burton, Jeffrey Kirkwood and Maria Vlotides. In Diedrich Diederichsen and Anselm Franke (eds), *The Whole Earth: California and the Disappearance of the Outside*. Berlin: Sternberg Press, 2013.

Hörl, Erich. 'Prostheses of Desire: On Bernard Stiegler's New Critique of Projection'. Trans. Arne De Boever. *Parrehsia* 20 (2014): 2–14.

Hörl, Erich. 'The Technological Condition'. Trans. Anthony Enns. *Parrhesia* 22 (2015): 1–15.

Hörl, Erich. 'Other Beginnings of Participative Sense-Culture: Wild Media, Speculative Ecologies, Transgressions of the Cybernetic Hypothesis'. Trans. Anne Ganzert and James Burton. In Mathias Denecke, Anne Ganzert, Isabell Otto and Robert Stock (eds), *ReClaiming Participation: Technology – Mediation – Collectivity*. Bielefeld: Transcript Verlag, 2016.

Hörl, Erich, and James Burton (eds). *General Ecology: The New Ecological Paradigm*. New York: Bloomsbury, 2017.

Hui, Yuk. 'Simondon et la question de l'information', *Cahiers Simondon* 6 (2015): 29–46.

Huntington, Samuel P. *The Clash of Civilizations and the Remaking of World Order*. New York: Simon and Schuster, 1996.

Husserl, Edmund. *On the Phenomenology of the Consciousness of Internal Time (1893–1917)*. Trans. John Barnett Brough. Dordrecht: Kluwer Academic Publishers, 1991.

IPCC. 'Global Warming of 1.5°C: An IPCC special report on the impacts of global warming of 1.5°C above pre-industrial levels and related global greenhouse gas emission pathways, in the context of strengthening the global response to the threat of climate change, sustainable development, and efforts to eradicate poverty: summary for policymakers' (6 October 2018), available at: <http://report.ipcc.ch/sr15/pdf/sr15_spm_final.pdf>.

Jacob, François. *The Logic of Life: A History of Heredity*. Trans. Betty E. Spillmann. New York: Pantheon, 1982.

Järvensivu, Paavo, et al. 'Governance of Economic Transition'. Invited background document on economic transformation, to chapter, 'Transformation: The Economy', for the *Global Sustainable Development Report 2019*, available at: <https://bios.fi/bios-governance_of_economic_transition.pdf>.

Johnson, Christopher. *System and Writing in the Philosophy of Jacques Derrida*. Cambridge and New York: Cambridge University Press, 1993.

Johnson, Christopher. 'Derrida: The Machine and the Animal', *Paragraph* 28:3 (2005): 102–20.

Johnson, Christopher. 'The Prehistory of Technology: On the Contribution of Leroi-Gourhan'. In Christina Howells and Gerald Moore (eds), *Stiegler and Technics*. Edinburgh: Edinburgh University Press, 2013.

Kaczynski, Theodore. *Anti-Tech Revolution: Why and How*. Scottsdale, AZ: Fitch and Madison, 2016.

Kant, Immanuel. *Political Writings*, 2nd edition. Trans. H. B. Nisbet. Cambridge: Cambridge University Press, 1991.

Karatani, Kōjin. *Isonomia and the Origins of Philosophy*. Trans. Joseph A. Murphy. Durham and London: Duke University Press, 2017.

Kisiel, Theodore, and Thomas Sheehan (eds). *Becoming Heidegger: On the Trail of his Early Occasional Writings, 1910–1927*, 2nd revised edition. Seattle: Noesis Press, 2010.

Klein, Naomi. 'Screen New Deal: Under Cover of Mass Death, Andrew Cuomo Calls in the Billionaires to Build a High-Tech Dystopia', *The Intercept* (9 May 2020), available at: <https://theintercept.com/2020/05/08/andrew-cuomo-eric-schmidt-coronavirus-tech-shock-doctrine/>.

Klossowski, Pierre. *Living Currency*. Trans. Vernon W. Cisney et al. London: Bloomsbury Academic, 2018.

Kofman, Sarah. *Freud and Fiction*. Trans. Sarah Wykes. Cambridge: Polity Press, 1991.

Kurosawa, Akira. 'Kurosawa on Kurosawa: Part Two', *Sight and Sound* 33 (October 1964): 200–203.

Lampert, Laurence. *What a Philosopher Is: Becoming Nietzsche*. Chicago and London: University of Chicago Press, 2017.

Laplanche, Jean, and Jean-Bertrand Pontalis. 'Fantasy and the Origins of Sexuality', *International Journal of Psychoanalysis* 49 (1968): 1–18.

Laplanche, Jean. *Life and Death in Psychoanalysis*. Trans. Jeffrey Mehlman. Baltimore and London: Johns Hopkins University Press, 1976.

Larsen, Brendan B., et al. 'Inordinate Fondness Multiplied and Redistributed: The Number of Species on Earth and the New Pie of Life', *Quarterly Review of Biology* 92 (2017): 229–65.

Lecourt, Dominique. *The Mediocracy: French Philosophy since the mid-1970s*. Trans. Gregory Elliott. London and New York: Verso, 2001.

Leroi-Gourhan, André. *Gesture and Speech*. Trans. Anna Bostock Berger. Cambridge, Massachusetts and London: MIT Press, 1993.

Lévi-Strauss, Claude. 'The Future of Kinship Studies', *Proceedings of the Royal Anthropological Institute of Great Britain and Ireland* 1 (1965): 13–22.

Lévi-Strauss, Claude. *Tristes Tropiques*. Trans. John Weightman and Doreen Weightman. Harmondsworth, Middlesex: Penguin, 1976.

Lévi-Strauss, Claude. *Introduction to the Work of Marcel Mauss*. Trans. Felicity Baker. London: Routledge and Kegan Paul, 1987.

Lewis, Thomas, Fari Amini and Richard Lannon. *A General Theory of Love*. New York: Random House, 2000.

Longo, Giuseppe, and Maël Montévil. *Perspectives on Organisms: Biological Time, Symmetries and Singularities*. Berlin and Heidelberg: Springer, 2014.

Longo, Giuseppe. 'Complexity, Information and Diversity in Science and in Democracy'. Trans. M. R. Doyle and S. Savic. *Glass Bead* (2018), available at: <https://www.glass-bead.org/research-platform/complexity-information-diversity-science-democracy/>.

Lotka, Alfred J. 'The Law of Evolution as a Maximal Principle', *Human Biology* 17:3 (1945): 167–94.

Lyon, James K. *Paul Celan and Martin Heidegger: An Unresolved Conversation, 1951–1970*. Baltimore: Johns Hopkins University Press, 2006.

Machiavelli, Niccolò. *The Prince*. In *The Portable Machiavelli*, ed. and trans. Peter Bondanella and Mark Musa. New York and London: Penguin, 1979.

Maine, Charles Eric. *The Man Who Couldn't Sleep*. Philadelphia and New York: J. B. Lippincott, 1956.

Marcuse, Herbert. *An Essay on Liberation*. Boston: Beacon Press, 2000.

Marx, Karl. *A Contribution to the Critique of Political Economy*. Trans. S. W. Ryanzanskaya. Moscow: Progress Publishers, 1970.

Marx, Karl, and Friedrich Engels. *The German Ideology*. Trans. Clemens Dutt and C. P. Magill. London: Lawrence & Wishart, 1974.

Mauss, Marcel. *La nation, ou le sens du social*, corrected edition. Paris: Presses Universitaires de France, 2018.

Mirowski, Philip. *More Heat Than Light. Economics as Social Physics: Physics as Nature's Economics*. Cambridge: Cambridge University Press, 1989.

Mirowski, Philip. *Machine Dreams: Economics Becomes a Cyborg Science*. Cambridge and New York: Cambridge University Press, 2002.

Mirowski, Philip. 'Philosophizing With a Hammer: Reply to Binmore, Davis and Klaes', *Journal of Economic Methodology* 11 (2004): 499–513.

Mirowski, Philip. *Never Let a Serious Crisis Go to Waste: How Neoliberalism Survived the Financial Meltdown*. London and New York: Verso, 2013.

Mirowski, Philip, and Edward Nik-Khah. *The Knowledge We Have Lost in Information: The History of Information in Modern Economics*. New York: Oxford University Press, 2017.

Moore, Gerald, 'On the Origin of *Aisthesis* by Means of Artificial Selection; or, The Preservation of Favored Traces in the Struggle for Existence', *Boundary 2* 44 (2017): 191–212.

Moore, Gerald. 'The Pharmacology of Addiction', *Parrhesia* 29 (2018): 190–211.

Morange, Michel. *Life Explained*. Trans. Matthew Cobb and Malcolm DeBevoise. New Haven and London: Yale University Press, 2008.

Morin, Edgar. *Method: Towards a Study of Humankind, Volume 1: The Nature of Nature*. Trans. J. L. Roland Bélanger. New York: Peter Lang, 1992.

Nancy, Jean-Luc. *The Sense of the World*. Trans. Jeffrey S. Librett. Minneapolis and London: University of Minnesota Press, 1997.

Neske, Günther, and Emil Kettering (eds). *Martin Heidegger and National Socialism: Questions and Answers*. Trans. Lisa Harries. New York: Paragon House, 1990.

Nietzsche, Friedrich. *Philosophy in the Tragic Age of the Greeks*. Trans. Marianne Cowan. Washington D.C.: Regnery Gateway, 1962.

Nietzsche, Friedrich. *Selected Letters*. Trans. Christopher Middleton. Indianapolis and Cambridge: Hackett, 1996.

Nietzsche, Friedrich. *The Pre-Platonic Philosophers*. Trans. Greg Whitlock. Urbana and Chicago: University of Illinois Press, 2001.

Nietzsche, Friedrich. *The Anti-Christ, Ecce Homo, Twilight of the Idols, and Other Writings*. Trans. Judith Norman. Cambridge: Cambridge University Press, 2005.

Pasquale, Frank. 'From Territorial to Functional Sovereignty: The Case of Amazon', *OpenDemocracy* (5 January 2018), available at: <https://www.opendemocracy.net/en/digitalliberties/from-territorial-to-functional-sovereignty-case-of-amazon/>.

Peeters, Benoît. *Derrida: A Biography*. Trans. Andrew Brown. Cambridge: Polity Press, 2013.

Polanyi, Karl. *The Great Transformation: The Political and Economic Origins of Our Time*. Boston: Beacon Press, 2001.

Ricoeur, Paul. *Time, and Narrative, Volume 1*. Trans. Kathleen McLaughlin and David Pellauer. Chicago and London: University of Chicago Press, 1984.

Robiou du Pont, Yann, and Malte Meinshausen. 'Warming Assessment of the Bottom-Up Paris Agreement Emissions Pledges', *Nature Communications* 9 (16 November 2018), available at: <https://www.nature.com/articles/s41467-018-07223-9>.

Ross, Daniel. *Violent Democracy*. Cambridge: Cambridge University Press, 2004.

Ross, Daniel. 'Traumas of the Image', *theory@buffalo* 10 (2005): 81–102.

Ross, Daniel. 'Democracy, Authority, Narcissism: From Agamben to Stiegler', *Contretemps* 6 (2006): 74–85, available at: <https://www.academia.edu/12687280/Democracy_Authority_Narcissism_From_Agamben_to_Stiegler_2006_>.

Ross, Daniel. 'Politics, Terror, and Traumatypical Imagery'. In Matthew Sharpe, Murray Noonan and Jason Freddi (eds), *Trauma, Historicity, Philosophy*. Newcastle: Cambridge Scholars Press, 2007.

Ross, Daniel. 'Pharmacology and Critique After Deconstruction'. In Gerald Moore and Christine Howells (eds), *Stiegler and Technics*. Edinburgh: Edinburgh University Press, 2013.

Ross, Daniel. 'Introduction'. In Bernard Stiegler, *The Neganthropocene*, ed. and trans. Daniel Ross. London: Open Humanities Press, 2018.

Ross, Daniel. 'Moving Images of the Anthropocene: Rethinking Cinema Beyond Anthropology', *Screening the Past* 44 (2019), available at: <http://www.screeningthepast.com/2019/03/moving-images-of-the-anthropocene-rethinking-cinema-beyond-anthropology/>.

Ross, Daniel, and Ouyang Man. 'Towards a Metacosmics of Shame'. In Ladson Hinton and Hessel Willemsen (eds), *Temporality, Shame and Social Crisis: Ominous Transitions*. New York and London: Routledge, 2021.

Sartre, Jean-Paul. *Critique of Dialectical Reason, Volume One*, corrected edition. Trans. Alan Sheridan-Smith. London and New York: Verso, 1991.

Schrödinger, Erwin. *What is Life?, with Mind and Matter and Autobiographical Sketches*. Cambridge: Cambridge University Press, 1992.

Secretariat of the United Nations Conference on Trade and Development. *Trade and Development Report 2018: Power, Platforms and the Free Trade Delusion* (New York and Geneva: United Nations, 2018), available at: <https://unctad.org/en/PublicationsLibrary/tdr2018_en.pdf>.

Semineiro, Maria. 'The Web Got You Down? Report Links Internet Use to Depression, Loneliness', *ZDNet* (31 August 1998), available at: <https://www.zdnet.com/article/the-web-got-you-down-report-links-internet-use-to-depression-loneliness/>.

Senatore, Mauro. 'Drive to Drive: The Deconstruction of the Freudian Trieb', *Derrida Today* 12 (2019): 59–79.

Shih, Gerry. 'Xi tells the world China will boost imports while swiping at Trump's "law of the jungle"', *Washington Post* (5 November 2018), available at: <https://www.washingtonpost.com/world/asia_pacific/xi-tells-the-world-china-will-boost-imports-while-swiping-at-trumpslaw-of-the-jungle/2018/11/05/c9b61f9c-e0bc-11e8-a1c9-6afe99dddd92_story.html>.

Shullenberger, Geoff. 'The Scapegoating Machine', *The New Inquiry* (30 November 2016), available at: <https://thenewinquiry.com/essays/the-scapegoating-machine/>.

Simondon, Gilbert. *L'individuation à la lumière des notions de forme et d'information*. Grenoble: Jérôme Millon, 2013.

Sloterdijk, Peter. *Neither Sun Nor Death*. Trans. Steve Corcoran. Los Angeles: Semiotext(e), 2011.

Sloterdijk, Peter. *Selected Exaggerations: Conversations and Interviews, 1993–2012*. Trans. Karen Margolis. Cambridge: Polity Press, 2016.

Sloterdijk, Peter. *Spheres, Volume 3: Foams. Plural Spherology*. Trans. Wieland Hoban. Los Angeles: Semiotext(e), 2016.

Smithson, Robert. *Robert Smithson: The Collected Writings*, edited by Jack Flam. Berkeley, Los Angeles and London: University of California Press, 1996.

Spengler, Oswald. *The Decline of the West, Volume 1: Form and Actuality*. Trans. Charles Francis Atkinson. New York: Alfred A. Knopf, 1947.

Steffen, Will, et al. 'Trajectories of the Earth System in the Anthropocene', *Proceedings of the National Academy of Sciences of the United States of America* 115:33 (14 August 2018), available at: <https://doi.org/10.1073/pnas.1810141115>.

Stein, Edith. 'Martin Heidegger's Existential Philosophy'. Trans. Mette Lebech, *Maynooth Philosophical Papers* 4 (2007): 55–98.

Stiegler, Barbara. *'Il faut s'adapter': Sur un nouvel impératif politique.* Paris: Gallimard, 2019.

Stiegler, Bernard. *Technics and Time, 1: The Fault of Epimetheus.* Trans. Richard Beardsworth and George Collins. Stanford: Stanford University Press, 1998.

Stiegler, Bernard. 'Derrida and Technology: Fidelity at the Limits of Deconstruction and the Prosthesis of Faith'. Trans. Richard Beardsworth. In Tom Cohen (ed.), *Jacques Derrida and the Humanities: A Critical Reader.* Cambridge: Cambridge University Press, 2001.

Stiegler, Bernard. 'The Discrete Image'. In Jacques Derrida and Bernard Stiegler, *Echographies of Television: Filmed Interviews.* Trans. Jennifer Bajorek. Cambridge: Polity Press, 2002.

Stiegler, Bernard. *Acting Out.* Trans. David Barison, Daniel Ross and Patrick Crogan. Stanford: Stanford University Press, 2009.

Stiegler, Bernard. 'The Magic Skin; or, The Franco-European Accident of Philosophy after Jacques Derrida', *Qui Parle* 18 (2009): 97–110.

Stiegler, Bernard, Alain Giffard and Christian Fauré. *Pour en finir avec la mécroissance.* Paris: Flammarion, 2009.

Stiegler, Bernard. *Technics and Time, 2: Disorientation.* Trans. Stephen Barker. Stanford: Stanford University Press, 2009.

Stiegler, Bernard. *For a New Critique of Political Economy.* Trans. Daniel Ross. Cambridge: Polity Press, 2010.

Stiegler, Bernard. *Taking Care of Youth and the Generations.* Trans. Stephen Barker. Stanford: Stanford University Press, 2010.

Stiegler, Bernard. 'Telecracy Against Democracy'. Trans. Chris Turner, *Cultural Politics* 6 (2010): 171–80.

Stiegler, Bernard. *The Decadence of Industrial Democracies: Disbelief and Discredit, Volume 1*. Trans. Daniel Ross and Suzanne Arnold. Cambridge: Polity Press, 2011.

Stiegler, Bernard. *Technics and Time, 3: Cinematic Time and the Question of Malaise*. Trans. Stephen Barker. Stanford: Stanford University Press, 2011.

Stiegler, Bernard. 'The Theater of Individuation: Phase-Shift and Resolution in Simondon and Heidegger'. Trans. Kristina Lebedeva. In Arne De Boever, Alex Murray, Jon Roffe and Ashley Woodward (eds), *Gilbert Simondon: Being and Technology*. Edinburgh: Edinburgh University Press, 2012.

Stiegler, Bernard. *The Lost Spirit of Capitalism: Disbelief and Discredit, Volume 3*. Trans. Daniel Ross. Cambridge: Cambridge University Press, 2014.

Stiegler, Bernard. *The Re-Enchantment of the World: The Value of Spirit against Industrial Populism*. Trans. Trevor Arthur. London and New York: Bloomsbury, 2014.

Stiegler, Bernard. *Symbolic Misery, Volume 1: The Hyper-Industrial Epoch*. Trans. Barnaby Norman. Cambridge: Polity Press, 2014.

Stiegler, Bernard, and Anaïs Nony. 'On Automatic Society', *Third Rail Quarterly* 5 (2015), available at: <http://thirdrailquarterly.org/wp-content/uploads/05_Stiegler_TTR5.pdf>: 16–17.

Stiegler, Bernard. *States of Shock: Stupidity and Knowledge in the Twenty-First Century*. Trans. Daniel Ross. Cambridge: Polity Press, 2015.

Stiegler, Bernard. *Symbolic Misery, Volume 2: The Katastrophē of the Sensible*. Trans. Barnaby Norman. Cambridge: Polity Press, 2015.

Stiegler, Bernard. *Automatic Society, Volume 1: The Future of Work*. Trans. Daniel Ross. Cambridge: Polity Press, 2016.

Stiegler, Bernard. 'The New Conflict of the Faculties and Functions: Quasi-Causality and Serendipity in the Anthropocene'. Trans. Daniel Ross. *Qui Parle* 26 (2017): 79–99.

Stiegler, Bernard. *Philosophising by Accident: Interviews with Élie During*. Trans. Benoît Dillet. Edinburgh: Edinburgh University Press, 2017.

Stiegler, Bernard. 'The Proletarianization of Sensibility'. Trans. Arne De Boever. *Boundary 2* 44 (2017): 5–18.

Stiegler, Bernard. *The Neganthropocene*, ed. and trans. Daniel Ross. London: Open Humanities Press, 2018.

Stiegler, Bernard. *Qu'appelle-t-on panser? 1. L'immense régression*. Paris: Les Liens qui Libèrent, 2018.

Stiegler, Bernard. *The Age of Disruption: Technology and Madness in Computational Capitalism*. Trans. Daniel Ross. Cambridge: Polity Press, 2019.

Stiegler, Bernard. 'Après les élections européennes, et en vue de preparer le séminaire des 2 et 3 juillet 2019. Considérations sur la question de la localité' (June 2019), unpublished.

Stiegler, Bernard. 'For a Neganthropology of Automatic Society'. Trans. Daniel Ross. In Thomas Pringle, Gertrud Koch and Bernard Stiegler, *Machine*. Minneapolis and London: University of Minnesota Press, 2019.

Stiegler, Bernard. 'The Internation and Internationalism'. Trans. Daniel Ross. *Alienocene* stratum 6 (2019): 9–10., available at: <https://alienocene.files.wordpress.com/2019/12/bs-internation.pdf>.

Stiegler, Bernard. 'Démesure, promesses, compromis', *Mediapart*, published in three parts: 1/3 (5 September 2020), available at: <https://blogs.mediapart.fr/edition/les-invites-de-mediapart/article/050920/demesure-promesses-compromis-13-par-bernard-stiegler>; 2/3 (7 September 2020), available at: <https://blogs.mediapart.fr/edition/les-invites-de-mediapart/article/070920/demesure-promesses-compromis-23-par-bernard-stiegler>; 3/3 (9 September 2020), available at: <https://blogs.mediapart.fr/edition/les-invites-de-mediapart/article/090920/demesure-promesses-compromis-33-par-bernard-stiegler>.

Stiegler, Bernard. 'Elements for a General Organology'. Trans. Daniel Ross. *Derrida Today* 13 (2020): 72–94.

Stiegler, Bernard. *Nanjing Lectures 2016–2019*. Trans. Daniel Ross. London: Open Humanities Press, 2020.

Stiegler, Bernard. 'Noodiversity, Technodiversity: Elements of a New Economic Foundation Based on a New Foundation for Theoretical Computer Science'. Trans. Daniel Ross. *Angelaki* 25:4 (2020): 67–80.

Stiegler, Bernard. *Qu-appelle-t-on panser? 2. La leçon de Greta Thunberg*. Paris: Les Liens qui Libèrent, 2020.

Strauss, Leo. *Natural Right and History*. Chicago and London: University of Chicago Press, 1953.

Streeck, Wolfgang. *How Will Capitalism End? Essays on a Failing System*. London and New York: Verso, 2016.

Supiot, Alain. 'The Territorial Inscription of Laws'. Trans. Saskia Brown. In Graf-Peter Calliess, Andreas Fischer-Lescano, Dan Wielsch, and Peer Zumbanssen (eds), *Soziologische Jurisprudenz: Festschrift für Gunther Teubner zum 65. Geburtstag am 30. April 2009*. Berlin: Walter de Gruyter, 2009.

Szendy, Peter. *Kant in the Land of the Extraterrestrials: Cosmopolitical Philosofictions*. Trans. Will Bishop. New York: Fordham University Press, 2013.

Taibbi, Matt. 'Why Aren't We Talking More About Trump's Nihilism', *Rolling Stone* (1 October 2018), available at: <https://www.rollingstone.com/politics/politics-news/trump-white-house-climate-change-731440/>.

Terrier, Jean. *Visions of the Social: Society as a Political Project in France, 1750–1950*. Leiden and Boston: Brill, 2011.

Thiel, Peter. 'The Straussian Moment'. In Robert Hamerton-Kelly (ed.), *Politics and Apocalypse*. East Lansing: Michigan State University Press, 2007.

Thiel, Peter. 'The Optimistic Thought Experiment', *Policy Review* (February and March 2008), available at: <https://www.hoover.org/research/optimistic-thought-experiment>.

Thiel, Peter. 'The Education of a Libertarian', *Cato Unbound* (13 April 2009), available at: <https://www.cato-unbound.org/2009/04/13/peter-thiel/education-libertarian>.

Toynbee, Arnold. *Mankind and Mother Earth*. Oxford: Oxford University Press, 1976.

United Nations Conference on Trade and Development. *Trade and Development Report 2018: Power, Platforms and the Free Trade Delusion* (New York and Geneva: United Nations, 2018), available at: <https://unctad.org/en/PublicationsLibrary/tdr2018_en.pdf>.

Urban, Tim. 'Neuralink and the Brain's Magical Future', *Wait But Why* (20 April 2017), available at: <https://waitbutwhy.com/2017/04/neuralink.html>.

Vernadsky, Vladimir I. *The Biosphere*. Trans. David B. Langmuir. New York: Copernicus, 1998.

Vitale, Francesco. *Biodeconstruction* Trans. Mauro Senatore. Albany: State University of New York Press, 2018.

von Uexküll, Jakob. *A Foray into the World of Animals and Humans, with, A Theory of Meaning*. Trans. Joseph D. O'Neil. Minneapolis and London: University of Minnesota Press, 2010.

Wei, He. 'Singles Day Achieves New Record', *China Daily* (12 November 2018), available at: <http://www.chinadaily.com.cn/a/201811/12/WS5be881a3a310eff303287e8d.html>.

Whitehead, Alfred North. *Science and the Modern World*. New York: Macmillan, 1925.

Whitehead, Alfred North. *Religion in the Making: Lowell Lectures, 1926*. Cambridge: Cambridge University Press, 1927.

Whitehead, Alfred North. *The Function of Reason*. Princeton: Princeton University Press, 1929.

Wiener, Norbert. *Cybernetics, or Control and Communication in the Animal and the Machine*, second edition. Cambridge, Massachusetts: MIT Press, 1961.

World Bank. *World Development Report 2010: Development and Climate Change*. Washington, D.C.: The World Bank, 2010.

Permissions

1. Bereft and Adrift in an Entropic Universe: After Bernard Stiegler. Written for this volume but also forthcoming in *Arena Journal*.

2. Protentional Finitude and Infinitude in the Anthropocene. Published in *Azimuth* 9 (2017): 127–42, in a special issue dedicated to 'The Battlefield of the Anthropocene', edited by Sara Baranzoni and Paolo Vignola.

3. Shanghai, 2018: An Introduction to Technics and Time, 1 and 2. An incomplete text composed as preparation for a set of ten lectures given at Tongji University, Shanghai, in November 2018, at the invitation of Lu Xinghua.

4. The Question of Elon Musk and the Aporia of Sustainability. Originally written as a background paper for the panel of the 2018 Serpentine Galleries 'Work' Marathon entitled 'Acceleration, Disruption, Bifurcation', presented on 22 September 2018. The other panel members were Gerald Moore and Shaj Mohan.

5. Carbon and Silicon: Contribution to a Critique of Political Economy. Originally written as a background paper for the Geneva 2020 project of Bernard Stiegler and the Internation Collective. Rewritten and included in Bernard Stiegler and the Collectif Internation, *Bifurquer: 'Il n'y a pas d'alternative'* (Paris: Les Liens qui Libèrent, 2020), English translation forthcoming.

6. Psychic and Collective Anaphylaxis: For an Organological Critique of Sovereignty. This text began as a talk given at ENMI, Centre Pompidou, Paris, in July 2019, and subsequently rewritten.

7. For a Neganthropology of Markets. This text began as a talk given at ENMI, Centre Pompidou, Paris, in December 2019, and subsequently rewritten.

8. Towards an Exergue on the Future of Différance. Published in *Derrida Today* 13:1 (2020): 48–71, and rewritten for this volume.

9 The End of the Metaphysics of Being and the Beginning of the Metacosmics of Entropy. This text was originally written for a conference at Nanjing University in April 2019, and published in *Phainomena* 29 (2020): 73–100. It has been rewritten for this volume.

10 Afterword: On Positive Pharmacology, by Bernard Stiegler. Translation by Daniel Ross of 'D'une pharmacologie positive', which was first published in German as Bernard Stiegler, 'Allgemeine Organologie und positive Pharmakologie', in Erich Hörl (ed.), *Die technologische Bedingung: Beiträge zur Beschreibung der technischen Welt* (Berlin: Suhrkamp Verlag, 2011). The French text is available at the Ars Industrialis website at: <http://arsindustrialis.org/d-une-pharmacologie-positive>.

www.ingramcontent.com/pod-product-compliance
Lightning Source LLC
Chambersburg PA
CBHW030101170426
43198CB00009B/442